ing out everywhere and always—a magical thing so very much worth saving somehow."

—Rick Perlstein, *New York Times* bestselling author of
Reaganland: America's Right Turn 1976–1980

"Ethan Michaeli has a gimlet eye for the people, texture, and contradictions of modern Israel. I'm in awe of his powers of observation and his ability as a modern-day Tocqueville to take us inside one of the most complex and confounding countries in the world."

—Jonathan Alter, bestselling author of *His Very Best: Jimmy Carter, a Life*

"Ethan Michaeli takes us on a series of jaunts around Israel, his keen observations and attention to everyday people creating a picture of the place and its inhabitants' lives far more comprehensive than in conflict-focused news reports. . . . *Twelve Tribes* is a joy to read, as breezy as a conversation."

—*American Jewish World*

"Ethan Michaeli has accomplished something of great value with *Twelve Tribes*. With his observant street-level reporting and vivid writing, he has broken through stereotypes to reveal the multiplicity of Israel and the promise of its diverse peoples. From these ground-level observations, I learned more about Israel than anything I'd read before."

—David Maraniss, Pulitzer Prize–winning author of *A Good American Family: The Red Scare and My Father*

"Marshaling an extraordinarily extensive network—from Palestinians to Haredim, from teenagers to nonagenarians, from kibbutzniks to businesswomen, from organizers to bystanders—Ethan Michaeli here proves himself an insightful guide through the many facets of today's Israel. Quietly and cheerfully nudging both his interviewees and his readers, he gets at the truth—not only that there are no easy answers but also that there are so many complicated ones."

—Yuval Taylor, author of *Zora and Langston: A Story of Friendship and Betrayal*

TWELVE TRIBES

ALSO BY ETHAN MICHAELI

*The Defender: How the Legendary Black
Newspaper Changed America*

MARINER BOOKS

New York   Boston

TWELVE TRIBES

Promise and Peril in the New Israel

ETHAN MICHAELI

HarperCollins books may be purchased for educational, business, or sales promotional use. For information, please email the Special Markets Department at SPsales@harpercollins.com.

A hardcover edition of this book was published in 2021 by Custom House, an imprint of William Morrow.

FIRST MARINER BOOKS PAPERBACK EDITION PUBLISHED 2022.

Designed by Lucy Albanese
Title page illustration © Menahem Kahana/Getty Images

Library of Congress Cataloging-in-Publication Data

Names: Michaeli, Ethan, author.
Title: Twelve tribes : promise and peril in the new Israel / Ethan Michaeli.
Description: First edition. | New York, NY : Custom House, [2021] | Includes index.
Identifiers: LCCN 2021029173 (print) | LCCN 2021029174 (ebook) | ISBN 9780062688859 (hardcover) | ISBN 9780062688866 (trade paperback) | ISBN 9780062688873 (ebook)
Subjects: LCSH: Michaeli, Ethan—Travel—Israel. | Israel—Description and travel.
Classification: LCC DS107.5 .M53 2021 (print) | LCC DS107.5 (ebook) | DDC 915.69404—dc23
LC record available at https://lccn.loc.gov/2021029173
LC ebook record available at https://lccn.loc.gov/2021029174

ISBN 978-0-06-268886-6

22 23 24 25 26 LSC 10 9 8 7 6 5 4 3 2 1

To my Ima, with love, appreciation, respect, and admiration,
for all you've done as a matriarch, educator, and role model

CONTENTS

PREFACE

The Pilots

In August 2014, I visited Israel for ten days that happened to coincide with the end of one of the wars with its Palestinian neighbors. That summer had seen an escalating cycle of violence beginning in June, when three Israeli Jewish teenage boys hitchhiking near the West Bank settlement where they lived were kidnapped and then murdered. Mobs of vengeful Jews rampaged through the streets of Jerusalem in retaliation, burning and destroying property as they searched for Arabs to lynch. One sixteen-year-old Palestinian boy was indeed abducted, beaten to death, and then set ablaze in a forest just outside of town. Palestinians on the West Bank responded to news of *that* murder with their own demonstrations, lobbing stones against the Israeli police and military sent to quell the unrest.

More intense fighting yet took place in the south, in the Palestinian enclave of Gaza, from which territory the Islamist group Hamas fired rockets and mortars into Israel, killing several people and injuring a score more. In a few cases, Hamas fighters entered the country through secretly dug tunnels, emerging into a kibbutz close to the border, where they killed a number of soldiers stationed there in the event of just such an attack. At first, Israeli Prime Minister Benjamin Netanyahu limited his response to strikes by fighter jets and drones. Then, in the middle of July, he ordered Israeli ground troops to invade Gaza, where soldiers engaged Hamas's irregular troops in brutal hand-to-hand combat amid tight warrens of homes and businesses, resulting in hundreds of casualties: combatants on both sides as well as civilians, including many children.

I watched the hostilities unfold over CNN from Okinawa, Japan, where my wife and I were visiting her family. Even with ground combat continuing, Hamas fired its missiles from Gaza deep inside Israel, coming close to Ben Gurion Airport on a few occasions. CNN also showed widespread destruction and death among Gaza's Palestinians as a result of Israeli military attacks from the air.

The images from Israel and Gaza alternated with scenes of combat in the United States: In Ferguson, Missouri, large groups of protesters, mostly African American teenagers and young adults, were shown running from phalanxes of police officers wearing black helmets and body armor and carrying shields, batons, and firearms. The officers were supported by multiple military vehicles, modified personnel carriers firing tear gas bombs from turrets on the top. CNN reported that the demonstrations, which began in protest of the killing of a young man during a confrontation with a police officer, had now devolved into looting and violence, broadcasting images of stores with broken windows and smashed doors.

I had been planning to fly from Japan to Israel on my own so that I could spend time with my brother Gabriel. Having been to Israel during other conflicts, I myself wasn't worried. Israel had faced foreign armies with serious capabilities in the past, after all, while Hamas was a homegrown militia of a few thousand fighters. Just two days before I was supposed to leave, moreover, Hamas and Israel ended up declaring a cease-fire. Still, it felt prudent not to have my wife and six-year-old child joining me; she was understandably terrified by even the remotest potentiality of being hit by a rocket.

Though biologically full brothers, Gabi and I are seventeen and one-half years apart—sixty-four and forty-six at the time of this trip—our respective generations as foreign to each other, really, as our nationalities. We didn't grow up together in the same house, or even the same country, our parents having been in entirely different phases of life when they raised each of us. Gabi was born on a kibbutz on the shores of the Sea of Galilee, and came of age in an Israel that was economically strapped and under constant threat of war. He was already thirteen when he came to the United States with my parents and attended Monroe High School in Rochester, New York. In contrast with the austerity and militant solidarity he grew up with in Israel, Gabi had arrived in the United States just in time to sample the prosperity of an unprecedented economic boom and to experience the impact of the ongoing civil rights movement as Monroe High School was integrating its student body. Baffled at first by American manners and racial dynamics, he nevertheless adapted well, became the school's tennis star, and fell just short of the state championship. I was born during Gabi's senior year at Monroe, 1967–1968, and within a matter of months, he had already returned to Israel to start his mandatory military service.

"Don't get killed over there," read one signature in his yearbook. "But if you do, it was great to know you."

My parents had initially planned to return to Israel as well, after my father had earned a bachelor's degree in engineering at the Rochester Institute of Technology, but then he found a series of rewarding jobs at factories in the area, and decided to pursue a master's at night while he worked. My younger brother, Dani, was born when I was two, and when I was four, our parents bought a house in the suburb of Brighton, known for its large Jewish population and excellent public schools. My mother began to teach Hebrew at a large synagogue's thriving day school.

My parents kept a room for Gabi in the suburban house where he had never lived, but I saw him in person only during visits to steamy Tel Aviv during summer vacation, and the incongruity between our lives stood out at several key junctures. I can recall coming home from Council Rock Elementary School in the fall of 1973 to find my mother perched over the radio, attempting to hear the latest details of the fighting between Arab armies and Israel, fighting in which Gabi was a front-line combatant. Later, as I made my way through middle and high school, Gabi went to law school, got married, and set about raising two children.

As adults, we have tried to compensate for the differences in our ages, geography, and life experience with short, intense visits—usually around weddings, birthdays, or other family events—a few days stolen away in the name of reclaimed brotherhood, or even just a few hours. Our longest time together was a ten-day trip in Sicily in 2007, when he was fifty-seven, his daughters all grown up, and I was thirty-nine, my son not yet born. Gabi had been there several times before, and he drove us around the island in a rental car, from its lush beaches to its snow-covered volcanic slopes, exploring crumbling hilltop villages and coastal towns whose histories were Roman, Byzantine, Arab, African, Ottoman, and Norman. Since that trip, however, our respective schedules had been dictated entirely by work and family obligations, and we knew the summer of 2014 was a singular opportunity to spend a few days together. War or no war, then, I resolved to go as planned.

I had never flown to Israel from East Asia before, and there were no direct flights from Tokyo to Tel Aviv at that time, but I discovered a flight from Hong Kong to Tel Aviv on El Al, the

Israeli national airlines. Reaching Hong Kong took just over an hour on one of the multiple daily flights offered by small airlines for tourists and business travelers from China, and my flight left Okinawa on time, as is the rule in Japan. My entry into Hong Kong's international terminal was smooth, facilitated by a perfunctory inspection of my American passport from the uniformed customs officer. Following the overhead signs indicating gate numbers, I made my way through the airport, an enormous, hypermodern complex containing, in addition to flights headed to hundreds of locations throughout Asia, Europe, Africa, and the Americas, a cornucopia of restaurants, multilingual bookstores, and duty-free shops, as well as free, ubiquitous, high-speed Wi-Fi. It even contained a mini-museum dedicated to Bruce Lee and, most usefully, clean bathrooms equipped with showers. Highly secure, the airport had multiple internal security checkpoints where bags were screened and passports were inspected by legions of stern-eyed officials in a variety of uniforms, each with their own elaborate epaulets. Finally, I arrived at my gate, where a seemingly exasperated Chinese attendant checked my passport, ticket, and boarding pass one more time, confirming that the necessary stamps and signatures were all in place before referring me to "them over there," a group of non-Chinese men and women in their early twenties, all dressed identically in large white cotton button-down shirts and dark slacks, each with their own stand to conduct interviews of would-be passengers.

I recognized these folks immediately as Israeli security, hired by the airlines as an additional layer of screening—an *Israeli* level of security legendary for its ability to sniff out terrorists lurking among legitimate passengers. El Al insists on installing these agents, mostly men and women just released from their military service, at every airport from which there are flights to Israel. I stepped up to a young woman with long, black curly hair and tattoos visible on her arms and neck. She looked through my American passport, noticed my Israeli name, and then asked if I spoke Hebrew.

"We can try," I answered back in Hebrew, smart-alecky enough to indicate I was fluent in the culture as well as the language.

She giggled, then asked me a series of questions about my reasons for going to Israel, who I knew in the country, how long I was planning to stay, etc.

Out of the corner of my eye, I noticed the Chinese woman next to me, whose English was passable but imprecise, being subjected to a far more rigorous interrogation after telling her security officer, a lean young man with a military-style buzz cut, that she was going as an independent tourist without any itinerary or reservations—a reasonable enough plan for someone headed to Paris but one that, when it came to traveling to Israel in a time of war, raised red flags. My security officer smiled, placed a sticker on my passport, handed it back to me, and told me to have a good journey. Her colleague, meanwhile, asked the unfortunate Chinese woman an increasingly intrusive set of questions as he went through her luggage, item by item.

Thus cleared, I proceeded through the terminal, passing capacious gates with ample seating to accommodate entire planeloads of passengers. I went by a flight to Jakarta, where a large group of people were speaking to one another excitedly, presumably satisfied with the course of their business affairs or sightseeing expeditions. At the next gate, a flight to Belgrade, I focused on a group of five or six Serbian men waiting for the trip home, looking exhausted and hungover, though still sporting mischievous grins at the memory of whatever adventure they were returning from.

The El Al flight had been placed strategically at the end of the terminal, but I knew I was close when a compact, middle-aged man in a plaid sports jacket approached me and, in accented English, asked with gritted politeness if he could help me. Recognizing that he was a senior airline security man, no doubt the supervisor of the brunette and her buzz-cut colleague, I answered in Hebrew that I was headed for the flight to Tel Aviv. He nodded knowingly. Still, before allowing me to proceed to the waiting area, he asked to see my passport and boarding pass.

In contrast with the cheerful animation I saw among the passengers about to board all the other international flights, the Israelis were somber, many staring hard into their smartphones or laptops, as if writing a final goodbye message, while others sat stiffly in their chairs, eyes darting, mouths fixed into frowns. Strangers avoided eye contact with one another. The older couple sitting across from me didn't even speak to each other, preferring to stare silently in different directions, as if preparing themselves for a journey they considered absolutely necessary, and yet gravely dangerous.

Slowly, after one more check of our boarding cards against our passports, all the passengers boarded the 747. Only when the aircraft's doors were finally closed and bolted did the dour faces finally begin to relax. One middle-aged man who, with his dress shirt and briefcase, appeared to be on a business trip, sighed, and then collapsed both into his seat and into an instant slumber. The sullen couple from the gate began chatting freely with a bald man sitting next to them, comparing notes about tourism in the Far East as well as various business schemes back home in Israel.

"We don't have oil," the bald man said, tapping his exposed pate, "so we have to use our brains."

It was a bit of conventional wisdom I'd heard often from Israelis of my parents' generation, though it no longer felt accurate. For a moment, I considered interrupting them to point out that Israel had recently discovered natural gas reserves in the

Mediterranean, to which the government was just then in the process of negotiating a multi-billion-dollar deal for access, but ultimately decided not to be a killjoy. This was August, usually the height of the tourist season, and the plane was half empty, no doubt the result of the war prompting cancellations of Chinese groups on Holy Land trips that had provided a vital stream of new income to Israel's tourist industry.

After stowing my bag in the overhead bin, I approached a nearby flight attendant. My cousin was an El Al pilot, I told her, and while he did not work this route, he had sent his colleagues an email to say I was coming, while instructing me to tell the captain once I was on board. Young, pretty, and perfectly made up, the flight attendant was attentive and warm as I fumbled through my explanation, and said she would pass along the message. I was, frankly, a little surprised by this show of courtesy and professionalism. The El Al of my youth had been staffed by gruff, ill-kempt, middle-aged apparatchiks trained, one would have assumed, in the Soviet school of public service. Back then, the reflexive response to any passenger query seemed to be "Do it yourself." I could hardly believe this was the same airline, with its cushioned seats, up-to-date electronics, and courteous staff.

I sat down in an aisle seat with two vacant seats between me and the window seat at the end of my row, occupied by a man wearing a tight black T-shirt. Just before takeoff, the head flight attendant, an elegant, middle-aged woman with perfectly coiffed hair and long, painted fingernails, came to my seat and introduced herself. She asked about my cousin, whom she knew well, and said the pilot would be glad to bring me to the cockpit a little later, after they'd reached a cruising altitude and finished the food service.

The takeoff was smooth and on time. As the plane made its ascent, I watched some television and ate a surprisingly delicious meal with fresh bread and fruit. Later that evening, just as promised, the head flight attendant reappeared at my chair with the captain at her side, a kindly, gray-haired man who introduced himself as Ron and offered to bring me up to the cockpit.

I tried to restrain my childish excitement. We walked through coach and first class up to a heavy, reinforced door where Ron rang a doorbell. The door swung open and I was welcomed inside. The cockpit had two rows of seats, and I was offered one of the well-worn black leather chairs in the second row. Ron introduced me to two of his copilots: Zvika, slight but lean, with a shock of gray-black hair swept to the side; and burly Yehudah, bald and robust. The plane had four pilots, led by Captain Ron, but, as per their regulations for a flight of this length, one was always outside of the cockpit, catching some sleep, which left an extra seat for me.

Like my cousin, these men were all veterans of the Israel Air Force, men whose exploits in F-16s, Phantoms, Skyhawks, and other jet fighters had thrilled and inspired me as a child. I had read voraciously about these daredevils who managed to surprise the entire Egyptian Air Force on the ground in 1967, obliterated Iraqi dictator Saddam Hussein's nascent nuclear weapons facility in 1981, and rescued Ethiopian Jews from war and starvation in 1991. Both Ron and Zvika were former fighter pilots, while Yehudah had commanded a Hercules, a transport plane that had to be loaded with a precise balance of men and matériel as it was flown in or out of combat areas.

For all of this fearsome history they'd lived and fought through, the pilots were jovial and talkative, engaging me in a conversation that was interrupted frequently as they adjusted one of dozens of dials or checked in with local air traffic control. Captain Ron was pleased to show off the cockpit's digital technology, even as he lamented the way the GPS had created crowded air lanes along standard flight paths, shortening flight times but making the pilot's job rather dull. Even the frequent bouts of turbulence we were experiencing, he explained, wistfully, were hardly more significant than a stiff breeze buffeting a passenger bus on the highway.

Flight attendants arrived every few minutes bearing espressos, specially prepared fruit salads, and other delicacies, and soon we were talking with the sort of familiarity and openness that so often characterizes Israeli conversation. Since their retirement from the military, these onetime warriors had clearly become not only well traveled but quite cultivated as well. Zvika discussed the restaurants he liked in Hong Kong and showed me photos on his iPhone of the natural hot springs in the mountains around the city to which he'd hiked with one of the flight attendants. The fourth pilot, Kalman, who came in when Captain Ron went to take his appointed break, had lived in Japan for a few years following his military service, learned to speak passable Japanese, and studied both martial arts and sushi making under great masters of these respective fields.

As the pilots nonchalantly steered the plane through the inky darkness over the hinterlands of China, the Himalayas, and into Central Asia, we kept talking.

"Look," Yehudah said at one point, extending his index finger excitedly toward a tiny red dot that I could barely see in the distance through the cockpit glass. "Another plane, just a few hundred meters away."

He lifted his radio microphone and announced himself with a series of numbers and letters, describing the type of vessel and destination, getting only a terse response back, an identification number with neither an aircraft description nor an affiliation.

"Probably Chinese military," he mused.

When the conversation turned to politics, it quickly became

clear that the pilots all felt Israel was, for the moment, safe from any foreign enemy, even a major power like Russia, which was just then stepping up its support for the beleaguered Syrian dictator next door, Bashar Assad. The so-called Islamic State had just declared its existence in a swath of territory they had seized from both Assad and Iraq; still, the pilots felt the military was well prepared for "Da'esh," as they called it, using the derogatory Arabic acronym. Nevertheless, they were all troubled by the current war in Gaza and worried about the general direction in which their homeland was headed. Kalman was particularly disturbed by the images of Palestinian children and other civilians killed and maimed by Israeli warplanes. True, Hamas was a terrorist organization that deliberately placed its rocket batteries in civilian institutions and homes, but it also functioned as the government in Gaza, operating schools, hospitals, and other social services for two million civilians. Kalman had flown over Gaza many times and knew it was densely packed, so he could picture exactly how much damage an F-16's missiles would do to an entire neighborhood.

Yehudah's son and daughter were in their late twenties, both of them married with children of their own, both prosperous from careers in the booming field of high tech. Nevertheless, Yehudah lamented that people with his liberal and secular values were increasingly eschewing careers in the Israeli military, jeopardizing the institution he knew best. Increasingly, key positions throughout the different branches and bureaucracies in the military, particularly in the combat units, were being filled by individuals who identified as "religious zionists," observant Jews who fused their faith with a militant political stance. Including large numbers of American-born Jews, the religious zionists were strong supporters of the settlements in occupied Palestinian territories and highly organized politically, with their own political parties and representatives in the Knesset, Israel's parliament. Many truly believed that living in Judea and Samaria, lands that in ancient times belonged to Jewish tribes but for generations had been home to Palestinian Muslims, would fulfill biblical prophecy and hasten the arrival of the messiah.

To Yehudah and the other pilots, the religious zionists were injecting a dangerous element into the most important institution in the country, an action that could have serious consequences on the battlefield: When it came to those crucial moments in which orders were given that might contradict a soldier's religious beliefs—during the evacuation of an illegal settlement as the result of a peace agreement, say—where would the loyalty of these religious zionist soldiers lie? "Will they obey their commanders," Yehudah asked, "or their rabbi?"

I spent five hours of the twelve-hour flight talking with the pilots, repeatedly asking if I was disturbing them, no matter how much they assured me that I was entertaining them on what would otherwise have been a long and boring trip. Finally, after so many espressos and treats I felt dizzy, I headed back to my seat, where I curled up under a blanket, halfway between sleep and exhaustion.

In my half-dreams, the journey itself became the destination, and I imagined the whole nation of Israel as one great vessel soaring through the darkness, a vessel full of my long-lost sisters and brothers, dressed in the costumes they had adopted during their long sojourns, pouring tea from intricately decorated samovars, or serving thick black coffee from little pots with grounds at the bottom, or passing around a bottle of schnapps as they negotiated, debated, and regaled each other with improbable stories, often in different languages from one another, but with the certainty and joy that their gathering together was itself evidence of their designated role in some cosmic design. They had each miraculously escaped brutal oppressors and mobs of murderers, hadn't they? Surely their course was now charted by divine hands.

And yet, up in the cockpit, the pilot guiding the vessel in my dream was growing increasingly anxious as he gazed out at the horizon. Not because of any external threats, but because he knew that in the not-so-distant future, one of those passengers would have to replace him, and he had real doubts that any of his potential successors would have that crucial ability to discern up from down, a basic necessity in keeping the plane from crashing into the ground.

TWELVE TRIBES

In those days there was no king in Israel; everyone did
as he pleased.

—JUDGES 21:25

I gave this book its title to employ, like many others before me,
the Tanakh's depiction of the ancient Twelve Tribes as a paradigm
for the complicated, often fraught dynamics among the religious
factions, ethnic traditions, and political affiliations within Israel
today. The modern "tribes" of Israel are not precise cognates for
those ancient tribes, but the interactions, conflicts, and collabo-
rations among these new tribal alignments, nevertheless, define
the country's culture and politics, not only internally, but with
Palestinians, the broader Middle East, and the rest of the world—
above all, the Jewish communities of the United States.

I have traveled to Israel many times since childhood, led several group tours, and organized many cultural exchanges, especially for journalists, authors, and other artists, but for this
book, I went to Israel on four extended trips: in 2014, during the
war with Gaza; and three times after that within a twelve-month
period from 2017 to 2018. My goal was to document Israel at
this crucial historical moment, and so I kept my literary lens at
street level, letting conversations unspool and allowing people to
speak for themselves. I interviewed hundreds of women and men

from a wide variety of backgrounds, occupations, and perspectives, utilizing my Hebrew skills to gain access to Israelis, and my American-ness to cross internal borders between Israeli "tribes" as well as between Israelis and Palestinians, abjuring pundits, politicians, and thought leaders in favor of those who could more forthrightly comment and reflect on the realities of daily life.

The ancient Tribes remain at the heart of Jewish identity, and understanding them is a prerequisite to understanding Israel. Israel is of course a modern nation-state standing on a piece of land sacred not only to Jews but also Christians, Muslims, Baha'i, and others, territory that has been a fulcrum in religious as well as political events for more than three thousand years. The name itself, however, comes straight out of the Tanakh, which states that "Israel," meaning "one who wrestles with God," was originally the second name given by a mysterious stranger to Jacob, Abraham's grandson. Jacob met this stranger on the banks of a river and they fought for hours, without resolution, even though Jacob was injured at the hip. Finally, at daybreak, the man asked Jacob to release him, but Jacob refused until the man blessed him, whereupon the man, an angel, or possibly a vision of God, bestowed on Jacob the new name "Israel."

The Tanakh relates that Jacob/Israel's twelve sons and their descendants maintained their unity throughout the centuries of exile and slavery in Egypt and then in the years wandering through the Sinai with Moses. Though Moses himself was barred from entering the Promised Land, his successor, Joshua, forged an army out of these former Egyptian slaves, leading them to conquest and settlement. Within a few generations, however, the Tribes had become fierce rivals more often than brotherly allies, robbing, raping, murdering one another, and conspiring with foreign enemies to advance their own interests over those of their brother tribes.

Saul, appointed the first king of Israel, failed to unify them, and tribalism remained an issue as well for his charismatic successor, David. Only David's wise son Solomon was able to unify the Tribes for the better part of his reign, and this is described as the kingdom's high point of peace and prosperity, when it held sway across the region. In time, though, intertribal tensions emerged once more, finally ripping the kingdom into two; nor were the kings of Israel and Judah any more successful at eliminating tribalism within their respective domains.

Ten of the original Twelve Tribes were uprooted by the Assyrian Empire's invasion in the eighth century B.C.E., becoming the original "Lost Tribes," while thousands of other Israelites were taken into exile by the subsequent Babylonian invasion, but the survivors held on to their dual identities as Israelites and members of their individual tribes. From Babylon to Warsaw, tribe was a fundamental component of Jewish identity. To this day, some Jewish families are recognized as Levites, and certain Levites are also Kohanim, considered the progeny of Moses's brother and lieutenant, Aaron. The Kohanim served as priests in the Temple in Jerusalem until its ultimate destruction by the Romans in 70 C.E. and then maintained their lineage over the millennia by passing traditions from father to son, and still today have special responsibilities in Orthodox synagogues as well as in certain ceremonies at the Western Wall in Jerusalem, just beneath where the Temple used to stand.

Though secular socialists, the founders of the State of Israel were fascinated by the Twelve Tribes, writing them into Israel's Declaration of Establishment as well as its fundamental legal codes. Among the first major policies they enacted was the Law of Return, which made Jews around the world eligible for Israeli citizenship, citing the prophet Ezekiel's vision that the Tribes would all find their way back to their ancestral home, and every new group of Jews arriving from a distant land is automatically labeled a "Lost Tribe" in mainstream media reports and political speeches alike. Israel's first prime minister, David Ben-Gurion, seeing parallels between the Twelve Tribes and the conflict with the Palestinians, not least in the story of Joshua's conquest of Canaan, created a study group to analyze the sacred texts. And after Israel won control over the West Bank and Gaza in the 1967 Six-Day War, religious settlers cited the Tribes as historic and religious justification for claiming territory from Palestinians, arguing that their ownership of the land was divinely ordained.

To this day, the Tribes have remained a potent metaphor for all sides in modern Israel, embodying the struggle to remain true to one's family, clan, homeland, or faith while also being a loyal citizen of the state. In a 2015 speech at the Fifteenth Annual Herzliya Conference, Israeli President Reuven Rivlin cited the Twelve Tribes to warn that the country was cleaving, perhaps irrevocably, along religious as well as ethnic lines because of its failure to respond to the rapid population growth of ultra-Orthodox Jews, or Haredim, and Palestinian citizens of Israel.

Tall and rotund, with a tuft of short-cropped, snowy white hair atop a bespectacled, cherubic face, Rivlin spoke to an audience of Israel's political, military, and economic elites, as well as selected American Jewish leaders, and used pie charts projected behind him to underscore his points: Palestinian citizens and Haredim were each contributing nearly 25 percent of the nation's first graders already, nearly half of the next generation of schoolchildren, and would surely grow as a percentage of the population overall. With an average birth rate of 7.1 children per woman, Haredim—a more accurate term than "ultra-Orthodox" for those highly observant Jewish families belonging to rabbi-centered movements that originated in Eastern Europe during the nineteeth century—already represented 12 percent of Israel's citizens, more than 1.1 million people overall, and could see their number double every sixteen years. Likewise, Palestinian citizens of Israel, sometimes called Israeli Arabs—distinct from the 5 million Palestinians in Gaza and the West Bank because they had full civil rights, at least theoretically, and were active participants in the nation's politics and economy—were outpacing secular Jews, numbering more than 1.8 million people, 20.9 percent of Israel's population, including Bedouin, Druze, and other ethnic groups, Christians as well as Muslims.

The consequences for failing to respond to these startling statistics, Rivlin warned, would be catastrophic. Haredim and Palestinian citizens had separate, government-funded school systems with their own curricula and bureaucracy, and, for the most part, neither Haredim nor Palestinians considered themselves zionists. Most Haredim and Palestinian citizens were exempted from the mandatory conscription into the Israel Defense Forces, an institution that, in addition to its primary function, had built national solidarity and provided practical benefits for education, housing, and employment. Israelis were also sharply divided by socioeconomics, whether they were recent immigrants or "old-timers," whether they lived in rural towns or major cities, and whether they were of European descent, otherwise known as Ashkenazim, or of North African and Middle Eastern descent, known as Mizrahim and Sephardim. The seemingly inevitable tendency for partisans of each of these camps to rally together in attacking the other camps, Rivlin observed, raised fundamental questions for the future of Israel:

Will this be a secular, liberal state, Jewish and democratic? Will it be a state based on Jewish religious law? Or a religious democratic state? Will it be a state of all its citizens, of all its national ethnic groups?

Tribe, by tribe, by tribe, by tribe, each tribe has its own media platforms, newspapers they read, the television channels they watch. Each tribe also has its own towns. Tel Aviv is the town of one tribe, just as Umm el Fahm is the town of another, as is Efrat, and Bnai Brak. Each represents the town of a different tribe. In the State of Israel, the basic systems that form people's consciousness are tribal and separate, and will most likely remain so.

We are not dealing here with the gaps between extreme Jewish nationalists on one side, and radical anarchists or Islamist fundamentalists on the other. We are dealing here with a cultural and religious identity gap and sometimes an abyss between the mainstreams of each of the camps.

From a political viewpoint, Israeli politics to a great extent is built as an inter-tribal zero-sum game. One tribe, the Arabs, whether or not by its own choice, is not really a partner in the game. The other(s), it seems, are absorbed by a struggle for survival, a struggle over budgets and resources for education, housing, or infrastructure, each on behalf of their own sector.

As president rather than prime minister, Rivlin wielded mostly ceremonial power; still, he carried an authority that came from a long and illustrious political career built on an impeccable biography that brought him a high regard as a voice of morality, decency, and restraint in a nation where these were especially rare qualities among elected officials. Born in Jerusalem in 1939, he had fond personal memories of the city from the time before the state was founded, and could look back to a long and proud family history there. Rivlin was descended from a great Torah scholar who had come to Jerusalem in 1809, and his father earned his own renown as a scholar who translated Arabic literature into Hebrew, including the Quran.

Rivlin himself had served as an intelligence officer in the IDF as well as a standard-bearer of the right-wing Likud, but where others in his party looked at the demographic growth among Haredim and Palestinian citizens as threats, he saw an opportunity to create a truly diverse Israel. Where some imagined that Palestinian Israelis could all be transferred out of Israel, or that they could dilute the numbers of Haredim by forcing them into military service, he dismissed these ideas as not only unworkable but unconscionable, mere political slogans that had no business even being considered, let alone implemented. Instead of banishment or discrimination, Rivlin proposed distributing resources and opportunities more equitably in order to create a level playing field that, respecting the integrity of each "tribe," would allow them all not only to benefit but to contribute. Mutual respect, shared responsibility, and equality: these would be the principles of the new society he espoused, along with most difficult of them all, "the creation of a shared Israeli character—a shared 'Israeliness.'"

"We are all here to stay," Rivlin proclaimed.

Haredim and secular Jews, Orthodox Jews and Arabs.

If we desire to live with the vision of a Jewish and democratic state as our life's dream and our heart's desire, then we need to look bravely at this reality. This should be done together, out of a deep commitment to find the answers to these questions, out of a readiness to draw together all the tribes of Israel, with a shared vision of Israeli hope.

Despite the challenges the "new Israeli order" poses, we must recognize that we are not condemned to be punished by the developing Israeli mosaic—but rather it offers a tremendous opportunity. It encompasses cultural richness, inspiration, humanity and sensitivity. We must not allow the new

Israeli order to cajole us into sectarianism and separation. We must not give up on the concept of "Israeliness"; we should rather open up its gates and expand its language.

Rivlin advocated that the integrity of each individual "tribe" be fully respected, that the tribes collectively recognize their shared diversity, and that those principles become the basis of a new national solidarity. Rivlin had already come out strongly in favor of extending these principles to the Palestinians on the West Bank and even in Gaza, to provide them with full civil rights based on a "One State Solution" in which Palestinians and Israelis would have nearly equal numbers. When questioned on the viability of this idea, Rivlin compared it with the Jerusalem he remembered from his childhood before the founding of the state, a city with Jews and Palestinians, Muslims as well as Christians, each with many varieties, along with a kaleidoscopic range of others.

At an historic moment when Israel and the United States have become the two poles of the Jewish world, the diversity and fierce sectarianism among Israel's Jews stands in stark contrast to the comparative homogeneity among American Jews. The twentieth century saw the mass murder, deportation, and evacuation of Jews from places around the world where they'd lived for millennia, and the United States and Israel together now contain more than 80 percent of the world's Jews, with a little over 6 million in each. There can be no doubt American and Israeli Jews share an indelible bond of ancestry and faith; still, there are vast differences of culture and language, all of which have a real impact on their complicated geopolitical partnership. And the relationship between American and Israeli Jews has changed dramatically in recent years in line with these new realities and the particular histories of the respective Jewish populations in each country.

Historically, Israel's society and institutions were profoundly shaped by the large number of survivors of the Holocaust who arrived in the country after World War II. While some 80,000 came to the United States from Displaced Persons camps by 1952, Israel absorbed more than 136,000, one out of every twelve people in the country that year. Many more arrived in the following years, and at the end of 2019, there were still 140,000 Holocaust survivors in Israel with an average age of eighty-five, according to the Finance Ministry's Holocaust Survivor Rights Authority. Those survivors shaped not only the national consciousness but also the state's institutions, which they staffed and dedicated to preserving whatever they could salvage from the Jewish world that had been destroyed. Avenging the Holocaust—or Shoah, in Hebrew—became as much a part of Israel's national mission as rebuilding the Jewish people.

There are other differences, too. While American Jews are increasingly diverse, the overwhelming majority are Ashkenazim, in terms of their religious traditions, with ancestors from Central and Eastern Europe who immigrated during the nineteenth and early twentieth centuries. Yet in Israel, more than 60 percent of Jews have ancestors from the Sephardic and Mizrahi communities of North Africa, the Middle East, and Central Asia. Many Israeli families are by now intermingled; still, those with roots in Warsaw, Prague, Berlin, or the Pale of Settlement are well outnumbered by those with grandparents and great-grandparents born in Baghdad, Marrakesh, Alexandria, or Bukhara.

Israel's population also includes a much larger proportion of recent immigrants and their descendants. Nearly 30 percent of Israeli Jews were born in another country, including most of the 121,000 Ethiopian Jews as well as 979,000 from the former Soviet Union. In 2017 alone, 3,157 French Jews immigrated to Israel along with 14,668 more from the former Soviet Union.

9

But even beyond the internal compositions of their societies, there are major differences in perspectives between Jews in the United States and those in Israel because of their relative political position. Where Jews in the United States are a tiny minority in a large country, dependent on coalition politics and policies of pluralism and tolerance, Israelis have faced existential war with their neighbors, while engaging for decades in an ongoing conflict with the nearly 5 million Palestinians in Gaza and the West Bank that has included campaigns of terror and low-level warfare. Where American Jews operate as individual citizens or as a religious minority in the world's dominant superpower, then, Israelis are used to national self-reliance.

Israeli and American Jews, moreover, have very little actual contact with each other. Forty percent of American Jews will visit Israel in their lifetimes, and most of those will come just once for a short tour. Among Israelis, however much as the elite may prize their degrees from American universities, even a brief visit requires significant expense, to say nothing of overcoming the bureaucratic obstacles to obtaining a visa. Even the tiny numbers of people moving permanently between the countries suggests a constrained flow of influence. In Hebrew, the word for Jews coming to live in Israel is *aliyah*, "an ascension," while emigrating from Israel is a *yeridah*, a "descent." And yet the truth is that more Israelis leave for the United States than come the other way, an average of 7,600 every year over the past twenty years, compared with just 2,800 Americans moving to Israel every year, on average.

In the past, American Jews have devoted considerable philanthropy to Israel while also advocating for U.S. assistance, but the financial aspects of the relationship have changed dramatically over recent years. Up through the 1990s, aid from the American government included a combination of grants, loans, and other subsidies for Israel's economy and military under the mandate of stabilizing a stalwart ally in a volatile, strategically vital region. But in recent decades, Israel has leapt into the first rank of national economies on the development of its high-tech sector while old alliances have dissolved among Middle Eastern nations, lessening hostility and the chance for new wars that threaten the supply of oil to the West. American support for Israel's economy was phased out while American military aid increased during the administrations of Presidents George W. Bush and Barack Obama, and in 2016, the United States and Israel signed a ten-year agreement to provide $38 billion for weapons, equipment, and other costs, including $5 billion specifically for missile defense programs. Most of that money will not go directly to Israel but will be used to purchase arms exclusively from American companies, and over time, the amount of American dollars that can be used for Israeli arms companies will be zeroed out.

Effectively, Israel has become a sizable, regular line item in the budgets of major American corporations while Israeli defense companies have gone international and enmeshed their operations with American military and law enforcement agencies just to stay viable. Israel's principal defense electronics firm, Elbit Systems, recently opened a headquarters for its American subsidiary in Texas and won contracts with the American military to create helmet-mounted combat vehicle systems, command and control systems, and to secure the border with Mexico using surveillance as well as drones. Elbit also operates in Great Britain, in Brazil, Colombia, and other South American countries, in Asia, and soon, very possibly, in the Gulf states establishing peace treaties with Israel.

It is undeniable that the voices of protest against Israeli government policy toward the Palestinians are bolder than in the past, registering greater influence in media and in academic and political institutions, and the loudest of these critics are frequently American Jews. And yet, Israel enjoys steadfast support from the overwhelming majority of American Jews—80 percent or more in opinion polls—not to mention from entirely new constituencies, such as evangelical Christians.

Circumstances within Israel, meanwhile, are so fluid that Americans debating Israel are talking very often about a country that no longer exists, proposing solutions that have long since been discarded to problems that have as likely multiplied as evaporated altogether. It is that fast-moving dynamic inside Israel that will determine the outcome of the conflict with the Palestinians, whether the vaunted Two State Solution is finally implemented, some other equilibrium is achieved, or the situation devolves into further chaos and bloodshed.

As during previous episodes in the long history of the Jewish people, the tensions and rivalries among the tribes as well as between the homeland and the diaspora are directly challenging Jewish solidarity even as the great powers scheme and plot over Israel's future. And as in other episodes of world history, what happens in this small slice of Earth has the potential to radiate outward with great influence and unpredictable consequences.

I set out, therefore, to identify the tribes within modern Israel and describe how their interactions play out in the country's politics, while also charting that complex dynamic against the context of the relationship with the United States, especially between Jews in both countries, tethered to one another despite their differences, deeply connected yet profoundly separated. For the nation of Israel today is engaged in an interminable struggle for its identity, trying to liberate itself from the restrictions of the past while simultaneously embracing its heritage.

1

GRETTI AND SHMULIK

On my first full day in Israel in August 2014, I got into the passenger seat of my brother Gabi's tan Buick sedan and we started heading south along a broad highway, with the transparent, azure water of the Mediterranean on our right. At sixty-four, Gabi's once bronze-colored hair had thinned and grayed, but he was fit and healthy, and ebullient on this day, thrilled to show me around his home turf. We were headed to see our mother's oldest and dearest friends, Gretti and Shmulik Berger, in the city of Ashqelon, near Israel's southern border with Gaza. Principal of his own small law firm with a busy practice in real estate transactions, Gabi was relatively free to hang out because it was the annual two-week holiday in the Israeli court system.

Under the cease-fire declared just two days before I left Okinawa, Israel had withdrawn its troops from Gaza, while Hamas had mostly restrained its fighters and other groups from launching missiles; still, the situation remained very tense. Ashqelon was well within range of Hamas's projectiles, but we drove in that direction without too much worry. If the rocket fire restarted, Gabi explained, he would receive a text message on his phone. Meanwhile, he took calls from his office and from various clients on the car's speakerphone while I gazed out the window, watching the busy towns on the coast give way to a sunbaked desert of sand and scrub on one side and the Mediterranean on the other.

About an hour after we left Tel Aviv, he pulled the car off the highway and turned away from the sea onto a side road. After two more turns, we stopped in front of a farmhouse with a workshop attached. A few Asian workers in triangular hats and cloths tied around their necks paused, tools in their hands, and greeted us politely. Gabi nodded at them and then gestured at what seemed to be a small office or toolshed perched atop the workshop itself.

"That was the first place we lived after we left the kibbutz," Gabi said, referring to my parents' decision to quit Ma'agan, the kibbutz on the shore of the Sea of Galilee, far to the north, where they'd been living since they arrived in Israel. Natives of Budapest, Hungary, my parents survived the Shoah as teenagers. My mother was in the infamous concentration camp at Auschwitz and a work camp for nearly a year, while my father, chased through the streets by Hungarian affiliates of the Nazis, was forced into the city's ghetto until the Soviet liberation in the winter of 1944–1945. In the war's aftermath, having decided independently that the Jews needed their own state to endure as a people, they each joined a zionist-socialist youth organization called Habonim, which is where they met and fell in love. They stayed active in the organization even after it was declared illegal by Hungary's new Communist regime, and later my father helped my mother slip across the Hungarian border, along with many other Jews, before fleeing himself.

When they arrived in Israel in 1949, just a few months after the War of Independence had ended, they changed their names from Vera and Andre to Chana and Avri, and selected Kibbutz Ma'agan for its affiliation with Habonim. They spent their first months happily living in a tent on the beach, while my father drove a tractor in the kibbutz's orange groves and my mother worked both in the kitchen and caring for the community's growing number of toddlers. They married in a field in the kibbutz, both taking the last name Michaeli, and Gabi was born shortly thereafter.

They soon found the kibbutz's rules and procedures grating, however. Collective living meant sacrificing even minor luxuries while governance was often a tedious, politically fraught negotiation. When my mother's aunt in Hungary sent her a package of clothing and other household items, the kibbutz members met and decided to distribute the contents according to need as well as seniority. The aunt's dresses, appropriate for maternity wear, were given to the many pregnant women, while a crisp white tablecloth was given to the older kibbutz members who sat at their own table in the dining hall. Also per the kibbutz's program, Gabi spent his first years playing, eating, and sleeping in the children's house, which he hated, darting across the kibbutz compound to reach our parents' cabin at any opportunity.

They stayed on the kibbutz for four years, long enough for my father to get an exemption from additional military duties. Because the kibbutz was very close to the Syrian border, living there was considered a kind of frontline service, and he was issued a uniform and assigned the rank of private, although he never had to go to boot camp and received only rudimentary training himself. They were ready to go by the time my father's term was up, and when a prosperous fruit farmer passing through the kibbutz offered my father a job as a mechanic on his orchard in the south, a position that came with housing, they decided to take it. Their new makeshift home, actually a converted toolshed, was cramped and hot in the summer, cold in the winter, but Gabi was a preschooler and they were still in their early twenties, satisfied to be independent, without any regrets at leaving behind the movement that had brought them to the country in the first place.

Gabi and I gazed at the shed for a few minutes before getting back in the car and driving to a nearby park, a few grassy knolls cooled by a grove of cypress and pine around a monument to an important battle in the 1948 war that followed Israel's founding. We stopped the car, got out, and I read the inscription on a memorial: *Here an ill-equipped militia held off the advance of Egyptian tanks and troops for enough days to give the fledgling Israeli army time to establish a defensive line.*

Gabi, though, was looking toward the clearing on the other side of the park. "It appears war isn't just history here," he said, pointing at a squad of soldiers in fatigues and berets a few yards away gathered around a large, camouflage-colored cube mounted on a wheeled, mechanized cart.

"The Iron Dome," he said, referring to the anti-missile system Israel had deployed only a few days earlier to fire interceptor missiles at Hamas's projectiles before they reached the ground. "That hill's got a good view on the whole area."

There were dozens of Iron Dome batteries like this one placed in strategic locations around the country, all of them connected through a highly sophisticated central command that attempted to compute the trajectory of Hamas's ordnance. It was a highly effective defense, if not a perfect screen, and a few rockets inevitably made their way through.

"I guess they don't have much confidence in the truce," Gabi added.

We got back into the Buick to drive on toward Ashqelon, where my parents moved in 1955, after three years on the farm. My father ultimately found a better-paying job on an American-owned oil rig in the Mediterranean while my mother got a part-time position as an assistant teacher in a public school established to absorb Jews from North Africa and the Middle East, hundreds of thousands of whom were arriving in Israel at the time. They bought half of a two-family house in a neighborhood of Ashqelon called Afridar, where Gabi immediately found a group of friends nearby. Without children of their own, Gretti and Shmulik fawned on Gabi as a surrogate nephew, and he visited often, not just because they lived conveniently close to the public beach.

Gabi pulled the car into Gretti and Shmulik's driveway and stopped before an iron gate with a heavy latch, whereupon Gretti emerged from the house, grinning broadly above her frock of patterned cotton. She teased us loudly for having aged dramatically— Gabi for having lost nearly all of his hair and me for getting "so fat." With still more affectionate insults, she conveyed us into their little living room, where Shmulik was waiting in his easy chair, feet up on an ottoman, reading spectacles perched on his nose, that day's newspaper folded in his lap. Before I could even ask Shmulik about his health, Gretti had foisted a familiar tin container into my hands, which I opened greedily to find a little stash of her cookies, a treat I had enjoyed ever since I first began visiting Ashqelon as a toddler.

I peered inside and made a show of frowning and saying, "That's all I get?"

I popped one into my mouth, and the cookie immediately dissolved on my tongue into a sandy consistency with a deep, buttery, slightly smoky flavor. "If this doesn't last the whole trip, I'll just have to come back and get more."

Gretti cackled with delight before changing the subject. She wanted to show us something, she said, beckoning us to follow her. Through the bungalow's back door, where there had once been a small garden, we now found ourselves in front of a concrete blockhouse with a heavy, metal door. Gretti produced a key that snapped into the door's lock with a satisfying click and led us inside.

Tidy and decorated nicely, if sparingly, the blockhouse's interior had a table and chaise longue as well as a few other chairs. One corner held a few brightly colored weights, ropes, and pulleys: Shmulik's exercise equipment, which he used with his physical therapists.

As the bombardments from Gaza had grown more frequent, Gretti explained, the municipal authorities ordered them to build the shelter, even granting them the funds for construction. In the past, when they were younger, they could have used the concrete bunker at the end of the block, but at this age, the authorities determined they needed something even closer. Nevertheless, Gretti had resisted their appeals for a long time, even dismissing the threat of poison gas, which military analysts warned might be contained within Hamas's missiles.

"If I get hit with a rocket, I get hit," she recalled telling the local officials who came to visit, with characteristic defiance. "Hitler wasn't able to kill me. Why should Hamas?"

In the end, of course, she acquiesced, and now that they had the blockhouse, Gretti admitted to using it whenever an attack was launched, her defiant attitude notwithstanding. Every time Hamas fired its rockets, the military sent text messages to the cell phones of everyone in the projected strike area, giving the residents of Ashqelon approximately forty-five seconds to get into a shelter. Hamas's missiles were underpowered and poorly aimed, and many were brought down by the Iron Dome, but a few Ashqelon residents had been killed and maimed.

I turned my attention to a framed photograph Gretti had mounted on one concrete wall, a portrait of her on the cover of a Hungarian magazine from the early 1940s, just before the war engulfed Hungary as it already had the rest of Europe. The photo showed her in her midteens, with wavy blond hair, clear blue eyes, and high cheekbones, posing wistfully in a lush grove of tall reeds at the Balaton, a lake in central Hungary that was the summer respite for many families in Budapest. Though there are more spectacular bodies of water in Europe, the Balaton was Hungary's own, the site of first love for generations of city dwellers. Whenever our parents and their Hungarian friends spoke of the Balaton, there was romance in their voices, and longing, too.

Gretti saw me looking at the photo and immediately snapped into the same pose as if she were that teenager once more, prompting Gabi and me to snicker.

"What's wrong?" she challenged us. "Do I look so different?"

Gretti had inherited her looks from her mother, who, though born a Christian, had converted to Judaism after she married Gretti's father, a staff biologist for a brewery. They lived in a fashionable neighborhood on the Buda side of the Danube, and in the dire months after April 1944, her father was arrested and sent to a military work camp. Gretti, her sister, and her mother stayed on in Budapest, walking the streets undisturbed because of their Aryan appearances. Still, they expected to be taken any day. Miraculously, they were unscathed by the Soviet army's siege in the winter, and Gretti's father returned home uninjured, so that the family resumed their lives more or less as they had been before being interrupted by the war.

Gretti rejoined her class in the Jewish high school, which had been more than halved by the Nazis, and met my mother there. The two girls were cordial, but as my mother lived on the Pest side of the Danube, they never became much more than acquaintances. After graduation, Gretti joined a zionist youth group, one that was less inclined than the group my parents joined to defy the Soviets by organizing mass escapes. She left Hungary for

Paris, at first, along with her family. There, she worked briefly for the Chanel company before moving on to Pamplona, Spain, where her father had been hired by a brewery. She came to Israel only a few years later, defying her family's wishes to try her luck in the unstable, undeveloped new nation.

In 1953, she ran into my mother by chance at the Tel Aviv bus station, with three-year-old Gabi in tow—my mother being recognizable for her exceptional height and for her thick, dark curls—and they struck up a lively conversation. Shortly after that encounter, Gretti came twice to visit them in Ashqelon, and during these conversations, my mother suggested that she meet a friend called Ravak. Gretti's Hebrew still being rudimentary, she didn't understand that *Ravak* meant "bachelor." When my mother and father went to visit Gretti in Tel Aviv a short while later, they brought "Ravak," their friend Shmulik Berger. It was love at first sight, and the two were married a few weeks later.

Shmulik was not from Budapest, but a little town in rural Hungary called Lula that was often the butt of jokes, as in "That's still fashionable in Lula." His father had a small shoe factory in the village that made shoes to order and cheap sandals without footbeds for peasants who usually went barefoot but needed something for the rocky roads between muddy fields. Hewing to family tradition, Shmulik earned a degree in shoemaking, his final exam being to make one shoe from beginning to end.

"I kept that shoe for many years, even though it didn't have a match," he told me when I interviewed him about his experiences during the war.

Shmulik was taken to a military work unit, where conditions were often terrible and the officers cruel, but he survived without incident and came home after the war. Only he was alone now, his whole family having been taken to concentration camps and murdered. Never a dedicated zionist previously, he decided then and there to go to Israel.

"I had no one," he explained, "so I decided to come."

When Shmulik's ship arrived a few months later, in May 1948, he disembarked into a port alive with celebration. Without intending to, he had arrived on the very day independence was declared, but his joyous arrival was soon deflated when war broke out. Fresh off the boat and as yet untrained, Shmulik was drafted as a guardsman, rather than in the regular army, stationed at a *yishuv*, a collective community similar to a kibbutz, near the border.

The *yishuv* had a line of concertina wire marking the border and one night, he remembered, a wild boar got stuck. The boar bayed and whined as it twisted in the wire until finally Shmulik and the other soldiers decided to put it out of its misery. Having spent a great deal of time hunting in the forests of Hungary in his youth, Shmulik was known as the best marksman in his unit, so he was the one selected to kill the boar. He took careful aim and fired, hitting the animal in the head so that it expired instantly. But as soon as that one shot was heard, everyone on both sides, figuring a battle had started, began to fire their rifles, machine guns, and mortars.

"It was terrible to be a soldier," Shmulik recalled, "but at least it was not in the army."

He was working as a truck driver by the time he met Gretti, and soon after they married he bought the very bungalow near the coast where we were now standing.

When we were done examining the blockhouse, Gabi and I took Gretti and Shmulik to their favorite restaurant, which they called the Romanian Place, though its proper name was Ha Nitzahon, meaning "the Victory"and referring to the time it was founded, in 1949, just after the armistice between the new state of Israel and its Arab neighbors. The town was still known as Majdal then, and though it had been occupied by the Egyptians for most of the war, the Israelis had evicted almost all of its eleven thousand Arab residents soon after seizing it in November 1948. The restaurant's founder received permission to build on the ruins of a pharmacy that had been bombed by the nascent Israeli air force during the conflict, and the restaurant struggled until 1958, when the Ashqelon municipality built an open-air promenade that connected it to other businesses. These were the Victory's glory days, when its menu fusing Eastern European classics with select Mediterranean dishes, especially Libyan specialties, attracted diners from across Israel.

We parked the car and strolled on the promenade among shops proffering cheap toys, groceries, sports clothes, and sundries, mingling with a crowd made up mostly of recent immigrants from the former Soviet Union and Ethiopia. Over the decades, the promenade had faded as brand-name stores relocated to the air-conditioned malls on the city's outskirts, while the Victory now had many competitors at every level, from fast-food drive-throughs to elegant, French-style fine dining and sushi. Ashqelon's population had changed as new waves of Jewish immigrants moved into the city center and native-born Ashqelonis headed out to the suburbs or to Tel Aviv and other cities.

Inside the Victory, we were greeted with vague recognition by the proprietors, who, Gretti and Shmulik whispered, were "not the original owners," but merely those who took over from the founders in the 1980s—more than thirty years earlier at this point, but still not quite authentic. The rest of it surely was, though, and we sat down at one of the very same Formica tables and stout wooden chairs with velvet cushions that I remembered from previous visits decades earlier. Nor had the menu changed, and we ordered an array of familiar favorites—hummus, a cod roe salad called ikra, and chopped liver for appetizers, and then various cuts of meat grilled on skewers, pickled onion soup, stuffed cabbage, and schnitzel—and when the food arrived, it carried all the aromas and flavors that had defined my childhood. The soup was just the right combination of savory and sour, the ikra, a salty, creamy treat. It was all far too heavy for the climate, but we ate heartily, a feast that left us overstuffed and a little stupefied.

We drove Gretti and Shmulik back home, and were back on the highway headed toward Tel Aviv when we heard on the radio that the Iron Dome battery we had seen that morning had intercepted two more rockets coming out of Gaza. Out of range by now, I stiffened at the thought that the rockets kept coming, even as the news announcer read statements from Hamas and Israel blaming each other for the breakdown of talks. My thoughts turned to the lovely old couple behind us. They would be fine, I did my best to reassure myself, wincing at the thought of them locked inside their blockhouse that night, gas masks at the ready as they digested the meal under the photograph of Gretti at the Balaton.

Late that night, in retaliation for the truce-breaking rockets fired by Hamas, Israeli jets destroyed the apartment building in Gaza that was home to Mohammad Deif, the head of military operations for Hamas. The bodies of Deif's wife and infant son were pulled from the wreckage and carried through the streets while more than a dozen neighbors reported injuries, but Hamas stayed silent on whether Deif himself had been killed. The body of Deif's three-year-old daughter was discovered a few hours later.

When I flipped through Israel's television news broadcasts the next morning, the anchors reported the attempt to kill Deif as their lead item, while commentators noted that this was the fifth time the military had tried to assassinate him. Had they failed again, the commentators agreed, it was a sure sign that the country's various intelligence agencies were slipping.

Hamas responded to the air raid by launching mortars at the communities and troop deployments near the border as well as volleys of missiles farther into Israel, even sending some relatively sophisticated Grad-type projectiles at Tel Aviv. The Iron Dome battery we'd seen intercepted four rockets over Ashqelon and its environs, and Israel scaled up its own attacks as well, sending planes and drones to continue wreaking havoc inside Gaza, striking dozens of targets while massing men and armor at the border and calling up thousands of reservists in preparation for another invasion. Even as the armies sharpened their swords, however, the diplomats in Cairo were still at work, sending messages through intermediaries.

2

HAIFA

Gabi and his partner, Nira, had arranged for me to join their regular walking group the next day. This would be a guided walking
tour of Haifa, a city just over an hour's drive north of Tel Aviv
along the Mediterranean coast. On the way there, I sat in the
backseat of the Buick while the two of them conference-called
with children, clients, contractors, and craftsmen; in addition to
being romantic partners, they were joint owners of the law firm,
and also in the midst of building out their own condominium, a
project that involved the coordination of multiple work crews,
inspectors, and deliveries.

Following the guide's instructions, we drove into the city limits of Haifa past the enormous port complex, through the shad-
ows of the docked cargo ships, and then up the slope of Mount
Carmel until we reached the particular spot where we would
meet the others, and Gabi parked. We had been instructed to wait
with the members of the walking group in a public park built on
a ridge that had a view of the whole Haifa peninsula, where we
could see large ships moving back and forth between the peaks
of the Levantine coastline.

The others arrived shortly, including Gabi's close friend Lezer,
a native of Haifa. The buddies greeted each other warmly, and
Gabi asked Lezer if he'd stopped at the falafel stand, to which he
shrugged: "Of course."

Back in his twenties, Lezer had opened a single falafel stand in a lively square at the summit of Mount Carmel, going on to open more restaurants throughout Israel and to follow that success with new establishments in Amsterdam and New York City, to the point where he was now working with his son to open an international chain of Italian-themed restaurants. Even now, though, he continued to stop by the falafel stand whenever he got a chance, shaking his head ruefully at its consistently meager profits and the inevitable disappointment of these spot inspections, given the poor work ethic of these employees today.

He was soon joined by our guide, his friend Nechamah, whose large, bright eyes above an embroidered blouse and cargo pants were framed by long, white hair that shone like newly fallen snow. In addition to her lifelong connection to the city, Nechamah had a Ph.D. in history and was thoroughly prepared with specially made plastic sheets she held up to superimpose over the view of the landscape, beautifully illustrating the history of Haifa. The first sheet showed a drawing of just a few rough homes near the natural harbor, as a proto-Haifa would have appeared during Neolithic times. Then she held up the second sheet, which showed the peninsula through the Roman era, when two towns, each small but with its own walls, grew until they merged, with populations that must have been diverse mixtures of Jews, Greeks, Phoenicians, and many others. The next plastic sheet was a jump forward many centuries to an actual photograph of Haifa in the late nineteenth century, which saw a small town of several thousand Arabs and Jews near the port, even as the Ottoman Empire decided to allow a few thousand members of the Templers to settle nearby. Nechamah noted that these Templers, an odd, messianic sect from Swabia in southwest Germany, were totally unrelated to the Knights Templar, a medieval order of Crusaders who operated out of their base in Jerusalem. Instead, the latter-day Haifa Templers created a tidy community of homes and businesses that still stands as the German Colony, though their most important contributions, in Nechamah's opinion, were the steam-fueled power plant, roads, and other infrastructure they built to stay connected with their compatriots in Jaffa and in other locations throughout the region. This was the first glimmer of Haifa's future as Israel's hub of technology, engineering, and education.

Nechamah put down the plastic sheets to point out some of the landmarks in the current cityscape. Now, instead of steamships paddling about, the harbor teemed with metal behemoths carrying containers filled with manufactured goods from Asia. The German Colony was still there, more or less intact, as well as the old Arab neighborhood Wadi Nisnas, but a downtown area with large municipal buildings as well as several recent glass towers had replaced another mostly Arab neighborhood that had come to be known as Haifa's Old City. From there, the city spread out in all directions, including right up the face of Mount Carmel, an expansion accommodating a nearly hundred-fold increase from the population in 1860 to just under three hundred thousand people, making it Israel's third largest city.

Stretched out directly beneath us on the slope was a spectacular, nineteen-tier hanging garden, the main feature of a Baha'i complex that included the golden-domed Shrine of the Báb, burial place of the faith's prophet-herald, an Iranian religious dissident named Siyyid Ali-Muhammad, who was tortured and executed in 1850. The Baha'i's prophet-founder, Mirza Hussein Ali, a follower of the Báb from a noble family who had been exiled from Persia into the Ottoman Empire, was placed under permanent house arrest in nearby Akko before dying in 1892. Ever since, the whole area has taken on great significance to the Baha'i, who brought the Báb's remains to Haifa and built the buildings and garden around him, opening them to the public in 2001. Today, . a few hundred Baha'i rotate through Israel to care for the Haifa complex as well as another garden and complex around the prophet-founder's former home in Akko.

From the ridge, we could also make out the campus of the Israel Institute of Technology, now the Technion, but originally called the Technikum in the 1920s, when it was the beneficiary of a fund-raising campaign by German Jews including Albert Einstein, who advocated for the Jews of the nascent state to have an academic institution dedicated to advanced scientific education and research. Since the state's founding, the Technion has had an incredible rate of success at producing breakthroughs, discoveries, mathematical proofs, and Nobel Prize winners, while its alumni, faculty, and student body have played an inordinate role in the technological superiority of Israel's military, from its satellite-guided jets, missiles, and drones to—more recently—its ingenious hackers and spying software.

Nechamah also pointed to a few nodes of one of Israel's less remarkable technological achievements: the Carmelit, Israel's only subway line, constructed in the 1950s to connect the port with the neighborhoods up the slope. A marvel when it was first opened, the Carmelit employs a French cable-pulled system, called a funicular, in which the cars going up and down are tethered together and stations have to be placed at even intervals. Many of the stations were located in remote spots far from population centers, and there are just six stops overall, including the two terminals themselves.

Connecting all these dots, Nechamah emphasized that Haifa's history, marked indelibly by all of the positives and negatives of Israeli history at large, could also be seen in the city's architecture and its urban design. It was an elaborate but brilliant introduction to our hike, which took us through the Baha'i Garden and the German Colony en route to downtown and then to the section of the old port where the streets are named for great Bulgarian Sephardic rabbis, who were also among those who had settled in Haifa under the Ottomans.

It was now evening, and we found a merchant-marine-themed gastropub near the harbor, where we sat outside on the cobblestoned square in plastic chairs. Lezer, who had grown up just a few blocks from where we were sitting, recalled his childhood among itinerant sailors and the prostitutes, pimps, and drug dealers who also called the port home. Inevitably, the conversation turned to the war. Though not generally a supporter of the current government, Lezer felt that both the government and the military were proceeding logically when it came to putting pressure on Hamas. Nor did he care, frankly, whether women and children, like the members of Deif's family, had to be killed in the process.

Gabi disagreed sharply, maintaining that the war was being waged in the least effective way possible, using tactics certain to drive up the number of casualties among both Israeli soldiers and Palestinian civilians while sparing the lives of Hamas leaders as well as the political careers of Israeli elected officials. It was ridiculous, in his opinion, to focus on the destruction of tunnels that would only be redug, especially when that meant sending soldiers on extended missions into the basements of Gazans' homes through neighborhoods where they had to fight the entire civilian population.

"I was in Gaza," Gabi sneered. "I fought in Gaza. It takes fifteen minutes to drive a tank to the center of Gaza. If they really wanted to get the Hamas leaders, they could just go in and get them."

29

Lezer threw up his hands in mock surrender. He knew that on this point, he had to concede to Gabi. They had both been soldiers in an elite paratrooper unit, participating in hand-to-hand fighting, often on the front line or even inside enemy territory, but Gabi had been Lezer's commanding officer.

3

<u>ORDER 8</u>

On my fourth day in Israel, I joined Gabi as he drove to Jerusalem for a meeting with a client, so that we could spend a few hours hanging out in the city afterward. The road to Jerusalem was familiar from my childhood visits, but when we reached a particular section on the ascent to the city, a forested slope of cypress and pine, there was something missing. As a child, I had been fascinated with a dozen rusted, damaged vehicles, armored cars that had been left by the side of the road during the 1948 War of Independence, part of a convoy that had run from Tel Aviv only to be disabled during an Arab ambush. But when we passed the spot where I remembered these hulks, rusting in their decommissioned days, they were no longer there.

I asked Gabi if I had missed them, and he smiled, explaining that just a few months earlier, the old war wagons had been removed and taken to a memorial park as part of a lane expansion project. The road was indeed quicker, and we were in Jerusalem within an hour.

Gabi's meeting was with another lawyer in an office building near the cluster of government ministries and courts, and, in the café on the ground floor, I bought a cappuccino to take with me to a table outside on the veranda, from where I watched a steady stream of customers, suited-up office workers, and the occasional young men in sunglasses and black cotton vests that just obscured their handguns and utility belts, part of the vast security apparatus dedicated to protecting the nation's political leaders. Just forty-five minutes later, Gabi emerged from his meeting and said he wanted to show me a place that figured in our family history.

We walked up King George Street, a main arterial street in West Jerusalem lined with important government buildings as well as synagogues, hotels, stores, and businesses, and then through the New City, built in the nineteenth and early twentieth centuries, during the successive eras of Ottoman and British rule, until, at last, we came to the Ethiopian Orthodox Kidane Mehret Church and Monastery, consecrated in 1893. Gabi led me around the back of the church complex to a dead-end street with a modest two-flat apartment building and a one-room house behind.

Smiling broadly, he produced a black-and-white photograph from his attaché case. The picture was from years before I was born, with a young Gabi lying on our father, who was lounging in a reclined canvas chair, my mother beaming down on the two of them. The photo also included my father's twin sister, my aunt Zsu, cradling a toddler—her oldest son, my cousin Roni, the future pilot—and my father's parents, standing by proudly. This grandfather had died before I was born, but I recognized him in the photo, bald, with octagonal glasses and a protruding belly. In the background, I could clearly make out the front of the very same shack I was now looking at.

I knew my grandfather's biography: During World War I, he had served as an officer in the Austro-Hungarian Imperial Air Force, a nascent corps with only a few biplanes. After the war, he ran the family teamster business for a time, but failed to switch from actual horsepower to trucks powered by combustion engines, and later found work as an engineer. During World War II, his status as a military veteran spared him and his family from some of the initial indignities of Hungary's antisemitic codes and prevented them from being in the first rounds of those sent to a concentration camp, but in the final months of the conflict, he and my grandmother along with my father were incarcerated behind the brick walls of Budapest's ghetto, spared only by the timely Soviet invasion. Afterward, he returned to his work as an engineer until the new Communist regime, declaring him a member of the "effete bourgeoisie," threatened to confiscate his property. He and my grandmother left Hungary in 1954, spending a few months at Kibbutz Ma'agan before renting an apartment in Jerusalem.

Saba Marzi, as Gabi called him, died of a stroke in 1965, two years before I was born, and I peppered Gabi with questions about him. Learned and intellectual, he was a popular fixture in the city's coffeehouses, Gabi recounted, leading conversations in German and Hungarian about politics and history. Our conversation was interrupted, however, by a man emerging from a garden apartment in the two-flat. Young, clean shaven, olive complexioned, wearing a tight undershirt and a kippah, which indicated he was religiously observant, he asked us suspiciously what we were doing there.

Explaining that our family used to live there, Gabi showed him the photograph, and the man warmed right up. Michael C., as he introduced himself, traced his family's ownership of the property to a great-grandmother, a native of Baghdad who had come to Jerusalem before the state's founding, after a pogrom in Iraq. As he spoke, Michael kept checking his phone whenever he heard the ping of an incoming text, apologizing that he was waiting for "Order 8." Knowing that I would have no idea what that meant, Gabi turned to me and explained in English that Michael was, like most Israeli men under the age of forty, also in the military reserves, and an Order 8 meant that he would have to report for duty immediately. An accountant in his day job, Michael was also a sergeant in a special forces unit that had been activated for the potential second ground invasion of Gaza.

Just then, a child yelled out from the garden apartment, "Dad, the rat is back."

Clearly embarrassed, Michael reflexively grabbed a long-handled rake with metal teeth and said he had to go deal with the persistent rodent. Marching back inside, he blurted out his Gmail address over his shoulder and asked us to send him a scan of the photograph of our family with the shack in the background. Gabi and I wished him safety in Gaza, to which we heard him respond with a hurried "Thanks," immediately followed by the sound of the sharp edges of the garden tool scraping the floor as Michael swatted at the rat.

That night, we were back in Tel Aviv, having dinner and drinks at a fashionable restaurant on Rothschild Boulevard, one of Tel Aviv's oldest streets, a broad, leafy thoroughfare with an incomparable collection of architectural gems: Bauhaus villas, Beaux Arts mansions, broad-fronted apartments, hotels, and many structures that housed foreign embassies and financial institutions, with a central strip that had lanes for bicycles and pedestrians as well as multiple stands set up to offer coffee, freshly squeezed juices, and snacks. Rothschild had been sleepy and ramshackle during my childhood, the central strip a dusty haven for backgammon competitions and little else. Since the turn of the millennium, however, downtown Tel Aviv had been positively transformed and Rothschild was the epicenter of activity, with multistory restaurants and bars that hummed with activity late into the night. The street was also known as a hub of political activity, particularly for the left-leaning population of Tel Aviv to protest Prime Minister Benjamin Netanyahu and his allies.

We found seats at the second-floor bar of a converted mansion, where the bartender persuaded Gabi to try his artisanal take on a gin and tonic, with added herbs and garnishes, and recommended a delicious vodka-based drink for me. We talked about economics and politics as we drank and forked up bites of tuna tartare, potato croquets, and other snacks, returning intermittently to family lore. My brother had been born just a few years after the end of the Second World War, when the memories of Budapest as it had been were still fresh, and I was fascinated with his stories of what our grandparents were able to salvage from their old lives, the memories they carried with them. But I also kept thinking about Gabi's own life, and how his experience was much closer to Michael C.'s, the accountant-soldier who would have to leave his family in their corner of Jerusalem for the battlefield as soon as he received Order 8, than it was to either my grandparents' or to my own.

With my days in Israel running out, Gabi and I visited my college friend Seth Cogan. In truth, Seth and I hadn't been close at the University of Chicago three decades earlier, when he was a sports fan from New Jersey pursuing a B.A. in economics, while I, a punk rock aficionado from Rochester, New York, was preoccupied with dreams of becoming a novelist. Though both Jewish, neither of us was particularly religious, and he, at least back then, had no particular connection to Israel. I'd lost touch with him even before graduation, but we had recently reconnected on Facebook, where I was surprised to see photos of Seth and his family—a wife and two teenage children—living in the city of Ra'anana, at the very center of Israel.

Regarding this latest war with Gaza, Seth had posted comments calling for maximum force against Hamas: "Bulldoze them all! Leave nothing! No retreat, no surrender, and not a moment's rest for these despicable villains!!!" I'd challenged him about this post and a few others, and he, in turn, had questioned my understanding of the situation in Israel, but we ended the argument on friendly terms, and he invited me to visit while I was in Israel.

Gabi was hesitant when I explained all of this, but I assured him it would be fine, that Seth was harmless, just another suburban American kid like me, and that was sufficient reassurance.

It was less than an hour's drive to Ra'anana, and the GPS guided us from the highway along one of the city's main streets into a neighborhood of freshly built high-rise apartment buildings. Seth was waiting at the door of his eighth-floor apartment with a broad smile and open arms, a thick, bristly beard with more than a bit of gray in it, the biggest physical difference from his college years. He and his wife, Lainie, and their children, eighteen-year-old Sam and fifteen-year-old Mimi, had just returned from summer vacation in New Jersey the day before, and half-unpacked suitcases lay on the plush sofa while a tiny white terrier ran about yapping excitedly.

Lainie graciously served us plump purple grapes as we sat in the living room, and Seth retraced his trajectory from the University of Chicago. After graduation, he had gone to New York City and found a job at a Wall Street investment firm. He and Lainie married, Seth succeeded in earning a good deal of money for himself and his clients, and they bought a large home near their parents in suburban New Jersey. Tragically, their oldest daughter died of cancer when she was just nine, and shortly afterward, Seth himself developed lymphoma. After his cancer was forced into remission, Seth experienced a religious awakening and convinced Lainie that they should move the entire family to Israel. They chose Ra'anana precisely because of its large American expatriate population, which supported a dual English-Hebrew track program in the public schools, and had become known as one of the best districts in the country.

The move had not been seamless, however. While Mimi and Sam absorbed Hebrew readily, Seth and Lainie struggled with the language. And, having given up a lucrative position at one of New York's most prestigious securities firms in hopes of finding new opportunities in Israel, he instead found himself confronted by one obstacle after another.

Seth quoted an old adage about doing business in Israel: "You want to become a millionaire? Start with $10 million, make a few 'wise investments' and pretty soon, you'll be down to $1 million."

To illustrate his point, Seth handed one bottle of red wine each to me and Gabi, then recounted for us how he had invested in a winery in the Golan Heights. "The day the owner of the vineyard got my check was the last day he lifted a finger," Seth explained, rolling his eyes.

Gabi nodded knowingly, having represented many Americans disappointed with the work ethic of their Israeli partners.

Nevertheless, Seth was determined to find his niche in Israel, even taking a course to become certified as a tour guide. He had continued his spiritual journey as well, spending time at the tables of several prominent rabbis and studying in a few different yeshivas.

Seth's son, Sam, would soon enter the military, and Gabi described to Seth his own military service, his years as an officer in a paratrooper unit.

Seth asked me if I'd served in the Israeli military, too.

"No." I laughed. "He wouldn't let me," I said, pointing at Gabi.

I explained that as a teenager, I'd fully expected to join the IDF, and looked forward to it, in fact. When I was sixteen, during our annual summer visit to Israel, I announced during a family dinner that I intended to join right after my high school gradu-ation. Gabi spoke up immediately, but where I expected him to be supportive, even enthusiastic, he said that if I tried to join the military, he would tell them that I was mentally ill, provoking uproarious laughter from the whole family.

"I wouldn't even be exaggerating," he added, while the family continued to laugh, "since you would have to *be* mentally ill to join the army when you don't have to."

Seth and Lainie looked to Gabi, who confirmed my recollec-tion.

"Life in Israel is hard, as you know," he said. "I didn't see the point of Ethan going into the military if he wasn't going to live here afterward."

Over Seth's shoulder on the living room wall was a large painting, a modernist portrait of Moshe Dayan, the former sol-dier, battlefield commander, and defense minister, with his recog-nizable eye patch.

"I like it," Gabi said, pursing his lips and nodding.

"Really?" asked Lainie, incredulous, but also casting a glance at Seth. "I think it's awful."

"He was a brave soldier," Gabi said weakly, "and a very good defense minister. He won the Six-Day War."

Lainie did not relent. She gave Dayan all credit for his personal courage and his military leadership, but said the war had left Israel in control of millions of Palestinians with no plan for peace.

"Ironically, he was as myopic politically as he was physically," Lainie went on to say. Looking at the painting, she paused for a moment, and said: "I guess in that way, it's accurate, that picture. Two-dimensional, you know? Just like Dayan."

Gabi sized up the family dynamic and, summoning his most lawyerly tone, turned to Lainie, "Of course—you're right," and then to Seth, "I still like the painting."

Seth sighed. He'd voted for a right-wing, pro-settler party in the most recent election, while both Lainie and Sam had voted for a centrist party.

"My daughter's too young to vote, but *she's* even more to the left," Seth said. "At home, I'm totally outnumbered."

Seth proposed the three of us go out to lunch, so we said goodbye to Lainie, and drove to a strip of businesses on Ra'anana's main street. Next door to a boulangerie started by French émigrés, we went into a pub attached to a microbrewery, sat in the shade under an umbrella on the porch, and ordered cold beers and sandwiches. Soon, the pub's owner, Seth's friend Jeremy Welfeld, came out to greet us.

An energetic redhead in his late forties, the same age as Seth and me, Jeremy had grown up in Washington, D.C., and visited Israel for the first time as a teenager, just after graduating from high school. Without a sensible elder brother to stop him, Jeremy enlisted in the IDF and participated in serious combat in both Lebanon and Gaza. Afterward, he moved back to the United States, working as a caterer, but felt a drive to return to Israel. More specifically, he dreamed of bringing to Israel the beer culture that was just then awakening in the United States. To that end, he studied microbiology and brewing at the University of California and, by then married with two young children, returned to Israel a second time.

Israel's beer market was dominated by two corporations, one of which produced two brands with vaguely nationalistic names, Goldstar and Maccabee, and a rival that produced two vaguely Scandinavian-sounding brands, Carlsberg and Tuborg. Jeremy struggled for years while his wife began to set deadlines for their return to the United States, reasoning that it would be far easier to make a living back home to support their by-now four children. Rescued by another American-born Israeli who invested in an abandoned factory in Petah Tikva, not far from Ra'anana, Jeremy started producing Jem's Fresh Beers. The timing was perfect for Israel's first microbrewery, and Jem's soon won a wide array of fans. It wasn't long before Jem's was served in all the fine restaurants, gastropubs, and boutique bars proliferating across the country.

"It's my personal zionist dream," Jeremy chuckled, before dashing off to handle the incoming calls, orders, and additional visitors. Gabi and I praised Jeremy's energy and enthusiasm, while Seth lamented the fact that he hadn't invested in Jem's when he had the chance. He then turned to the waitress and, after trying a few words in Hebrew, asked her in English to take our picture. A pretty young woman in fashionable clothing that allowed her to show off her pierced belly button, she handled the iPhone he handed her with familiarity. *"B'simcha,"* she said, "with pleasure."

Moments later, Seth posted the photo on Facebook:

"The world is truly an amazing place. Just back to Israel and my first visitor is Ethan Michaeli and his brother Gabi. Spent time at Jem's laughing about the South Side and old memories. Thank you, Ethan. You made my Shabbat Special already!!!"

On my second-to-last night, I joined Gabi and Nira at the movies. The cinema was located in downtown Tel Aviv on the third floor of the Dizengoff Mall, Israel's first indoor shopping center—a marvel of architectural design and air-conditioning when it opened in the late seventies, now a kitschy behemoth in this increasingly sleek metropolis. We sat down in the theater to see *A Most Wanted Man,* a political thriller set in Germany starring

Philip Seymour Hoffman, one of my favorite actors, who had died of a heroin overdose shortly after finishing the movie.

Midway through the film, cell phones throughout the theater began to buzz and shriek. At first, not yet comprehending what was going on, I snorted at the rudeness of Israelis who had neglected to silence their devices, but when Gabi's and Nira's phones began to chirp as well, I glanced at their screens, and saw an official-looking text message. Finally, it dawned on me: this was a warning of an imminent rocket strike in the area. The film stopped and as the lights went up in the theater, I saw most of the people get up and, just as they had been trained, stand in archways and other places where the building's structural integrity was strongest. Gabi and Nira, however, stayed in their seats, having calculated that the actual risk was very small, and I sat next to them, doing my best to display a similar sangfroid.

Scanning the theater, I noticed a man about my age wearing a plaid, short-sleeved shirt and khakis standing under one of the archways. He was clean shaven with close-cropped blond hair under a pinned kippah, and our eyes met for an intense moment in which I saw his genuine fear.

Within a few minutes, everyone received another text that the rocket had been intercepted by the Iron Dome, the lights were lowered, and the movie restarted. The incident had revealed, however, that no matter how useless Hamas's rockets were on the battlefield, these low-tech projectiles sent hurtling into space to land randomly on anyone at any time were quite effective strategically in that they could be counted on to sow widespread terror among Israelis.

After my tenth day in Israel, Gabi and I embraced each other at an espresso bar inside the airport departure terminal and said our goodbyes, making promises to see each other again soon. It was just 4:00 A.M., and I watched him leave through the sliding automatic doors into the hot, humid predawn air toward the parking garage where he had left the Buick. He was working on several large real estate deals that were about to close, and the courts were back in session later that week, so I knew that he'd be heading straight to the office for what would likely be the beginning of an extra-long workday.

This was the normal hour for departures from Israel to the west, and because this was the end of the summer, the airport was filled with those returning to Europe and North America: Haredi couples with multiple children pushed metal carts piled high with overstuffed suitcases alongside tour groups of bleary, sunburned American teenagers wearing headphones, Arab families with men in jeans and women in hijabs, and elderly Christian tourists with identical, brightly colored baseball caps.

There were several layers of security, of course, but none of the tension I'd encountered in Hong Kong because just hours earlier, after days of false hopes, Israel and Hamas had agreed to a legitimate cease-fire. Both sides had repeatedly agreed to previous truces and violated them, and this time, too, they had fought until the very last possible moment—mortars fired from Gaza just minutes before the cease-fire was to take effect had killed two Israelis and wounded two more at a town near the border. Mohamed Deif's status was yet unknown, though rumors continued to reach Israel that he had survived the efforts to assassinate him.

Still, the war was over, at least for now, and the expansive departures lounge was already back to its normal state of frenzy. With an hour or so before boarding, I made my way through the throngs in the main duty-free shop, considering a few items only to be put off by the interminable line of groaning customers. I remembered then from a previous visit that there was a smaller duty-free shop tucked away among a set of gates at the end of a hallway, and when I got there, it was much less crowded, just as I'd hoped. I picked out a few items—foot cream made with Dead Sea minerals, a package of snack-size chocolates inscribed with Hebrew, a pair of key holders in the shape of camels with the word "Jerusalem" on them—and got into the briskly moving line. At the counter was an Arab woman in a full veil, who was trying to count out a combination of Jordanian dinars and dollars while two small children tugged at her wrists. The cashier, a chunky Haredi man with a large black hat and two long ringlets of curled, red-blond hair dangling over his pallid cheeks, punched a few keys on a calculator and then showed the figure to the woman.

"You can give me this many dinars," he said softly, in Arabic, "and this many dollars," he added, showing her another figure on the screen.

Her eyes wide in astonishment above the veil's silky fabric, the Arab woman paid the Haredi cashier and thanked him sincerely as she gathered up her bags and took her children by the hand. "You are most welcome," the cashier responded in Arabic before moving on to his next customer, a middle-aged Russian woman with a massive mane of straw-colored hair spray-plastered into place, who was buying a serious cache of chocolates and cigarettes. To this woman, he spoke in Russian, and said something that I didn't understand, but which made her giggle.

The cashier was just as congenially professional with me in Hebrew, and after bagging my items, I walked to my gate, a LOT Polish Airlines flight to Warsaw, from where I would catch a direct connection to Chicago, a route designed for the thriving Polish community on my home city's Northwest Side. The plane to Warsaw was a cramped, older aircraft built for short hauls, filled mostly by stout, apple-cheeked Poles returning from Catholic-themed tours, modern-day pilgrimages, contentedly reviewing the photos on their cell phones and comparing Christian curios and souvenirs. I passed the hours in Warsaw's international terminal waiting for my connecting flight to Chicago without incident, and flew home on a 787 Dreamliner loaded with passengers speaking German, French, English, and Polish, whiling away the hours with an assortment of on-demand movies, both Hollywood productions and European offerings.

Eight months after the Gaza war was over, I spotted a news report that Israeli intelligence sources believed Mohammad Deif had indeed survived the various attacks on him during the war and was back in charge of Hamas's military wing, preparing for the next confrontation with Israel. The circumstances within Gaza continued to be grim by all accounts, with Israel sealing its border as punishment for the war, and Egypt closing its crossing to punish Hamas for its close ties with the Muslim Brotherhood and Iran, which Egypt's new military rulers considered their principal domestic and regional rivals, respectively. The blockades meant that imports of fuel, medicine, building supplies, and other necessities were severely restricted, making it all the more difficult to leave for business, education, health care, or any other purpose.

4

THE KING OF FALAFEL

Three years later, in July 2017, I returned to Israel accompanied by my good friend Nathaniel Deutsch, a professor of Jewish studies at the University of California–Santa Cruz. A Guggenheim Fellowship recipient, Nathaniel had also won multiple awards for his books focusing on Jewish history. We arrived separately on the same day and spent most of that first day recovering from the long flight, but roused ourselves enough for a meeting at Gabi and Nira's law office the next morning.

Gabi was meeting with a client, but Nira sat with us at the long, fine-grained table in their conference room amid shelves of legal books, going over a calendar she had produced with a positively action-packed schedule for the ten days Nathaniel would be in Israel, including visits to Jerusalem, Nazareth, and an Israeli settlement in Palestinian territory. We had blocked off one day for a special event that was my reason for inviting Nathaniel, an expert in Haredi history and culture: a festival to commemorate a long-dead Romanian rabbi.

Looking over the schedule, Nira noticed that the next day remained open. "What do you want to do tomorrow?" she asked.

"A good day to look for the King of Falafel," I answered.

Nira studied my face impassively, waiting for elaboration.

I explained how Gabi had taken me as a teenager to eat at a falafel stand in the Bezalel Market that was the first to come up with the fill-your-own pita idea, where the customer buys an empty pita, then stuffs it with salads, chips, and falafel balls. It was hugely popular, attracting people from throughout the country until there were regularly lines around the block. Eventually, the King was challenged by nearby competitors, other stands in the same market, including—not to be outdone for royal prerogative—a Queen of Falafel and a Prince, too. I tried to go back every time I came to Israel, but over time, even as the crowds thinned out, the falafels got a little soggy, and then one year I came back, and the falafel stand was gone altogether. I always wondered what happened to the King, so I thought we'd walk around that part of Tel Aviv and try to find him.

Nira, nonplussed, just stared at me. "You're going to walk around Tel Aviv in the heat," she asked finally, "looking for the King of Falafel?"

Nathaniel looked on with interest.

"Yes, that's my plan," I answered, with as much confidence I could muster.

The next morning, I asked Nathaniel if he was willing to brave the broiling streets of Tel Aviv in search of the legendary monarch of fast food, but he agreed readily, as I thought he might. We had been friends since our first day as undergraduates at the University of Chicago, and I knew that, not having been in Israel for seventeen years, he would be just as excited as I was to get out and see the country, no matter how quixotic the quest.

We charged boldly outside, but within a few minutes under the combined forces of piercing sun and intense humidity, my resolve melted, along with the sunscreen coating my face, which quickly became a relentless, pasty mess flowing from my forehead into my eyes and onto my glasses. As we reached a bus stop, I proposed we board the first bus that arrived, wherever it was going. Nathaniel immediately concurred.

The first bus to pull up was a #42, and I asked the driver, a middle-aged woman with a thick wave of chestnut hair, whether she went anywhere near the Bezalel Market. The closest she got was several neighborhoods away in South Tel Aviv, and we would be better off with the #63, she explained, kindly offering to drop us off at the stop for that line without charge. I interjected that we really were planning on walking anyway, so we could just get there as long as she didn't mind telling us where to disembark and pointing us in the right direction.

"Walk?" She frowned. "In this heat?" But then she smiled, shrugged her shoulders, and instructed us to sit near the front door.

From Givatayim, the small city on Tel Aviv's eastern border where my brother's family lives, the bus proceeded south past the Asrieli Mall, a new, multistory complex with shopping, housing, and a hotel, through a zone where every lot was fenced off for construction, with cranes, scaffolds, and piles of materials peeking out amid structures that were, by turn, half demolished or half built. According to the murals printed on the fences, some of these would soon become gleaming high-rise apartment buildings and stores—websites and phone numbers conveniently placed at the bottoms of the attractive images of families playing around fountains and swimming pools—while others would comprise portions of the city's forthcoming light rail system.

The construction ended when we turned west into the Tikva and Shapira neighborhoods in South Tel Aviv, where, instead of gleaming high-rises, we now encountered boxy, low-rise concrete buildings from the 1950s and 1960s, well-worn apartment blocks interconnected by webs of clotheslines. The main boulevards were lined with small grocery stores, specialty shops, beauty salons, and cheap restaurants. On several walls, Nathaniel spotted graffiti that transliterated to English read "Na Nach Nachma

Nachman," words whose Hebrew letters had mystical, kabbalistic meanings that honored Nachman of Breslov, an eighteenth-
century Hasidic rabbi. The Breslovers, as they were known, were
fond of scrawling phrases on every available surface as part of
their program of proselytizing to other Jews.

As we proceeded through the neighborhood, the bus started
to fill up with passengers who reflected the area's varied demo-
graphics: with Tel Aviv's central bus station nearby, these neighborhoods had for decades been a port of entry for new arrivals to
the country, most recently for those from the former Soviet Union
and a range of African countries. Immediately behind us sat a
couple of stout, Russian-speaking seniors, the woman wearing a
flowered dress and a kerchief while the man had on a blue short-
sleeved shirt and polyester slacks. And now an African man,
gaunt and wild eyed under his ragged suit jacket, boarded along
with a companion and showed the driver a printed photograph
of a particular branch of Bank Leumi where he wished to be let
out. The driver attempted to explain to the men that Bank Leumi
had many branches, but the man kept pointing to the photograph
while his friend attempted to explain in desperate, broken English
that the man needed that particular branch. They tried and failed
to communicate for some time before the driver simply shrugged
her shoulders and nodded for the man in the suit jacket to sit
down in the seat immediately behind her. Satisfied, his companion left the bus.

At Shalma Road and Abarbanel Street, the Russian couple
behind us got off to join a throng clamoring for entry into a large,
solid building festooned with national flags. This was an office of
the Institute of Population and Immigration Authority, one of the
myriad agencies handling the absorption of the large numbers of
immigrants from the former Soviet Union.

The driver instructed us to get off at the next stop, pointing us in the direction of the market. Thanking her, we disembarked into the miasma of humid heat, down a narrow street of low-rise workshops and small factories with walls of plywood and tin, and a buzz of small trucks loading and unloading on the narrow sidewalk. The few pedestrians tended to be either fashionably tattooed twentysomethings or middle-aged men in paint-spattered work clothes. This was Florentin, a neighborhood founded in the 1920s by working-class Jews from Greece, Turkey, North Africa, and Bukhara, though lately, quite trendy for young artists and professionals.

At the entrance of a carpentry shop, Nathaniel paused to examine a meter-high wooden cylinder placed outside on an unfinished table. It had ridges carved into the top, like a castle for a giant chess set, while on the cylinder itself were Hebrew blessings engraved in rings along the top and bottom with leaves carved in relief bearing images of the Temple in Jerusalem in their centers.

Nathaniel identified this beautiful item as a Torah scroll container, something used by Jews following Sephardic practices. The original Sephardim were the Jews of Spain who were targeted and finally expelled in a series of decrees that culminated in an infamous 1492 edict by King Ferdinand and Queen Isabella. Scattered throughout North Africa and the Middle East after their exile, the Sephardim were highly influential on Jewish custom and law in their new homes, supplanting or fusing them with local ways. Judaism has no formal hierarchy, and all the Jews from different lands brought their own respective approaches with them when they came to Israel, such that Sephardim have continued their different practices and maintained separate congregations side by side with Ashkenazim, who trace their traditions back to Central and Eastern Europe. Thus, on issues such as the proper covering for a Torah scroll, Sephardim continue to use a hard cylinder, where Ashkenazim employ cloth covers instead. Except for the small number who are actually descended from the Spanish and Portuguese exiles, however, being Sephardi was a religious designation, while in ethnic terms, those with ancestry in North Africa and the Middle East refer to themselves as Mizrahim. The Jews who adopted a Mizrahi identity found solidarity in their common religious and cultural practices as well as in opposition to Ashkenazi-dominated state institutions that discriminated against them.

In that regard, Nathaniel hypothesized that the scroll holder showcased the carpenter's skills, certainly, but also made a political statement. Inside the workshop, a handful of carpenters were making tables, stools, and other items for household use, just as so many other small factories in Florentin had when it was a working-class community whose residents attended the nearby Sephardic synagogue. Florentin's newest residents were increasingly secular Ashkenazis, however, hipsters at first, but inevitably, ever greater numbers of educated professionals, some with young children. Near the scroll holder, the workshop's owner had planted a meter-tall Israeli flag, a patriotic statement where Florentin's gentrifiers were more likely to fly a rainbow flag of support for LGBTQ rights or a black flag of protest against the government.

We didn't have to look far to find evidence of Florentin's newcomers. Just a few doors down, a shop selling posters and T-shirts displayed an enlarged, colorized reproduction of a dollar bill—only in place of the central portrait of George Washington was a head shot of the deceased Lubavitcher Rebbe, with his luxuriant white beard and the wide-brimmed black hat he always wore in public. Among Haredim, the Lubavitchers were the most dedicated to outreach among other Jews, distributing menorahs during Hanukah and standing on street corners offering to help male, adult passersby wrap phylacteries called *tefillin* and guide them through appropriate prayers. But the Lubavitchers were also controversial among Haredim, since a faction had extolled the Rebbe's purported messianic qualities when he was alive, and continued to make the case even after his death in 1994.

Regarding the irreverent poster thoughtfully, Nathaniel noted that the Rebbe had become a figure in many pop culture representations, a frequent stock image not only for Haredi Jews, but for Jews in general.

"It's a perfect metaphor for Israel," he said. "American imperial influence with a stubbornly Jewish core."

We advanced along Eilat Street, past storefronts displaying boxy women's dresses in flashy colors and sleek fabric and short-sleeved, button-down shirts for men. On the sidewalk were great round racks of T-shirts, sweatpants, and underwear priced for bulk purchases. This was Israel's garment district, but on what should have been a busy summer workday, the showrooms and streets were nearly empty. The textile industry in Israel and Palestine employed some ten thousand people, mostly in tailoring shops and small factories scattered throughout the region, but these days, nearly everything was being manufactured, assembled, or sewn more cheaply in the People's Republic of China, while consumers increasingly bought goods from multinational chain stores or simply ordered them online.

From Eilat Street, we turned onto Pines Street to find the very oldest section of Tel Aviv: Neve Tzedek, or Oasis of Justice. Founded by an Algerian Jewish businessman and other Arabic-speaking Jews in 1887, during Ottoman imperial rule of the region, Neve Tsedek was originally a suburb of nearby Jaffa, though it became known among European Jews in the mid-twentieth century as a haven for émigré architects and engineers fleeing the Nazis. These were the artists who designed thousands of buildings in the Bauhaus style, a district known as the White City, which, indeed, soon enough became Tel Aviv's signature architectural feature.

They were still there, these Bauhaus buildings—three- and four-story apartments, stores, and institutional buildings with rounded balconies, usually painted plain white—but as we walked, every other lot seemed to be a new condominium building that towered above them, with a loudly designed placard advertising the latest amenities and technological innovations.

We weren't far from the Bezalel Market now, but we were enjoying the walk, despite the heat, so we detoured, going south instead of north, and crossed the unmarked border to Jaffa, the ancient Mediterranean port city contiguous with Tel Aviv. The streets became narrow lanes as we walked, packed tight with skinny three- and four-story nineteenth-century buildings stacking homes over workshops, stores, and restaurants.

At the end of one lane, we found an open courtyard that had been converted to a flea market and browsed assorted curios, worn clothing, and framed paintings by modest talents laid out on tattered sheets while the vendors clustered inattentively in a shady corner, thoroughly absorbed in a backgammon game. From the flea market, it was a short walk to Jaffa's town center, where the municipality had very deliberately preserved its Ottoman flavor as a tourist draw, with a clock tower, two mosques, and a host of restaurants serving Palestinian cuisine and seafood, as well as souvenir shops, boutiques, artists' studios, antique shops, and galleries. Across the street from the clock tower was a formidable building built by the Ottomans as a police station and jail, utilized for the same purpose, successively, by the British and then the Israelis, only to be transformed now into a luxury hotel.

We found a road that ascended to an outcrop overlooking the Mediterranean, where a decommissioned, muzzle-loading

Ottoman cannon was still aimed at Napoleon's approaching fleet, and savored the spectacular view of the blue waves crashing against the rocky coastline with Tel Aviv's impressive skyline as the backdrop. For all the Ottoman-themed marketing, in truth, just 16,000 of Jaffa's 46,000 residents were Palestinian Muslims and Christians that year, and the city had long been legally incorporated with much larger Tel Aviv, with more than 430,000 residents. All the tourist sites and plaques, then, served to obscure the city's long, complicated history, not to mention the economic and political tensions simmering just below the surface.

During the era recounted in the Tanakh, Jaffa's perfect, natural harbor had been a Canaanite port until it was seized by the Egyptians, who were eventually beaten by the Philistines, who, in turn, lost it to the Assyrians, only to be succeeded by the Babylonians and then the Persians. Alexander the Great's armies were stationed there, but the Maccabees won it during their war against the Seleucid Greeks, and the Romans razed the town during their war against Jewish rebels. Rebuilt and ruled as a Christian city by the Byzantines, it was taken by the Arab Muslims in their sweep across the Near East with the birth of Islam, and then wrenched from *them* by the Crusaders, who made it the main port for Christian pilgrims on their way to Jerusalem.

The great general Saladin and Richard the Lion-Hearted fought bitterly over Jaffa, but it was finally absorbed into the expansive Ottoman Empire in 1515. In the first few centuries of their occupation, the Ottomans kept only a small garrison there, but after those troops were overwhelmed and massacred by Napoleon's expeditionary force, it was fortified with soldiers and settlers, Arab Muslims as well as Jews, Armenians, Turks, and others from throughout the dominions. Jaffa thrived, and at end of the nineteenth century, a trickle of European zionists began to arrive as well. Tel Aviv, adjacent to Jaffa, was founded in 1909 as a suburb for those Europeans, and remained smaller and dependent on Jaffa in these years. This was a bloody period, with mob murders of Jews by Arabs in 1920–1921 and again in 1936, and then, during the 1948 War of Independence, a mass expulsion of Arabs, followed by military control for those who remained until 1966.

From Jaffa, we marched along the promenade built along the gorgeous Mediterranean beach back into Tel Aviv, past signs advertising condominiums for sale offering luxury amenities and views of the sea. With swimmers and sunbathers frolicking in the sand to our left, we reached a corner that had the high-rise Inter-Continental hotel on one side and the Hasan Bey Mosque on the other, another Ottoman-era institution with its two domes, one large and the second smaller, and its stately minaret jutting out in the midst of a courtyard and complex ringed by tall palm trees. Once marking the northern edge of Jaffa's municipal authority, the mosque was now dwarfed by all the steel and glass high-rises surrounding it.

We turned inland and rounded Tomer Square to enter the Carmel Market, one of Israel's greatest *shuqs,* a honeycomb of streets of stalls stacked high with fruits and vegetables, meat and fish, olives and candy, clothes and cookware, with proper stores and restaurants behind that sold nearly everything else. A few of these stalls hawked kitschy T-shirts or other items geared to tourists, but the *shuq*'s mainstays were mothers and grandmothers of every background bargaining over each fresh tomato, each bunch of bananas, indifferent to whether the person they were elbowing aside was an oblivious German tourist or a world-weary, middle-aged writer. Many of the stalls were manned by the descendants of the Russians and Yemenites who had first erected them back in the 1920s, men and women who still bought their strawberries and mangos from wholesàlers or farmers with whom they had long-standing personal relationships.

Emerging from the market's northern node, we walked up and down fashionable Sheinkin Street, tempted by several cafés that offered cold beers, but pressed on, since the Bezalel Market was nearby. A few meters along Allenby Street, named after the British general who finally dislodged the Ottomans, and then around the corner from King George, the street named for the monarch who ruled during the United Kingdom's mandate, we found it: an opening in the middle of the block with racks of clothing spread out under a massive blue plastic tarp.

The Bezalel Market had always been a much more modest enterprise than the Carmel Market, but now all the more so. It seemed to specialize in second-tier facsimiles of major brands, T-shirts, bathing suits, flip-flops, sandals, and athletic apparel. It wasn't busy, and so we browsed the stalls until we reached one staffed by a woman who appeared quite friendly.

Explaining that I was an American writer, I told her that I was looking for the King of Falafel, who had operated a food stand there in the 1980s. I didn't know his name, but the King had been a stall vendor at Bezalel and was renowned throughout Israel as the first with the idea to let people fill their own pita. Would she have any idea who he was or what happened to him?

As I spoke, the woman vendor looked puzzled, at least at first, but as I finished my spiel by assuring her I was a writer, not a government official or a debt collector, a flash of recognition showed on her face.

"Could you mean Eli?" she said. She nodded briskly, "Yes, you must be talking about Eli Noy," she said. "Come on."

She escorted me to the other stalls, explaining to the other attendants that I was looking for "Eli the King."

"All of the kings have disappeared," quipped one. But his

neighbor reported that Eli was still there. He had gone to pray but would be back soon.

We had been waiting a few minutes, looking through the racks of T-shirts, when Nathaniel noticed a man rush by. Of medium height, with a graying beard, thick, though neatly trimmed, and wearing a crisp white T-shirt and a kippah, the man, Nathaniel couldn't help thinking, had something regal about him.

"That must be the King," Nathaniel whispered.

A moment later, he was proven right as the woman vendor brought over Eli Noy and introduced us. He greeted us with a firm handshake and a direct, curious glance of his hazel-colored eyes. The King's T-shirt was imprinted with an eagle in attack mode, talons out, on a rustling American flag. In blood-red letters underneath were the words "USA #1."

I explained to Eli my idea of including him in my book, and he agreed without hesitation. Still, I knew that also meant we would have to do it on his terms. Eli began to walk through the market, narrating the history of his kingdom as he went.

He had started the concept of fill-your-own pita at the King of Falafel in 1982, and it was an immediate hit. People came from all over the country and tried their best to stuff the bread pockets to the bursting point while every day, they went through enormous quantities of hummus, tahini, and eggplant, chopping endless piles of cabbages, lettuce heads, radishes, carrots, tomatoes, and cucumbers. Eli the monarch stood behind the counter with a broad smile, magnanimously wielding his ladle to dispense glistening, golden brown falafel balls and crispy chips while the cauldrons of oil bubbled behind him. At its peak, the stand sold one thousand pitas a day, employing twelve people, who served lines of customers stretching onto King George Street from morning to evening.

But tastes changed, Eli lamented, and falafel fell out of mode.

"Pizza and hamburgers became popular," he said, sighing deeply. "Eventually, the people stopped coming."

I tried to imagine Eli as he had looked behind the counter at the height of his glory.

"Back then, I didn't have a beard," he said, noting that he was a Baal Teshuva, meaning that he had become religiously observant.

By now, we had stopped in front of a bank of stalls at the edge of a market along a little lane covered by dirty canvas, across from a wall made of metal sheets, beyond which were the scaffolding and concrete skeletons of two new nine-story buildings, which Eli said proudly would soon contain apartments, a shopping mall, and an attached parking garage. I asked Eli who owned the land, whether it belonged to the market or the municipality.

One of the vendors, overhearing my question, pointed at Eli and said, "It belongs to *him*."

Eli smiled enigmatically, neither denying nor elaborating on the vendor's assertion. I programmed Eli's number into my phone, promising to return soon to do a proper interview.

THE WESTERN WALL

Two days later, at the Arlozorov Terminal in North Tel Aviv, Nathaniel and I boarded the #480 bus bound for Jerusalem, with a plan to visit the Western Wall, the Kotel ha Ma'aravi in Hebrew, as well as a neighborhood that was an historic stronghold of the Haredi movement, Mea She'arim.

The route from the Mediterranean coast to the mountain city of Jerusalem is a much storied journey, but today it takes just under an hour on a multilane highway, and for many is a quotidian experience. Our bus contained mostly conscripted soldiers in their faded green or gray uniforms, and high school students enjoying their summer breaks, all absorbed in their mobile devices.

Heading southeast out of the city on Highway 1, the traffic thinned out after we passed sprawling Ben Gurion Airport, and we soon reached the Ayalon Valley, where the road was bordered on both sides by harvested fields of fruit and grains operated by collective communities called *moshavim*, while in the distance a massive industrial plant belched clouds of ominous-looking smoke. From there, the bus ascended a steep incline into the foothills of the Judean Mountains, through slopes with picturesque little towns of neat stone cottages in sparse forests of pine, some punctuated by minarets standing tall, others with church steeples, and a few with synagogues at their center.

At the final approach to Jerusalem, looming over us on the

ridge above were rows of neatly placed graves in the Har ha Menucha, the Mountain of Rest, a cemetery that had opened just after the War of Independence and now housed the remains of many prestigious rabbis and public figures. The bus turned off the highway at Ben Gurion Boulevard, where we caught sight of large, white Hebrew letters spelling out the words *Bruchim ha Ba'im*, meaning "Blessed are the arrivals." Around a bend, Ben Gurion Road, named for Israel's founding prime minister, changed into Chaim Weizmann Boulevard, named for the country's founding president, and now the buildings and structures of Jerusalem came into view, dominated by the immense Chords Bridge directly in front of us. Anchored by a curved white base with thin white strands soaring into the sky, the bridge was designed for a light rail line as well as pedestrians by the Spanish architect Santiago Calatrava, who imagined it as an homage to King David, whom the Tanakh describes as a lyre player of great skill.

At ground level, as the bus stopped in thick traffic, I glanced out of the window to the left and saw the Hello Yemen restaurant adjoining a gas station. A popular spot for kosher shawarma, shredded, spiced meat cooked on a spit, inspected by rabbinic authorities, the restaurant was among the few echoes of the Yemenite Jews who had founded Givat Shaul, the neighborhood we were passing through. Driven by religious fervor, with many believing that the messiah's appearance was imminent, the Yemenites started coming in 1905, just after the Ottoman Empire reconquered their home kingdom and it became possible to reach the Holy Land.

The bus ducked into the underground parking garage of the central station and deftly pulled into its assigned slot. We disembarked and scuttled forward with the other passengers until we reached the security checkpoint, where a squad of soldiers scanned everyone head to toe, quietly instructing people to place their handbags and knapsacks on the conveyor belt of an X-ray machine. There was a metal detector for individuals as well, but without bags, the soldiers waved Nathaniel and me through. The bus station was crowded, a multilayer complex with fast-food eateries, banks, and shops selling cell phones and curios as well as religious items like skullcaps and prayer books, and we managed to thread our way to the exit, and then out onto Jaffa Road.

We stood in the shade for a moment, attempting to get our bearings in the chaotic, cacophonous scene. Directly in front of us sat a weathered little man with a snowy white beard, worn suit, plastic sandals, and a satin skullcap, a prayer book open in his lap, dispensing blessings to a long-skirted religious woman who had stooped down to hear him. Another woman, neatly put together but wearing a short-sleeved red dress and her hair uncovered, waited patiently for her turn to place a few coins in the old man's cup and hear his words of wisdom.

Not far from this scene, in front of a kosher ice cream shop, a cluster of a half dozen young women soldiers in faded fatigues carrying heavy backpacks, Mizrahim, Ethiopians, and Ashkenazim, were engaged in an intense discussion; just inches away, on the other side of the store's window, a woman in a head scarf eagerly consumed a dish of creamy vanilla soft-serve, one heaping spoonful after another. Young Haredi men, some in their uniform black suits, black hats, and white shirts, others sans jacket on account of the heat, darted about quickly in every direction, their sidelocks swaying in the rhythm of their stride, past secular men and women in cotton, short-sleeved shirts who moved at a more languid pace, pausing frequently to glance at their phones or adjust their headsets. A good percentage of the passersby were Arabs—the women, some bareheaded but mostly in hijabs and long cloaks; the men in suits and neatly trimmed mustaches if they were middle-aged, or jeans, sneakers, and T-shirts if they were young.

Jaffa Street teemed with private cars, taxis, and buses, and just across from the bus station, a sleek new silver light rail car glided to a stop. Our plan was to walk through the Old City to the Western Wall, and I checked with a young Ethiopian Israeli police officer leaning on his blue-and-white car to make sure we were headed the right way.

The officer replied that we were indeed on the right path, but the Old City was quite a way off, so he politely suggested that we might want to take the bus or the new light rail. We were determined to make this pilgrimage on foot, however, and truthfully, it was far less humid here than in Tel Aviv, with a slight breeze that made it actually quite pleasant.

Many of the buildings on Jaffa Street were Ottoman-era structures, solid yet ornate, if a bit decrepit, and an Arab man sitting on the steps of one apartment building—neat brown suit, trimmed mustache, and polished black shoes—gave me a thorough visual inspection, nodding his chin in approval of my black T-shirt and khakis, before grimacing in disapproval at my black running sneakers. I couldn't argue with his judgment of my fashion sense, and had no choice but to press on and suffer Nathaniel's snickering for the rest of the day.

The bustling Mahane Yehudah Market took up several city blocks, with a central, pedestrian-only street made of cobblestones with rows of stalls selling the finest olives, fruit, vegetables, meat, fish, cheese, halvah, spices, and other produce, with butchers, fishmongers, and a wide assortment of restaurants on the back streets. It was one of the only true rivals to the Carmel *shuq* in Tel Aviv, and we were certainly tempted, but, as we planned to return for lunch after the Old City, we walked quickly past for now, averting our eyes to avoid temptation. Likewise, we resisted the urge to tarry at lively King George Street or Ben

Yehudah Street, pedestrian-only promenades packed with restaurants, cafés, bars, and stores.

Finally, we reached the end of Jaffa Road, where the northwest corner of the walls of the Old City appeared before us, continuing in straight lines south and east, with the green hills and valleys of the West Bank visible beyond. These were not the walls built by the original Solomon, but rather by the latter-day Solomon, the Ottoman Sultan Suleiman I, in the sixteenth century, to enclose the medieval town around the holy sites of Jews, Christians, and Muslims. We followed the flow of people along a pedestrian path to the Jaffa Gate, one of six entrances Suleiman had carved into the walls to facilitate the passage of pilgrims, traders, soldiers, imperial bureaucrats, and their beasts of burden. Once inside, we passed the currency changers and eager, would-be guides to the narrow stone stairs leading down to a proper bazaar with an endless array of small shops on both sides, though this section catered mainly to tourists, with restaurants, juice stands, and shops selling curios and souvenirs, costume jewelry, and T-shirts with silly slogans. One had a crude drawing of an Israeli fighter jet over the words "Don't worry America, Israel is behind you," while another displayed a familiar Pokemon character called Pikachu, with added sidelocks, beard, a brimmed black hat and labeled "Pika-Jew." Yet another T-shirt had the shield of the Israel Defense Forces, under which were the words "My job is so secret even *I* don't know what I'm doing."

We edged around sunburned Europeans and Americans, backpackers and organized tour groups with leaders carrying flags of various colors and patterns, until we reached the security point before the Wall complex, where a group of soldiers in a Plexiglas shack manned a metal detector and an X-ray machine to screen all would-be visitors. There was just one couple ahead of us, in T-shirts and jeans, a man and woman in their early twenties with dark brown hair and slightly olive complexions. They placed their cell phones, wallets, and backpacks on the X-ray belt and stepped through the metal detector casually, but something caught the interest of the soldier standing there, a short, stocky corporal.

Pointing at the young woman's T-shirt, the soldier asked her in English, "What does it say?"

"Michigan," the woman said, then added, "University of Michigan."

"I can read it," the soldier said brusquely. "It's not good."

She responded too quietly for me to hear, turned to collect her phone and backpack, and walked off with her partner, clearly irritated. She turned slightly, and I saw that the words printed on her T-shirt were in Arabic.

The soldier cleared Nathaniel and me without a question, and we walked down a flight of stairs into the huge plaza before the Western Wall. The Wall itself, composed of huge, unevenly sized limestone blocks that showed all the scars of their eventful two-millennia life span, loomed sixty-two feet above us, some sprouting spiky green shrubs. At the top of the stairs, we could see the area beyond the Wall, what in English is known as the Temple Mount—the "Har ha Bayit" in Hebrew and "al Haram al Sharif" in Arabic—with the golden Dome of the Rock on the left and, on the right, the smaller, darker dome of the Al Aqsa Mosque. But the Temple Mount became invisible at the bottom of the stairs, as the angle changed and the sun gleamed on the polished stone of the plaza before the Wall itself.

We headed for the larger northern section of the Wall, which, set aside for men, is separated by a partition from a smaller women's section. It had become customary for all men to cover their heads before the Wall, and there was a clear bin filled with white, polyester kippahs for anyone who needed one, but Nathaniel had thoughtfully brought kippahs for both of us, simple black felt circles he produced from his pocket. It was not too busy just then, a nonholiday midweek in the summer, too hot to sit in the plastic chairs that were placed in the plaza, and the squad of Lubavitcher men who regularly staffed a post in which they tried to entice passersby to lay phylacteries lounged under a white umbrella, too enervated to muster much of an effort.

Still, there were a few dozen men praying at the Wall, enough so that Nathaniel and I had to find vacant spots some distance from each other. I placed my right hand on the stones, worn smooth by the touch of so many palms over so many centuries. It had become a practice to inscribe prayers, requests, pleas, and wishes on tiny slips of paper, and insert those into cracks or crevices in the Wall, and there were so many of these folded notes that they spilled onto the floor in great piles. Twice a year, before Rosh Hashana and Passover, the notes were collected and taken just outside of the Old City to be interred at the Mount of Olives cemetery just outside the walls, a Jewish burial site since ancient times.

This wall was not built by Solomon either, but by Herod I, the Roman ally who for more than three decades in the first century B.C.E. ruled as King of Judea. Herod ordered a massive reconstruction of what was known as the Second Temple, the facilities erected by the Jews who had returned from exile in Babylon hundreds of years earlier. His engineers used earth and stone to turn the slope of Mount Moriah into a level platform, an artificial plateau, then added new structures that contemporary accounts described as among the most magnificent in the Mediterranean world.

Well-known for his cruelty and mendacity, Herod kept a lid on anti-Roman sentiment during his long reign, but Judea became increasingly restive following his death, and after four years of revolt, his temple was destroyed by the legions and their Syrian auxiliaries in 70 C.E., a moment that would be memorialized as one of the great cataclysms of the Jewish people. And yet, while the Romans razed Jerusalem and built a new city in its place, eventually consecrating a temple honoring Jupiter on the Temple Mount, they left Herod's support structures intact, including the Western Wall. The Jews themselves, moreover, did not disappear from Israel, and continued to rebel despite repeated Roman massacres, bans, and enslavement, always managing to have a presence in Jerusalem, if only as pilgrims during those periods when they were banned from actually living in the city.

Beginning with Constantine in the fourth century, the Roman Empire's Christian emperors deliberately left the Temple Mount desolate, building churches honoring Jesus's life elsewhere to distinguish themselves from the Jews. In contrast, the Muslim Arabs who seized Jerusalem from the Byzantines in the seventh century, seeking to assimilate the Temple Mount as a vindication and sanctification of their new iteration of the One True Faith, consecrated the Dome of the Rock to house the Foundation Stone, a holy relic that had been part of the sanctuaries of the First and Second Temples, which they found buried under a garbage heap. The Foundation Stone also figures in the Quran's depiction of Muhammad's Night Journey to Heaven, while the Western Wall is mentioned as the place where the divine steed al Buraq is tethered.

In the same spot where Herod placed a substantial public building, Umayyad caliphs and their successors constructed the Al Aqsa Mosque, making the Temple Mount the third most important site in Islam, after Mecca and Medina. In 1099, Jerusalem was taken by Christian European Crusaders, who murdered thousands of Jewish and Muslim inhabitants and made it the capital of their new kingdom, converting Al Aqsa into their king's palace, with one section remade into a stable, and the Dome of the Rock recast as a church. The Crusaders ruled for more than a century before Muslims took back Jerusalem, and the city continued to change hands many times thereafter, suffering devastating raids from Mongols and Bedouin, among others, until 1516, when the city was absorbed by the Ottoman Empire.

A latter-day Solomon in ambition as well as name, Sultan Suleiman spared no expense in refurbishing the Dome of the Rock and Al Aqsa, adding beautiful new buildings to the Temple Mount along with his other improvements to the city, building the Wall along with numerous bazaars and other public works. The Ottomans had welcomed Jews in their empire, including the exiled Jews of Spain, and Suleiman allocated a section of Herod's Western Wall as their special prayer site. To many outsiders, this was the Jews' "Wailing Wall," a poignant spot amid the wreckage of a shattered city for a broken people to lament the destruction of their once great civilization.

Nevertheless, for the Jews themselves, the Wall became a symbol of dignity, a physical connection to their ancient past, which was, after all, the root of both Islam and Christianity. They had prayed in many spots around the Old City, and parts of the Wall were buried under the accumulated detritus of centuries of urban life, but the spot the Sultan designated for them was located just beneath the Dome of the Rock, adjacent to the cave beneath Solomon's sacred chamber in the First Temple, which some believed was a gateway to holiness. Jewish sentiment for the Wall, therefore, evolved separately from the Temple Mount, and some rabbis even recommended that Jews refrain from visiting the Temple Mount altogether.

In the wake of the First World War, the British Empire tried to maintain their Ottoman predecessors' policies when it came to the use of all the holy sites in Jerusalem, but the Wall and the Temple Mount had become part of the political struggle between Jews and Palestinians, the site of protest, combat, and massacre. The Jordanian army captured the Old City during the 1948 War of Independence and effectively blocked access to the Wall for nearly two decades after Israel's establishment. IDF paratroopers drove out the Jordanians during the Six-Day War in 1967, and just two days after the fighting ended, army engineers created the Wall's expansive plaza by forcibly evicting 650 Palestinian Muslims from a neighborhood that had been known as the Mughrabi Quarter, demolishing 130 homes as well as a seven-hundred-year-old mosque and other community buildings in the process. The Israeli government subsequently ceded administration of the Temple Mount to a Muslim religious agency based in Jordan, dividing the areas of authority in an effort to create a new order that carved out a space for Jews while avoiding international protest.

Since that time, Israel has focused on developing the Wall while generally leaving the Temple Mount to the Palestinians, though the arrangement has been marred by occasional riots and clashes, sometimes provoked by religious militants who advocate for building a new Jewish temple. The Wall has been the subject of protest as well from the Women of the Wall, an organization that wants equal access to all portions of the complex. But Orthodox rules predominate at the Wall with the tacit support of the state, and it has been incorporated into Israeli life as the site for the induction of soldiers and for annual ceremonies in which the Kohanim, the descendants of the Temple priests, converge to give blessings to the Jewish people.

On Saturdays, the Wall was busy with bar mitzvahs, and I recalled my own bar mitzvah at the Wall nearly four decades earlier, during one of our family trips to Israel. I'd attended several of my friends' bar mitzvahs in the synagogues of Brighton, the suburb of Rochester in upstate New York where I grew up, but wanted something more authentically Jewish. Gabi phoned the Western Wall's office to make a reservation, and, on the appointed Saturday, our family drove in several cars from Tel Aviv along the old road past the wrecked military vehicles until we reached Jerusalem. My mother, both grandmothers, aunts, and the other women in the family found spots along the barrier marking the border of the men's side and looked on while my father, uncle, cousins, brothers, and I entered the plaza.

The scene before us was cacophonous and disorderly, with men as well as boys running about in various directions, all of them shouting or laughing at top volume, while behind us, the row of women cheered on their bar mitzvah boys with cheers, ululations, and volleys of candy. We quickly discovered there was no reservation system—whoever had taken Gabi's call had a good laugh at our expense—and all the necessary components of a bar mitzvah, not least a willing rabbi and a table to read on, were in very high demand. Gabi eventually found an available rabbi in the crowd, but had to hold on to him by the lapels of his coat and drag him over to where we were standing against the efforts of others to secure him for their own ceremonies. Meanwhile, my cousin Ami found a table and promptly lay down on top of it to keep other bar mitzvah families from moving in.

Finally, the rabbi led us in song as we paraded together to the northern edge of the Wall plaza, where we entered a cavelike chamber and procured a Torah scroll before returning to the table, which Ami continued to defend with his body while enduring threats of violence. In addition to the main rabbi, we got a specialist who carried a long, thin, silver wand shaped into a craggy finger—the wand was called an *etzba,* or "finger"—to help me keep my place in the text.

We unfurled the scroll and I prepared to read the portion I

had studied for the past year, *"Ve'etchanan"*—"I beseeched"— recounting the moment Moses stood on the far side of the Jordan River and pleaded with God to forgive him and allow him to enter the Promised Land. I had painstakingly learned not only how to read the ancient Hebrew text but how to sing most of it in trope, rehearsing hundreds of times, and yet the word the *etzba* pointed to was unknown to me. I looked up at the rabbi in confusion.

We soon realized I had learned the wrong portion. There is a specific portion of the text designated for each week, and I, alas, had learned the one for the prior week. The family friend who trained me had miscalculated the date on the Jewish calendar, which incorporates lunar as well as solar elements, and does not accord with the standard Gregorian calendar.

This was a problem, in that the Torah was not usually rolled back, which meant I would have to wait an entire year to read it again.

I glanced back helplessly at my mother, grandmothers, and aunts while Gabi and my father negotiated with the rabbi. I began to cry. Finally, I saw that the argument was over, and the rabbi nodded before ordering, mercifully, "Roll the scroll back."

Now I saw *"Ve'etchanan,"* the first words in the portion I had studied. My voice creaked and lilted, inaudible in the din, as I sang about God rebuffing Moses, commanding him to stand on a nearby mountain and gaze upon the country he would never touch, trying my best to ignore the hard pieces of candy striking me as well as the little boys running beneath me, gathering up the errant sweets.

Emerging from this poignant, not to say humiliating, recollection, I spotted a dark, peaked portal on the northern edge of the plaza, an entrance to that very cavelike chamber where I'd obtained a Torah scroll for my bar mitzvah. Nathaniel came over and we stepped through into a long, dimly lit chamber with a high, vaulted ceiling. The chamber was actually the excavated under-side of millennia-old bridgework now known as Wilson's Arch, and inside was a whole new section of exposed Wall, against which were dozens of men with their palms pressed up against it, nodding back and forth with their eyes closed, or reciting prayers out loud from open books as they did outside. It was cooler in here, so others took advantage of the shade inside this artificial cavern to pray seated in plastic chairs before the Wall or mill around in groups. Most were Haredi, but there was a wide mix represented, and those wearing finely tailored suits over fitted white shirts *davened* shoulder to shoulder with men in tattered, sweaty rags. Here, too, the notes stuck in the cracks overflowed onto the floor, and a huge, ornate wooden cabinet with satin curtains had been placed against the Wall, its chambers housing the Torah scrolls used for bar mitzvahs and other sacred rituals.

Wandering around this hivelike arrangement of rooms, we noticed a heavy door cracked open, and peeked inside to see a group seated around a thick wooden table engaged in an intense debate. Bookshelves lined the interior walls, and we read the small brass plaques affixed to them with the names of families in Montreal and Los Angeles who had donated the funds for this sacred library, tomes that contained law and interpretation dating back two thousand years to the very beginnings of rabbinic Juda-ism, arranged according to whether the authors were Ashkenazi or Sephardi.

6

RAV NACHMAN'S CHAIR

Stepping back into the bright sunshine, we decided to try to find a way to get up to the Temple Mount, but the wooden plank structure that led up there was closed. Instead, Nathaniel suggested we get there through one of the gates in the Old City's Muslim Quarter, which was just a few minutes' walk through another bazaar. Removing the kippahs from our heads and putting them in our pockets, we left the Wall's vicinity through a side street.

Moments later, on a quiet, sunny street, a man with a thick, black mustache and goatee wearing a battered, dark suit sidled up to us and asked, in English, "Hello, how can I help you?" We glared at him briefly but didn't respond, pretending not to understand, and walked on. He tried again, throwing something to the ground and saying, "Sir, you dropped something. Look."

We didn't look back.

We found the bazaar covered by a structure of high peaked arches that ended in the Cotton Merchants Gate to the Temple Mount, but immediately noticed a different mood. On the way down from the Jaffa Gate, the owners had all been sitting outside their shops on stools and chairs, hawking their wares, smoking and kibitzing with their colleagues. But here the shop owners and their stools were all inside, many shops closed altogether, with metal screens and padlocks in front, and there were just a few women in hijabs with children in tow doing their necessary daily shopping for produce and household goods. At the end of the street, a squad of police officers in dark green uniforms, wearing bulletproof vests and carrying assault rifles, scanned every face of those going in both directions through the gate to the Temple Mount. We did our best to blend in, but as soon as they saw us, the officers shook their heads at us and pointed firmly in the other direction.

The police did sometimes close the Temple Mount area to non-Muslims, but how would the soldiers know we weren't Muslims, we wondered, considering whether to try to bluff our way in. The soldiers' demeanor dissuaded us from that folly.

Well, if we couldn't visit the Muslim sites, perhaps we'd try the Christians: the Church of the Holy Sepulchre was nearby. As we approached the church, the flow of people was greatly thickened by tour groups of Russians and Filipinos all carrying color-coded flags streaming in that direction. We were jostled left and right as we approached the main entrance, until Nathaniel spotted a rusted and damaged sign that read simply "Church" pointing up a steep stone stairway. As intrigued as we were eager to extract ourselves from the throng, we ascended the stairs while the tour groups all lumbered down the road.

After a winding climb, we reached a broad, flat space that looked like a courtyard with several structures in it, including a small chapel and a barrackslike hall. This was a portion of the roof of the Church of the Holy Sepulchre, with the dome of one of the chapels bulging out in the middle. In the shady places of the rooftop, under a large weeping willow and near the walls, a score of lean, dark-complexioned men and women dressed in gauzy white and black robes chatted with one another in small groups. These were monks and nuns of the Ethiopian Orthodox

Church, just one of the Christian denominations with a presence in this sprawling medieval complex.

Discovering an entryway, we ducked our heads to avoid the low ceiling and entered a chapel with a few benches before an altar to Jesus and a large painting on one wall depicting a meeting between King Solomon and the Queen of Sheba, ruler of a significant empire that included Ethiopia as well as Yemen. Ethiopian tradition holds that Solomon and the Queen's liaison produced a male heir, Menelik, ancestor of a long line of emperors and custodian of the Ark of the Covenant, the container for the tablets on which Moses inscribed the Ten Commandments. Though the artist had done his best to replicate the idealized style of ancient Ethiopia, giving all the characters ovular heads and large, round eyes, the painting had features that revealed it to be a decidedly modern production—King Solomon's entourage, for instance, appeared in Haredi style, complete with long, curly sidelocks as well as black coats and broad hats that were adopted only in the nineteenth century.

Beyond the chapel was a narrow internal stairway leading down to another, even smaller space, where a monk seated in the gloom glared at us as we walked past him into the main courtyard of the Church of the Holy Sepulchre.

The original church was built in the fourth century on the orders of the Roman Emperor Constantine, who, after converting to Christianity, dispatched his mother, the Empress Helena, to Jerusalem to find artifacts and sites related to Jesus. Empress Helena determined that a temple to Venus built during the reign of Emperor Hadrian was occupying the location of Jesus's crucifixion, subsequent preparation for burial, and temporary entombment, so she had it razed and replaced with a church. But that original structure was destroyed by fire in the sixth century, and its replacement, too, was severely damaged by fires and at least one earthquake, so that the current church is mostly a medieval construction from the eleventh century, when it served as the spiritual center of the Crusaders' kingdom.

The courtyard was filled with modern-day pilgrims, monks from Armenian, Orthodox, Coptic, Syriac, and Roman Catholic orders all interspersed among them. While the Ethiopians were relegated to the upper floors, these other orders controlled different monasteries and chapels on the ground and were involved in long-running arguments over duties and privileges that sometimes led to physical violence.

The church's enormous front doors were propped open and, just inside, pilgrims took turns kneeling over an uneven stone slab worn smooth by many millions of hands over the centuries. A sign indicated this was only a replica of the original stone used to prepare Jesus's body for burial, but the pilgrims' faces showed deep feeling and connection.

Beneath the largest dome of the church was an aedicule built to encase the remains of Jesus's burial place, the cave whose cliffsides had been reduced by Empress Helena. I stared up at the dome's interior, admiring the giant, star-shaped skylight in the center surrounded by beautiful starbursts, until a monk began yelling at me in Armenian to move along. Nathaniel and I exchanged looks, and decided we'd had enough.

Pushing past the pilgrims who were struggling to press inside, we soon made it back out the main doors to the courtyard. In an alcove in the shade, I spotted a young man perched near the door. His matted brown hair and beard, as well as the filthy, torn rags in which he was shivering, marked him as one of many unfortunates whose mental illness manifested in a city replete with holy sites, mystical symbols, and messianic movements. Turning from that poor fellow, I spotted a Greek Orthodox priest wearing an immaculate black cassock and a round hat as he very approvingly took in the posterior of a young, blond German woman in short pants. Lower-ranking Greek Orthodox clerics were not obligated to celibacy, so who was I to judge, but the young priest, who must have detected our amusement, quickly straightened up and picked up a discarded plastic cup in what seemed an impromptu act of penance.

We left the Old City and, just outside the unlocked gate, paused to gape at a Birthright group equipped with ropes and harnesses being urged by their guides to scale the Old City walls, with mixed results. Some of these young, foreign Jews were fit, daring, and willing, but a majority were either reluctant or unable, though the guides egged them on with the volume and urgency of an IDF sergeant at boot camp.

Perhaps, I proposed, this was intended as a reenactment of the paratroopers during the 1967 Six-Day War? Nathaniel didn't know and suggested we move on.

Hiking past the Damascus Gate on an incline, he pointed to the right at the entrance to East Jerusalem, a mostly Palestinian enclave with half of the city's population. Instead, we turned left and presently were standing at the beginning of Mea She'arim Street, the main thoroughfare in the eponymous neighborhood that was Jerusalem's most important Haredi neighborhood.

A little boy on a tricycle, dressed in a miniaturized version of the black-and-white uniform of Haredi men, sat poised on the edge of the sidewalk, considering whether to cross the large street before him. Presently, a slightly older boy appeared, and dragged his little brother and the tricycle back toward one of the gray buildings beyond. A sign in English and Hebrew warned tour groups and other tourists not to enter, explaining that such visitors offended the community. Those who chose to come anyway were expected to dress modestly, the sign continued, which meant women in particular had to have their hair covered and wear long sleeves and ankle-length skirts.

Mea She'arim (One Hundred Gates) was built in 1874, while Jerusalem was still an Ottoman dominion, one of many developments constructed to accommodate the fast-growing Jewish population. This wave of immigration, known as the Old Yishuv, was made up of tens of thousands of highly observant women and men, Ashkenazim from Europe as well as Sephardim and Mizrahim from North Africa and the Middle East. Rather than nationalism, they were motivated by religious fervor, and most lived pious lives of prayer, text study, and careful ritual practice. Mea She'arim's residents had a wide range of feelings about the secular nationalists who began coming in ever larger numbers in the twentieth century, with many expressing strong opposition to a state of Israel. But after the Second World War, Mea She'arim became the base for survivors of several Hasidic movements all but destroyed by the Nazis. Over the following decades, these groups reconstituted their rabbinic courts and their families multiplied until they filled, and then overflowed, the neighborhood's network of modest apartments and town houses.

Mea She'arim today shows the wear and tear of these generations of large families in overcrowded, mostly impoverished conditions, with shabby buildings along gloomy, narrow streets and significantly greater amounts of litter than other areas in Israel. Cars and trucks are permitted, but the tiny sidewalks are much too small for all the foot traffic, especially the large number of oversize strollers loaded with two, three, and even more young children, so pedestrians spill out into the road. Men from different Haredi movements wear distinctive styles of outerwear, some with stripes and others made of satin instead of wool, as well as hats in a variety of shapes with or without fur linings so that they are instantly recognizable as Satmar or Gur or another group. Women dress in parallel uniforms, with small but noted variations in clothing as well as hair coverings to distinguish one Haredi group from another. The drive to demonstrate modesty has even driven some women to wear head-to-toe black coveralls, like the burka required in some parts of Afghanistan.

Pulling the kippahs out of our respective pockets and replacing them on our heads, we stopped to read the *pashkevilin*, posters affixed to a wall as a sort of analog community bulletin board with public notices of funerals, religious gatherings, and proclamations by prominent rabbis, all written out in formal Hebrew and laced with religious references. Some were tacit advertisements, such as a service that organized tours of the Jewish holy sites in Hebron, a city mostly under the administration of the Palestinian Authority, but with one Jewish enclave cordoned off by the Israeli army. One centrally placed message admonished against the use of computers, mobile phones, and tablets to watch "unapproved" material—not only anything with sexual content but also anything touching on a wide variety of secular topics: everything from music videos to paleontological descriptions of dinosaurs, which might contradict Torah-based versions of the Earth's history. Haredim are not prohibited from using electronic devices or technology generally, the way Amish are, but Nathaniel commented that the last time he'd been in Israel the broadsides all prohibited the watching of "unapproved" videotapes and cable television programs.

Just a few blocks in, we saw the Breslover Synagogue, a long, flat structure made of the same dune-colored bricks as the rest of the city. At least from the outside, the building looked like it was in bad shape; the unswept stairs of the main entrance had collected wrappers, paper scraps, and empty liquid containers, while the battered front doors looked as if they were at risk of falling off their hinges. A few of the windows were cracked, while others had been replaced with pieces of cardboard.

Nathaniel had brought me here many years earlier to visit the synagogue's library, which contained a chair that had belonged to Rebbe Nachman, among other artifacts. We decided to see if we could find it again. The door was unlocked and we ascended a narrow, dusty staircase, squeezing past a Haredi man chatting animatedly on his cell phone and several groups of young boys jumping down the stairs. No one paid any attention to us, and at the top of the stairs, on the third floor, we reached a hallway with classrooms and offices, which we realized was the wrong place.

We were just making to go back down when Nathaniel stopped a little boy about six or seven wearing a kippah, his thick, light brown sidelocks coiled on his padded, pink cheeks all the way down to his neck, and asked him in Yiddish where the "Tzadik's chair" was?

The little boy gazed up at us with wide eyes, nearly breathless. A *tzadik* was a holy man, and the little boy surely knew instantly that we meant the chair of Rebbe Nachman, but he couldn't stammer out a response.

"It's OK," Nathaniel reassured him, "you can tell us in Yiddish."

Language was a complicated issue in Mea She'arim. Some Haredi groups, including this faction of Breslovers, persisted in speaking Yiddish, the Germanic language that originated among the Jews of Central and Eastern Europe, and refused to speak Hebrew in protest of the "Zionist Project," which they saw as a secular defilement of holy institutions. What that meant practically is that this little boy grew up in a Yiddish-speaking household but was aware that non-Haredim spoke Hebrew. Nathaniel surmised correctly that the boy was surprised and confused by a secular person speaking Yiddish, and indeed, it took him a moment to summon up his courage. His voice quavering, the boy finally whispered that we should head back to the second floor and turn left through the antechamber.

Following the child's instructions, we returned to the second floor, turned left through the antechamber, a spare room with a concrete floor, and entered through the swinging double door into the *beis midrash,* the synagogue's main prayer hall, which resembled a library, with shelves holding heavy hardbound books floor to ceiling. Men of various ages sat on wooden benches in front of desks and tables reading and conversing quietly, albeit with animated gestures.

Nathaniel addressed an older man with a black, gray-flecked beard sitting at a table reading nearest the door: *"Shalom alei-chem."* Peace to all of you.

The man glanced up briefly, nodded, and returned to his book.

We made our way to the back of the room, past the tomes on Jewish law and the sages' commentaries, until we were intercepted by a tall, thin Breslover with a scraggly gray beard and square gray wire-frame glasses. He introduced himself as Yosef, the *gabbai,* the warden of the synagogue.

Nathaniel and Yosef spoke to each other in Yiddish, chit-chatting about their respective family lineages, but I don't speak Yiddish, and when I tried to participate in the conversation using a combination of Hebrew and German, Yosef merely glared back at me with a mixture of horror and pity, before switching to German himself, and asking me pointedly where I'd learned *that* language.

He was not impressed when I explained that I had studied German in high school and mastered the language as an exchange student in the city of Bremen when I was sixteen, but he withheld comment as he turned back to Nathaniel.

"Well," he said, glancing at me again with unspecified concern, "let's go see the Tzadik's chair."

There it was behind a glass case built into the wall, an ornately carved wooden chair for a man of small stature, with vines sprouting flowers and fruit and even animals, both realistic-looking birds and mythological winged mammals that resembled griffins. When Nathaniel and I had visited the synagogue seventeen years earlier, the chair had been in the center of the room, set aside if otherwise exposed, but in the intervening years, it had been moved to this more protected location.

Was it true, I asked, that the chair had been smuggled out of Ukraine to Jerusalem?

Yosef nodded. The chair was carved in 1808 by a kosher butcher from a village in the Pale of Settlement, a heavily Jewish region controlled then by the Russian czar. The Breslovers were just a tiny group of only a few hundred devoted followers, and Rebbe Nachman was suffering from the first stages of tuberculosis, the disease that had just killed his wife and would claim his life within just two years. The chair survived as a precious relic among the Breslovers for over a century, but during the chaotic years after the Russian Revolution, as many Jewish communities were destroyed by their neighbors in frequent pogroms, the chair was disassembled and hidden away for a decade before being brought to Jerusalem in 1936. Restored at the Israel Museum in 1959, it was refinished in 1984 and finally placed on display at the synagogue.

Yosef continued to hover nearby until Nathaniel asked, "Do prayers to the Tzadik reach God directly?"

A bit taken aback, Yosef answered, "The Tzadik could only be helpful while he was alive, and in any case, *all* prayers go to God directly." But then he retreated, leaving us alone to contemplate the chair.

It was time for us to make a strategic exit. We backed out slowly, studying the titles of the books on the walls as we made our way out. Yosef reappeared in the anteroom, directing our attention to a strange-looking device he described as a "computer," which we quickly realized was an interface designed to collect donations using credit cards, complete with screens of instructions in English and French as well as Yiddish, but certainly not in German. We were able to politely refuse, however, repeating "thank you" in multiple languages as we went out to the stairway.

Back on the street in Mea She'arim, we made one last stop at a stall on the sidewalk with photos of famous rabbis, portraits as well as images of the rabbis reading or strolling alone in a forest. Though it had been erected on the sidewalk, the stall was semi-permanent, with shelves in the back piled high with documents, along with videotapes and other items, and Nathaniel asked the proprietor in Hebrew if he had photographs of any sages other than those displayed.

The proprietor, neatly dressed, with a trim gray beard and a black kippah, but not the black-and-white Haredi uniform, smiled confidently.

"I've got everybody," he said. "Who are you looking for?"

Nathaniel thought for a moment, and then asked if the proprietor had an image of the Satmar Rebbe, Joel Teitelbaum?

"Of course," said the proprietor with a huff.

He reached behind him to a folder and produced a color print photograph of the Satmar Rebbe, with his large, soulful eyes and loose white sidelocks. Born in 1878 in Transylvania, the Satmar Rebbe fled Europe during the Second World War, and reestablished his branch of Hasidism in Williamsburg, Brooklyn. Thoroughly and stridently anti-zionist, the Satmars believe it is rank heresy to declare the reconstitution of Israel before the arrival of the foretold messiah, though some Satmars have lived in Israel for many decades anyway. Indeed, many other Haredim in Israel respected and admired the Satmars precisely *because* of their anti-zionist stance.

"It's twenty-five for one or forty for two," the proprietor proposed, "if there's someone else you're looking for?"

Nathaniel glanced at me briefly, and asked the proprietor, "Do you have the Ben Ish Chai?"

The proprietor nodded. "Of course." He disappeared into the back room, and emerged a moment later with a black-and-white photograph of a man with intense, coallike eyes over a curly, black beard, his forehead wrapped in an ample turban.

Based in Baghdad's Grand Synagogue, the Ben Ish Chai—known, like many rabbis, by the name of his most famous religious text—led Iraq's venerable, prosperous Jewish community for the second half of the nineteenth century, corresponded with other rabbis across Europe and North Africa, and traveled to Jerusalem in 1909 to support the Jewish community there.

Nathaniel handed over forty shekels and took the brown envelope containing the portraits.

He looked my way seriously: "The Ben Ish Chai will be a gift for you."

Nathaniel had an afterthought, however, and turned back to the proprietor.

He asked, "Do you think it matters that we have these and we are neither Iraqi nor Satmar?"

"As long as you're Jews," the proprietor answered.

7

EL MARSA

Less than thirty-six hours later, at 7:00 A.M. on Friday, July 14, three men ran out of the Temple Mount through the Gate of the Tribes and fired pistols at a squad of Israeli border police officers stationed in front of the nearby Lion's Gate into the Old City. Two border officers suffered fatal wounds and two others were injured before the attackers retreated back into the Temple Mount. Within minutes, they were encircled by more border police responding from all directions, and all three attackers were shot to death.

According to news reports that morning, the murdered officers were Druze, a religious minority within Israel who often served in the border police because they spoke Arabic, while the attackers were Israeli Arabs from the city of Um al Fahm who had joined the cell of a banned Islamist group. Investigators were looking into whether the attackers had stashed their weapons in the Temple Mount and had closed the area.

The attack made a return to the Old City of Jerusalem impossible, but did not disrupt the rest of the country, and on Saturday, Gabi and Nira offered to drive Nathaniel and me to Nazareth to continue our tour of religious sites.

We drove north from Tel Aviv for one hour and twenty minutes in their new car, a Cadillac SUV, until we reached Nazareth, its winding streets tucked into the hills with two- and three-story apartment buildings and large family homes with shops on the ground floor and homes and apartments above. There were just a few taller buildings, sleek new glass-and-steel structures for apartments or offices.

In Hebrew, the word for Christian is *Notzri,* derived from the word for someone from Nazareth, and there are roughly 120,000 Palestinian Christians in Israel, concentrated in Nazareth, Haifa, and other northern cities. Palestinian Christians, divided primarily between Greek Orthodox and Catholic churches, collectively have the highest levels of educational achievement of any sector in the country, Jews included, and commonly speak fluent Hebrew as well as Arabic. As such, they are well represented in health care, media, and the courts; there has even been a Christian justice of the Supreme Court of Israel. But Christians were not only enmeshed with Muslims, they were also outnumbered by them. Even Nazareth, Israel's largest Arab city with a population of approximately 76,000, now had a Muslim majority.

We parked and walked back to the central plaza near the Basilica of the Annunciation, which was ringed by shisha cafés and kebab shops, banks with ATMs, and a tourist information center. Just up the narrow little road, a crowd of people stood shoulder to shoulder as they passed through the gate into the basilica's spacious, clean grounds.

Nazareth was old, to be sure, but not quite as old as many places in Israel. Just a village, if that, during the time of Jesus's childhood, it really was put on the map by the early Christians, above all Roman Emperor Constantine's mother, who, stopping in Nazareth on her tour of the Holy Land, ordered a church built to contain the grotto where, according to tradition, the angel Gabriel informed Mary she was carrying Jesus. Reconstructed most recently in 1969, the current basilica is the latest structure to occupy that space, an explicitly Catholic structure that has become a major tourist draw.

Among the busloads of West African tourists dressed in dazzling printed patterns and Eastern Europeans in solid black, gray, and blue ensembles, we lingered in the arcade, reviewing a display of mosaics on religious themes contributed by Catholic congregations around the world: a Philippine scene of an angel descending in front of Mary, depicted as at the bath with her long, straight hair uncovered; Ukrainian peasants in colorful clothing kneeling in front of an icon of Mary before fertile farmland; an Italian Mary with her exposed heart in her hand before a pyramid, an amphitheater, and a large, columned palace; a delicately composed Japanese portrait of the Madonna holding her child, both dressed in kimonos, standing in the sky amid clouds; and Korea's version, the Madonna and Child before a spare background laced with blossoming flowers.

The grounds included a convent and several other buildings, but the basilica itself was made up of two floors, with the upper level a modern prayer site that had pews before an altar and dais, and the bottom level part archaeological dig, part prayer site, housing the ruins of the church chartered by Empress Helena and the unfinished structure commissioned by the Crusaders during their tenure. The Franciscan monks who now ran the basilica held services in this space, so that a table with a white cloth and candles as well as stacks of folded chairs were set up in front of the ruins of the Byzantine church that contained the grotto where Mary had purportedly lived.

We emerged from the church complex and walked back down the lane to the plaza. A mosque located on the edge of the plaza hung a banner just below its loudspeakers that held a long

quotation from the Quran in Arabic with an English translation
in a larger font below:

> Say, "We have believed in Allah and what was revealed to us
> and what was revealed to Abraham, Ishmael, Issac, Jacob,
> and what was revealed to the Descendants, and what was
> given to Moses and Jesus and to the prophets from their Lord.
> We make no distinctions between any of them, and we are
> Muslims (submitting) to Him."

Gabi suggested we try some pastries at a bakery he knew
around the corner. An expansive establishment with seating on
two floors, Al-Mahdi Sweets was operated by an eponymous
family who had been baking for more than three generations.
We chose between dozens of varieties of baklava, cake, and
cookies, all made with purified butter and filled with cashews,
pine nuts, almonds, and pistachios, spiced with cardamom and
cinnamon, soaked in honey or syrup or cream, and shaped into
cones, cylinders, cubes, balls, triangles, discs, and squares, which
we finished off with thick, black espressos.

Properly fueled, we strolled the streets of Nazareth, past ar-
tisan jewelry makers and through the local market to a coffee
vendor Gabi liked, a shop that smelled of sawdust where fresh
sacks of beans from Ethiopia and Central America were piled
up behind a battered counter. Gabi greeted the heavyset store
owner, and after a few minutes of friendly exchange, requested
his "special blend." The owner combined an Ethiopian bean with
a Colombian and one or two others, filling the paper sleeves and
weighing the mix in a durable metal scale in a series of seamless
motions.

We stopped at a wine bar that doubled as a youth hostel, taking our glasses up to an airy lounge on an upper floor where we

sat amid black-and-white portraits of Nazareth's previous generations as we watched European tourists come in and out of their rooms. We had planned on eating lunch at Diana just up the hill, known as one of the country's best restaurants for Arabic cuisine, but Gabi seemed unsatisfied. Turning toward Nira, he conceded that Diana was great, but perhaps we could do better?

She raised an eyebrow pensively while Gabi kept brooding, and, after a few moments, snapped his fingers triumphantly.

"El Marsa," he proclaimed.

Nira wasn't sure: "You want to drive all the way to Akko?"

"We'll get there in thirty minutes," Gabi vowed. "No problem!"

Nira didn't protest. "OK," she said. "I'll see if we can get a reservation."

We walked back to the car past shisha cafés where groups of young men and women sat together, the men dressed in jeans and fashionable shirts with short haircuts and bushy beards, while the young women wore jeans and had their hair uncovered. On a long white wall, I caught sight of a mural, a map of Palestine encompassing Israel, Gaza, and the West Bank colored in black, red, green, and white strips like the Palestinian flag. Alongside the map was a painting of a key, and a cartoon character with his back turned, next to a few paragraphs translated into Arabic, English, and Hebrew:

On the day
of the Palestinian
Nakba on
May 15 1948
More than 780,000
Palestinians were
Forced out of their

Homes and Land
More than 500 Villages
Were Destroyed by Zionist
Forces. More than 50
Civilian massacres were
Committed. More than
15,000 Martyrs.

The wall was in a politically sensitive spot on a major tourist route, the Pilgrim's Road, designated to convey Christian tourists along sites significant in Jesus's life and times. On further research, I learned that the mural had been erased and repainted several times as the subject of an ongoing legal and political battle. Originally the work of a group of youth activists in 2014, the painting we were looking at was, in fact, its seventh iteration, carefully restored using a projector with an image of the first mural, which was traced over.

Farther down the road, on a brick wall overlooking a significant ridge, a sign in both Hebrew and Arabic, signed by Israeli police and Arab municipal authorities, warned in legalistic language that discharging firearms was prohibited and could result in significant civil and criminal penalties, especially if someone was injured by one of the rounds, which could result in up to ten years' incarceration. At the bottom of the sign, a sentence in bold, red Arabic as well as Hebrew declared, "In Our Village, We Do Not Shoot."

Gabi explained that firing weapons in the air was a traditional way to celebrate a wedding, say, or some other happy event among Arabs, but that it could very easily alarm Israeli police into thinking a terror attack was under way, quite apart from the risk of being hit as the bullets returned to the ground.

Driving directly west, downhill toward the coast, we arrived at the gate to Akko's Old City, another Ottoman installation, in just over a half hour. As we passed under the watchtower in the thick medieval walls onto a narrow road that wasn't truly wide enough for the cars that were flowing in each direction, let alone the cars parked on the sidewalks, Gabi steered the Cadillac deftly through it all, even slipping around a police operation in which two battered patrol cars with their blue overhead lights flashing had pinned a third vehicle, a battered, ancient Renault, to the wall. Gabi didn't pause long enough for us to figure out what was going on, and we continued on until we could see the waves of the Mediterranean. Finally, we rolled into the restaurant's little lot.

Akko's intact Ottoman-era walls had been given a UNESCO designation, and like Jaffa, the city had a long history as a port that had changed hands repeatedly, not least significantly as the Crusaders' last redoubt in the Holy Land in the thirteenth century. As in Jaffa, the Ottomans developed and populated Akko with Arabs, Jews, and other denizens of their dominions, though the current residents of its old city were almost entirely Muslim and relatively poor, reliant on tourism and fishing, both of these seasonal and fickle.

The marina was chockablock with restaurants, charming shacks advertising fish and hummus on sandwich boards amid boats, nets, and the other necessities of seafaring, but El Marsa was in a different category, a modern sandstone structure built on top of an old foundation. Checking off our reservation, the host led us through the airy, spacious dining room to a table along the front wall, all glass, looking out to the boats anchored in the harbor, their masts tied down, and the blue water of the Mediterranean beyond, all framed by the walls of the Old City.

Our waitress, Lina, short and slight, with an aquiline nose and raven hair pulled back into a tight ponytail, spoke to us in fluent, efficient English, though she could manage excellent Hebrew as well, both with a very slight Arabic accent: a trilled *r* and an aspirated *w*. She surveyed our interests, made a few recommendations, and soon brought out a first wave of small plates that included creamy whitefish pâté and red tuna carpaccio as thin as lace, a calamari salad with goat cheese and black olives, pickled sardines, a delicate whipped hummus topped with toasted almonds, and a spicy red *muhammara,* eaten on crusty housemade breads.

The base was traditional Arabic cuisine, but with liberal infusions of Mediterranean and European flavors. We washed the first course down with a dry Italian riesling from their finely curated list before the even more spectacular main courses emerged, a sea bass cooked whole, a vegetarian fettuccine, and a local fish called a *seneyia,* breaded very lightly and served over a bed of green beans, radishes, and lentils.

Lina lingered after we ordered dessert, answering our questions. She was born in a town near Akko in a Christian family, had recently graduated from high school, and planned to study medicine in Italy to become a doctor. In the meantime, she preferred to hang out in nearby Haifa, which had a thriving Arab social scene with shisha cafés, bars, and theaters.

"Akko is boring," she said.

Nira jibed that her confidence and ambition would make it hard for her to get married.

Lina glanced around at the men working in the restaurant, then nodded in agreement. "No doubt."

She returned a short time later with our desserts, small scoops of sherbet, apricot and pistachio, almond-infused rice pudding, chocolate pudding, house-made baklava, and—best of all—a round skillet with fresh kanefa, the traditional Palestinian treat, thin semolina noodle pastry layered with cheese, soaked in sweet syrup with rose water, saffron, and crushed pistachios sprinkled on top.

After this feast, we tried to rouse ourselves with more espressos as we stared at the fishing boats' masts teetering in the waves, but Lina came over and laughed out loud when she noticed our food-blissed stupor.

I approached the bar and introduced myself to the manager and co-owner, Marwan Su'ed. His English was poor, so we spoke in Hebrew as he explained that the building, which contained the kitchen, storeroom, and office, was built originally by the Crusaders in 1210, and later used as an Ottoman custom house. The dining room had been the custom house's courtyard, which was enclosed as part of the renovation.

Marwan was a childhood friend of El Marsa's visionary chef, Alaa Musa, and both were born and raised in Akko, in Arab Muslim families. Musa began his cooking career when he was just fifteen, a few blocks away at Uri Buri, the restaurant of pioneering seafood chef and hotelier Uri Jeremias, who was known for his enormous white beard and for an autodidactic epicureanism picked up along his youthful world travels. An Israeli Jew, Jeremias has trained generations of Arab chefs in his restaurant. Musa began as a dishwasher and fish cleaner, but was noticed and trained as an apprentice during his high school years. After graduation, he attended the Israel Center for Culinary Studies, then worked at restaurants in the Red Sea resort city of Eilat and in Tel Aviv as a sous chef.

At twenty-one, Musa met and fell in love with a Swedish woman, and ended up staying in Scandinavia for several years, landing positions at a series of Michelin-starred restaurants. These were establishments of a grander scale than any of Israel's much smaller restaurants, with an entirely different cuisine drawing upon items unfamiliar to him, like truffles, oysters, and lobsters. He returned to Israel to find Akko's food culture "trapped in the 1980s," as he told an interviewer, and, in 2012, opened El Marsa—the Anchor in Arabic.

I asked Marwan whether the attack in Jerusalem had affected the restaurant, and he paused pensively before saying no, they hadn't had any cancellations. Everyone watched the news, of course, but what happened on the Temple Mount seemed remote, at least for now. As a port city, moreover, Akko had a different perspective; it had always been open to outside influences, and was home even today to Muslims as well as Christians, Jews, and Baha'i, if one counted the entire municipality well beyond the old city walls.

"We need each other as partners to progress and develop," Marwan said, "even if not everyone knows it."

Gabi, Nira, and Nathaniel were already waiting outside, taking in the languid, salty breeze off the sea. I joined them, but our meditations were disrupted by a crowd of men who erupted into an intense argument on the dock, not far from the entrance to El Marsa. In the center, one man, bald and wearing a greasy white sleeveless undershirt, was holding the stirrup of a donkey laden with saddlebags, confronted a taller, thinner, hirsute man in a blue work shirt while a crowd of other men encircled them, egging on one side or the other, or standing by silently, arms folded, as they assessed the conflict.

I excused myself to use the washroom at El Marsa before we drove back to Tel Aviv. When I emerged, the bartender who had been standing with Marwan was waiting, a young man with that fashionable look I had seen in both Nazareth and Brooklyn, hair cut short on the sides with a heavy beard. His name was Ali, and he said he was happy to run into me as an American journalist because he wanted to elaborate on what Marwan had said. Ali agreed with Marwan's sentiment about Jews and Arabs needing each other in Israel, but he didn't think productive, peaceful coexistence would be possible in Israel, given the actual power dynamics in the world today. I asked him to explain, and he said that the only power capable of restraining the Israeli government from mistreating Palestinians was the United States, but instead, the United States only empowered and abetted the Israelis. Why? Because of Jewish control over the U.S. Congress, American politics generally, and the mainstream media.

In particular, he cited the American Israel Public Affairs Committee (AIPAC) as the principal organization that was allegedly orchestrating this domination of state and corporate American institutions.

"Where did you get all this information?" I asked him.

"The Internet, of course. In Arabic and in English," he said. "The truth can only be found online."

He wasn't accusing me personally of involvement in this conspiracy. Rather, he spoke earnestly, with all the fervor of having made a recent revelation that he felt had to be urgently shared. But I was momentarily dumbfounded to be confronted with a new form of the classic antisemitic conspiracy theory of secret Jewish control, a version of the *Protocols of the Elders of Zion* updated for the Internet age. I tried to counter with facts of the relative size of the pro-Israel lobby as compared with the oil lobby, the latter being many times larger, or the military hardware lobby, which was likewise comparatively huge.

I might have gone on, but noticed I wasn't getting anywhere with Ali, and cut my argument short. We parted on friendly terms anyway.

I emerged from the restaurant to find that the argument on the dock had by now escalated into a full-fledged street fight, with the bald man and his hirsute rival trading blows while the donkey brayed miserably. I looked across the road to see Gabi's hand waving at me from the Cadillac's window, so I dashed over, and got inside quickly. Nira, Nathaniel, and Gabi wondered what had taken me so long, but my answer was drowned out by the sirens of the approaching police cars.

8

<u>THE GENAZIM</u>

Though El Marsa was a harbinger of an original cuisine emerging in the country, Israel also had an established tradition of excellent restaurants located adjacent to gas stations, often evolved from roadside truck stops. The following evening, we ate at a prime exemplar, the Ayalon Inn. Its name was both descriptive and nostalgic, near the on- and off-ramps of the Ayalon Highway and harkening back to the days when trade caravans used the road. It served what was now called classic Israeli cuisine—chopped salads, hummus, pickled beets, and cabbage as appetizers, and then, for the main course, grilled meats on skewers. It was hardly a hip spot. The waiters were all thick-necked, middle-aged men with buzz cuts wearing long-sleeved blue work shirts with sleeves neatly folded above the elbows, but the prime cuts, kebabs of liver, and other innards were all cooked until the meat had a soft, buttery texture.

The next morning, Nathaniel and I walked from Givatayim into Tel Aviv to visit an archive for Jewish writers located within Tel Aviv's central library. On Kaplan Street, we stopped to get an iced coffee at a café in the Sarona Market, an area of several neat rows of sturdy stone cottages with spacious lawns with restaurants and boutiques that was actually a refurbished village built by the Templers, the German cult who also settled in Haifa in the 1870s.

At the same time they founded Haifa's German Colony, the Templers built Sarona adjacent to their fruit fields on what was then the outskirts of Jaffa. Over the next decades, the fast-growing Jewish metropolis of Tel Aviv enveloped Sarona on three sides, and during World War II, the Templers showed their support for Hitler and the Nazis, sending recruits to the German military, organizing a secret cell to spread propaganda, and plotting to help General Erwin Rommel's Afrika Korps in nearby North Africa. Inevitably, British authorities arrested the Templers, seized their property, and turned the neat cottages into a prison camp before expelling most of them to Australia. After the State of Israel was established, its military used the Templer homes as offices, building a huge military-government compound in the former fruit fields. The Templers sued the Israeli government from Australia, and in 1962, became the extremely rare case in which Israel ended up compensating German citizens for property that had been seized.

In the center of the land where the Templers once grew grapes and citrus, the military built the Marganit Tower, a thin concrete structure with a knot of wires, antennae, and an aircraft beacon blinking red on top. By the twenty-first century, the tower was crumbling and slightly tilted, so that it seemed like an artifact from some ancient extraterrestrial civilization. Just seventeen floors high, the tower was the second tallest building in the country when it was built in 1987, but today, with ever more high-rises coming on-line, it ranks only the twelfth. The commercial redevelopment of the cottages in 2015, however, proved highly successful, with Sarona attracting regular weekend crowds, despite a terrorist attack just one year after it opened in which two Palestinians from the West Bank sitting in the Max Brenner chocolate shop opened fire with automatic rifles, killing four and injuring thirty-seven.

A few blocks from Sarona, we reached Tel Aviv's central public library, called the House of Ariela, after the daughter of its primary benefactor. It is a massive, squat structure built in 1977 in the brutalist style in vogue then, with huge concrete plates affixed to its exterior. Inside the lobby was a veritable cross section of Israeli society, with many religious people in kerchief or kippah as well as bareheaded young people in shorts and T-shirts, from babies in strollers with their mothers to adult scholars.

To reach the Genazim Institute of the Hebrew Writers Association in Israel, we descended one flight on the central staircase to a landing between main floors, down a short hall, and through a door into a bright, open office with broad, clean desks and tables arranged for research as well as curation and preservation. A literary treasure trove, the Genazim held correspondence, manuscripts, drafts, drawings, photographs, paintings, contracts, promotional brochures, press releases, press clippings, video and audio files, balance sheets, bills, receipts, and other assorted documents from more than 750 writers, poets, and playwrights in Hebrew, Yiddish, Russian, English, French, and many other languages, some of the objects dating back to the early nineteenth century. Simply stated, it was the largest archive of materials related to Jewish literary figures in the world.

Nathaniel hadn't called ahead about our visit, but he was well acquainted with the Genazim's staff, having worked with them previously through email, and the board chairman, Adiva Geffen, came out to greet us warmly. Effervescent and charming, Adiva, a well-known author of novels, children's books, and plays, recounted the Genazim's history as she showed us through the offices and then took us into the archives: windowless, climate-controlled chambers with row upon row of shelves containing folders, papers, and books in a wide variety of paper stocks and trim sizes. Adiva explained the Genizam had been founded in

1951, just a few years after the end of the Shoah, with the oppression against Soviet Jews still ongoing, and it incorporated many items saved from Nazi fires and Stalinist purges, some from authors who had not themselves survived.

The Genazim was originally stuffed into a cramped, dilapidated space in the headquarters of the Hebrew Writers Union on Ibn Gabriol Street, and moved into this larger space within the library only in 2011. It was the perfect setting for the Genazim, whose name was derived from the word *geniza,* a storage space in synagogues where books and any document that contained the Hebrew names of God were kept, often for decades or even longer, while they waited for ritual burial. In practice, *genizas,* such as the famous one in Cairo, stored large quantities of text for indefinite periods, ponderous tomes alongside receipts, letters, and contracts, and this was the spirit that also animated the Genazim, which was a kind of *geniza* for the Writers Union.

Adiva clearly enjoyed administering the Genazim despite what she admitted were ongoing difficulties with fund-raising, to say nothing of managing the relationships between irascible artists, coldhearted bureaucrats, and self-interested politicians. But it wasn't too different from supervising any other artistic venture, really, so the precariousness felt natural.

"For me to run something is like dancing on the ice in Alaska," she laughed.

The Genazim's creation was a team effort spearheaded by Asher Barash, the president of the Hebrew Writers Union, an author, editor, publisher, and translator who wrote in Yiddish, Hebrew, and Polish. Born in the Austro-Hungarian province of Galicia, Barash had received a religious as well as a secular education, like many of the writers of his generation. He came to Israel in 1914 but kept in close touch with the vibrant world of Jewish writers in Europe, which would be destroyed during the Second World War.

Barash served as editor, for example, to the novelist and poet David Vogel, who was murdered in the Auschwitz concentration camp in 1944, following which Barash somehow acquired Vogel's papers, including unpublished manuscripts for various poems and novels. Barash turned over most of Vogel's papers to the Genazim before he died in 1952, but two more caches of documents were later found in his apartment, including one package of papers that was discovered decades later stashed within a hidden compartment in a wall. Once they were edited and published, a book of Vogel's poems and a novel both became bestsellers.

A placard hanging in the study room quoted Barash on why the Genazim was necessary:

> In the past, there were sons who kept the endeavor of their spiritual fathers. Today this "institution," meaning sons, is collapsing. The existing libraries cannot absorb the estates. There is a growing attitude of disrespect toward the past. Therefore, the time has come for us, the writers, to act. While the literature of the Middle Ages is being taken care of by institutions in Israel and abroad, almost nothing has been done for the current literature. This flaw must be corrected. Every day something is forgotten, every day something is lost. It must not be delayed. The immediate goal: to open an "account" for each writer, consisting of small or large items. Nothing is to be underestimated. A minuscule detail sometimes brings results to better understand the writer and his creative work.

In addition to Adiva, we also spoke with Yitzhak Bar-Yosef, a man in his sixties with short gray hair, blue eyes, and a reassuringly kind smile. In keeping with the Genazim's tradition of hiring writers as staff, Yitzhak was himself an award-winning novelist, not to mention the son of another acclaimed author, Yehoshua Bar-Yosef.

I asked Yitzhak about the practicalities of publishing in Israel.

Making a living in Israel as a writer was as difficult as in any small country, he responded, but at least there was a ready pathway to the global market here, translators who could render Hebrew texts into English, French, German, Russian, and other languages, along with publishers, editors, and marketing personnel in those countries, many of them Jewish, who could reach local Jewish readers as well as general audiences.

Nathaniel and I had worked up an appetite in the Genazim archives, and when we were done, I texted Gabi to ask if he had any suggestions for where we should go for lunch.

"Miznon," he wrote back promptly. "There's one right there on Ibn Gabriol Street."

Miznon was a casual chain founded by celebrity chef Eyal Shani, a regular judge on Israel's *Master Chef* television program who has no fewer than seventeen restaurants, not just in Israel, but in Paris, Vienna, Melbourne, and New York City as well. It was indeed a short walk to Ibn Gabriol, a broad boulevard named for the eleventh-century Andalusian Jewish poet and philosopher, and we could spot the restaurant easily from the crowd. It was an open storefront with a kitchen visible behind a counter, where the half dozen seats were all taken by a group of young men with motorcycle helmets while other diners sat at stools and at metal tables that sprawled out onto the sidewalk. The menu was written in multicolored chalk above the counter, but we could see racks of violet-and-purple eggplants, yellow onions, vermillion peppers, ripe cinnabar-colored tomatoes, and, displayed on their own wooden shelf, blossoms of cauliflower in their green leaves, the house specialty.

Nathaniel ordered a cauliflower sandwich and I got the eggplant sandwich, both with hummus, pickles, and spicy sauces. We found a recently vacated table, brushed off the crumbs, and dug in, devouring the mixture of textures and flavors, crunchy and creamy and pasty, tangy and spicy and sweet, vinegary and peppery all at once. The pita was delicate and fluffy, the eggplant roasted and smoky, firm to crispy on the outside but a steaming liquid on the inside, and the cauliflower was deliciously salted and roasted, with a granular crust and a milky interior that swirled with the hummus and coated the pickles.

"Not bad," I said.

"Not bad," Nathaniel repeated, "but not as good as the gas station Gabi took us to yesterday."

9

KABBALISTIC KUGEL

It was evening by the time Nathaniel and I hiked back to Givatayim, and when we arrived at Nahalat Yitzhak Cemetery, the memorial celebration was already well under way, just as we'd hoped.

I'd timed this particular visit to Israel to coincide with this event, an annual festival commemorating a long dead rabbi from Romania that brought many thousands of Haredim into Givatayim, the small city adjacent to Tel Aviv where much of my family lived.

I'd visited Givatayim since childhood and was frankly surprised to learn that a massive Haredi event of any kind was held there, since it was undoubtedly one of the bastions of secular Israel. Founded in 1922 by zionist-socialist workers, Givatayim was like any other secular area, with cafés and restaurants that served nonkosher food, and nonreligious public schools, among Israel's best, that offered a curriculum based on science, history, mathematics, and literature to mixed classes of boys and girls. Its municipal swimming pools, parks, shopping malls, and movie theaters were likewise fully gender-integrated and accepting of LGBTQ families as well. Election data showed large majorities of Givatayim's sixty thousand residents regularly voted for Israel's left-leaning political parties, and overwhelmingly opposed restrictions on Shabbat such as closing businesses and stopping public transit, as well as exemptions for yeshiva students to avoid military conscription.

Well aware of Givatayim's reputation, Haredim reveled in provoking its secular population with this gathering, held every year on the rabbi's death date, according to the Jewish calendar. The headline of a story about the annual gathering on a popular Haredi website translated as "The Memorial for the Rabbi from Shtefanisht Shines a Light Among the Goyim in Red Givatayim," using the derisive word for non-Jews to describe the city's population.

The Romanian rabbi honored by the Haredim at this memorial had died and been buried far away, making his unlikely journey to Israel only long after his death. Born in 1847, Avrohom Mattisyohu Friedman was the Second Shtefanisher Rebbe, the son and grandson of great Hasidic leaders at a time of general penury for the Jews of Eastern Europe, and particular impoverishment among Romania's Hasidim. Avrohom Mattisyohu's father, the First Shtefanisher Rebbe, had been a bold figure who inspired his followers by authoring important commentaries on Jewish law, keeping a large rabbinical court, wearing fine clothes, and riding horses like a nobleman. When his father died, Avrohom Mattisyohu was just twenty-one years old, and, cajoled into taking his father's mantle, he soon proved himself a very different leader. A pillar of humility and restraint, he rarely spoke during the gatherings of Hasidim, never issuing an opinion on a religious topic at all. He prayed silently for hours at a time, ate little, gave most of his wealth to widows and orphans, supported the many Hasidim who came to study at his home, and dispensed unpretentious advice to those who sought his wisdom, Jews as well as Christians.

"Do you have faith?" he would ask the supplicant. "Go home and God will help you."

One legend held that when he was approached by the desperate father of a girl critically ill with typhus, the Rebbe gave the man the spoon he used for breakfast as well as bread from his table. Although the girl had not eaten in days, she devoured the bread and ate even more with the spoon, eventually recovering completely. Another tale asserted that secular Jewish leaders sought his advice to counter the maneuvers of antisemites in the Romanian parliament, and that the Rebbe's legal analysis prevented atrocities from being committed.

Abstemious in his personal life as well, the Rebbe divorced his first wife after eleven years without producing children, and later married a cousin, a widow with three children from her previous husband. To the Hasidim of Romania as to many others in the Jewish world, his behavior was so righteous that many theorized he was a Hidden Tzadik, a holy man who concealed his greatness behind a mask of simplicity.

Even his official portrait radiated pious humility: hunched and elderly, his eyes open wide in astonishment, his lips pursed pensively, a fluffy white beard draping down over the lapels of his black coat, topped by a unique hat, black and conical, with a thick fur brim.

When he died in 1933, after sixty-five years as Rebbe, his funeral was attended by tens of thousands, and afterward, according to his instructions, the silverware and other valuables in his expansive home were used to endow a yeshiva on the site. There, small cadres of Hasidim studied sacred texts until 1941, when it was destroyed by Romanian allies of the Nazis. Approximately 15,000 Jews, including many Hasidim, were slain during a pogrom in Iasi, where the Rebbe was buried, and overall, some 400,000 Romanian Jews were killed during the war, including most of the country's Haredim.

Still, 350,000 survived the conflict, becoming one of the largest remaining populations in Europe and a bargaining chip in a particularly cynical episode of the Cold War. Israel, aligned with the United States, and Romania, aligned with the Soviet Union, were in opposing camps, but each enjoyed a modicum of independence within their blocs. Israel was anxious to collect Jews from the world, while the Romanian government was hungry for cash and technology, and their negotiations resulted in a small number of emigration visas being issued to Jews to leave for Israel. When Nicolai Ceausescu came to power in Bucharest in 1965, he stopped the Jewish exits at first, claiming solidarity with Palestinian organizations and their Soviet allies, but soon issued a formalized price list that placed a greater value on those with status, degrees, or notable skills. According to one researcher who dedicated years to documenting the scheme, between 1968 and 1989, Ceausescu sold visas for 40,577 Jews at an average of $3,000 each, generating more than $112 million.

In this context, the Ceausescu regime turned its attention to the Shtefanisher Rebbe. His grave site had been unmolested throughout the Second World War, and afterward became a pilgrimage site for Jews and Christians alike, such that the tentlike structure placed over his grave overflowed with notes on which people had written their wishes, hopes, and pleas. Officially Communist and atheistic, the regime could not allow such displays of religiosity, and it informed Jewish leaders that the Rebbe's grave was in danger, though the government would be willing to facilitate the relocation of the remains. Surviving Romanian Hasidim in the United Kingdom, the United States, and Israel took charge of the effort to rescue the Rebbe's remains, debating for a time whether to bury him in Tiberias, near the Sea of Galilee, before finally deciding on Nahalat Yitzhak Cemetery in Givatayim, where several other prominent members of their movement were already buried.

In October 1968, the Rebbe's coffin was disinterred from

the Jewish cemetery of Iasi under the supervision of Hasidic and secular Romanian Jewish leaders and brought to the airport in Bucharest, where it was placed on a plane belonging to the Romanian Aviation Association and flown to Israel with Israeli authorities on board.

The Rebbe's remains arrived in Ben Gurion Airport on a Thursday evening, and the coffin was officially greeted before being brought to a yeshiva in Bnai Brak, a city adjoining Tel Aviv where relatives of the Shtefanisher had established yeshivas, and rituals were performed throughout the night. At 10:30 A.M. the following morning, a hearse arrived to bring the Rebbe's remains first to the main synagogue in Tel Aviv, and finally to Nahalat Yitzhak Cemetery.

Today, Nahalat Yitzhak holds thirty thousand graves set among sloping hills, including a mass burial site for soldiers of Israel's pre-state militia, the Haganah, as well as cenotaphs for several communities destroyed during the Holocaust, all enclosed by a high wall topped with metal stakes. The grounds were bisected by a single street called Avnei Zikaron—which translates into "Stones of Memory"—and this was blocked off to allow the memorial festival, with a sign issued by the municipality at the entrance politely warning "honored guests who are coming to pray" not to park illegally, light candles outside of designated zones, or disturb the neighborhood's senior citizens, who had lodged many complaints in the past. The sign also urged the "honored guests" to use the public toilets and informed them cold drinks and kugel, a traditional casserole with reputedly mystical qualities, according to the Kabbalah, would be served free of charge. Only in the vicinity of the grave site were the memorial's organizers allowed to offer passersby a kippah or a pamphlet containing prayers.

Hundreds of men and women were strolling up and down Avnei Zikaron Street, women dressed modestly in skirts or dresses with their shoulders covered, with kerchiefs, berets, tams, and caps in a kaleidoscopic range of colors and shapes, but a good number had their hair exposed, and no one seemed to be bothering them. Likewise, not all the men wore kippot, and there were many clean-shaven faces among those with unkempt beards of the highly observant.

A few young boys and teenagers moved in and out of the long, air-conditioned prayer tent, which pulsated with rather improbable disco lights, and a bookseller barked into an electric megaphone to advertise his bestsellers, illustrated tales of famous rabbis for children, at low, low prices, three for the price of two, while a long line had formed at the table where a tall, heavyset man with an expansive snowy white beard dispensed blessings as well as "official" memorial candles, prayer books, and mezuzahs, engraved metal cylinders containing tiny prayer scrolls fixed to door frames. Those in line stepped forward to speak with the white-bearded man for a minute or two, collect an item, and then drop a few coins into a small metal box on the table before moving on.

Nathaniel approached a group of men in Haredi uniform— black suits and broad-brimmed hats, long-sleeved white shirts, beards and untrimmed sideburns called *peos,* an ancient practice for religious Jews that stems from an interpretation of a Torah passage which specifies not to cut the corners of one's hair.

He addressed them in Yiddish, but they looked back blankly.

He switched to Hebrew: "You don't speak Yiddish?"

The tallest of the men quipped back an answer, "Why not Arabic?"

"Well," Nathaniel countered, "You are dressed as Hasidim

and are attending the memorial for a Hasidic rebbe from Romania, so it's only natural that I thought you were Hasidim."

"People of all kinds come to the Tzadik's memorial," shrugged the Tallest.

Nathaniel laughed. "So I guess that's why we we're speaking Hebrew."

The Tallest laughed as well and shook Nathaniel's hand vigorously. These men were Mizrahim whose ancestors had lived in North Africa or the Middle East and spoke Arabic, rather than Yiddish—hence their quip. Nevertheless, they came from the large number of highly observant Mizrahi families who had adopted Haredi ways in Israel but had their own rabbis who adhered to Sephardi traditions, maintained their own yeshivas, and even their own political party. Even as the numbers of Mizrahi Haredim had grown rapidly, however, when it came to clothes, they had fully adopted the Ashkenazi style.

The Tallest looked us over and asked what our story was.

"We're from the U.S.," Nathaniel answered. "He's from Chicago; I'm from California."

"Oh, yeah," replied the Tallest, knowingly. "I used to live in Brooklyn."

They asked us how we'd heard about the Tzadik. I explained that my family lived in Givatayim, and that I'd seen the memorial and wondered what it was all about.

The Tallest explained helpfully that the Tzadik was from Europe, that he had died a long time ago, but that Haredim had brought him to Israel. Miraculously, when the body was transferred, they saw that the Tzadik's corpse was not decomposed, as if he had been buried just the day before, rather than decades earlier.

Had the Tallest seen the body himself? I asked.

No, he laughed. That had all happened well before he was born, but he had heard about it from those who were there.

At this point, a woman in a colorful kerchief came up to the Tallest and asked him a question. She was accompanied by a West African woman in a colorful, patterned dress and matching head wrap, and Nathaniel asked her what brought them to the Shtefanisher's memorial.

After hesitating for a moment, the woman nodded toward her African friend and explained, "She needs help . . . with a family matter."

We nodded sympathetically, and they proceeded toward the cemetery's entrance.

The man with the white beard who had earlier been disbursing commemorative items was now distributing slices of kugel, the kabbalistic casserole, from enormous pans.

"That looks good," I said. "Do you want some?"

Nathaniel shook his head skeptically.

I asked the white-bearded man: What was the connection between the kugel and the mystical traditions of the Kabbalah?

He smiled slyly as he dished out slices: "Kugel and Kabbalah [which means "The Received" in Hebrew]? At this memorial, we *receive* kugel and we're happy."

The crowd roared with laughter, and I slunk away, doing my best to make myself invisible.

Though it hasn't yet been discovered by culinary elites, kugel is something special at its best, having a fluffy, creamy texture and a delicate sweetness or savoriness, depending on the recipe. Unfortunately, this kugel was rubbery and bland with a strange, bitter aftertaste. Still, I ate it while we observed a small crowd gathered around a fortune-teller, a ruddy-faced, older woman with dramatically arched eyebrows, a plush brown cloth covering her thick gray hair, and an embroidered shawl on her ample shoulders. Before her stood a middle-aged, secular Russian woman, pinching a neck scarf at her chin to veil her well-coiffed hair, listening intently as the fortune-teller shouted at her in rapid-fire Hebrew. I hadn't heard the initial question and couldn't quite hear the answer either through the din, but the secular Russian woman and her friends nodded and stuffed bills into the woman's tin box, apparently impressed.

I turned to Nathaniel and asked him about the Tallest's account of the Rebbe's unspoiled corpse, which I'd read several times on different Haredi websites.

"It's a legend that's associated with many Hasidic figures," Nathaniel said. "Like the healing properties of the food from the Rebbe's table."

I forced down the rest of the kugel, then tossed the plastic plate and fork into the trash as we proceeded to the cemetery entrance, a gate in the wall that had been flung wide open. Dozens of men and boys of various ages were milling about in the wide courtyard, swaying in prayer separately or together. Outside the walls, men and women mixed freely, but here the space was male-dominated, with women consigned to their own designated path to the grave site. The Rebbe's grave was conveniently located near the entrance, with tape and barricades installed to direct the memorial-goers, along with armed security guards positioned at key junctures to prevent any ecstatic celebrants from wandering too far.

Following the flow, we got into the thick of the fast-moving line along with the Haredim and the other men with short sleeves until we all stood under a great, green plastic tarp that served as the tent over the Rebbe's grave. Like other graves, the Rebbe's was a solid horizontal slab of Jerusalem stone with a headstone inscribed in Hebrew. A nervous police officer looked on while the restive stream of men took turns pressing their palms onto the slab, most of them praying audibly as they rocked back and forth. A plastic curtain had been draped at the back of the slab and headstone, but as it rustled, it opened slightly and I caught a glimpse or two of an equivalent flow of women at the rear of the mausoleum, quieter and more orderly than the men.

Back outside on Avnei Zikaron Street, we milled around for a while before deciding to get an evening snack. Weizmann Boulevard nearby had a good number of restaurants and pubs that were still open, so we cut through the neighborhood up Taiber Street's steep, tree-lined, blossom-scented slope, past bungalows and apartment buildings with little yards and low walls and then down to Weizmann, where our choices were Slyder, serving hamburgers and french fries in booths with vinyl seats and laminate tables resembling an idealized 1950s American diner, and Favela, which specialized in Brazilian cuisine presented amid furnishings of rough, handcrafted wood designed to evoke the Amazonian frontier. But at the edge of the strip, we noticed an unnamed falafel stand with a skinny young man behind the counter in a T-shirt, jeans, and kippah who, when he noticed us, called out, "Come on over. We have the best falafel in town."

We spoke to him and another slender young man his age, likewise in a T-shirt and jeans, but of East African descent. The East African youth used tongs to give us sizzling falafel balls straight out of the oil. Every falafel mix is a little different, based on chickpeas mashed and fried, but with scallions and various other spices added, and theirs was indeed tasty, at least while it was crispy and fresh, so we each got a sandwich in a pita stuffed with pickles and chips, drizzled generously with tahini and hot sauce.

We returned to the memorial just over an hour later, and there were many people there still, with long lines of both men and women waiting for their turn to touch the Rebbe's tombstone. But it was after sunset now, the crowds were definitely thinning, and the vendors and soothsayers were all packing up or had already moved on. At the spot along the cemetery wall closest to the Rebbe's tomb, people were lighting small memorial candles.

We walked past the barricades and waited for the light to change on busy Aliyat ha Noar Street next to a middle-aged Haredi man approximately our age, portly but with a regal carriage, his beard thick, black and curly at the chin and on his cheeks, but wispy on his upper lip. He nodded and smiled as we approached.

"Good evening," I greeted him in Hebrew, to which he responded in kind.

I asked, "Were you just at the memorial for the Tzadik?"

He looked pleasantly surprised. "I was," he answered. "You two were there, too?"

"It was a very special experience," I said. "Powerful. I've never been to anything like it."

He nodded, thoughtfully. "Sometimes you just need a . . . a recharge, you know what I mean?"

"It was different from many other events," Nathaniel said. "When I tried to speak Yiddish with people, they refused. 'Here we all speak Hebrew,' they said. When I asked them if they were Gur or Breslov, they said, 'Here we are all the people of Israel.'"

The man nodded vigorously. "The Tzadik's memorial is the perfect place for Jews like me," he said. "I don't have a rebbe. I do my own thing."

By now, we were at the corner of HaShalom Street, a busy, six-lane thoroughfare, and the independent Haredi guy was headed left where we were turning right.

"Good night," we said in Hebrew.

"Good night," he responded, began walking, then turned

back again, smiling and waving. "Here we are all the people of Israel," he called out, with good humor.

Between the Genazim and the memorial to the Second Shtefanisher Rebbe, we'd spent the day in two very different, equally Jewish spaces dedicated to re-creating the world that had been destroyed by the Shoah. The Genazim aimed to preserve every scrap of writing, no matter how mundane, from every writer and artist, regardless of their level of recognition. The memorial, meanwhile, glorified a man whose life had been dedicated to humility and personal contemplation, whose community had been nearly wiped out, but ironically, where the Genazim was just hanging on, neglected by a secular society that valued literature only as a commercial enterprise, the Shtefanisher's legend was only growing, buoyed by rapid expansion of the Haredi world.

I had ample opportunity to contemplate these grand ideas and deep contradictions until very late that night while the gourmet cauliflower, kaballistic kugel, and teenagers' falafel battled it out in the molten landscape of my digestive system.

The next morning, Nathaniel helpfully pointed out that his stomach was fine, which he attributed to avoiding the kugel. Food at the Rebbe's memorial, he mused, did not have the same power as food from the Rebbe's table.

10

PSAGOT

Two days later, Gabi drove Nathaniel and me to a winery in Psa-got, an Israeli settlement deep in the Palestinian territories on the West Bank of the Jordan River. We left Givatayim late in the morning, after the rush hour traffic, and crossed the so-called Green Line—the official border between Israel and the Palestinian territories—just about an hour later. There was no checkpoint and no discernible boundary or even a marker on the highway, but on the hills above the road, we now noticed high fences topped with razor wire as well as watchtowers and electronic cameras on high posts. The road curved oddly, and Gabi explained that this was in order to connect the various settlements and military bases in the area, while circumventing the expansive Palestinian capital of Ramallah and its suburbs.

Soon, the road became one lane in either direction, with many trucks as well as private cars bearing green license plates that identified their owners as Palestinians from the occupied zone. Only here, several kilometers inside the Green Line, did we cross through the separation barrier, a high concrete wall topped with armored watchtowers that was constructed beginning in 2002, after a series of suicide bombings during the Palestinian revolt against Israeli military control called the Second Intifada. All of the towns and villages visible from the road were Palestinian now, with minarets rising out of mosques in neighborhoods of single-family homes and low-rise apartment buildings. Most of the municipalities in this area were under direct control of the Palestinian government based in Ramallah, but the complicated, ongoing negotiations between the Palestinian Authority and the Israeli military meant that some towns or parts of towns were no-man's-land. These areas had little or no government services, obvious in the unpaved streets, uncollected garbage, and hulks of stripped, burned-out cars by the side of the road.

As the Cadillac neared Psagot, we saw a cluster of trailers on a hilltop behind several concentric layers of high fencing, along with parked military vehicles and bunkers bristling with antennae. The first bunker, unoccupied in the midday heat, was covered in camouflage netting with a torn Israeli flag affixed to the front. On the rocky ridge above, a large black sign with an electronic counter marked the number of days the former residents of Migron, a settlement the Israeli courts had determined illegally built on Palestinian land, had been waiting for replacement housing promised them by the government in exchange for their peaceful departure. Previous evacuations had sparked violence as settlers and their supporters fought against police and military units, creating videos of Jews fighting with other Jews that were shared widely on television and social media. These video clips were a great embarrassment to Prime Minister Benjamin Netanyahu, whose current coalition of right-wing parties generally supported unchecked expansion of the settlements.

The entrance to Psagot was guarded by soldiers in a fortified checkpoint and by electronic surveillance, but we passed through easily enough, and ascended until we reached the hilltop. There we parked in the lot, and walked to the visitors center, a wide, low building made of large, rough stones, with an ample, glassed-in veranda and a tiled roof held up with arches and columns. It was a scene that could have fit easily into Tuscany or California wine country, marred only by the battered IDF jeep in the foreground, its windows covered by a metal grill, and the bustling Palestinian city visible on the nearby hills.

Gabi had arranged this visit through a lawyer in his office, who was a cousin of the winery's owner, and we were met by a brightly smiling woman in her twenties dressed in something of an updated hippie style—embroidered blue denim skirt, long-sleeved shirt, and a thick red head wrap. This young woman (who said I could describe her and her work at the winery but asked that I not use her name) led us into an air-conditioned conference room. The winery's founder, Yaakov Berg, would join us shortly, she said, but first, she would be giving us a tour. To begin, she brought out an important relic for the winery, a tiny gold coin stamped on the front with the words "For Freedom of Zion," and "Year 2," referring, apparently, to the second year of a revolt against the Roman occupation, the year 67 C.E., along with the image of an amphora, an ancient wine container. The coin, which she said had been found in a cave discovered during the construction of a new storage space for the winery, had been taken as a symbol that this was indeed land promised to the Jews, and that their task of producing wine here, therefore, was a righteous restoration of its true purpose. Producing a map of ancient towns that were now modern settlements, though it left out every Palestinian city or village, she pointed to Psagot—meaning "Peaks"—as one of the communities mentioned in the Tanakh as belonging to the Tribe of Benjamin.

The visitors center also housed the winery's production facilities, and our guide brought us into a hallway with large interior windows overlooking the vats used in fermentation as well as the filtration equipment before moving to the next room, where she showed us hundreds of oak barrels used to age the wine. Her presentation was laced with references in the Tanakh and other sacred texts to winemaking, but she was careful to underscore that she wasn't really interested in politics. She hadn't chosen to live in the West Bank as some sort of statement, she explained. Her parents were born in Hungary, and she had been raised on a nearby settlement, had recently married, and started a family in Psagot. This region was just her home, simple as that.

We returned to the conference room, where our guide had laid out bottles of wine, cheese, nuts, and dried fruit, and Yaakov himself arrived shortly, charging into the room and apologizing for his tardiness, carrying several more bottles of wine by their necks with his fingers. A fit, clean-shaven fellow of about forty in a dark-colored polo shirt, jeans, and a kippah perched on an unruly patch of blond hair, he sat down and started opening the bottles, quizzing us about our backgrounds and interests as we sampled the wines, including a robust but refined cabernet/shiraz blend the winery called "Sinai," a merlot that was rich and warm, and a complex Bordeaux blend called "Edom."

Yaakov was born in Moscow, and his parents immigrated to Israel when he was three, first to Jerusalem, and then to a settlement nearby when he was thirteen. He had served as an enlisted soldier in the Golani Brigade, a famed infantry unit, and studied law after his service before returning to the West Bank, where he planted his first vineyards in 1998 and founded the Psagot Winery in 2003. The land he used to build it all was hotly contested, not only in violent confrontations between Palestinians, settlers, and the Israeli military but also in Israeli courts, where Yaakov had sometimes lost, he admitted. Indeed, he was even facing a demolition order on his own house and swimming pool—a court edict that remained unenforced. But Yaakov insisted that he had paid, and paid well, for all of the land he had claimed and culti-vated. Now Psagot was the largest of thirty or so wineries in the

West Bank, comprising sixty-two acres and producing upward of 400,000 bottles per year to be sold around the world, especially in places where there were Jewish communities with many who drank only kosher wine.

As the conversation turned from his life story to politics, Gabi asked Yaakov if the settlers saw themselves the same way as the founders of the kibbutzim during the early years of the state, as pioneers in a new land, but Yaakov rejected that idea. Certainly he didn't identify with the socialist ideology behind the kibbutz movement, but more fundamentally, he and his fellow "settlers" were, in their self-conception, really just reclaiming the land promised to the Jewish people by sacred covenant.

Nathaniel asked Yaakov whether those who settled in the West Bank believed they were catalyzing the events prophesied to occur before the return of the messiah, but he demurred—he was no Haredi either, though he adhered to orthodox practice.

I picked up Gabi's point, noting that settlers constituted only 10 percent of the country's Jewish population, something like 600,000 people, and yet had come to dominate the national conversation. It had become controversial, I observed, even to refer to the military control of the conquered Palestinian lands with the Hebrew word for "occupation," or to say "occupied territories" rather than Judea and Samaria. Nevertheless, it remained an occupation under Israeli law, so I asked about the settlers' endgame. Did he hope for these territories to be incorporated fully into Israel with a formal annexation?

Yaakov said the popular use of Judea and Samaria showed that the rest of the country was finally catching up with the settlers' position and acknowledging the historic role of these lands in the Jewish world. Psagot was Israel, just like Tel Aviv or Haifa or Jerusalem, and it was going to stay Israel in the future. There were already seventy thousand Jews in dozens of settlements of varying sizes in the Benjamin area, and Yaakov was confident they would keep growing.

Nevertheless, there was significant international opprobrium, I pointed out, including the fast-growing Boycott, Divestment and Sanctions movement (BDS), which was gaining traction in Europe, on American college campuses, and even among American Jewish groups who advocated for peace with the Palestinians.

BDS only increased his sales, Yaakov scoffed. Every time a BDS organization targeted the winery in a public campaign, he saw a surge in orders from those who wanted to show their support. Still, he railed against the European Union, which had recently ruled that wine from Psagot and other West Bank wineries would have to be labeled as "produce of the West Bank (Israeli settlement produce)" or "Israeli produce of the occupied Palestinian territories." This, he raged, was akin to forcing Jews during the Holocaust to wear yellow stars.

As for American Jews who criticized the settlements, they were simply soft in their support for Israel, as Yaakov saw it, because they didn't understand what Israelis were dealing with, the existential threats they faced. But he received plenty of support from American Christians, including a visit from John Hagee, a leading evangelical pastor who had written several popular books interpreting current events in Israel as prophesied in the Bible for the final days before the arrival of *their* messiah. Dozens of American Christian volunteers came to help pick grapes every year, though Yaakov had to tell them not to touch the wine, as contact with non-Jews during key points in the production process would obviate a kosher certificate.

Yaakov counted international authorities up to and including the previous American president all as rank hypocrites, citing a scenario that was close at hand to make his point. A few families were living in trailers that had been parked on land he said belonged to him and the community of Psagot, but this "community" had been declared illegal by Israeli courts under international pressure. Comparing the situation to America's 1846 war with Mexico, in which large sections of North America were seized through military conquest, Yaakov said the trailers had become the target of international outrage only because of the undue and unjust attention given to anything Israel does.

"If Obama saw the caravans, he would complain," Yaakov said, "but if they were in Texas, he wouldn't notice."

And what, I asked, changing the subject slightly, did he envision would happen to the Arabs under annexation?

Yaakov responded that he had a high regard for Arabs individually, and had many Arab friends as well as longtime employees. He spoke about an Arab family who lived nearby with whom he had a warm relationship, visiting each other's homes on holidays and special occasions.

The real story of the West Bank, he asserted, was one the mainstream media refused to tell. For the most part, Jews and Arabs got along well, and many Palestinians actually appreciated the Jews' injection of commerce and jobs, such as those who worked on construction projects in the settlements earning wages that were far beyond what they would have received doing similar work just a few meters away with their brethren.

But how close was that relationship really, I asked him? Did he go, for example, to the nearby Palestinian city of Ramallah?

No, he had never been to Ramallah; it was illegal for Israeli citizens, Yaakov explained, and unwise as well.

So, I wondered, what would happen in the long term? Would the Palestinians be forced out? Or did he subscribe to a vision in which Palestinians would be absorbed into the country, with full civil rights?

"Look," Yaakov said. "The Palestinians themselves know they are incapable of running a state. What they had established in Ramallah was a joke, completely dependent on U.N. funding and corrupt to the core. No one's going to hurt the Palestinians, and they can certainly participate in commerce and have some other rights, but they cannot be allowed to govern or to vote."

But did he trust the Israeli government to stand by the settlers? Was he sure that Prime Minister Netanyahu would continue to expend the money and soldiers, as well as the water and electricity needed to keep Psagot and other settlement enterprises viable?

Here, Yaakov was unreserved in his praise. "Bibi works twenty hours a day," he said. "Nowhere else in the world will you find a government that works harder."

Yaakov invited us to explore the vineyards and the settlement in general. "Walk around," he said, grinning. "You'll see. It's a normal place."

We hiked among the neat rows of vines, sampling the ripe blue grapes, which, though small, were plump and juicy, tasting at once tangy and earthy, with thick, chewy skins that gelatinized in our mouths. We were alone and it was quiet, save for the birdsong and pleasant hum of insects. On one edge of the vineyard, in an exposed, dusty yard, were a few rough trailers propped up on makeshift piles of bricks and stones, with heavily barred windows that were wide open. No one was hanging around outside, but the trailers seemed to be inhabited and fitted for a long-term presence.

Yaakov's house stood at another corner of the vines, a stately, stone structure topped by green shingles, with a capacious yard and swimming pool past the driveway. Beyond the house on the next hill, we could see the buildings of a Palestinian town in the Al Bireh district, punctuated by the golden dome of a mosque and an even taller muezzin to call the faithful.

We got back in Gabi's car and drove on an internal road from the winery to the Psagot settlement proper, a cluster of streets with neat rows of well-appointed single-family homes along with the expected public buildings, a school, and a community center. It was by no means teeming right now, in the middle of the day, but we saw a few mothers pushing babies in their strollers, some other adults running errands—for all appearances, a typical suburb. We parked, got out, and walked around for a few minutes, stopping at a point where the street had been built to the very edge of the hilltop, beneath which was a steep drop to the security barriers below. Through the tree branches across the little valley below was a Palestinian neighborhood built on the opposite slope, close enough for us to see into people's living rooms and even to make out what they were watching on television.

Nathaniel was leaving early the next morning, so we decided to have a farewell dinner in Abu Ghosh, an Arab village in the Judean Hills near Jerusalem, about a half hour's drive from Psagot. The Abu Ghosh clan traces their lineage to Chechens who arrived in the early sixteenth century and set themselves up as a military power that controlled the route from Jaffa to Jerusalem during Ottoman times. Even before the War of Independence in 1948, they had friendly relations with European Jews and that amity allowed Abu Ghosh to remain intact while many other villages were emptied. Now a town of six thousand Muslims and Christians, Abu Ghosh was studded with churches from the Crusader era as well as the largest mosque in Israel, built in 2014 with a donation from the Chechen government.

Our favorite restaurant, Caravan, was a popular spot for lunch, especially on the Shabbat, when most of the restaurants in nearby West Jerusalem were closed. We arrived late on this

weekday afternoon, however, and Gabi found a parking spot easily on the village's main street, just in front.

Up a steep flight of stone stairs, we were welcomed by a waiter
who recognized Gabi and me, clasped our hands firmly, and led
us into the dining room past a neatly dressed older man with a
wide nose and a bristly, pure white mustache sitting behind a
counter. This man, too, greeted us warmly, if briefly. The walls
were amply decorated with handicrafts, brass coffeemakers and
serving trays, antique paintings of the local landscape, lush hills
with a smattering of Arab villages, minarets as well as steeples
poking out from clusters of homes.

We sat at a table by the window and ordered the standard
array of salads and meats on skewers, drinking from a pitcher of
lemonade with fresh mint leaves while we waited for the meat.
The waiter had lived in Chicago years ago, he said, reminiscing
with me about the Albany Park neighborhood, where he'd spent
many happy years. I asked if the bitter cold of the Midwestern
winter had bothered him, but he insisted, in English with a grav-
elly Chicago accent tinged just slightly with Arabic *r*'s, that this
was precisely what he missed most of all: the crisp, clean air of
the winter, the primal beauty of Lake Michigan frozen as far as
you could see.

After the meal, we started to drive back to Tel Aviv, but just
before the ramp to the highway, I noticed a modernist, single-
story building with two-tone paneling in red and gray and a white
awning attached to a gas station. This was the Elvis Inn, an appropriate final stop on Nathaniel's tour: a last image of American
influence on Israel, in this case transforming the typical truck-
stop diner into a shrine to American culture.

Gabi guided the Cadillac through the large, mostly empty
parking lot until he came to a halt in front of a several-meter-
high statue of a man in a white suit with a thick helmet of hair,

a guitar strapped to his back, shoulders back, hips forward, left arm outstretched while the right was pulled in tight to hold a microphone. Instantly recognizable, the statue nevertheless bore an inscription on its three-tiered base, a Hebrew transliteration of "Elvis Presley" alongside the English. Behind this simulacrum King of Rock 'n' Roll, the verdant Judean Hills shimmered in the afternoon sun.

Closer to the entrance, a second, more abstract statue depicted Elvis in a gold-colored material, a guitar attached rather oddly to his calf. Inside, everything that could be Elvis themed *was*, set amid a convincing facsimile of a semimythical 1950s American restaurant, a long countertop with attached vinyl-upholstered stools, vinyl booths with benches, floors tiled in alternating back and white, mirrored walls and columns. Hundreds of photographs chronicled every phase of Elvis's life, from his childhood through his early success and his service in the U.S. army, all the way to his latter days as an obese superstar bristling with rhinestones. There were also paintings, plates, placards, clocks, cups, flags, and even an acoustic guitar that Elvis may have once played.

The establishment's owner, Uri Yoeli, had been a devoted fan since he was twelve, when a girlfriend gave him his first photo of Elvis and a 45 record of "One Night." A seventh-generation Jerusalemite, Yoeli had at that point never heard of Elvis and had no idea what the English lyrics even meant. Still, he felt a profound affinity for the music, to say nothing for the showmanship, and began obsessively acquiring Elvis-related materials as well as receiving them from friends and associates who caught on to this bug. After his military service, Yoeli traveled to the United States to gather records, photographs, and other memorabilia, proudly displaying the collection at home until he married and his new bride objected to the décor.

Yoeli opened the gas station and restaurant as a standard truck stop in 1974, hanging a few portraits of Elvis behind the cash register. Only when he heard several truck drivers refer to his restaurant as "the Elvis place" was he inspired to showcase his hobby as a marketing strategy, transforming the restaurant and its environs step by step, hauling his artifacts out of storage and expanding upon it all with even more items during research trips to the United States that included pilgrimages to Graceland, the Elvis museum in Memphis, Tennessee.

The menu, alas, was typical fare for Israeli restaurants—kebabs and chopped salads—only with the addition of hamburgers and french fries. The gift shop, however, was a fascinating refraction of American culture, with shot glasses, key chains, gag license plates, coffee mugs, and other trinkets, all emblazoned with images of Elvis along with the words "Elvis Inn" and "Jerusalem" printed in Hebrew and English. Bottles of "Elvis cabernet" were lined up in long rows and in a pyramid affixed with signs in English, Hebrew, and Russian. Best of all were the T-shirts, replicas of those portraits of the King on black velvet that saw a surge in popularity in the 1980s, "Elvis" spelled out bilingually in a font that resembled illuminated marquee lights.

11

<u>ALAM</u>

That Thursday, I had arranged to have lunch in Jerusalem with Alam, a Palestinian citizen of Israel and an attorney who worked for the government. Alam's father had been friends with Gabi for decades, and Alam interned in Gabi's office while he was in law school.

I got on the #480 bus at the Arlozorov Terminal at 10:30 A.M. and made it to Jerusalem's central station less than an hour later, passing perfunctorily through the security checkpoint and navigating the restaurants, kippah vendors, and cell phone providers to Jaffa Street.

The old soothsayer was seated in his usual spot at the edge of the shade, his long white sidelocks merging with his beard and the whole mat laying on his threadbare purple suit, a creased, leather-bound prayer book open on his lap. He was momentarily unoccupied, and I came over to him, kneeled down, placed a shekel in the plastic cup he was holding, and asked him if he had any advice for me.

His eyes were barely visible behind wildly overgrown eyebrows and the many folds of his lids, but he had clearly seen my type come and go many times, so that he answered immediately, in a quiet, raspy voice that was nonetheless confident and unwavering.

"Happiness," he said, "is the most important thing."

I thanked him for the advice, which was sage, if less Talmudic than I'd expected, and stood up, just in time to see Alam coming across the street. He looked fit and professional in workday casual clothing, a short-sleeved sport shirt, slacks, and buffed black leather shoes, with a short beard, and we embraced warmly.

I suggested we go have lunch at Pasta Basta, in the Mahane Yehudah Market, which I knew was kosher as well as halal. Alam knew the restaurant from his time in Gabi's law firm—Gabi's friend Lezer was a co-owner, and the head chef was Lezer's son.

Instead of walking, though, Alam suggested we take the light rail.

There was a short line in front of the ticket machine, and we waited patiently while several teenagers pushed in front of us, but we managed to get our tickets just as a new train was arriving. The door slid open easily, and we entered a comfortably air-conditioned car packed with every manner of Jerusalemite carrying every sort of luggage, from school backpacks to oddly shaped packages wrapped in brown paper.

The ride was smooth, quiet, and brief, just two stops from the station, and we disembarked into the throngs of shoppers and tourists in front of the market. I let Alam lead the way, and he used polite, formal Hebrew as he asked a few of the vendors for directions through the maze of stalls, shops, and restaurants.

We found Pasta Basta in a corner of the market shaded by a roof just next door to a classic hummus and shawarma spot, and across the lane from a stylish fish and chips stall decorated in angular navy blue and silver furnishings, and an older establishment that sold fresh squeezed juices with purported spiritual and physical benefits, according to the signs decorated with images of Buddhist and Hindu legends and quotations from prominent rabbis.

We ordered at the counter—I got gnocchi with red pesto while

Alam chose spaghetti with cream sauce—before finding a cozy table with a view of the market.

While we waited for the pastas, we reminisced about the last time we'd seen each other. Several years earlier, Gabi had brought my wife and child to Alam's family's home in Um al Fahm, a bustling, densely packed Palestinian Israeli city of fifty-five thousand built into the hillsides near Haifa. With space at a premium and family relations tight, the majority of the structures in town were family homes with adult children's apartments stacked right on top of the parents' dwellings. Alam's family's house was spacious and airy, and his mother brought dish after dish while we chatted: lamb and beef stews with rice and many different kinds of salads. At the end of the evening, his parents presented us with a bottle of olive oil produced from their own trees, which had the slick consistency of melted butter and a distinct but ephemeral sweetness.

When Alam, now thirty, was a child, his father owned a successful car wash near Tel Aviv. Gabi had initially been a customer, only later coming to represent the business as its attorney.

I shared the concept of my book with him, explaining that it was important for me to include the voices of Palestinian Israelis, who had always been an essential part of the country, and were a rising force economically and politically—20 percent of the nation's citizens, as evinced by the recent success of the Palestinian citizens' political parties, who had formed a party called the "Joint List" out of a fractious bunch that ranged from dedicated Communists to conservative Muslims, driving up turnout and becoming the third largest party in the Knesset in the last election.

Pleased that I was recognizing Palestinian citizens, Alam felt that those metrics, in fact, represented a deliberate undercount: Palestinians accounted for at least 25 percent, perhaps as much as 30. As for the kind of electoral engineering I'd just mentioned, he personally abstained from voting, not wishing to validate the discrimination faced by Palestinians on an official level.

"If you want to sit with me with respect, as an equal, that's fine," Alam explained, "but I won't sit with you as a second-class citizen."

The Joint List's success would only provoke a backlash from the Israeli right wing, Alam predicted. Whenever Arabs voted in large numbers, that prompted an even larger response from those who explicitly called for forcibly ousting Arab citizens from Israel.

I asked whether, in the end, he supported two states or a single state in which all Palestinians would have equal rights with Jewish Israelis?

Alam did not see how one state would produce equal rights for Palestinians. Jewish Israelis would always dominate the politics, the military, and the economy. No, it would be better for the Palestinians to have their own state. Nevertheless, the United States was the dominant power in the region, and the world, with ultimate control over the situation in the Middle East, and it would never allow a Palestinian state to happen, since American policy on Israel was dictated in turn by lobbyists such as AIPAC.

I asked him where he'd read information about AIPAC, and he cited Arabic-language news websites.

I argued that AIPAC and other Israel lobbyists were far less influential than American oil and arms in shaping American policy in the Middle East, but Alam remained skeptical, citing America's unflagging support for Israel as evidence the relationship was different from that with any other of the superpower's allies.

"Even if your friend is right," Alam said, referring to America's political relationship with Israel, "he's not right all the time."

I asked Alam about the relationship between Palestinian citizens of Israel and Palestinians in the territories under military control.

He rolled his eyes a bit. Those in the territories called Palestinian citizens *shamenet*, meaning "cream," due to a presumption of privilege and opportunity. The friction between the two extended to many business transactions, in which those in the territories would vastly overcharge citizens.

That said, apart from the real tension over the two groups' relative economic situations, he still felt solidarity with other Palestinians due to strong cultural, historical, and family ties. His grandfather's brother had just died in Jenin, a Palestinian city just twenty kilometers from Um al Fahm, but on the other side of Israel's official border. Because of that, Jenin's residents were not citizens and were subject to the rule of the Palestinian Authority and the IDF.

In his family, as in many others, there was a common memory of expulsion and dispossession. Alam had heard his grandfather describe the family's life in a village near Megiddo, land that they had been frightened into leaving during the 1948 war. While his grandfather's brother fled to Jenin, Alam's grandfather ran to Um al Fahm, which until then had been a small town of several thousand but grew rapidly with the influx of refugees.

I asked Alam about cultural connections between Jewish and Palestinian citizens, mentioning my trips to Acre and Haifa, where there were mixed populations of Jews and Palestinians. I was particularly curious about a theater in Haifa where Shakespeare was performed in Arabic.

This theater dated back to Ottoman times, Alam said, but under the current right-wing government, the culture minister had threatened to cut their funding if their productions strayed into topics or voiced opinions she didn't like.

Expanding on the subject of discrimination, Alam noted that while Israel's major universities all admitted Palestinians, there were no academic institutions located in Palestinian towns, and while there are many Palestinian doctors and nurses, many more than proportional to their share of the population, there is still no hospital in any Palestinian Israeli town. The separation was so complete, Alam explained, that for those Palestinian citizens who chose to go to university, it was usually the first time in their lives they were in a multicultural environment, an experience that could be jarring as well as confusing.

In terms of employment, the reality is that ambitious, educated Palestinian citizens have limited options. Not having served in the military, for instance, they would not be able to get a job in aviation or security, or even in high tech. Palestinian citizens who study math, physics, or computers are more likely to end up being teachers with very low salaries.

"No one will say, 'I didn't give you the job because you're Arab,'" Alam said matter-of-factly, "but we know the reason."

In terms of his own career, he was completely satisfied with his decision to become a lawyer, and grateful for the support of Gabi and others who had helped him along the way.

"I've found myself," he declared.

His job at the Justice Ministry was to investigate the inheritance claims of foreigners with relatives who'd died in Israel. The work could be both challenging and fascinating, regularly putting him in touch with different nations and their customs. He spent his days determining, for example, if the Parisian nephew of a man in Tel Aviv was legally entitled to his property. Work like this required him to be sensitive and cautious, as people were, not surprisingly, often aggrieved if their claim was denied.

But it had often been a lonely journey, Alam admitted, fraught with obstacles that were institutional as well as personal. He had a Jewish friend in Ramat Gan, a suburb of Tel Aviv adjoining Givatayim, in whose house he lived for seven months while he was in law school. One time, this friend agreed to come to Um al Fahm, even though he was terrified. To show his friend he had nothing to worry about, Alam sent him on a roundabout way that took him through the whole town. He continued to call Alam on his cell phone along the way, and each time, Alam instructed him to go inside a particular establishment, a store and a bakery among them, to ask for directions. By the time his friend got to Alam's home, he had bought some kanefa and reported that he enjoyed talking with the friendly residents.

Some weeks later, he was sitting in his friend's salon in shorts when a few others came in to play poker. At first, the poker players didn't realize that an Arab was sitting there. When they did, they asked him where he was from, and then immediately began to talk about how bad Um al Fahm was, how high the poverty and crime rates were, and how dangerous it would be for Jewish Israelis to go there. His friend remained silent, declining to dispel the stereotypes or even to reveal that he'd been there at all. That hurt Alam's feelings, he confessed.

Even now, as a recognized attorney working for the Ministry of Justice, Alam felt like a second-class citizen. To illustrate, he asked me if I had passed through the security checkpoint in the basement of the bus station when I came from Tel Aviv.

I had indeed, I told him.

"Did they ask you for ID?"

"They did not."

Alam said he takes the bus to Jerusalem daily from Um al Fahm, and goes through that checkpoint each time, and every day the security officers ask to see his ID. The same officers see him every day, and yet every day these men ask for his ID in the same hostile manner. For more than two years, Alam has tried to joke with them, even to greet them simply, but they only glare at him as they inspect his laminated identification card and the card from the Ministry of Justice.

Housing being very expensive in Jerusalem, many of his colleagues at the ministry also lived in their hometowns and commuted. One was a young woman of Ethiopian descent, and they often arrived at the same time from their respective locations, but she was on a first-name basis with the guards, who smiled and waved her through whenever they saw her.

But how do they even know you are Palestinian?

"It's written on your ID," Alam explained. But even if it weren't, people in Israel can tell who is Palestinian and who is Jewish. It's hard to quantify, maybe, because Jews and Palestinians have the same range of complexions and similar clothing, but something in the combination of appearance and mannerisms makes it clear. Sometimes, it's as simple as the word to greet an acquaintance. Most of the time, Jews use the greeting "Shalom" while Palestinians use "Alahn," for example.

"But on the street, people can somehow tell you're an Arab," Alam maintained, adding that he can tell other Arabs as well.

We had talked for nearly two hours, and I thanked Alam for sharing his insight with me. I said I also needed his advice, though. I was planning to include the voices of Palestinians under military control as well Palestinian citizens, but needed help with logistics and contacts. I wanted to visit Ramallah, for example, and wondered if there were public sites such as museums or monuments.

Alam had acquaintances in Ramallah, but he said they wouldn't feel free to talk to me.

Perhaps I might try to contact another writer, I asked. There were several who I knew lived in Ramallah. Alam thought this was an excellent idea and offered to call any of these individuals for me, and even to go with me to Ramallah.

I was grateful but asked if it was really necessary.

He laughed. "What, did you want to go by yourself?"

We walked out through the market, chatting as we navigated around clumps of shoppers and tourists. Alam consented to walk with me along Jaffa Street back to the bus station, and we strolled slowly, savoring the slight breeze. He was giddy and excited about getting married in October. He and his new wife would be going to Zanzibar for their honeymoon. Though he'd had relationships with women he had met on his own in the past, he had undergone a religious turn lately, and this marriage had been arranged by the local imam.

Alam and I said goodbye warmly at the bus station's entrance, before the security guards and metal detectors, and I caught the next #480 bus back to the Arlozorov station in Tel Aviv. The bus was packed with soldiers, young men and women in faded uniforms with their weapons slung over the shoulders or cradled in their arms, going home for the weekend, in a jovial mood, sharing music or viewing videos on their phones.

Just fifty minutes later, I was back in Tel Aviv, walking home to Givatayim. My route took me just past Nahalat Yitzhak, so I decided to check on the Shtefanisher Rebbe's tomb. The festival long since over by now, Avnei Zikaron Street was quiet and bare, and the sun was setting by the time I passed through the gate into the courtyard, which was also empty. There was no line in the row of tombstones that led to the Rebbe's, but the canopy above the tomb and its surroundings was intact, and a desk had been placed in a space between other tombs, attended by the heavyset white-bearded man who had dispensed kugel during the memorial, who smiled and nodded when I arrived. Then I noticed he was not alone: seated on the stone pavement just past the Rebbe's tomb was a rail-thin Haredi man with a wispy, straw-colored beard, his pasty skin damp in the summer heat under his thick, dark suit, talking on a cell phone in English while a young girl next to him acted out an imaginary story.

I put a shekel in White Beard's *tzedakah* box, and then placed my palms on the cool stone of the Rebbe's tomb, meditating silently for a few moments. When I was done, I turned back to White Beard, told him I'd been at the memorial a few days earlier, and found it very moving.

The thin Haredi man interrupted to ask me, scoffing, if I really felt something or if I was just saying it.

"Why do you doubt me?" I retorted. "Because I'm a secular guy? Even non-Jews feel something from the Rebbe."

White Beard validated my assertion, noting that he had been to the Rebbe's former grave site in Romania and goyim still go there to pray. He had personally spoken to non-Jews who were there when the Shtefanisher's body was exhumed for its transfer to Nahalat Yitzhak, and they testified that the corpse was intact, as if he had been buried just the day before.

The Haredi man was growing increasingly agitated, firing skeptical questions about the organization behind the memorial, but White Beard answered calmly, explaining that after the body arrived in Nahalat Yitzhak, the organization had been built around a nucleus of the few followers of the Rebbe still alive and in Israel. The Rebbe never had children himself, and that was what made him so effective in helping those who were trying to have children as well as those who were trying to heal sick children.

White Beard offered us all something to drink from a plastic cooler he kept behind the table. The Haredi man's little girl asked for orange juice from a large jug, and White Beard graciously poured her a plastic cupful, but after taking a sip, she announced she didn't like it. I asked for a glass of cold water.

The Haredi man declined to drink anything. "Where are you from?" he asked me pointedly.

"Chicago," I said.

"Me, too," he said. "Which part?"

"Wicker Park," I answered.

"Never heard of it," he scoffed before announcing proudly, "I'm from Rogers Park."

In the global geography of the Haredi world, Rogers Park, a neighborhood on Chicago's far North Side, is notable for its large number of yeshivas and *shuls,* whereas Wicker Park, a fast-gentrifying area just northwest of downtown, is nearly devoid of Jewish institutions.

Not about to be calm in the face of so much sinful behavior, the Haredi man accused White Beard of laxity, citing his validation of my feelings about the Rebbe's memorial as evidence. How could a guy like me have felt anything when it clearly had no effect? Where by contrast, *he* had been moved to do *mitzvot*—good deeds—all day long. Doing more and more *mitzvot* was all he thought about, unlike this—

"Don't bring me into your argument," I interjected. "You obviously know nothing about the Shtefanisher Rebbe, who didn't gather his followers around his dining table and didn't write books the way that other rabbis did. The Rebbe was fine with reaching out to common Jews who weren't learned or perfectly observant, so who are *you* to be so high and mighty?"

The Haredi man refocused on White Beard, continuing to refer to me in the third person, essentially accusing me of spiritual tourism, performing an empty ritual or two without absorbing any actual meaning.

I wasn't having it and told him that it was obvious his argument wasn't with me, but with himself. He should look to his own behavior, I suggested, failing to show respect to his elders, for starters, and not even trying to show another Jew the way, totally unconcerned with the example he was setting for others. How would he convince me—or anyone else—that his path was the righteous path with the way he was acting?

He wasn't trying to convince me, the Haredi man said.

"That's obvious," I retorted.

White Beard handed me a booklet and told me to use it to pray at the tomb. Printed in full color, the booklet contained the text of appropriate prayers as well as instructions for rituals that purported to bring recovery from illness, success in financial matters, and the health and prosperity of one's children, grandchildren, and other relations. Its back cover was an idealized portrait of the Rebbe, posed as if caught midstudy in his library, one hand on the page of an open book, the other hand hovering, ready to turn the page.

I flipped through the booklet for a few seconds, but then asked White Beard if he would help me use it to pray. White Beard did his best, though I stumbled through the prayers, with the pallid Haredi man moaning with glee every time I made a mistake. When we finally finished, White Beard looked at me with unmistakable pity, told me to take the booklet home, and study hard.

I thanked him heartily and told him he had helped me greatly before heading off into the summer night without looking back.

12

OFER LIKES TO COOK

On Friday evening, my niece Orian, Gabi's younger daughter, had arranged for me to join an alternative tour of Jaffa led by a political activist. As a result of the age difference between Gabi and me, I was actually closer in age to Orian, thirty-four, and her elder sister Maya, thirty-nine, than to Gabi. A professional dancer and choreographer, Orian was then also working as a teacher in Jaffa at one of the few preschools in Israel with a mixed Jewish and Palestinian population.

Orian used a phone-based app, Gett Taxi, to order a cab for me, and the driver arrived promptly, a clean-shaven Palestinian with the same short-on-the-sides, long-on-top haircut that seemed to be popular in Nazareth and other Palestinian areas.

I asked the driver about the app, and he was effusive with praise. "I rarely drive with an empty cab anymore, and never wait in line at a mall, or at the airport," he raved. So much had the app improved his productivity, in fact, that he had been able to stop working as a truck driver as his main gig.

"I'm doing this to work," he said, "not to chitchat in a line with the other drivers."

The streets were quiet on the evening of the Shabbat, and the taxi dropped me off at the tour's starting point, a small plaza at the intersection of Yehudah Hayamit and Dror Streets, a little early.

Throughout that week in Jerusalem's Old City, Muslim religious leaders had organized thousands of Palestinians for prayer in the streets outside the Temple Mount to protest the installation of metal detectors, cameras, and other security devices. With all the mosques in East Jerusalem and across the West Bank closed in solidarity, Palestinians had gathered every day for prayers and speeches, along with the traditional Friday services. Mostly these large crowds gathered peacefully, but violence broke out afterward in East Jerusalem and all over the West Bank between small groups of Palestinian men throwing rocks and other improvised weapons and Israeli police, who responded by firing live rounds. Hundreds were wounded, dozens arrested, and three young Palestinian men killed. In the taxi, I'd heard a radio report that protesters had taken the men's bodies from the hospital before they could be confiscated by Israeli police.

But Jaffa appeared totally calm now, with just a few Palestinian women in hijabs and a few pairs of men strolling by. Orian and her partner, Shmulik, soon rode up on bicycles, followed by Maya, who found a parking spot nearby. We were joined shortly thereafter by two Austrian men whom Orian had met at a dance festival in Edinburgh, and their two American friends. I introduced myself to everyone, and the Americans were happy to announce they, too, had Midwestern connections. Matthew, who towered above me at something close to seven feet tall, was a Methodist minister originally from Ohio who was now stationed in Austria. Sergio, fit and energetic, was from a Filipino family in Los Angeles, but had recently moved to Chicago.

Our guide, Ami Asher, walked up soon thereafter. Slim, with close-cropped black hair and a matching beard, he was wearing a white T-shirt emblazoned with the name of the Israeli-Palestinian school where Orian taught, which translated from Hebrew and Arabic into "Hand in Hand."

Ami A. introduced himself as forty-six years old, Jewish, with parents originally from Bulgaria. He was married with two kids, fourteen and nine years old, and lived in a condominium here in Jaffa. He had chosen to begin the tour on this corner because it contained many of the elements of the gentrification of Jaffa, which he saw as a continuation of the military eviction of Palestinians during the 1948 War of Independence. He pointed first to the offices of the Israeli military radio station, which broadcast music and news, and then across the street at a five-story apartment building. Producing a black-and-white photocopied image of the structure, an Ottoman-era apartment building, he pointed out the renovations that had turned it into luxury housing.

Ami A. then led us west on Yehudah Hayamit Street, pointing out decrepit buildings targeted for demolition or rehabilitation, some of them emblazoned with faded Arabic addresses and advertisements, before taking us under a bridge. The street above had been called Ajami Street originally, Ami A. noted, after the Persian saint whose name was also attached to a Palestinian neighborhood in Jaffa, only to be renamed Yefet Street, after one of the sons of Noah.

We reached a turnabout that had just been named for Sheikh Bassam Abu Zayd, the recently deceased chief imam at the Mahmoudiya Mosque, a complex of buildings around the corner from the clock tower. Though this imam surely deserved the recognition, Ami A. noted that it was rare for places or roads in Jaffa to be named for Arabs; in fact, the number of streets and public spaces named for Arabs was shrinking rapidly.

My niece Maya pointed out a restaurant on the street above, Abu Hassan, often rated by magazines and websites as serving the best hummus in Israel. Its proprietor, Ali Karavan, started at a stand with just two pots at the nearby port, and opened the restaurant itself in 1972 as a modest establishment that soon became immensely popular with locals. With the advent of the Internet, Abu Hassan was featured on many local blogs as well as travel sites, Maya explained, and now people sometimes waited hours in line to get inside. Unless they were lucky enough to find a seat at one of the communal tables inside, many of the customers ate sitting on the curb.

I asked Maya if Abu Hassan's hummus was really good enough to warrant waiting in line. "It's definitely good," she answered, shrugging, "but I mean, it's hummus, right?"

Perhaps what those who waited in line wanted was not just the hummus, she proposed, but the encounter with authenticity, most of the patrons being young adult Jews who came in from Tel Aviv and its suburbs.

We arrived at the port just in time for a glorious sunset, which turned the clouds into slivers of pink and purple set against a sky of deep, glowing orange at the horizon. Ami A. pointed to the dockside warehouses, recently converted into fashionable new restaurants and theaters, and said the area had been completely evacuated during the 1948 war, later used only as temporary housing for Jewish refugees from Europe. Not far from this, we entered a labyrinthine warren of restored Ottoman structures, all connected by narrow staircases and crooked paths housing cafés and restaurants, as well as shops for artists and craftsmen, painters, woodworkers, and jewelry makers. Here, too, Ami A. pointed out, the Arab inhabitants were cleared out in 1948, with the area opened to Jewish artists only years later to change the population dynamics in this strategic location near the sea.

We found ourselves now in the gardens where Nathaniel and I had gazed at the Mediterranean a week and a half earlier. In the cool of the evening, the space was filling with city residents as well as tourists. In one plaza, several dozen people were taking a ballroom dancing class, and couples twirled and dipped while music blared from the speakers.

Ami A. scowled. The hill we were walking on had been constructed from the ruins of buildings demolished during the 1948 war and its aftermath, he explained.

Now the group joined together in demanding that Ami A. explain his personal commitment to the antigentrification movement in Jaffa. We'd asked him about his own story several times and each time, he'd demurred, saying that it was irrelevant.

People always wanted to know about his personal motivation, he complained.

I did my best to convince him, though: "Well, it's relevant as well as interesting, and it could only help your cause, right?"

Facing this united front, Ami A. capitulated, and we gathered around him near the stage of an empty, replica amphitheater, the crashing of waves audible in the background, to listen to his story.

His parents arrived in Jaffa from Bulgaria, and when he was a child, they would bring the whole family here as a place for recreation and remembrance. Little Ami would often roam the neighborhood, and one day he found an empty mosque that was unsecured. He climbed the minaret, avoiding spent needles, soiled condoms, and feces as he ascended to the top, from where he sang out, in his best impression of a muezzin, *"Allau akbar,"* "God is great" in Arabic.

In the early nineties, as an adult, he returned to Jaffa to look for the mosque in which he'd played as a child. He thought he remembered exactly where it was, but somehow could not find it anywhere. It was mysterious because he had always been told that the State of Israel had a policy of maintaining religious sites. But when he checked newspaper archives, he discovered that the mosque had indeed been demolished, not because it was a mosque but because it was an "unsafe structure," according to the reports.

Now, from the folder he'd been carrying with him throughout the tour, he produced a black-and-white photo of the mosque in a clear plastic cover. Lifting the photograph to our line of vision, Ami said the mosque had stood very near where we were standing, and showed us where its dome had fit into Jaffa's skyline.

The revelation of the mosque's destruction had left him wondering what other truths were being obscured, and he continued investigating the state's official history, especially its conduct toward Palestinians. As he unraveled that official narrative, Ami grew disillusioned, deciding that he opposed any type of Jewish state. Jews were more creative and more moral, he concluded, when they were minorities in the diaspora.

"Jews should not rule themselves or others," he said.

Joined by more friends, we ate dinner as a group at one of the restaurants in the restored port area, sitting at a long table digging into plates of mezze and salads, many made with fresh fish caught by one of the little boats whose masts were still visible against the indigo sky. Afterward, Orian and Shmulik suggested we go to a pub nearby where Jews and Palestinians danced together. Maya and Ami declined, but the other tour group participants, the two Austrians and the Americans, Matthew and Sergio, were enthusiastic.

It was a short walk to Rehov Hapninim (Pearls Street), just a narrow alley near the clock tower, and it was obvious where the bar was from the thin, fashionably dressed hipsters standing outside and sitting on the curb smoking tobacco and cannabis. We steered around them to approach a burly, mustachioed bouncer guarding a heavy iron door to an Ottoman-era building; despite his fearsome posture, he welcomed us with a broad smile and instantly let us in.

Inside was a narrow chamber with a well-stocked bar, a dance floor, and a DJ's station all packed in under a high domed ceiling. The place was already crowded, with a clientele of Jews as well as Palestinians, including, most remarkably, many Palestinian women in jeans and short skirts, their hair loose and flowing as they rocked the dance floor. Red neon Arabic letters on the wall read "Lou Lou," Arabic for "pearls."

The DJ played an alluring, seamless mixture of hip-hop, house, rap, electronic, and pop music, with Arabic, Israeli, American, European, and even occasional African and Indian songs. Likewise, the cocktails included house specialties made with arak, the anise-flavored, milky spirit popular all over the eastern Mediterranean and Middle East.

I chatted with Khalil, a Palestinian Israeli who was born and reared in Jaffa but had spent the past five years in Germany studying medicine. When he met Orian's partner, Shmulik, Khalil laughed, then explained that his father always called him Shmulik, presumably because of his studious, Jewish-like behavior. Down a narrow corridor was the bar's back room, a smaller, quieter chamber with chairs, benches, and tables, where couples sat talking, smoking, and making out.

Founded in 2011, the bar was named Anna Lou Lou, in full, an approximate transliteration for the Arabic sentence "I am pearls," which was chosen by the bar's original owners, an Israeli Jewish Ashkenazi couple named Ilana Bronstein and Niv Gal, in an homage to the bar's street address. Soon after opening, Bronstein and Gal recruited a Palestinian Israeli DJ, Muhammad Jabali, who used the freedom of his position at Anna Lou Lou to experiment and improvise, bringing in many friends from across the musical spectrum. It all set the tone for what would become known through social media and word of mouth among Palestinians and Israelis of all stripes, gay and straight, trans and cisgender.

After five years, about a year before my visit, Bronstein and Gal grew tired of running the bar and sold it to a consortium of eight people, a diverse, eclectic group that included former employees as well as patrons of the bar, Jewish Israelis as well as Palestinian Israelis. The new owners were all educated millennials who had formed lasting friendships, found romances, and built community at Anna Lou Lou—a few of them had even moved to Jaffa to be closer to the bar—so as a collective, they were all motivated to keep the bar operating just as it had been.

My time at Anna Lou Lou ended at approximately 3:00 A.M., and Shmulik offered to use the Gett Taxi app to summon a cab to take me back to Givatayim. When he completed the order a few moments later and my designated cab appeared on his screen, Shmulik announced, "Your driver's name is Ofer. His profile says he likes to cook."

The taxi arrived, and after a few minutes, when we were moving quickly through the empty streets, I leaned forward a little bit in my seat to speak with this Ofer.

"Ofer, do you mind if I ask you something?" I asked.

Clean shaven with square, wire-frame glasses, Ofer nodded good-naturedly.

I mentioned his profile on Gett Taxi and inquired if it was true he really liked to cook.

"I do," Ofer answered, turning as he drove to flash a bright smile. "Very much."

Ofer explained that his father was Ashkenazi, from Poland, while his mother was from Tunisia, which has a rich Jewish culture that is, in fact, one of the world's oldest. His parents were a rare combination in their day, and Ofer's mother tried her best to bridge the cultural gap, especially in the food she prepared at home. After being introduced by Ofer's father's family to gefilte fish, pickled seafood remnants favored by Ashkenazim, she altered the recipe to add black pepper and other spices.

Ofer was fascinated by her efforts, to the point that he eschewed the activities of his brothers and other boys. "When my brothers were playing sports, I was in the kitchen watching my mother cook," he explained.

I asked if he had a family, and if he cooked for them.

He nodded proudly. He had three grown daughters, and his wife, who was born in Bulgaria, happened to be a very good cook herself, drawing on the flavorful cuisine of her own homeland. Nevertheless, Ofer did most of the cooking at home, mainly just because he enjoyed it so much.

Had any of his daughters inherited his interest in food?

"One of them," Ofer answered, and luckily, she lived nearby. On those days when he was tired or didn't feel like cooking, they had kind of a game: he would call his daughter and ask her to make dinner for them, and she might agree, but wouldn't reveal what she was making.

When they arrived at her apartment, she would already be cooking, and they would sit in the living room, trying to guess what she was making from the scents wafting out of the kitchen.

Right or wrong, he added, it didn't really matter, since the food was always delicious.

13

THE SATURDAY MORNING CREW

I slept only a few hours, as I had committed to pick up my mother that morning and drive her to regular Saturday morning brunch with a group of friends, all of whom, like her, were Hungarian survivors of the Shoah. I'd asked my mother to check with her friends if I might attend to document their feelings and perspectives for my book, to which they readily and graciously agreed.

She lived in a cozy, one-bedroom apartment on the first floor of a four-story concrete apartment building on the same street in Givatayim as Gabi, just a few steps away from busy Weizmann Boulevard, and when I arrived, she was sitting in the salon in her padded easy chair watching the news on a large-screen television. Dressed up in a pretty blue floral, short-sleeved shirt and a pair of gray slacks, she greeted me with a smile, then quickly turned back to the television and frowned. On the screen were images of a kitchen with the tile floor covered in red blood while the baritone of the announcer's voice somberly described the details.

"Terrible," she exclaimed.

The previous night, a nineteen-year-old Palestinian man had infiltrated the West Bank settlement of Halamish, a hilltop community of about 1,400 families, similarly sized to Psagot, but north of Ramallah. This native of the nearby Palestinian town of Khobar had skulked through Halamish until he saw a home emanating light and came through the front door to attack a family

151

celebrating Shabbat dinner, stabbing a seventy-year-old man and his wife as well as two of his adult children, both in their forties, before a neighbor, a soldier on weekend leave, heard the commotion and shot the Palestinian with his issued firearm.

The wounded were all taken to a hospital in Jerusalem, but only the mother could be saved. Several other family members, including young children, had been in the house at the time, but managed to hide behind a locked door and were not injured.

Injured by the soldier's bullets, the Palestinian attacker was being treated at an Israeli hospital in the city of Petah Tikva and was expected to recover, according to the news. He reportedly revealed under questioning that he had been incensed by the new Israeli security measures at the Temple Mount and intended the attack as a suicide mission, writing on Facebook, "All I have is a sharpened knife, and it responds to the call of Al-Aqsa."

He would be charged with a long list of crimes, Israeli authorities promised, and his family's home in Khobar was already set to be demolished under a preexisting policy designed to punish the families of terrorists.

"Terrible," my mother repeated, before pressing a button on the remote control to turn off the television, and then, with a little effort, raising herself out of the chair.

She had moved back to Israel more than twenty years ago, when I was in my late twenties, after more than three decades in the United States. I hadn't been surprised when she announced she was returning, since she had always spoken of Israel as her true home. My parents had moved from Israel to the United States in 1963, ostensibly to give my father the opportunity to study at an American university, but their tenure in upstate New York dragged on, as their obligations and commitments mounted. My younger brother, Dani, and I were raised in Rochester but spoke

Hebrew at home and called our mother "Ima," the way Israeli children did.

My mother worked as a Hebrew school teacher from the time Dani and I were in preschool, and after my parents divorced when I was twelve, she went back to college and earned American degrees in addition to her Israeli teaching certificate, ultimately becoming principal of the Hebrew school attached to the largest synagogue in the Rochester area, a Reform congregation founded in 1848. Through her entire career, she taught thousands of young Jews, and then reached thousands more, Jews and non-Jews, as a lecturer on her experience during the Shoah.

She had been fourteen when Hungarian allies of the German Nazis seized control of the country, and her father was soon required to report for conscription into a military labor unit where conditions were notoriously poor. Shortly after that, her mother, my grandmother Ibolya, purchased false Christian papers and left Budapest for a small town in rural Hungary. But they were recognized as Jews there and arrested, and then taken by sealed cattle car for days until they reached Poland.

In Auschwitz, all of the prisoners in their section colluded to conceal from the camp guards the fact that there was a mother and daughter in the same bunk. Had this been discovered, they would have been separated, if not killed on the spot. After six months in Auschwitz, they were taken to a work camp in what is now Slovakia, where they assembled munitions for the Nazi war machine under conditions that were nearly as terrifying, but after four months there, with the Soviet army approaching quickly from the east and the Americans from the west, the guards fled an assault by partisans, giving my mother and grandmother the opportunity to escape.

They made it to a nearby village, where a kind woman found

them, emaciated and exhausted, picked them both up, one in each arm, and brought them to her home. She fed and nursed them until they were healthy enough to make their way back to Budapest, a journey that ended with a ride in a coal train, so that they arrived covered in a thick black dust. Only then did they learn my mother's father had died while he was a Nazi prisoner.

In the years immediately following the war, my Ima did not adopt the identity of "survivor." Everyone around her, after all, had "survived" something—war and invasion, oppression and terror from one side or the other. No, in her years in Israel and then in the United States, she was focused on the present, with little time or motivation to revisit the atrocities of the past. But having landed in the United States just in time to see the civil rights movement firsthand, she was inspired by the resilience and dignity of African Americans who testified about the abuses and humiliations of segregation and discrimination. As one of a handful of survivors in the Rochester area, she accepted invitations to speak about the Shoah as a duty, visiting prestigious universities and city high schools alike.

Once back in Israel, however, there were many survivors willing to lecture about their experiences; the Shoah was woven right into school curricula, and commemorated in a reverently observed national annual holiday. Instead, my mother kept up a busy routine of social activities and swimming whenever she wasn't conversing on social media, often entertaining her former students or visitors from the United States or Europe. She'd suffered a stroke just a few months before this visit, and this slowed her down just a little, but at eighty-eight, she remained as incisive and compassionate as ever.

I drove her car, a tiny but reliable fifteen-year-old Daihatsu, about twenty minutes north to Ramat ha Sharon, a large suburb of Tel Aviv, and parked just a few doors away from Edna, a popular restaurant that the group had been able to agree upon as a "temporary" compromise. It had a broad menu that offered something for everyone, my mother explained, and was conveniently located for Mari, who couldn't drive very far.

Mari happened to arrive at just the moment we did. A vivacious ninety-year-old woman with a mane of chestnut hair framing a wonderfully wry smile, she and her husband had owned a store in Haifa. He had passed away some years earlier, and now she lived nearby on her own here outside Tel Aviv, close to her daughter and son-in-law, their adult children, and her great-grandchildren.

As soon as we stepped through the doorway into the air-conditioning, the hostess smiled and told us that the others in our party had already arrived. At a large table in the back were Esti, her red hair held back with a fashionable headband; her husband, Mordi, robust and lean with close-cropped hair, aviator sunglasses, and a black sport shirt; Chava, charming and bright; and Zeru, a neat, quiet man in a purple polo shirt. The Saturday morning crew's roster had shifted slightly with illness and availability, but they were all from secular families in Budapest, the conversation was heavily peppered with Hungarian, and everyone called my mother by her original first name, Vera.

We ordered from the eclectic menu, which included pastas and sandwiches along with more traditional fare, and I ordered schnitzel, the Israeli version of the breaded, fried Viennese classic. In the Middle East, thin, pounded chicken breast was substituted for veal, and it was so popular that a franchise called Schnitzel King operated in Israel as well as the Palestinian territories.

I had planned on being a fly on the wall, and writing about anything that came up, but Mordi insisted that I ask the group questions, so I began by asking about their reception in Israel when they first arrived as Shoah survivors. Were they treated well?

To this question, they had a unified answer: "No."

Mordi had been taken as a sixteen-year-old to the same labor camp as my mother's father in Mühldorf, Germany, a satellite of the Dachau concentration camp where Jews worked under brutal conditions without adequate rations and were often killed outright. But when Mordi first arrived in Israel, he quickly realized it was shameful to admit to being a survivor. The survivors were seen as having failed to resist the Nazis, Chava explained, a serious weakness in the militant Israeli ethos of the day.

"We accepted the narrative that we didn't fight back," she summed up.

This attitude had prevailed among Israelis until very recently, despite the official recognition on the Day of Remembrance and all the rest. Esti added that conversations with her own children about the Shoah were highly fraught, and only now, for the first time, were their high-school-aged grandchildren asking them to detail their experiences.

Esti had had a particularly difficult childhood in Hungary, as both of her parents were deaf, and they sent her to live on a farm in a rural village, where she was captured after the Nazi invasion. She was then taken to the Bergen-Belsen concentration camp in northern Germany, where Anne Frank, her sister, and more than fifty thousand other people were killed or allowed to die. When British forces entered the camp in April 1945, they freed sixty thousand people, mostly Jews but also Roma, homosexuals, prisoners of war, and political prisoners. In the process, they also discovered thirteen thousand unburied corpses.

Once she made it to Israel, Esti worked in a watch repair shop and compensated for the education the war had interrupted by taking courses in art, music, and literature. Mordi taught mechanical engineering in high school, and they had one daughter and one son, who each went on to have two children of their own.

A few years earlier, their son had launched a software company that he later sold at a particularly propitious moment and made an enormous sum, which he shared generously with his parents.

All the members of the lunch crew were comfortable financially, Mari noted with relief, but they were hardly typical of survivors. She mentioned a report in the newspaper that found more than one-quarter of Israel's remaining survivors lived in extreme poverty, and there were nods around the table as they mentioned friends or acquaintances in dire circumstances.

I shifted the conversation to Israel's future, mentioning the demographic projections cited by President Rivlin that show nearly half of Israel's children were either Haredi or Palestinian, two communities that would not send their children to the military. How would Israel continue to function?

Mordi responded that he didn't think Palestinians *should* serve in the army: "Should they go and fight relatives and family members?" he asked, rhetorically, cocking his head to one side. "That's not logical."

In general, he expressed dissatisfaction with the callous treatment of Palestinians, both those who were citizens and those who lived on the West Bank and in Gaza. He shook his head in disapproval, for instance, as I described Alam's situation as a lawyer for the Ministry of Justice, enduring a daily humiliation of a checkpoint just to get to work.

"It's the problem of any minority living in a majority," he said, raising his hands in frustration.

Mari agreed, noting that she hadn't imagined dealing with the Palestinians would be such a problem when she first arrived in Israel. Young and naïve, she longed to help create a modern, Western, socialist country and, in pursuit of that ultimate goal, did her best to ignore what the state had done to the Arabs. The evidence was never far. Her brother was assigned a house in Haifa that had belonged to Arabs; it still had their furnishings when he moved in. Nevertheless, Mari was patient, sure that an equitable resolution would be worked out.

"The Jews, with all their knowledge and wisdom, surely could find a solution," she recalled thinking. "And because of what we had just experienced, I expected that it would be a just, humane, compassionate solution."

Mari said her disappointment at the ongoing conflicts with the Palestinians had shaken her faith in zionism. Like my mother and everyone else around the table, she had risked life and limb for the cause, but she couldn't even call herself a zionist anymore.

"The biggest problem is the occupation," she said in summary, with everyone around the table nodding in understanding and solidarity.

14

MA'AGAN

Gabi and I spent the next two days in the north around the Sea of Galilee, where he had a business meeting and where our mother had arranged some other interviews for me. We left in the morning, driving east and then northeast for more than an hour on highways hugging the edges of the West Bank territories conquered in 1967, past Um al Fahm, Alam's home, and Megiddo, the site of an ancient town foretold in the New Testament as the location of a future battle between the forces of good and evil— i.e., Armageddon, which was drawn from the Hebrew words "Har Megiddo," the foothills of Megiddo. The SUV's speakers hummed with the rough but tender crooning of Willie Nelson and Merle Haggard singing Bob Dylan songs as we rolled across the broad plain with ridges and hills in the distance, the perfect place for an epic military confrontation, as it had been for the armies of Pharaoh Thutmose III and the Canaanites during the fifteenth century B.C.E., for the soldiers of the British and Ottoman Empires in 1918, and many others in between.

Gabi and I argued most of the way there. It began when I mentioned my visits to the Shtefanisher Rebbe's tomb and Gabi grew annoyed, telling me that I was giving the Haredim too much credit and too big a voice in my book. I explained that the Haredim represented a continuity with the Jewish past, and that their influence on modern Israel was profound, far greater than was generally acknowledged. But Gabi wouldn't have it. To him, the Haredi vision of Israel was impractical at best and, at worst, truly dangerous, based on superstition and the petty agendas of scheming rabbis, while entirely dependent on the religious nostalgia—and attendant largesse—of the majority. I was being duped by the great Haredi con, and was allowing myself to be a sucker.

"The conversation wasn't about 'why,'" Gabi continued. "See, that's the thing. Among Haredim, you're never allowed to ask why."

After Beit She'an, we turned north, keeping to our east the Jordan River, the border with the nation of Jordan, until finally we began a steep descent. Gabi stopped the Cadillac at a vista where we could see the whole Sea of Galilee, a great, ovular pool of placid, turquoise water surrounded by hills with steep, nearly barren slopes and lush, green peaks. We got out to savor it.

A small lake by North American or even European standards, the Sea of Galilee had the geographical distinction of being the second lowest body of water in the world, after the Dead Sea in Israel's southern desert. The sea's modest size, however, was out of proportion to its significance in both Jewish and Christian traditions, as it was the location of Jesus's sermons and miracles, and the place where some Jewish sages retreated after the Romans expelled them from Jerusalem. Parts of the Talmud were written in Tiberias, a city just a little farther up the shore, and the region had been a haven for Jews fleeing the Spanish Inquisition as well. Regardless of whether it was properly a lake or an inland sea, Israelis now referred to this body of water as the Kinneret, reviving an ancient word that resembled the Hebrew word for "harp," but with an even older, unknown origin.

We drove a little farther down the slope, parked, and got out in front of a row of nine solid, gray-brick structures just a few steps away from the water. This was the preserved Kinneret Colony, launched in 1908 by the Zionist Organization (renamed the World Zionist Organization in 1960) with support from Baron Edmond Rothschild on a former Ottoman plantation near the spot where the Jordan River exited the Galilee. The plan was to replace the Arab laborers of the area with Jews fleeing Russian antisemitism, who would be directed by an agronomist-foreman training them in the agricultural skills necessary to become entirely self-sufficient in this challenging environment. Within a year, however, most of the Jewish workers—among them a former yeshiva student from a rabbinical dynasty in the Pale of Settlement, an experienced farmer from Romania, and a feminist from Russia who arrived in Israel with a group of friends—revolted against the foreman and went on strike, demanding communal self-rule.

Granted a section of the farm, the workers moved into mud huts previously housing Arab workers, and soon their commune had proved more productive than the plantation itself. They named themselves Degania, after the grains they cultivated on the farm, and built wood-and-brick buildings to replace the original mud huts. The World Zionist Organization had intended for the Kinneret Colony to serve as a model for the zionist enterprise, but it was the radical experiment on this second farm that became far more influential. And so, Degania became the very first kibbutz, a place where socialist principles were debated, refined, and applied to create an ever more egalitarian community. Other kibbutzim, the more individualistic *moshavim,* and other types of communes soon began to appear around the Kinneret plantation and elsewhere throughout Israel, such that by 1930, there were about 3,900 people living in 29 kibbutzim, and by end of 1941,

26,552 living in 82 kibbutzim. During the 1948 war, alas, many kibbutzim were on the front lines, and Degania was destroyed by the Syrian army.

Once the state was established, the number of kibbutzim and their population rose dramatically, to 67,550 in 240 communities, representing about 7.5 percent of Israel's Jews by 1950, the year Gabi was born on nearby Kibbutz Ma'agan. Ranging from the southern deserts to the Mediterranean coast, large kibbutzim boasted thousands of members working in factories while smaller communities eked out a living in isolated corners of the country. These highly visible social experiments captured the public's imagination despite their small numbers, and were now seen as incubators for a new kind of Jew, modern and self-reliant, proud of their heritage and liberated from the humiliating restrictions of the diasporic past.

The young men who grew up on the kibbutzim tended to do well on the military's aptitude tests, such that they were disproportionately represented in elite special forces units, as officers, and as pilots. Israel's first prime minister, David Ben-Gurion, lived on Kibbutz Sde Boker in the Negev, the desert that made up much of Israel's south. Aspiring officeholders and cultural figures alike saw affiliation with a kibbutz as a meaningful expression of their political philosophy, while in the 1960s and 1970s, volunteering on a kibbutz became a rite of passage for international travelers from around the world.

With the Likud takeover of the government in 1977, however, the kibbutzim experienced a turnaround in their public perception and a plunge in economic status to go with it. Criticized for discrimination against Mizrahim and Sephardim, who were rarely admitted as members, and for the substantial government subsidies they received, the kibbutzim saw dwindling numbers of foreign volunteers, while the number of paid employees in factories and farms surged, undermining the movement's very economic rationale of self-sufficiency. As a majority of those who grew up on the kibbutzim opted not to return, complaining of the lack of opportunity and a restrictive lifestyle, economic reforms soon forced the kibbutzim to sell off their assets, allow members who worked outside to keep their income instead of contributing it to a common fund, and even permit property that had previously been commonly held to be bequeathed to one's heirs, whether or not they had even lived on the kibbutz. By 2017, three-quarters of kibbutzim were paying their employees competitive wages, rather than a common stipend.

From the Kinneret Colony, we drove just a few minutes around the southern tip of the Sea of Galilee, passing huge fields of date palms and bananas, before we saw the entrance to Ma'agan Holiday Village, a resort hotel built on kibbutz land, and then finally to the entrance to the kibbutz proper.

There was a guard post resting on tall metal stands, but it looked forlorn and rusty, while the gate through the metal fence topped with barbed wire was flung wide open. Nearby, a large, concrete storage facility that looked similarly neglected bore a graffiti message at least ten meters off the ground, which said "Hello, from the Australians, '75" in sharp, linear Hebrew. Beyond these dispiriting relics, however, we saw a few rows of half-finished cottages, a hopeful sign of growth.

Gabi found a parking spot and turned off the car. He paused, looked out through the windshield, and sighed. "I feel connected here," he said. "You know? I was born here. This is my kibbutz."

Outside, it was 39 degrees (102 degrees Fahrenheit), and the air was thick with humidity, but this did not deter Amnon Ben Shoushan, who soon appeared at the edge of the parking lot.

He and Gabi had been communicating by cell phone as we approached, and he insisted on coming out and greeting us in person.

According to my mother, Amnon was the last of the kibbutz members of her generation still there. Many had died, others had moved away, but Amnon, originally from Morocco, who had been at Ma'agan since the beginning, was still in good shape, and when she called him, he generously agreed to let me visit.

Tall and fit, his skin fair yet unwrinkled, he was dressed in a baseball cap, a white and striped polo shirt with a retractable pen clipped to his pocket, khaki pants, and sandals. After shaking our hands vigorously, he then led us along the kibbutz's winding paths at a brisk pace past pomegranate trees, tall palms, thick shrubs, and flowering cacti between rows of cottages with steep, slanted roofs covered with rust red shingles. Most of the homes were neat, with well-trimmed lawns and closed screen doors. More than a few had small, plastic Israel flags hanging over their thresholds.

Amnon's cottage was tidy, tucked between one neighbor with bicycles, toys, and a couch hung precariously from a swing on their front lawn on one side, and another who preferred wild shrubs, overgrown plants, and wooden sculptures to decorate their entrance on the other.

We sat down in his living room, sparsely furnished, tidy but comfortable, shady and cool from the humming air-conditioning unit. The house phone rang, and Amnon answered in French and then left the room to speak to the caller, only to return a few moments later with tall glasses of cold, sweet pineapple juice. He had lived here alone for the past nine years, he explained, ever since his wife, Esti, had died. His wife didn't want a full kitchen because she didn't like to cook, but she did bake, so an oven was included. Suddenly, gazing deeply at Gabi, he remembered that our father had recently died, and said, shaking his head: "He was *beseder gamur*," Hebrew for "just fine," a high compliment from men of his milieu.

Gabi thanked him for his condolence and asked how long he'd lived in this particular cottage.

"Since 1964," Amnon announced proudly. It was conveniently located near the kibbutz's accounting office, where he continued to work as he had for many years. He could have retired, of course, but he enjoyed the intellectual exercise.

"It's a reason to keep getting up in the morning," he said. "Keeps the head clean."

Amnon was born Edmund Shoushan in Morocco in 1928. His father had been born in a Sephardic family in Great Britain but came to Morocco through his business as a fabric merchant, married a Moroccan Jewish woman, and learned to speak Arabic. Amnon said his father somehow remained "thoroughly British" in outlook throughout his years in Morocco, achieving the rank of prince in the Freemasons. Indeed, Amnon and his brothers and sisters—he was the fifth of nine children—all grew up with a tangible connection to Europe as well as Morocco, at the time a French protectorate. Practicing Judaism according to Sephardi traditions, with a kosher household, his family was otherwise quite liberal; the men did not wear kippot or grow beards, and the women did not cover their hair. They kept the Shabbat and prayed in synagogue in the morning, but afterward were perfectly free to go to the club or the beach.

During the Second World War, after France's capitulation to Nazi Germany, Morocco fell under the control of the German-controlled Vichy regime, with antisemitism now sanctioned by official policy. Jews fell victim to assaults and mob violence, and authorities confiscated Amnon's family's cars, demanded their gold and silver, and prohibited them from attending school. At least his family was not interred, however, and survived without casualties.

As with so many young Jews, the war changed Amnon into a zionist, though this conversion was strongly opposed by his father. His father prayed to Jerusalem, but in the years after the war, did not want Amnon go to what was still a British colony while the British military was actively stopping Jewish immigration.

Nevertheless, after he turned eighteen, Amnon made contact with local agents of the Palmach, the Jewish militia, who helped him get to France. There he joined Habonim, the zionist movement of which my parents, too, were members, and boarded a tiny ship with 650 other Jews—some Hungarians, others French, as well as several other Moroccans. They had no food or water, and storms rocked the ship violently enough that many of his fellow passengers died. Whenever British ships approached, they hid among boxes of sardines in the hold, and did their best not to be discovered.

Relating all of this to me, he shook his head and pursed his lips. "It reminds me of the current refugees crossing the Mediterranean," he said.

Not far off the coast of Israel, they were intercepted by a British destroyer demanding their surrender. Audaciously, they fired at the destroyer, which returned a warning shot, and then, when they still refused to give up, a burst of machine-gun fire, killing one of the passengers. With no other choice, they surrendered as ordered. Ironically, they were brought to Haifa, but only briefly, before being put on British boats bound for the island of Cyprus, also a British possession, where they were placed in internment camps. "We called them summer camps," Amnon quipped, capturing the defiant spirit of the Jewish internees.

The Palmach sent two agents to infiltrate the camps and train them in weapons and other military topics as well as Hebrew, which Amnon now added to the French, English, and Arabic he already knew. As my parents and other zionists had done, he Hebraized "Edmund" to "Amnon," after the oldest son of King David, and made his last name "Ben Shoushan," which translates as "son of Shoushan." As the months dragged on, more Jews arrived.

"The British were exasperated," Amnon recalled. "They didn't know what to do with us." By then, it was early 1948, nearly a year after they'd arrived, the establishment of the State of Israel was imminent, and the British had stopped trying to prevent Jewish immigration. The two Palmach agents asked Amnon and five other Moroccans where in Israel they wanted to go.

"We want to go to a kibbutz," he told them, "but don't know which one."

The agents, Hungarian natives, recommended the kibbutzim in the Kinneret, where they were based, and made a call on their behalf. The kibbutzniks, however, were not enthusiastic. Moroccans? How would this even work? How will we speak to them? They protested, "What about the cultural differences?"

But in the end they relented, and in January 1948, Amnon and the others arrived at the Kinneret Colony, which was then being used as a jumping-off point to launch kibbutzim all around the Sea of Galilee region. A group of Hungarians, in fact, had already formed an association called Ma'agan, but they had not yet established the kibbutz.

"It was a big surprise," Amnon recalled. "A small place, pathetic, a few small buildings and tents, but it was close to the Kinneret."

Their fellow kibbutzniks, mostly Hungarian speakers from Transylvania, were thrilled to discover the Moroccans spoke Hebrew. Still, they separated them from one another just to make sure they assimilated properly. Given work uniforms and jobs, they all became soldiers when war broke out in May, for months fighting on the front line against the Syrian army. Amnon participated in tank battles around Kibbutz Degania, driving a bulldozer to dig trenches. He was luckier than many, including one of the other Moroccans, who lost his life during one of the episodes of combat.

Kibbutz Ma'agan was established in 1949 on land technically on the Syrian side of the armistice line, replacing a British military base and an Arab village, Semakh, whose inhabitants fled when the war started. The members who had been there during the war were now joined by more young Hungarian Jews, Habonim members including my parents as well as Esti, a young woman who arrived with her twin sister and soon caught Amnon's eye. These young men and women quickly paired up.

The kibbutz lacked basic twentieth-century infrastructure when they first arrived, but its new members, all dedicated to the cause, adapted quickly. Though nearly everyone was Hungarian, they insisted on speaking Hebrew, as everyone there threw themselves into the menial tasks involved in building a new community from the ground up. My parents were city kids who grew up in apartments in dense neighborhoods on the Pest side of Budapest, and yet they rose to the challenge, my mother working in the kitchen and with the children, while my father drove a tractor in Ma'agan's fields while doing his best to ignore the Syrian soldiers looking on from the hills above through the scopes of their rifles. All the men on the kibbutz wanted to be farmers, if only to make a defiant statement about Jewish determination to plant themselves there for good.

"I remember your father as if it was yesterday," Amnon said, his eyes gleaming. "Working on farming, on the border—that was the dream."

He also remembered my parents' wedding in 1950, a happy occasion in the burgeoning little community. My mother was tall and thin, her thick, dark curls flowing to her delicate neck, while my father was short and robust, with a cherubic smile. Gabi was born just under nine months later, and the following year, Amnon's first son, Dani, was born. Following socialist thinking that adults should be provided with child care to allow them to work, all the children, including babies, spent most of their days separate from their parents. Because of the ever present threat of incoming weapons fire, they slept in a bunker with one of the parents.

My mother had described that aspect of kibbutz life as particularly difficult, I explained, and cited Gabi as an example of a child who found the practice onerous as well. Amnon looked at Gabi skeptically, but Gabi, with a sheepish nod, confirmed that he had escaped the children's house as soon as he was able. I asked Amnon whether his wife went along with the separation from the children.

Amnon shrugged. "Of course, it hurt her—taking a baby there." But they accepted the science behind the kibbutz policy, that the children's house would create an environment conducive to educating the children even as it allowed the parents to be maximally productive. His two sons were both raised that way and stayed at the kibbutz until they went off to their military service.

"No, my kids never ran home," he said, looking askance at poor Gabi.

In 1954, Amnon served as a guard at a ceremony to honor Peretz Goldstein, a founder of the Ma'agan group before the establishment of the kibbutz, who had volunteered to parachute into Europe behind enemy lines during the Second World War. A Hungarian native just twenty at the time, Goldstein was part of a small team of thirty-two recruited by the British to infiltrate Jewish communities in Hungary, Romania, and other Eastern European countries. With the support of zionist organizations, Goldstein was selected by the British for his language skills and was sent in with Chana Senesh, a twenty-three-year-old from Budapest who lived on Kibbutz Sdot Yam on the Mediterranean coast near Haifa. In the course of the mission, Goldstein and Senesh were captured, Senesh was tortured for months before being shot by a firing squad, while Goldstein was killed in a concentration camp. Senesh was lionized by many Hungarian zionists, and my mother took the name Chana in her honor.

It had been just a decade since the parachutists' failed mission, and with the war's memory and its consequences still so salient to Israelis' daily lives, the ceremony attracted some 2,700 people, leaders of kibbutzim from around the country, veterans of the pre-state struggle as well as the War of Independence, and Prime Minister Moshe Sharett himself, along with other senior government officials. Among the guests of honor were four of the paratroopers who had survived the Nazis, and the Aero Club of Israel agreed to fly two Piper propeller planes to drop a greeting from Israel's president, who would be laying the cornerstone for the Yad Vashem Holocaust museum in Jerusalem at the same time.

Amnon watched as the Piper planes approached. The president's message was contained in a metal tube with a parachute attached, but when the pilot tried to throw it out of his window, the parachute's strings got caught in the plane's wheels. The pilot flew back over the Kinneret to make another pass, put the plane on course back toward the kibbutz, told his passenger to grab the plane's stick and hold it straight, and then leaned out of the cockpit to retrieve the parachute, a highly dangerous maneuver he had to try several times before he finally succeeded in freeing the tube, and throwing it. By then, however, it was too late to regain control of the plane as it headed toward the crowd. Seventeen people were killed, and twenty-five others were injured, an event that the newspapers and radio stations described as a national tragedy.

Amnon was particularly aggrieved by the loss of those four parachutists who'd survived the Nazis only to be "killed in this useless way," on the ground at the ceremony.

Despite the plane disaster, the kibbutzim remained at the center of the state's identity, and Amnon was employed in a series of important jobs at the Youth Workers Association in Tel Aviv as well as several other organizations. In 1959, the Jewish Agency, an international charitable organization that collaborated closely with the Israeli government to bring Jews to Israel, asked him to go to Algeria and recruit Jews from the substantial community there. His knowledge of French and Arabic as well as his familiarity with North Africa would all help him, but to Amnon, not only did this assignment require leaving his family behind on the kibbutz, it was also a dangerous one, because Algeria was just then in the midst of a violent revolution against the colonial French government.

He recalled the chaotic situation in Algeria. Frequent blackouts. Terrorist acts as well as reprisals by the secret police. "They killed people every night," he said.

As an Israeli, Amnon was considered neutral. The Arabs asked him for help, noting that the Israelis had fought the British colonial government, eventually forcing them out, even as the French authorities, also seeing the Israeli experience as relevant, asked Amnon for tips on fighting Arabs. Nevertheless, he had to operate secretly, since neither side wanted the Jews to leave for Israel; the Arabs saw the Jews' presence as a mark of confidence in their postrevolutionary state, while the French were offering them citizenship and jobs on the mainland. In the end, Algerians voted en masse for independence in 1962, with the vast majority of Jews opting to depart for France, and Amnon's mission was effectively over.

"Our world ended" with Algerian independence, he observed ruefully.

After that, he was dispatched to Marseille and Paris, where he was able to bring his family from Israel, and from where he was able to visit his family in Morocco. He hadn't seen them since fleeing the country, and since then, his father had died, but he had a happy reunion with his mother and sister. His wife and sons learned French, adopting a French lifestyle for two years, following which they returned to their cottage on the kibbutz. After the glamour of these foreign assignments, Amnon was back to driving a tractor through the banana trees. He even won an award for managing to keep that tractor functioning. "It's a big machine, but it needs to be handled with care," he explained.

Did he mind going from a position where he had international responsibilities back to farmwork? Amnon shook his head. He liked working on the tractor, and was willing to perform whatever duty the kibbutz assigned him. "You always agree with whatever is needed," he said, simply.

On one evening in 1968, Amnon was driving a truck near Beit She'an after spending the evening with friends when he was attacked by terrorists. Shot in the back, he was nevertheless able to keep going until he found a nurse, who kept him stable until the ambulance arrived and took him to a hospital. The surgery saved him, though it left pieces of the bullet that had struck him in his lung, along with shrapnel from the truck. Since then, he's been unable to run and even a trip up a flight of stairs winds him easily, so he stopped doing physical work.

The ensuing years saw great changes on the kibbutz. In 1969, a section of its land on the shore of the Kinneret was opened for tourists and camping; later, it was developed as a luxury resort with a full complement of services, including kosher meals. Then, in 1970, the kibbutz abolished the children's house. Amnon didn't protest; his kids were already grown, after all.

He got a new foreign assignment as well, this time at the Israeli headquarters for Habonim as the representative for the whole French-speaking world, a position he held for two years before being recalled during the aftermath of the 1973 Yom Kippur War, as Arab nations exerted international pressure by tightening the oil supply and terrorists stepped up attacks on Israeli targets overseas.

Since 1976, he had been back on the kibbutz, leaving only for trips to visit his large extended family in San Francisco, Spain, Australia, and Paris. His own children had not come back to live on the kibbutz either. One son lived near Tel Aviv, while another lived in Australia, married to a woman he'd met when she was a foreign volunteer at Ma'agan. This younger son had studied to be a date farmer in Israel, but in Australia, he worked in water management, an essential job on that perennially parched continent. He came to visit every year, and Amnon was also close with his nieces and nephews in Rishon le Zion and Herzliya, who frequently came to visit him on the kibbutz.

A staunch zionist to this day, Amnon wished out loud that all his family members lived in Israel, and he was "very disappointed" with capitalism—with the wealthy, their lack of service to the poor and to people at the margins of society. Still, Amnon described himself as an optimist by nature. "You can't fight against everything," he said.

I asked if he'd returned to Morocco since he emigrated.

He had indeed visited two times. On his first trip, he went by himself to see his hometown, and was immediately approached by a young man who offered his services as a guide. Amnon accepted, but said that he would actually be the guide. "I'll show *you* the town," Amnon told him.

The guide was surprised and a little wary, but went along with Amnon as they visited the coffee shop where he'd whiled away many hours as a young man and the school where he'd taught for more than a year. When they found the house where Amnon had grown up, still a stately structure, the guide became nervous.

"Don't be scared," Amnon reassured him. "I won't take the house back."

The last time he went to Morocco, fifteen years ago, he'd organized a tour for his family in which he rented a car to show them all the sites of his childhood. With everyone speaking French, which is commonly spoken in Morocco as well as Arabic, they had a grand time.

Amnon took us on a tour of the kibbutz now, his pace undiminished by his age or the still formidable afternoon heat as he charged along the lush paths. At the edge of the Kinneret, he pointed out how low the water was, the result of decades of overuse as well as the increasingly visible effects of climate change. But his tone was matter of fact; this, too, was just another problem to be solved with an adjustment of policy, a tweak of habit, a bit more grit.

We passed the old communal cafeteria, which had been an important gathering place for the kibbutz and one of the last hallmarks of their socialist ideology. It had been closed more than a decade earlier, after an intense argument among the kibbutz members. Amnon and his wife Esti were among the last to eat there, he said. "We couldn't keep it open for a few people," he said. At the end, the members who fought for the cafeteria had to acquiesce.

At first, the young people still on the kibbutz wanted to install a disco in the space, but now the space was rented out to a high-tech company.

We soon reached a sturdy structure with walls of unevenly shaped stones and a tall, cylindrical roof painted in fanciful colors reflecting the blue of the Kinneret beyond as well as the palate of a hedge of flowery thickets that, strategically planted in front, had since proliferated throughout the kibbutz. This was the museum for the kibbutz, the parachutists, and the seventeen killed in the 1954 airplane disaster, Amnon explained. The museum was empty and locked, but Amnon got the key from another kibbutz member. We entered and, after switching on the air conditioner, perused the well-designed placards and photographs telling the story of the whole kibbutz, from the time of its founders and those who arrived in the years after the war—striking images of young women and men with dark, shaggy hair and a range of expressions, from unrestrained optimism to pensive reserve. One photo showed Amnon and the other five Moroccans on Cyprus, fit young men in shorts or pleated cotton pants, waiting for their opportunity to reach Ma'agan in the Promised Land.

After the airplane tragedy, Amnon explained, he was all the more determined to construct a permanent memorial to the parachutists, and the structure was erected just two years later. Some had objected that the memorial museum would block the view of the Kinneret, so Amnon used his bulldozer to dig a huge hole to lower the structure below ground level.

After the museum, Amnon took us on one more stop in this tour of the kibbutz, a spacious, clean, windowless room that served as a gallery for his wife Esti's artwork. Esti had been the kibbutz's kindergarten teacher for many years, but she exhibited her work in Europe and Israel, and within this gallery was a treasure trove of sculptures, paintings, and mixed-media works, naked, undulating human forms, works exploring Jewish cultural themes, resistance in the face of capitalism and religion as well as images of the Kinneret and the kibbutz itself in bright, bold colors, textured paints, very often including found objects.

It was time for us to go, and as we walked back to the car, I asked Amnon how he felt about the changes to the kibbutz system. He thought for a moment before answering that he owns his cottage as an individual piece of property, and thus can pass it on to his children. An outside administrator was hired to manage the kibbutz, and the finances were solid as a result. There was a facility to take care of the old and infirm, all on the kibbutz's account, and with sufficient funds to hire caretakers up to twenty-four hours per day, as needed. Those members unable to work have a minimum guaranteed income, and there was a common fund for extraordinary medical expenses. He missed eating at the communal cafeteria, certainly, but was grateful for the catering every day except for Shabbat, when a Yemenite family living nearby was kind enough to step in.

This was all a safety net that simply didn't exist outside the kibbutz, and he was more than a little critical that the rest of the country had failed to provide the same basic security to its citizens. At least they had it better than those in the United States, who were basically left to fend for themselves, no matter how dire the circumstances, which he considered a colossal failure of the capitalist system. He asked, pointedly, "What will happen to the old or to the poor?"

Reaching the parking lot, we looked up at the mountains around the Kinneret, from which Syrian snipers had once fired down onto the kibbutz. These were the Golan Heights, seized from Syria in 1967. Just on the other side, the Syrian civil war was raging on between the regime of President Bashar Assad and jihadis affiliated with the so-called Islamic State. Assad was just then bringing in forces from Iran, Israel's nemesis within the region, and positioning them close to the border, though the Islamic State had likewise pledged to destroy Israel.

I asked Amnon if he was worried about a new war.

He stifled a chuckle. Israel might want to go to war to stop Iran from setting up in Syria, he mused, but the state was in a far better strategic position than it had been when Amnon first arrived at the Kinneret nearly seven decades earlier.

"Now we have the Golan Heights," he answered, sweeping his hand over the brown and green slopes. "So the war is much farther away."

15

RAZALLAH

It was late afternoon by now, and Gabi had a business meeting to attend in Kiryat Shmona, a gritty, industrial city right up against the border with Lebanon. This was to be the culmination of a long negotiation in which Gabi's client, Abu Kaf, a Bedouin entrepreneur, was agreeing to lease a factory space to produce canned tuna.

Gabi had met Abu Kaf a decade earlier at Ben Gurion Airport, where, on their return flight from Hong Kong, they were both selected for security screenings. Gabi was plainly annoyed to be selected for the extra screening. He'd been an officer in the IDF, after all, and continued to work with government agencies as an attorney, but the young soldier who pulled him aside said it was merely a random screening, and escorted him to a nearby room where a few others, mostly East Asians, sat waiting. Gabi took his seat next to a tall, stout man with a shaved head who smiled and welcomed him genially. Abu Kaf introduced himself and explained the procedures to Gabi.

Grateful, Gabi asked, "You've been through this before?"

"Every time I come through." Abu Kaf laughed.

The scion of a prominent Bedouin clan in the Negev, he had built a sizable business empire with investments in Israel and East Asia, an occupation that required frequent international travel, and he was searched every time he returned.

Abu Kaf became Gabi's client soon thereafter, and they had worked closely together on several projects, but the tuna factory was by far their biggest deal to date. Abu Kaf lived a world away from this particular industrial space in Israel's far north, just a few kilometers from the border with Lebanon, amid scrubby hills studded by pine and cedar trees.

We met the facility's owner in an industrial park on the edge of town, but, not entirely sure how to get there, Gabi coordinated with Abu Kaf by cell phone along the way, driving through factory lots until we spotted Abu Kaf's car, a black BMW with tinted windows, parked outside an enormous metal warehouse. We got out and approached the warehouse just as the owner, Avraham Shoshani, came out to greet us. Diminutive and bald with a belly protruding out over his jeans, this fellow projected the formidable work ethic that had earned him success in his hooded eyes and thick, callused fingers. His warehouse was immaculate, spacious, and modern, fully equipped to handle the machines necessary for tuna canning.

Abu Kaf had inspected the facility before, so Gabi was just there to finalize the legalities of the deal. They all embraced, posed for photos, and we got back in our cars to drive to Avraham's office in Kiryat Shmona.

Situated on the "Finger of the Galilee," a narrow strip of Israeli land in the Jordan River valley surrounded on three sides by Lebanese territory, Kiryat Shmona, with well over twenty thousand residents, was the site of the agricultural settlement of Tel Hai, which predated even the Kinneret Colony by a couple of years. Kiryat means "city," and Shmona means "eight," referring to eight Jewish militiamen who were killed in a 1920 battle with Arab militiamen that destroyed Tel Hai. It was not only the ruins of Tel Hai, however, that Kiryat Shmona was built upon, but also those of a Bedouin village called Al Khalisa, whose residents were expelled during the 1948 war. Repurposed thereafter as a transit camp, its first residents were Yemenite Jews, followed by Romanians and Moroccans. In 1953, with an infusion of government support, Kiryat Shmona was designated a development town.

Still it lagged economically in subsequent decades, bearing the brunt of Israel's violent history with Lebanon. Palestinian militant organizations set up operations in Lebanon in the 1970s, launching terror attacks and firing rockets at Kiryat Shmona until 1985, when Israel succeeded in occupying much of southern Lebanon, which they did not leave until 2000. In 2006, Kiryat Shmona was evacuated during a bombardment of more than one thousand missiles launched by Hezbollah, the Iranian-backed Lebanese militia; and though no resolution was ever reached with Hezbollah or Iran, the ensuing lull over the past decade plus had seen the city's population grow considerably.

We drove into a mostly residential neighborhood of modest, single-story bungalows approximately the same size as the cottages on the kibbutz, each with its own fenced-off garden. Avraham's office took up an entire lot, but the office was a converted shed with most of the yard used for truck parking. Inside was just enough space for a few desks whose surfaces were covered with contracts, construction drawings, and folders of varying sizes and materials. Avraham's adult son, a scaled-up, younger, less weathered version of the man himself, appeared and greeted us, as did his lawyer, Dudi, who was about my age and sported what I recognized as eighties-style, slicked-back hair held in a tight, short ponytail and a pink striped shirt.

Everyone was too happy and excited to mind that I was sitting there jotting down notes while they negotiated the final details of the contract. Avraham betrayed only the slightest hint of anxiety when he grew a little short ordering his son to bring us fresh-cut fruit—he clearly wanted everything to go smoothly. While the two lawyers hashed out a few fine points of the argument, I was the only one to partake of the thick slices of watermelon and cantaloupe set before us. But the conversation stayed cordial, and after a few handwritten changes to the contract, the signatures were all applied, and the first rent check handed over.

Avraham stepped out of his office and popped a cigarette into his mouth, as the edges of his lips turned up into a smile so that the crags and wrinkles in his face cracked and deepened. He had been working as a builder since he was ten years old, he told me, and had been in the city through all of its various military conflicts. The factory space was a sizable investment for him, something of a gamble, in fact, and he was just very pleased it had all worked out.

He was proud to work with Abu Kaf to produce the canned tuna, which would be sold throughout the Middle East. It was food that accorded with the dietary rules of both Jews and Muslims, and was as popular among Ashkenazim as it was with Mizrahim and Palestinians. There was significant competition in the tuna business, of course, but Avraham and Abu Kaf were both willing to roll the dice on their unique partnership.

It was evening now, almost sundown, and Gabi had arranged for us to stay in a guest house in a Bedouin town called Tuba-Zangariye. We drove just thirty minutes from Kiryat Shmona on a main highway before turning onto a road that wound through the hills around the Kinneret, until we reached the town of expansive family homes behind high concrete walls. The Cadillac's navigation app stopped functioning at the town's entrance, but Gabi knew the way and drove until he reached a particular bend, where he stopped the car and called our hosts. Presently, a young man in a long dishdasha—an ankle-length, long-sleeved robe traditionally worn by Arab men—came out, smiling, and waved to Gabi before opening the gate to allow the car into a long driveway leading to a large two-story stone house.

We got out, stretched, and grabbed our bags. From this ridge, we could see all the way down to the northern edge of the Kinneret, and we paused to draw in the fresh, cool air before ascending an iron staircase into a spacious courtyard with a bubbling fountain. In the doorway stood Razallah, the matriarch of this household, a lithe woman of medium height with a complexion the color of dates and a bright, full smile. She hugged Gabi closely and welcomed me with warmth and enthusiasm as well.

We were late for dinner, but Razallah had kept the food warm, she insisted, as she escorted us into a spacious chamber decorated with shelves and cabinets holding metal *finjans,* cups, pitchers, and candleholders. On the wall opposite these hung a realistic painting of a woman in robes standing in a landscape of scrubby hills. Her husband, Ali Al Heib, joined us as we sat at a large wooden table, and she immediately put down a plate of pita to dip into a bowl of olive oil that glowed with a lime hue and tasted especially tangy. Gabi brought out a few bottles of white wine he had brought along, but studied the labels for a moment and decided instead to open the cabernet/shiraz he'd bought at Psagot, saving a bottle of riesling from his collection for later in the night. Gabi poured glasses for Ali and me, but we had barely sipped our first glass when Razallah brought out the mushroom soup and laid out couscous, creamed cauliflower, roasted red peppers, pickled cabbage, baked okra, zucchini in tomato sauce, and black and green olives. Of course, there was hummus, too, which had that same special tang I recognized in the olive oil.

When I remarked on this, Razallah smiled proudly. She had

pressed the oil herself from olives they picked in an annual harvest she had participated in since childhood. She brought her daughters, too, when they were small, and now brought her granddaughters, and looked forward to these joyous annual picnics as a chance to pass on the skill set and traditions to the next generation of women.

I stuffed myself, as did Gabi, but we barely made a dent in the feast Razallah had prepared, and I felt guilty despite her assurances that we'd eaten sufficiently. Still, when she brought out generous slices of sweet, cheesy kanefa to "go with" the thick black coffee that finished the meal, I devoured the whole thing.

We retired to the courtyard, where we sat at a large round table with Razallah, her husband, and two other guests, Israeli Jewish men in their early sixties who introduced themselves as Ronni and Avni.

Gabi shared the cabernet/shiraz and then the riesling before Ali brought out a thick, rectangular, blue bottle of arak. Avni slurped down the wine and the anise-flavored liquor, but Ronni only took occasional sips of each, and where Avni grew more loquacious, Ronni just smiled silently. Avni explained that he was a tank commander during the 1982 war in Lebanon, when Israel invaded that country to dislodge Palestinian militias, and Ronni was a soldier in his crew. Lebanon was then in the midst of a civil war between militias from their own Christian, Druze, and Shi'ite communities, as well as the Palestine Liberation Organization led by Yasser Arafat, which also frequently fired rockets and artillery at communities throughout Israel's north. Assisted by Christian Lebanese allies, the IDF drove on into Lebanon until it besieged the capital of Beirut. Severely injured during combat at the American University of Beirut, Ronni had been left with physical and cognitive impairments.

Avni explained that this was, in fact, his last name; he had been born with the European family name Weinstein, but after the war, changed it to the Hebrew Avni, meaning "My Stone." Even after becoming a successful salesman for a high-tech firm, he never forgot about his former comrade in arms Ronni, visited him regularly, and took him on holidays like this one.

Avni "loved his simplicity" as a relief from himself, he explained. "I'm not simple or straightforward."

Avni tried to bring Ronni into the conversation, but Ronni demurred, and after a few minutes, he whispered to Avni that he was ready to retire. Avni apologized for both of them, and then helped his friend stand up and walk slowly back to their room.

Ali poured another glass of arak, and the young man in the dishdasha reappeared, introducing himself as Ali and Razallah's son. Tall and thin, with a fashionable mustache and goatee, he had just married, and proudly showed off a photo of his bride, a beautiful young woman with a proud smile and large, shining eyes. He didn't stay long, having entered the house only to retrieve a *nargileh* (a hookah), a knee-high water pipe composed of a water basin at the bottom protruding with hoses tipped with mouthpieces. His friends, he said, were waiting for him at the gate.

Ali explained that the entire town was composed of a single Bedouin tribe who had been there for more than five generations, now numbering some six thousand people. I mentioned our meeting earlier that day with Abu Kaf, a Bedouin from the Negev, and asked Ali if his family had common ancestors with these Bedouin, but he said the Bedouin of the north were only distantly related, if at all. The Bedouin of the north were Muslim, he added, but distinct from Palestinian Muslims, and were less numerous than the Druze, who also lived in several towns and villages in the area, or even the Palestinian Christians.

During the 1948 war, as the forces of the Haganah Jewish

militia approached, Ali's grandfather fled to the neighboring Jewish town of Rosh Pinna. The Al Heib tribe had a long, cooperative relationship with the residents of Rosh Pinna, which was founded in 1878, and Ali's grandfather conferred with a Jewish friend who urged Ali's grandfather to return quickly to his land, warning that it would be confiscated if he was absent. Ali's grandfather thus returned to his property while his brother fled to a refugee camp on the edge of Jenin, which was then in Jordanian hands. Jenin was captured by Israel in the 1967 Six-Day War, and though Ali's grandfather and his brother had long since passed away, he continued to visit his cousins there to this day.

"It's not easy being an Arab in Israel," Gabi observed.

Ali responded that life had become easier since he realized he could register his home as being in Rosh Pinna versus Tuba-Zangariye. Now, when he traveled back and forth to Jenin, the IDF soldiers who inspected his identification card assumed he was Jewish, and were confused when they saw he had been to Jenin, which was known as a particularly dangerous place for Israelis.

The soldiers always looked at him and asked, "What were you doing *there*?"

Razallah and Ali's eight-year-old daughter came to the table with a stack of her drawings, colorful unicorns and smiling bears, waterfalls and enchanted trees with smiling faces. Gabi praised the girl's work effusively and asked if she had any more work to show us. Her face lit up, and she ran back into the house.

Razallah beamed, and explained she was their youngest of five. She kept the girl close, determined that she get a university education. Casting a wry smile at Ali, Razallah said she had been "snatched" by her husband at fifteen, at which point she stopped going to school. That had been the case with her older daughters as well, and while some husbands were open-minded, others were not. One of her daughter's husbands was so deeply conservative he refused even to let his wife go to the market by herself.

"A woman needs to keep living," she protested, anger and frustration audible in her tone. "Don't shut women up. Don't separate women."

Razallah breathed out deeply and then turned to me directly.

"Boys and girls marry early in our community because there is no premarital sex, so when they fall in love, they have to get married," she said. "Engaging in premarital sex would cause a loss of honor for the entire family."

The little girl returned with an armful of drawings and graded homework assignments, including writing projects in Arabic, Hebrew, and English—all with the highest marks.

Inspecting each item, Gabi marveled at the fine work before him, passing them to me for further praise.

He asked Ali and Razallah if they'd ever traveled to Europe.

They hadn't, so he suggested that they try it, for the sake of their little daughter. It would surely be eye-opening for all of them, but for the little girl it could be a truly formative experience. They could join a guided tour in Arabic, and it was less expensive than they imagined, he assured them. He'd visited London recently, and told them about the unparalleled collection at the Tate Modern gallery, among other attractions.

Ali and Razallah smiled at each other at the thought of a trip to Europe but were noncommittal. It was quite late by now, Gabi and I were drunk and sleepy, so we said good night and walked to our room.

We slept fitfully, and I awoke before Gabi in the spacious, airy room. The sun was already bright, flooding into the room through the gaps in the curtains, the temperature rising minute to minute. Just outside our front door was Razallah's garden of flowering cacti and lush little trees in a multitude of geometric shapes, glorious in the morning light.

Breakfast was eggs, bread, olives, and several kinds of home-made cheeses, as well as dates and fresh-squeezed orange juice, all of which Razallah prepared and served while her daughter watched *SpongeBob SquarePants,* dubbed into Arabic, on a big-screen television in the adjoining living room.

Gabi and I still had one more appointment before we returned to Givatayim, and Gabi asked for a strong coffee from the *finjan* to fuel the drive. Razallah obliged graciously, presently bringing us two glasses of the black, oily liquid, which left tiny grinds on my tongue. She sat with us as we sipped the coffee. I asked Razallah if she ever drank strong coffee in the morning, and she said no. Still, she managed to rise every morning at 5:00 A.M., to pray and be silent. That was her moment to gain perspective on her family and friends, and on the world generally.

"People are like the coffee in a *finjan,*" she said. "Sometimes you have to let the mud settle."

The front door opened suddenly, and a much older woman with a deeply lined face, her head wrapped in a colorful hijab that matched her dress, came in and said something to Razallah, gesturing with a craggy wooden cane as she spoke. Razallah excused herself and got up.

"I have to make tea," she said.

We finished breakfast, and went downstairs to collect our bags and load up the car before we went back to the house to say a final goodbye to Razallah and Ali. By then, they were both drinking tea with the older woman in the shade of the courtyard, but Razallah rose to see us off.

16

TOMIKA

It was only a few kilometers from Tuba-Zangariye to Safed, but the road snaked along a barren landscape of jagged, sunbaked volcanic rocks, where just a few green tendrils had managed to establish a precarious foothold despite centuries of effort. Safed was an ancient town that became an important site of Jewish learning in the late sixteenth century, especially with the arrival of Rabbi Joseph Caro, a Spanish exile who was a master scholar of Torah, Talmud, and the mystical traditions of the Kabbalah. Jerusalem-born Isaac Luria settled in Safed later, and his transcribed teachings became central texts of kabbalistic traditions, cementing the city's significance for religious Jews around the world.

Only by 1948, Safed had a Palestinian Arab majority of 12,000 as compared with approximately 1,700 Jews who lived in their own quarter. During the war, pitched battles were fought in the city and nearly all of the Arabs were expelled, and afterward, the city was repopulated with Jews from around the world. Safed remained a site for new immigrants over the following decades, and by the end of 2017, it was Israel's highest-elevation city with more than 35,000 people.

Our destination was the Memorial Museum of the Hungarian Speaking Jewry, housed near the town center inside Safed's old Ottoman government complex in a stout, Jerusalem-stone bungalow with an ample porch. Pulling up to this landmark, we were greeted by the museum's executive director and driving force, Chava Lustig, a serious, fit woman of boundless energy, who now took us on a whirlwind tour of the museum's holdings.

Into just a couple of small rooms and storage spaces, she and her tiny staff of two paid employees and five dedicated volunteers had packed 15,000 books, 100,000 photographs, paintings, clothing, and documents, wedding portraits, graduation certificates, marriage licenses, religious objects, Torah scrolls, and teapots—every conceivable item of daily life, religion, folk tradition, and high culture for thousands of Hungarian-speaking communities, some 4,500 different congregations across Central and Eastern Europe that had existed for one thousand years before the Shoah. Over decades, each item had been painstakingly collected and catalogued, and in addition to the actual artifacts, there were rows of neat folders and binders with laminated lists of rabbis and synagogues as well as many other finding aids, all thoughtfully arranged to help visitors conduct research.

With particular pride, Chava showed off the terminal of a digital, touch-screen interface with a sign above that read in Hebrew, "Touch. Know. Remember." The museum had installed this device, which allowed users to interact with various databases, with a grant from the Conference on Jewish Material Claims Against Germany, the main compensation fund for survivors of the Shoah.

We went into the back room, which, serving as a collective office, was lined from floor to ceiling with shelves of books and even more color-coded binders, while the floor space was filled with desks and tables. Chava used a metal, screw-top coffeemaker in the museum's tiny kitchen to produce strong, Hungarian-style mochas, and we sat down to talk with her and Judith, one of the museum's volunteers.

Now twenty-eight years old, the museum survived on ticket sales and limited private grants with very little government support, despite being the only institution of its kind. Most of the visitors to the museum had parents or grandparents from Hungary, she explained, and were "looking for their roots."

"Miri Regev doesn't answer our letters," Chava said, referring to Prime Minister Netanyahu's culture minister, who was notorious for her opposition to any institution she suspected of harboring a leftist agenda.

Officially, Chava had turned over the helm of the museum to her son, but she still came in every day to lead her crew, and worried about what would happen to the museum in the future. "It hurts me," she confessed. "I don't know how it will work out."

Chava expressed her condolences to Gabi and me for our father's death, and said she'd known him in Budapest even before the war. She first met him and his twin sister, my aunt Zsu, when they were all in the youth scouts together, and they lived a short distance away on the Pest side of the Danube River. In those days she'd been a tomboy who preferred to play soccer and other sports with the boys, despite gender separation in the scouts and other activities, and had a friend in the same building, so she saw my father quite frequently.

"He was nice and quiet," she recalled. "Everyone loved him."

Chava was still Evi Kandel back then, fourteen in the spring of 1944, when the Germans and their Hungarian allies in the fascist paramilitary organization called the Arrow Cross seized control of the government. Her parents were both doctors, and the Arrow Cross ordered all physicians to the front lines, ostensibly to military hospitals. Before her mother left, she told Chava and her eleven-year-old brother, Erno, that if conditions were nice where they would be stationed, she would return to bring them there.

"Until we immigrated to Israel," she said, "we were sure they would come back."

Bolstered by the idea that their parents would soon return, Chava and her brother kept going to school and managing their household even as the weeks turned to months. In November, Jews were ordered to leave their homes and go into a walled ghetto, and Chava and her brother, allowed to bring twenty kilograms of material with them, brought bread, biscuits, and sardines, as well as schoolbooks, because they were concerned about keeping up their grades. Among the last to arrive in the ghetto, which was purposefully too small to contain all the Jews, they were assigned to a three-bedroom apartment that had previously belonged to a cosmetician, where they shared a room with thirty other people. There was one toilet and no water after a few days, and German soldiers took away anyone who was older than sixteen and younger than seventy.

In Chava's apartment, there were four children and dozens of seniors left behind. By now, it was nearly Christmas and the Soviet army was approaching, shelling the city with artillery while Allied planes dropped bombs regularly, so that everyone spent the nights huddled together in the basement under whatever blankets they had. No food was coming into the ghetto, to the point that some people peeled the paint off the walls and ate that, but Chava, discovering the cosmetician's makeup, organized the children to write uplifting messages on the walls using the lipstick and rouge.

Pushed into grim desperation, the old people were angered, rather than inspired. "You don't even know where your parents are," one told her, "even if they are still alive."

One night, she felt someone rubbing her leg, and when she turned around, saw that it was an old woman who'd lost feeling in her leg and was trying to massage it, but mistook Chava's leg for her own.

Then, on a cold, snowy day in early January—by then, they had no idea what date it was—the bombing stopped. The quiet continued for minutes, then hours, and Chava dared to venture out of the basement into the street.

As she stepped through the new-fallen snow, she saw bodies all over. In the distance, she saw someone coming her way, a soldier wearing an unfamiliar uniform, neither German nor Hungarian. The soldier was holding a very strange-looking object which Chava realized was a musical instrument, which he now began to play, producing an odd, haunting sound.

This was a Soviet soldier with a *garmushka*, a Russian-style accordion, and as he played, people came out of their hovels and surrounded him. "I'm Jewish, too," he repeated over and over in Yiddish, as more and more bedraggled survivors emerged from their hiding places. They were saved.

Gabi and I had grown up with nearly the same story from our father, who had been incarcerated with his parents in the Budapest ghetto just a few blocks away from Chava. He had dodged several efforts by the Arrow Cross to arrest the Jewish students at his school, including one episode where he slipped away just before his classmates were marched to the shore of the Danube, shot, and thrown in the river. In the end, though, he and his parents were forced into the ghetto, along with all of Budapest's remaining Jews, and endured the weeks of hunger and deprivation in a tiny basement until the timely arrival of the Soviet army, much as Chava had.

With the end of the German occupation, Chava and her

brother tried to return to their home, but as one of a minority of buildings in the city that were still standing, it had been occupied by homeless people. The new residents allocated Chava and her brother their former maid's room, where they tried to reestablish themselves, though all the house's windows had been blown out, and it was still the middle of the winter.

In April, the schools reopened, including the Jewish high school that Chava and her brother attended. There were only twenty-five to thirty students left in her class, and at the break, when the students broke out their snacks, Chava asked where they got the food. From their parents, they answered.

When she got home, her brother was waiting in the doorway.

"Evi," he asked her, "did you know that some people still have their parents?"

Some of their friends' mothers invited them over, but they didn't want to be indebted to anyone. Focused now on simply finding a stable supply of food, they gave up on school.

They heard of one house in Pest where a good bean soup was being served, and when they arrived, they found a large, properly equipped villa populated by good-looking, jocular young people in blue shirts who immediately invited Chava and her brother to stay.

They returned to their house to leave their parents a note in case they came back, and then moved into the villa, the Budapest base for Habonim, where they were assigned beds with sheets and allowed to eat as much bean soup as they wanted. The head of the organization, nineteen-year-old Yosef Lustig, caught her eye, and they were soon married. It was here that Evi changed her name to Chava and her brother changed his name from Erno to Moshe, the way so many others in the zionist movement had.

My father moved into the Habonim villa at the same time,

and my mother began hanging around as well, joining the cohort of confident young people who sang Hebrew songs in the streets and invited other young people to join them.

"That's how we built the movement," Chava explained. "There is no stronger people than the children. They gave us everything." Soon, she was doing the same; more than once, she gave her shoes to a new arrival who was barefoot.

Chava rose through the ranks of Habonim, becoming secretary and then director, organizing Jews in Budapest and other Hungarian cities. She had resumed her studies by now, but was so busy she dropped out of school once more.

Soon it was time to leave for Israel. The last thing Chava did before departing was to take out of her pocket a can of sardines she'd kept since they first moved into the ghetto. She'd held on to the sardines through the weeks in the ghetto and all the months afterward, promising her brother they would share it with her parents to celebrate their reunification. This she left on the table, resigned to the reality they would never return.

Many years later, after she'd already launched the museum, a visiting American researcher told her the Hungarian doctors taken to the front in 1944 had been brought to the western, rather than the eastern front; after two days, the Arrow Cross culled out all the Jewish doctors, and murdered them.

It took months for Chava and Yosef to travel through Austria and Italy en route to Israel, finally making it there in the winter of 1948. The first weeks they spent on a kibbutz and then in a farming community before friends suggested they come to Safed, which became their home. Here they had two children, who in turn gave them three grandchildren; one grandson lived in London, while a granddaughter was studying medicine in Budapest. Chava's younger brother lived in Petah Tikva, near Tel Aviv.

Not all of the museum's staff had such personal connections to Hungary, however. Judith, a vivacious woman with thick, coal black hair and an incisive gaze, explained she'd been born in Israel; though her mother was Hungarian, her father was Moroccan, and she did not speak Hungarian. Judith was there to help the visitors, who were often on highly personal quests.

"When we find something," she said, "it gives us such a good feeling."

Some time ago, a woman in her sixties had come into the office bringing a black-and-white photo of a toddler with curly, blond hair. On the back was written "Tomika." The boy in the photo was her husband, the woman explained, and he'd been brought to Israel alone as a two-year-old and placed on a kibbutz. The man refused to come in himself, but his wife knew that her husband had a sister named Zsusika, and she asked Chava to help learn anything about Tomika's family.

This was a tough one. They had name lists of children who had been orphaned, but these were organized by family name. When they began looking through their lists of first names, "every other name was Zsusika."

After a painstaking search through the lists, they found one brother and sister named Tomika and Zsusika, whose mother had died in 1946. It seemed like a match, but how could they be sure? Consulting their records, they learned that Tomika and Zsusika were placed in an orphanage after their mother's death and found the address.

As soon as the wife saw the address of the orphanage, tears burst from her eyes. She had been in the same orphanage as a girl herself.

They consulted an album of photos of children in the orphanage from the appropriate dates, and there they saw little Tomika, with his blond curls, next to his sister, Zsusika. From there, they were able to establish that Zsusika was still alive and also in Israel, and arranged a meeting between the long separated siblings.

There was no happy reunion for Tomika and his sister, however. They met briefly, but having lived apart for so long, they were not truly able to reconnect. Tomika did travel to Budapest to conduct research into his family, going on to write a book documenting their lives. He found his mother's grave and discovered that his father had been killed in a concentration camp.

It was late afternoon by now, well past the museum's posted closing time, and Chava and Judith were headed home once we left.

We offered to drive them, but Judith declined, saying she lived just a few steps away in downtown Safed. Chava, too, was reluctant, insisting she was happy to take the bus, but we persisted until she agreed. Still, she pointedly refused my invitation to take the front seat.

As we drove along Safed's winding streets, Chava narrated the history of each neighborhood, usually by ending with a word I hadn't heard before, *mitchared*, which meant "to become Haredi." Haredim now occupied 80 percent of the city, she said, drastically altering its character. What had once been a relatively liberal, secular place with a mystical tradition that had attracted many hippies, artists, and New Agers had become a Haredi-dominated town where any overt expression of sexuality or gender mixing, even something as innocuous as a painting of a woman placed in a studio window, was increasingly taboo. On Shabbat, the whole town closed up, with all public activity ceasing.

Chava wondered aloud how long she would be able to continue living in Safed, and more important, how long a museum dedicated to the history of Hungarian Jews—religious as well as secular, women as well as men—could endure in this context.

We reached the end of her street, and she demanded that we drop her off there, rather than at her front door. This was a more convenient place to turn the car around, she said, closing the door firmly behind her before hiking off in the direction of her home.

Gabi drove the Cadillac down the mountain out of Safed and tuned into a news broadcast on the radio. The main headline was about an apparent resolution of the crisis at the Temple Mount. After days of standoff, Prime Minister Netanyahu had met with King Abdullah of Jordan, who had nominal authority over the holy sites in Jerusalem, and the Israeli government was agreeing to remove the metal detectors, cameras, and other security elements they'd recently installed. Palestinians in East Jerusalem and throughout the West Bank were dancing and distributing sweets in the streets, celebrating what they regarded as a huge victory of their protest movement. The leaders were venerated, along with the young men who had been killed in confrontations with Israeli forces.

17

THE WOLVES AND THE KING

Back in Tel Aviv the next day, I had an appointment with Simona Weinglass, an investigative reporter who'd broken a series of articles about the dark side of Israel's thriving high-tech sector. We got together at the Landwer Café on Rothschild Boulevard, one of a chain of casual restaurants built on the legacy of a coffee company founded by a German family who fled Berlin in 1933 after Adolf Hitler came to power.

I'd met Simona in Chicago more than a decade earlier and followed her work with the *Times of Israel,* an English-language, web-based news source that debuted in 2012. She'd written about foreign workers in Israel, Israeli settlements in the West Bank, and other controversial topics, but her series "The Wolves of Tel Aviv" had major international implications, exposing billions of dollars bilked from hundreds of thousands of people around the world, attracting the attention of the law enforcement agencies of several nations, not least the U.S. Justice Department.

The first installment of her investigation, published on March 26, 2016, profiled immigrants to Israel who had struggled to find decent-paying jobs until they found the field of "binary options." One man, Dan G., had moved to Tel Aviv from Australia when he was twenty-eight years old and worked a series of low-wage jobs that didn't pay enough to live on in a city with notoriously high rents, rivaling those of New York City or Tokyo.

As soon as he put his resumé online, however, he was recruited for jobs as a salesperson in binary options that paid more than double what he was previously making. He quickly landed a position at a firm in Herzliya, the coastal city north of Tel Aviv that had become the country's high-tech center, with rows of shiny new glass office buildings that included the Israeli headquarters for Intel and Microsoft as well as many locally grown companies.

Impressed by the fancy office and the free food and coffee, not to mention the salary, Dan was excited to work alongside native speakers of other languages: Spanish, French, Russian, Arabic, and Turkish, as well as English. During a weeklong training period, he was taught high-pressure tactics along with a basic knowledge of financial markets before being set loose to phone people around the world, trying to persuade them to invest their money in binary market or binary forex funds, ostensibly in order to trade foreign currencies. Dan was told to say he had studied at Oxford and worked at the Bank of Scotland, and as the weeks went on, he began to suspect that the business in which he was involved was unethical. His customers' accounts dwindled, seemingly regardless of their investing strategies, and when they tried to withdraw their money, Dan was instructed to delay and otherwise impede them, using the excuse of paperwork and, whenever that failed, verbal persuasion that could escalate from gentle to outright bullying. Worrisome to Dan, too, were the company's deliberately opaque business practices, using VoIP technology to appear as if they were based in the United Kingdom, while selling only to people in Canada, Australia, Europe, and the Middle East, but never in Israel or the United States.

Through additional interviews with recent immigrants and a careful scan of international finances and laws, Simona's investigation revealed that the binary options customers were all but certain to lose their money. The United States had banned binary options trading for that reason in 2013, but in Israel, there were at least one hundred binary options companies employing more than five thousand people, generating at least $5 billion a year for the country's economy.

"The Wolves of Tel Aviv" earned a record number of hits for the *Times of Israel* site, attracting the attention of several Israeli politicians, the FBI, and European Union law enforcement. Simona kept up the pressure with new reports on the victims of binary options, including a sixty-eight-year-old woman in rural England who'd lost her life's savings and had to sell her house and a sixty-one-year-old Canadian man who fatally shot himself after losing more than $228,000 to the scam. She kept tabs as well on the progress of the legislation to ban binary options as it progressed through the Knesset, noting which ministers supported it and which ones had absented themselves on days of discussions or key votes.

We ordered iced coffees and a cookie plate, and I proceeded to interview Simona about her background and life in Israel. She was born in Bucharest, Romania, in 1972 to secular parents who'd met at the Polytechnic Institute. Her father had survived the Shoah as a child, while her mother was from Iasi, the historic center of Jewish life where the Shtefanisher Rebbe had been buried before his remains were relocated to Givatayim. Romania's Jewish community was deeply zionist, and several of Simona's family members had already immigrated to Israel. They paid extensive attention to any media reports about Israel and, the horrors of the Shoah looming large in their collective memory, held on to their Jewish identity tenaciously.

"It was a miraculous thing," she said of the Romanian Jews' perceptions of Israel, "full of high hopes, the kibbutzim and the pioneers. The Jewish people coming back to the land after their terrible trauma."

She was still a toddler when one of her grandparents utilized dictator Nicolai Ceausescu's sub-rosa channels to allow Jews to leave in exchange for substantial bribes and paid for her family's emigration. Presenting themselves to the appropriate government office to get the papers for their departure, Simona's parents were surprised, however, to learn they were headed to the United States, rather than Israel.

Simona thus spent her elementary school years in Philadelphia, far away from any other Romanian Jews. But her parents yearned for a more European lifestyle, a life enhanced by walkable cities with welcoming cafés, so when Simona was fourteen, they moved the family to Israel.

The Israel she experienced as a teenager during the 1980s had a strong sense of community, with relatively small differences in lifestyle between rich and poor. Glancing outside the Landwer's window, she recalled Rothschild Boulevard as being a sleepy place then, without any bars or restaurants, its architectural treasures dilapidated.

Returning to the United States to go to college, Simona married, divorced, remarried, and then finally moved back to Israel. Much as she'd loved working as a journalist in Chicago, Israel, in the end, was the place she felt she could make a real difference.

"Chicago is higher profile in many ways, but it doesn't matter if I'm there or not," she explained. "In Israel, I can be important. I have a role to play."

She used her journalism skills to write for the *Jerusalem Post*, the Foreign Ministry, and *Haaretz* before landing a job as a translator at *Israel Hayom,* a Hebrew-language, free-distribution daily newspaper owned by the American casino magnate Sheldon Adelson. Her husband, Ilan, a business intelligence analyst who consults on corporate and political issues including terrorism funding, established himself as well during these first few years.

Israel Hayom displayed a distinct bias toward Prime Minister Netanyahu, to the point that Simona felt she was working for an Israeli version of the notorious Soviet propaganda publication *Pravda*. She soon left and found other jobs, but jumped at the opportunity when the illustrious editor David Horovitz offered her a spot as an investigative reporter at the *Times of Israel*.

Simona struck a vein of interest when she began writing about the high cost of living in the country, a topic she and Ilan knew all too well. Despite having serious jobs, they were constantly daunted by the costs of living in Tel Aviv, from child care and education to the dizzying cost of housing. Rents were exorbitant, but the for-sale prices were simply out of reach for most middle-class families.

"If you don't own an apartment already," she lamented, "there's little hope of ever getting one. You can only inherit an apartment."

Her story about the cost of living was shared thousands of times, leading many readers to contact her with ideas for other stories. "English speakers come to Israel full of idealism," she explained, "and they're surprised by the corruption and how expensive everything is. It's more corrupt than the U.S."

One of the readers who contacted her was Dan G., the Australian native who became her first source for the binary options investigation. He called with what she initially thought was an outlandish story. "You're not going to believe this, but it's all true," Dan told Simona. "Thousands are moving to Israel from idealism and ending up working for organized crime."

Simona thought Dan's description sounded more like Nigeria, which had a reputation for Internet scams, than Israel. The more she investigated, however, the more she realized the scope of the binary options fraud. Still, she hesitated out of concern that the image of Israel would be damaged in a way that might fuel antisemitic canards of Jews as avaricious and deceptive. "I wanted to make an excuse for Israel," Simona said. "How can this be happening in broad daylight?"

She soon learned that binary options had grown along with the high-tech sector, which now employed 130,000 people—9 percent of the workforce—and accounted for a majority of the nation's $60 billion in average annual exports, bringing in money that diffused into construction and real estate as well as food, entertainment, and retail. Unlike the entrepreneurs of Silicon Valley in California, Israel's Silicon Wadi had emerged from the military, which had a special unit that developed sophisticated hacking techniques, spyware, and other clandestine digital tools.

Embedding itself within the Israeli world of high tech, binary options camouflaged its activities to appear as just as another part of the sector. As Dan G. indicated, the firms concealed their identities and where they were calling from. And so that the trail would disappear, they often used shell companies based in the British Virgin Islands, where secrecy laws prevailed. Many of the victims of binary options didn't even know for sure they had been scammed, and frequently gave up when their inquiries led to apparent dead ends.

The binary options companies, moreover, hired high-profile attorneys and lobbyists in Israel, Canada, various European nations, and the United States, and they weren't afraid to use rough tactics. An attorney from one of the country's biggest firms representing a number of binary options firms soon threatened Simona and the *Times of Israel* with lawsuits, while she and some of her sources, past and present binary options salespeople as well as victims, were threatened by anonymous phone callers.

"People in very high levels of society are involved in this," Simona said.

In a country with low levels of crime, where terror threats were handled by the intelligence agency known by its Hebrew initials Shin Bet, Israeli law enforcement was ill equipped to confront these well-financed and devious companies. While binary options companies filled whole floors of slick high-rises in Herzliya, the police offices were cramped, decrepit facilities with dirty walls and carpets. Israel's other media outlets, moreover, not yet attuned to these types of stories, failed to follow up on "The Wolves of Tel Aviv."

Nevertheless, Simona was relentless, and the issue eventually caught the attention of Israel's state comptroller while the nation's Securities Authority had received many complaints as well, and a few lawyers in Israel were now representing binary options victims. The prime minister's office issued a blanket call to ban all binary options trading worldwide, and the cabinet was working toward an outright ban of binary options, though too slowly for Simona.

She hadn't totally surrendered her idealism about Israel, but the story had shaken her faith in the nation's leadership. The country wasn't irredeemably corrupt quite yet; still, she looked at her two young sons, who, if she stayed in Israel, would eventually have to serve in Israel's military, and wondered aloud whether the state they were defending was truly "a just and decent society.

"In wartime, Israel has solidarity and comes together, but the country is becoming corrupt. Who would want to, God forbid, risk their child's life for that?"

It was a short walk to the Bezalel Market from Rothschild Boulevard, but I had to rush: I was already a few minutes late to meet the King.

This was my follow-up interview with Eli Noy, the semi-retired King of Falafel, and I found him among the racks of billowing T-shirts and bathing suits engaged in an intense conversation with several vendors. He shook my hand warmly and then invited me to follow him through the market to Shaul Tchernichovsky Street, named for a poet who was born in the czarist empire and died in Jerusalem in 1943, and whose archives are housed in the Genazim in the Beit Ariela library.

Eli led me into a neat, compact, air-conditioned falafel restaurant called Johnny's, where Johnny himself—tall, blond, and sporting an impeccable white chef's apron—stood at the ready behind an impressive array of salads, a few balls of raw falafel mix poised in front of the fryer and a vat of boiling oil at the ready. Eli instructed Johnny to bring us two cold drinks, and Johnny turned to his juicing machine and the stack of oranges next to it.

Eli directed me to sit on a stool at the counter mounted on the wall, so that I was facing him while he could see Tchernichovsky Street through the window. Periodically, he would notice someone outside, pause our conversation, and go outside to exchange a few words with these passersby. Johnny brought us the fresh-squeezed orange juice mixed with ice in foam cups, cool and refreshing on my throat and all the way down into my chest.

The King was born Ahron Eli Noy in Jerusalem's Sha'are Zsedek Hospital to parents from the Iranian city of Yazd, who had immigrated to Israel shortly before the War of Independence. His parents moved to Tel Aviv when he was a child, but as a fourteen-year-old, he returned to Jerusalem for the two-month summer break to work with his grandfather, in the Bukharan quarter, selling vegetables and fruit in a market. They specialized in watermelons, but his grandfather was an excellent salesperson who taught him skills applicable in many situations, and he loved being in Jerusalem working alongside his uncles and cousins. In his time off, he bought toys, housewares, and towels, which he then resold at the central bus station.

After finishing high school, he returned to Jerusalem to join one of his uncles who had a small falafel restaurant, learning that business as well. Soon he opened his own restaurant on King George Street serving falafel, shawarma, and fresh-squeezed juice. He and his partner quarreled, however, and he moved back to Tel Aviv, where he opened his own falafel shop on Allenby Street, naming it the Blue and White Restaurant after the colors of the Israeli flag. The street itself, named for the British General Edmund Allenby who had defeated the Ottomans in the Middle East during the First World War, was Tel Aviv's most fashionable street during this era, and Eli was successful in this spot. He even met his wife at the restaurant.

Later, a friend of his rented him a prime spot in the Bezalel Market, and in 1980, he opened the King of Falafel. An overnight success, the stand grew big enough to require twelve employees. True, he had competitors and imitators, various "princes" and "queens," but such pretenders never approached his own level of success or fame. He had three children, two boys and a girl, and, from the profits at the King of Falafel, paid not only for *their* education and extracurricular activities but also the school fees and expenses of many nieces and nephews.

In time, though, falafel began to lose out to "pizza and hamburgers," as Eli saw it, and it all ended in 2012 when, after more than twenty years in that spot, the city of Tel Aviv decided to sell a part of the Bezalel Market to a billionaire developer. Eli negotiated an exit agreement with the municipality, but that turned into a protracted legal fight, and after several negative verdicts and reversals, he was awarded an apartment in the new development and a store space in the new mall as a settlement. He gave the apartment to his daughter as a gift, while he expected the store space to be rented to a fish restaurant or a coffee shop.

I asked Eli how he felt Tel Aviv had changed over his years in the city.

Tel Aviv had become a much wealthier city, he observed, and everything had become easier as a result. People drove air-conditioned cars to air-conditioned malls, where they shopped and saw movies in luxurious theaters.

What about the poor, though? I asked. Wasn't there a big difference now between rich and poor?

There was indeed a big wealth gap in Israel today, Eli allowed, but that was the same in the United States, wasn't it? He'd read about Americans who, after making poor investments, were evicted from their homes, left with literally nothing. At least in Israel, private foundations and corporations tried to help, making grants and small loans, so that no one ended up on the streets.

Now Eli asked me if I ever ate at any of the new restaurants in Tel Aviv, and I told him about Captain Curry on Dizengoff, a casual, Indian-style place opened by Jonathan Roshfeld, whose name Eli recognized from Israel's popular edition of the television show *Master Chef*. Johnny listened in when I described what we'd eaten there, the bowls of rice with vegetables cooked according to Roshfeld's creative take on South Asian cuisine.

But after I was finished, Eli shook his head slightly and explained that he ate only kosher food now. Twenty-six years ago, he had traveled to Ukraine to participate in Rosh Hashana festivities around the grave of Rabbi Nachman of Breslov. He'd gone for an entire week, and experienced powerful feelings that inspired more practice of Jewish prayers and rituals when he returned to Israel.

"I got stronger in the faith," he said, repeating a common way for Jews to describe their increasing observance. "I started doing a lot more *mitzvot* [righteous acts]." Among these, he was supporting a Sephardic yeshiva in Tel Aviv that taught five hundred boys and girls and had paid for an impressive library of religious texts. Nor was he alone: more and more Israeli Jews were demonstrating an interest in their faith traditions in the last decade, he said.

Eli was impressed when I mentioned that I'd been to see Rabbi Nachman's chair in Mea She'arim, but he was firmly aligned with Sephardic practices, especially the opinions of Ovadia Yosef, the recently deceased Sephardic chief rabbi, who was renowned for his wisdom, generosity, Torah scholarship, political acumen, and Sephardic pride.

"Rabbi Yosef was very wise," Eli said. "He gave the law to all of Israel."

I asked Eli about Israeli politics, whether he was active in any of the parties or supported any particular candidate. He voted in every election, he said dutifully, usually casting his ballot for Shas, the party founded by Rabbi Yosef to focus the numerical power of observant Sephardim. Sometimes, though, he voted for the Likud of Prime Minister Netanyahu, whom he thought of highly, generally speaking.

I closed my notebook and thanked Eli for his candid recollections, but asked him one final question: Had he ever heard of the Shtefanisher Rebbe's memorial in Nahalat Yitzhak Cemetery? Eli paused for a moment and then reached into his pocket. He brought out a laminated card slightly larger than a business card and placed it in my hand. On one side was the familiar photograph of the Shtefanisher Rebbe, his eyes wide with wonder and astonishment, his mustache drooping onto the curls of his beard, the distinct, black conical hat perched on his head. On the back of the card was a prayer for "success, safety and health," with instructions written in tiny text shaped like a menorah.

"I go to the Tzadik's memorial every year, and it's always one of the most meaningful events I attend," Eli said. "I have kept this for luck for years, but now I want you to have it."

We both thanked Johnny and stepped back out onto Tchernichovsky Street, where he disappeared into the market's racks of fluttering T-shirts and bathing suits as I contemplated the odd intersections of the day—a long dead Romanian rabbi, a reporter born in Romania investigating the corruption in Israel's high-tech sector, and the King of Falafel, who had adapted to this new age of air-conditioned malls and fancy restaurants.

18

<u>VILLAGE OF PEACE</u>

With my days in Israel winding down, Gabi agreed to drive me to Dimona, a city in the Negev that was the home of the African Hebrew Israelites, a community founded by African Americans from Chicago who arrived in Israel in 1969. I had been writing about the Hebrew Israelites since 1991, when I was a reporter at the *Chicago Daily Defender*, and had been to Dimona several times, but this visit was my first after the death of the Hebrew Israelites' leader, Ben Ammi, whom many had regarded as nothing less than a messianic figure.

We headed south from Tel Aviv along a new highway that bypassed Be'er Sheva, Israel's fourth largest city, with over two hundred thousand people. We whisked past forests and green hills in the foothills of Jerusalem before the foliage disappeared abruptly, alerting us we were in the Negev proper, a landscape of barren, sun-bleached rocks. Within two hours, we'd reached Dimona.

Like Kiryat Shmona, Dimona had been founded in 1955 as a development town, with the same concrete apartment blocks, broken up by the occasional park or light industrial complex or small plaza of stores. Dimona enjoyed some renown as the home of Israel's nuclear power research facility—and, many believed, the main site of its nuclear weapons program—but this small and secretive scientific facility alone could not float the whole city's economy, and its thirty-four thousand residents had relatively

211

high rates of poverty and unemployment. Evidence of deprivation and a real lack of opportunity was everywhere to be seen, from the decrepit apartment buildings with cracked or boarded-up windows to the profane graffiti scrawled across many buildings' walls.

When we rolled up to the Hebrew Israelites' compound, however, it looked the same as it had the last time I visited, two decades earlier. Dubbed the Village of Peace, it was composed of cottages that had been freshly painted and tidy lawns, the trees and bushes all neatly trimmed, with pretty flowers growing everywhere. In the center of the front courtyard, I spotted a large placard with the words "Celebrating 50 Years Since the Great Exodus" commemorating the time from the community's arrival in Liberia to 2017, with photographs of thirteen "Kingdom Pioneers"—eight women and five men—arranged in a ring around a portrait of Ben Ammi, who was identified as "The Mesiakh," the messiah.

Born as Ben Carter in Chicago in 1939, he was working in a foundry in his twenties when a colleague introduced him to the idea that African Americans were descendants of the Twelve Tribes of Israel. Impressed and inspired, he changed his name to Ben Ammi Ben Israel, "Son of my people, Son of Israel," and became an influential leader of a small group whose intense analysis of biblical prophecies led them to decide to leave the United States. In 1967, the nucleus of the Hebrew Israelites left for Liberia, the West African nation founded in 1847 by freed American slaves, with the plan of creating a self-sufficient, communal farm where they could practice their faith. But with little experience in agriculture and limited resources, their numbers were dwindling after just two years, and Ben Ammi experienced what he called a "prophetic vision" that the group should move on to Israel itself.

Soon 138 Hebrew Israelites arrived in several groups with the intention of claiming citizenship under Israel's Law of Return, and at first, Israeli officials did provide them with visas, housing, and other benefits allotted to new Jewish immigrants. Most of the Hebrew Israelites were assigned to a dilapidated former absorption center for new immigrants in Dimona, but in 1973 authorities formally rejected their claim to Jewish identity. When the government tried to pressure the Hebrew Israelites to leave, however, they responded with an international public relations campaign and organized protest marches in Dimona. The Hebrew Israelites found allies in the United States among African American leaders and legislators as well as Louis Farrakhan of the Nation of Islam, despite his penchant for making antisemitic comments that outraged Jews in the United States and Israel. Negotiations with the Israeli government were frequently fraught, therefore, even after 1990, when several state legislators from Illinois brokered an agreement to allow the Hebrew Israelites to stay and receive work permits.

The following year, coming on board the *Chicago Defender,* the African American–owned newspaper founded in 1905, I began covering the Hebrew Israelites. I saw Ben Ammi for the first time in 1993, when he spoke to an all–African American church on the South Side. Thin and lithe, with piercing blue eyes, a long beard, and an aquiline nose, a knit tam covering his hair and dressed in a long robe, Ben Ammi looked every bit the biblical-era prophet, and he riveted the crowd in the packed church with his accounts of the Hebrew Israelites' paradise in the Holy Land, where the people lived close to nature, free of crime and drugs.

My mother insisted on coming with me the first time I visited Dimona in the spring of 1996, and Ben Ammi was especially gracious to her, giving us a personal tour of the Village of Peace, its communal cafeteria, and its health center, and introducing her proudly to the community's midwives, who boasted that they had assisted in the birth of more than six hundred children, raising the community's population to over two thousand. My mother commented that it reminded her of Kibbutz Ma'agan, and Ben Ammi responded that indeed the village was modeled, in many ways, on the kibbutzim, in that they believed in communal living.

The children attended an accredited school with a specialized curriculum in both Hebrew and English. Hebrew Israelite teachers taught religion and culture while Israeli teachers, including newly arrived Russian immigrants, taught subjects like math, science, Hebrew, and history. Some of the adult members of the group had been able to translate their American skills and experience into careers here in Israel, while the community itself was collectively engaged in several entrepreneurial ventures, including a vegan fast-food restaurant in Tel Aviv. They had even formed popular musical groups, the Soul Messengers and the New Jerusalem Fire Choir, that performed original works as well as R&B classics with spiritual themes, including free concerts for IDF soldiers on their bases. Dimona had become a regular stop for African American celebrities, luminaries, and elected officials who traveled to Israel, including superstars like musician Stevie Wonder, whose photo Ben Ammi proudly displayed.

Ben Ammi was upfront about the more esoteric aspects of their faith as well. The Hebrew Israelites ate a strictly vegan diet and practiced their own strict regimen of fasting, holistic medicine, and physical exercise, which they believed would give them everlasting life. Most of the adult men had multiple wives, and many children.

As we walked through the community, everyone addressed Ben Ammi as "Abba," meaning "Father," and he explained that children were required to bow to the community's elders as they passed in the street. When I interviewed him then, Ben Ammi described huddling with fellow Dimona residents in a bunker while Iraqi President Saddam Hussein fired Scuds at the city during the

1991 Persian Gulf War, targeting the nuclear facility with these notoriously imprecise, Russian-designed missiles. His concerns were Israel focused, Ben Ammi explained, and he saw an expansive role for himself and the Hebrew Israelites in the country's future in which they would be a vanguard of a union between Israel and Africa.

"Our priorities are quite different from those of African American communities," Ben Ammi observed. "We see the redemption of our people there [in the United States], in Israel, and all humanity coming via the achievements and the redemption of the children of Israel."

I returned to Dimona in 1998, this time leading a group of sixteen young people from Chicago's public housing developments, youth journalists whom I'd trained through a yearlong program I was administering as an official with the city's housing authority. Having won a special grant from the federal government for this international trip, we'd spent several days in Jerusalem and around the Kinneret before arriving at Dimona. It was the first trip overseas for most of these young people—indeed, the first trip outside the city for some of them—and, after days of listening to lectures from government officials and historical guides, they found the Hebrew Israelites familiar and welcoming. They jumped at the chance to speak English, and found the Hebrew Israelites' vegan versions of soul food far more palatable than the hummus, shawarma, falafel, and other dishes I'd forced them to try, thoroughly enjoying the macaroni and soy cheese, BBQ seitan strips, and collard greens cooked in vegetable oil instead of lard.

Ben Ammi did preach at the youth journalists, encouraging them to immigrate to Israel, but they left unconverted, seeing their visit to the Hebrew Israelite community as just one more experience in the overall adventure beyond the bounds of their lives in Chicago.

Ben Ammi died in 2014 in a hospital in Be'er Sheva at seventy-five, survived by four wives, twenty-five children, forty-five grandchildren, and fifteen great-grandchildren. Not having been back to Dimona since, I wondered how his death had affected the Hebrew Israelite community overall.

Gabi and I were greeted warmly by Ahmadiel Ben Yehudah, the Hebrew Israelites' minister of information and national spokesman, whom I'd met on my previous visits, and he invited us into the cottage they used as the press office, where we sat in the comfortable air-conditioning drinking cold, sparkling water as we talked. Speaking in English, he spent the first few minutes recalling our prior conversations over the years. Tall and thin, with a narrow mustache and full beard, Ahmadiel remembered my mother's tour of Dimona and graciously accepted her condolences for Ben Ammi's death.

Though not an original member himself, Ahmadiel had held important positions in the community for decades, serving in nine locales over twenty years, including Zaire (now the Democratic Republic of the Congo), where they had just a small group, and South Africa, where there were over one thousand members. He had arrived in Israel in 1978 and played drums with the Soul Messengers, before becoming the minister of information as of 1984 and community spokesperson since 1994. He proudly counted twenty-two children from three wives, including four who were adopted. All those who had reached the age of conscription had served in the IDF, and some had even served in combat units. "There is no greater service," he said of his children in the military. "Most parents don't want their children in combat units, but it's their choice."

I asked about the community's size now, and Ahmadiel said

they did not keep an exact count, though he was sure it was well over three thousand in Dimona alone. Ben Ammi had finally received his Israeli citizenship two years before he died, but Ahmadiel noted with frustration that many Hebrew Israelites were "still in limbo" when it came to their citizenship applications, while additional immigration from the United States or elsewhere was effectively blocked. But overall, there had been great improvement in their circumstances since my last visit, he said. In the past, after all, many community members had been deported from Israel and prohibited from legal participation in the workforce. Now Teva Deli, which the community founded in 1995, was selling a line of products in supermarkets—vegan shawarma, tofu, and seitan packages, as well as BBQ patties in flavors they called "New York," "California," "Texas," and "Kabab"—and also supplied restaurants across the country, providing patties for the signature dish at Buddha Burgers, a fashionable vegan spot in Tel Aviv, and nondairy cheese to the Israeli branches of Domino's Pizza. To formalize their communal efforts, the Dimona community had incorporated as a municipal kibbutz called Shomrey Ha Shalom, or the Guardians of Peace.

"They no longer call us a vegan, polygamous cult," Ahmadiel said.

Acceptance and legalized status came with their own consequences, however. The young people all wanted cell phones, while among those families who had received residency status and work permits, as well as those who had served in the military, some had rented private apartments, bought cars, and taken jobs independent from the community, to the point where they resisted paying tithes and fees.

"They're strapped in their own debt," Ahmadiel said with regret.

Younger members who did remain inside the community were

contending with their own responsibilities as well, even as many of the community's original members were now in their sixties, seventies, and eighties. There were a few cases of intermarriage, he conceded, which were of particular concern, since a young Hebrew Israelite woman would have little experience with the habits and practices of most secular Israelis.

"If she marries someone who smokes or eats steak," he explained, "she doesn't know anything about that."

Nor was this concern over the Hebrew Israelites' exposure to broader Israeli society just a theoretical concern for Ahmadiel; one of his children, Elamar, a successful musician, had introduced another child, Ahtaliyah "Tali" Pierce, to the industry, and just a few years earlier, she had become a successful contestant on the popular television show *The Voice: Israel*, making it all the way to the semifinals. Several other Hebrew Israelites had embarked on musical careers, too—the brothers Gabriel and Eitan "Eddie" Butler represented Israel at the Eurovision international musical competition in 1999, and Eddie Butler represented Israel in Eurovision a second time in 2006.

Ahmadiel was ambivalent about his daughter's success. Tali was just seventeen when she competed on *The Voice,* and he objected outright to her wearing makeup as well as the choice of her songs, such as the Patti LaBelle hit "Lady Marmalade," which he regarded as unduly sexualized. The conflict with Ahmadiel was played up as part of the show, becoming a principal theme of a background video that was aired to build anticipation for Tali's performance in the semifinal. In the video, Tali's mentor, Israeli superstar Sarit Hadad, recalled her own father's objections to her singing, while Tali announced, "*The Voice* is my ticket out."

In the video, Tali brought Sarit to Dimona to meet members of her family, her siblings, and her mothers. Ahmadiel was interviewed and expressed his disapproval frankly, though he admitted to watching the show, and was shown attending one of her performances along with her mothers and many other family members.

More than four years had passed by the time I interviewed Ahmadiel, but it was clear that he was still stung by the experience, even as he continued to question the decisions of the TV show's producers.

"I was seen as a father who wasn't supportive," Ahmadiel complained, "but why would you choose that song for my daughter?"

Tali made it as far as the semifinals before going on to serve in the IDF as part of a unit of entertainers that had been a training ground for generations of Israeli musicians. After finishing her service, she moved "up north," as Ahmadiel put it, and joined a band. In fact, four of his children had moved up north.

Shifting the conversation to a related topic, I asked Ahmadiel how the community had processed Ben Ammi's death.

He sighed heavily. "We took it hard," he admitted. "His transition came as a surprise to those who didn't know his condition." Without specifying the malady, Ahmadiel explained that Ben Ammi had suffered a "prolonged illness" over several years, one from which he'd suffered highs and lows, so that some in the community assumed he would recover from the final bout, and were therefore shocked when he died.

But if the messiah was gone, Ahmadiel said the "messianic people" remained, with the whole community striving to fill Ben Ammi's shoes and fulfill his vision that they be a cultural and political bridge to Africa, a "light unto the nations," as the prophet Isaiah instructed. "Ben Ammi's energy didn't dissipate," Ahmadiel said. "That legacy remains for us to step into." The Hebrew Israelites had an essential role to play in upcoming world events, and they were paying close attention to political developments within the United States and around the globe.

"We are telling people, 'Keep your bags packed,'" Ahmadiel said.

Particularly worrying were the deteriorating relations between the United States and Russia, with their arsenals of nuclear missiles threatening a devastating world war in the near future. That war would not end all human civilization, however, and he predicted Africa would be the cradle of the new order to emerge—a world in which the Hebrew Israelites were positioned to lead humanity.

"We see a cataclysmic end for America, prophetically," Ahmadiel said. "We see Africa as a geopolitical landmass set aside for a new beginning."

With this heavy prophecy still settling in our minds, Ahmadiel took us on a tour of the village, which had definitely grown in the years since I'd been there. As we passed the school, Ahmadiel boasted of the high matriculation rate at the high school—88 percent, far above the national average of 65 percent for high school graduates. The Ministry of Education assigned the teachers, 75 percent of whom were not Hebrew Israelites, and oversaw the curriculum, which covered Hebrew, English, Arabic, and Bible studies—according to the Hebrew Israelites' interpretation. The student body even included two Bedouin, Ahmadiel noted, a sign, he felt, of how advanced the school was. All students were required to wear modest clothes and were prohibited from smoking or eating meat.

From there, we went on to the housewares store, a one-room building with shelves filled with cleaning supplies. Ezreyah, a handsome woman in a blue batik-pattern dress who had arrived in the community in 1982, explained that everything she proffered was made of natural, non-chemical-based products according to the community's strict standards, and all the items were bought in bulk, so that the savings could be passed on.

Next door was the grocery store, which was well stocked with fresh fruit and vegetables in bins and the full line of Teva products in coolers, which Ahmadiel said were made with an Israeli partner according to the original concepts and standards of women in the village.

Gabi theorized that the food line's success was a direct result of the experience women had in feeding the whole community nutritious, vegan meals on a tight budget.

"It's coming from a real kitchen," Gabi observed.

From the store, we walked on to the vegan ice cream parlor, a new endeavor launched by some of the village's young people. While we waited, an older woman in a pale lime-green dress approached the booth as well, steadying her slow but even gait with a heavy wooden cane. She beamed at us as Ahmadiel introduced her as one of the community's oldest members. She informed us proudly that she was there for her daily dessert—a combination of chocolate flavors in a foam cup, which she carried with her carefully and deliberately as she walked back home.

Once the lady in the green dress had her ice cream, the attendant inside the booth served us generous samples of several different flavors—pistachio and coffee for Gabi and mango with a side of melon for me.

To Ahmadiel, the ice cream parlor was a positive sign that the community was continuing to innovate and expand while they were still reeling from Ben Ammi's death. Ben Ammi had always loved ice cream, and they even had a soft-serve machine in Liberia. But the community's young people wanted to improve and innovate, and had added a wide number of new tastes and styles, all of which had proved immensely popular. "The only flavor was vanilla, and we were happy," Ahmadiel said. "The next generation has more than twenty flavors and now we're happier."

Next we visited the art gallery, a large hall where a score

of Jewish Israelis were checking out an assortment of paintings, photographs, fabrics, multimedia works, and more abstract pieces made by Hebrew Israelite women and men, as well as a few original animation videos shown on screens that were created by youths from the community. The village received visitors regularly, Ahmadiel explained, almost all of them Jewish Israelis from other parts of the country.

Amid the bustle, I interviewed Avidaliah Rafa Afrah, fashionable in a blue batik tunic, skirt, and matching sandals, standing in front of two of her paintings: one a realistic scene from the village with children playing while their mothers looked on, and the other an image of a woman's hand holding a globe of the Earth, with the continent of Africa facing the viewer. This second painting, she explained, was a depiction of the special role Hebrew Israelite women play in the divine orchestration of global events.

Avidaliah's artistic skills had been honed when she studied art at Kent State University, and she had been in the community for thirty-three years, married to one of the founders who had come through Liberia. Having raised four children there, she was candid about the difficulties faced by the Hebrew Israelites in their early years.

"When we first came, it was a challenge," she said. "The language, the weather, the different culture. We had a whole community in the States, and it was more convenient there. Here, we make everything, including the catsup and mustard at the store."

One of Avidaliah's children ultimately returned to the United States, but even now they remained close, and she had returned to the United States three times to see her daughter and her family, including, most recently, her twin grandchildren.

"That was a good trip," she said with a distinct glimmer in her eyes.

Among the gallery visitors, I saw Prince Immanuel Ben Yehudah, one of the community's senior leaders, whom I'd met on my previous visits and knew had been very close to Ben Ammi. I asked Prince Immanuel how governance of the community had changed since Ben Ammi's passing.

Thoughtful and mild mannered, Prince Immanuel answered frankly that the internal decision-making process was more deliberative and democratic now, with women playing a much larger role. "We can take more time to adjudicate things," he said.

Prince Immanuel spent his days handling immediate concerns, such as the community's ongoing housing crunch, which they hoped to alleviate by building new housing on land they'd purchased nearby. But he, too, forecast a special role for the Hebrew Israelites in global events. Israel was not destined to go the way of other countries, following science, technology, and consumerism blindly, becoming a place where people measured themselves by their possessions. No, Israel was intended to be a place for spiritual development, the prince maintained. That was why the Hebrew Israelites had left America behind—for this higher, spiritual mission.

"There's a misconception that we were misfits in America," he said. "We had jobs, lives, and we left them behind to come to the desert and live with the coalition of the willing."

Ironically, the spiritual nature of Israel was today under constant assault by American culture and economic power, he went on. "American society is encroaching," the prince said. "*That's* a concern."

19

<u>SAMI AND SUSU</u>

Back on the road, I turned to Gabi and observed, "You really hit it off with the Hebrew Israelites."

Gabi had enjoyed his conversations there, he said, nodding, and the whole atmosphere at the village, really, noting that Ahmadiel and Prince Immanuel were approximately his age, and that they had all shared the experience of being teens in the United States in the late sixties. Gabi's port of entry to the United States had been Monroe High School in the city of Rochester, one of many institutions being integrated in those years, and he remembered the political turmoil clearly. Seeing the Hebrew Israelites as embodying the bold experimentation of that time, he understood full well why the Hebrew Israelites wanted to leave the United States and why they saw Israel, with all its problems, as a kind of paradise.

"They brought with them something of the best of that era. There was a lot of spiritual awakening then," Gabi said, "But it disappeared quickly."

Then he turned toward me with a mischievous grin. "So, that vegan stuff was good," he said, "but how about some meat now?"

We pulled off the highway at Be'er Sheva, and Gabi, through a combination of memory and use of the Waze app, navigated through the city to the old municipal market. Located in a valley with substantial water cisterns on the precipice of the Negev and mentioned in the Tanakh as a place where Abraham and Isaac dug a well, Be'er Sheva had been settled and destroyed many times since Chalcolithic times. In 1948, it had been an Arab, mostly Bedouin town of a few thousand with an Egyptian garrison when it was attacked, evacuated, razed, and repopulated. One of the last vestiges of the pre-state Be'er Sheva was the Bedouin Market, held every Thursday, where merchants on camels and in trucks arrived to trade in rare goods and handicrafts, spices and house-wares, as well as metal- and leatherwork, carpets, clothing, and ceramics, along with antiques, actual and facsimile. Only lately, having survived into the twenty-first century, the market had be-come yet another venue for cheap manufactured products from China, and earlier that year, the city government had announced plans to close it.

Be'er Sheva was just then undergoing an extensive renovation and had received large government subsidies for its universities and tech sector, but the area we drove through looked forlorn, dozens of empty concrete stalls with scraps of desiccated garbage blowing past in the hot afternoon breeze. We pulled up in front of one of the few inhabited spaces, a storefront restaurant with a large sign in Hebrew that read "Sami and Susu: Specialty Grill—Beer on Tap" and the blinds on its windows drawn low.

In response to my inquiries, Gabi only smiled enigmatically, so I warily followed him inside. The interior was surprisingly pleasant and homey, with Formica tables and wooden chairs, and old yet clean wallpaper with small circular patterns in warm, dark colors. The walls were decorated with racks of wine bottles, Israeli flags, photographs of the owners, and, in one corner, tap-estries from Romania. Just one other table was occupied at that moment, two men quietly finishing off their glasses of beer. From a speaker in the corner, we heard Swedish pop stars ABBA's 1980 megahit "Super Trouper" fading out in favor of Alphaville's 1984 "Forever Young."

We sat down at a table against the wall, and shortly after, a smiling woman with straight, dark hair in a fashionable cut came out to greet us, introducing herself as Natasha. Gabi ordered a large glass of draft beer for me and a small glass of white wine for himself, as he was driving, and Natasha returned shortly with the beer, wine, and a plate of mashed, roasted garlic accompanied by a basket of white, crusty bread.

I used the bread to grab pats of garlic, which I wolfed down with the cold beer too quickly. When Natasha returned a few moments later, Gabi ordered for both of us, and before long, she returned with little plates of various meats, brains, and liver on plates, kebabs of sausage, and bull testicles—the meat grilled until perfectly tender to bring out the particular flavor and texture of each piece—as well as ikra, all of which I ate with a second beer and even more garlicky bread.

Gabi recounted the restaurant's history for me: Sami and Susu was opened in 1970 by a Romanian native named Marcel Lehrer, who had arrived in Israel just six years earlier and wanted to give his new venture a "catchy commercial name," so he chose the name of a popular Arabic-language children's show that aired on Israeli television beginning in the late 1960s. Produced by a government ministry as part of an early effort at public relations with Israel's Arab citizens and neighbors as well as its own Arabic-speaking Jews, the show had become a major hit with Hebrew-speaking families, too, and Lehrer saw it as symbolic of Israel's evolving culture in the region.

"I understood I had arrived in the Middle East," he told the newspaper *Haaretz*. "I was no longer in Europe."

Lehrer launched the restaurant with a fellow worker at the

nearby chemical factory, but his partner soon left, put off by the long hours and meager profits. Lehrer kept going, however, with a basic menu of Romanian classics, especially *chorba* stew, and distinguished himself by becoming the first restaurant to serve beer on tap and sell meat by weight. By the late seventies, Sami and Susu had become a favorite for Israeli celebrities—musicians and movie stars, politicians and army officers—and Lehrer kept the restaurant going into his seventies, even as his three children pursued other careers and interests.

By now, we had moved on to espresso, and Gabi asked Natasha to sit with us and finish the restaurant's history. She happily agreed, and Gabi asked her how she had come to run Sami and Susu. Natasha and her husband had originally stepped in to help Lehrer, she said, but these days, he spent less and less time there. He taught them to make the restaurant's specialties, but they had added their own items to the menu as well.

Natasha had come to Israel from Moscow with her daughter in 2005, when she was thirty, at the tail end of a massive wave of Jewish emigration from the Soviet Union and its successor states after 1989. In 1990, after Premier Mikhail Gorbachev opened the borders, 185,000 Jews arrived, nearly 150,000 the next year, and then more than 50,000 annually for the next decade. When Natasha came, the torrent had slowed to about 10,000 per year, though by then, more than 1 million people had come to Israel from the former Soviet Union.

For Natasha, moving from cosmopolitan Moscow to Dimona, where she was initially assigned by Israeli authorities, was a severe adjustment in lifestyle as well as culture and language. Natasha recalled that on her first Saturday in Dimona, she was stunned to go out and find nothing to do, quite a change from lively Moscow. Be'er Sheva, though, was a different story, with plenty of theaters and cafés that were open even on Shabbat. She met her husband, a native of Moldova, and together they bought a house in Be'er Sheva. She went back to Moscow occasionally, but each time, within a week, she'd had enough. Russia had changed for the worse, she felt. The people had lost their sense of solidarity, and there was much more antisemitism. In material terms, too, it seemed clear to her, Russians had fallen behind. "They don't have what we have in Israel," Natasha said.

I asked her if she ever went back to Dimona.

Yes, often, she said. Her mother and sister had come to Israel after her and settled in Dimona. She tried to persuade them to move to Be'er Sheva, but they were very happy there.

Had she ever encountered the Hebrew Israelites in Dimona?

"Of course," she said. "They really add something special to the city, and together with the Russians, make Dimona a much more interesting place.

"The Hebrew Israelites are such nice people," Natasha added. "On the street, they say *shalom* to everyone, whether they know them or not."

Perhaps it was remarkable that these towns at the edge of the desert would be havens for African American Hebrew Israelites and for Russian Jews, but Natasha regarded it casually, just another place in Israel where all kinds of Jews from all over the world wound up. Likewise, she had stepped up to the helm at Sami and Susu—a restaurant founded by a Romanian émigré and named for an Arabic-language children's TV program from decades earlier—with a shrug, taking over one of the country's minor culinary institutions from one of the living legends of Israel's founding generation, ensuring this unique menu would continue to be available.

20

<u>HADSH</u>

On my third-to-last day in Israel for this trip, I spent a few hours with my cousin Ami Sonnenfeld, eight years older than me, younger brother of Roni the pilot; Ami was the one who had dutifully lain down on the table in front of the Western Wall at my bar mitzvah, defending it from all comers. Ever charismatic, clever, and pragmatic, Ami had been a rebellious teenager and a restless student, but during his military service, he displayed a natural talent for organization as a loadmaster for Hercules transport planes, a skill set that translated into his later entrepreneurial efforts.

He began by selling helium balloons and other trinkets on the street in Tel Aviv, to finance his studies, and soon was managing a team of other salesmen. Sensing the opportunity, he dropped his college classes and launched a distribution company, Fly Balloon, inevitably moving from retail into wholesale quantities and becoming one of the country's largest importers of balloons, toys, and other items.

I took a train out to Fly Balloon's new warehouse in Modi'in, a recently developed city thirty-five kilometers from Tel Aviv. Built along Israeli's Green Line dividing Israel from Palestinian territory on the West Bank, Modi'in was in ancient times the home base of the Maccabee family, whose revolt against the Seleucid

231

Empire is commemorated in the holiday of Hanukah, but otherwise hadn't been inhabited before 1948. Ami had been among the early businesses in his particular part of town, building a large facility with an ample loading dock, warehouse, and office space.

My visit ended with the workday, and Ami drove me to the train station along with Hadsh Berhane, one of the dozen staffers of Fly Balloon, who was taking the same train as me back to Tel Aviv. Hadsh was one of Ami's most long-standing employees, a native of Eritrea who was one of about 42,000 Africans seeking asylum in Israel. The status of asylum seekers was the subject of heated political debate at that moment, but Ami, with his typical dexterity at handling bureaucratic obstacles, had been able to obtain a permit for Hadsh to work legally at Fly Balloon.

The station was deserted when we arrived, aside from one attendant and an electronic ticket vendor, so Hadsh helped me buy a ticket and we boarded the near empty train, easily finding a pair of comfortable seats facing each other.

I asked Hadsh if he would mind answering a few questions about the lives of asylum seekers for my book, and he agreed, saying it would be good to practice his English.

Fit and neat, with a well-trimmed mustache, Hadsh lived near the Ha Tikva Market in South Tel Aviv, he said, alongside many other Africans as well as Jewish Israelis. Eritrean men comprised close to half of the asylum seekers, but there were many Sudanese as well, and some women with young children from various other countries. Most of the people lived in overcrowded conditions and lacked work permits, receiving very limited support from government agencies and private philanthropies, while sustaining themselves with low-paying, off-the-books jobs in restaurants and hotels or as domestic workers.

Prime Minister Netanyahu had wavered on his policy toward the asylum seekers, calling them the Hebrew word for "infiltrators" and attending protests organized by right-wing activists in South Tel Aviv who cast them as violent and dangerous, often with decidedly racist language. But the asylum seekers had also attracted many supporters, who organized unexpectedly large popular demonstrations on Rothschild Boulevard—liberal Israelis as well as humanitarian-minded religious leaders, physicians, and tolerant neighbors who saw a Jewish duty in admitting refugees. As a result of their efforts, Netanyahu had not followed through on his threats to deport the asylum seekers en masse.

Israeli media reports described Eritreans walking days across the deserts of Sudan to get to Egypt and then crossing the Sinai peninsula to reach the border with Israel with the aid of criminal organizations who sometimes held and tortured these unfortunates to extort a ransom from their relatives. If they survived and managed to cross the border, Israeli authorities confined them in detention camps in the desert, only to be released at the Tel Aviv bus station with neither resources nor contacts.

Hadsh, who had arrived in Israel six years ago, pushed back against these reports as exaggerated. "Yes, there were hardships," he admitted, "but when you have your mind set on something, you don't feel it."

He continued, "I didn't walk the *whole* way, and we had been warned the smugglers could charge tens of thousands of dollars, only to rob and murder us, so we avoided them. And I only spent twenty days in an Israeli detention camp."

That said, Hadsh wasn't so deeply impressed by Israeli society. Though Eritrea had far less material wealth, its citizens were unified behind their leader and their national purpose. There was no corruption, and President Isaias Afwerki walked among his people without bodyguards, while Prime Minister Netanyahu had to be accompanied by a phalanx of security agents wherever he went in his own country.

I was surprised by this, since Afwerki's regime was usually described as a dictatorship, and many of the Eritrean men in Israel were fleeing military service that could last decades. Hadsh said his father was a career soldier, and he'd been a proud soldier himself, but he had eight brothers and sisters, and coming to Israel was his way of contributing to the cause. He was there principally to earn money, because Eritrea was poor due to its long-standing conflict with its neighbor, Ethiopia.

Ethiopia and Eritrea had both been ruled by the Derg regime of Marxist-Leninist former military officers from 1974 to 1987, when they were removed by a guerrilla army in which Afwerki and the Eritreans were a sizable component. Relations deteriorated in subsequent years, however, and war broke out over a disputed border in 1998. A cease-fire two years later failed to lead to a permanent peace, and the two country's armies skirmished often.

Unable to defeat the resilient and united Eritreans, the Ethiopians enlisted Russia and especially the United States to block commerce and strangle Eritrea's economy. Seeing Eritrea's strategic position on the Red Sea coast on the Horn of Africa, the United States orchestrated the international opprobrium over Afwerki's supposedly dismal human rights record to legitimize their policy, Hadsh explained. Afwerki's repression of a free media and democratic politics, however, were fully justified by these ongoing efforts to undermine Eritrea's independence, Hadsh said.

It was complicated, this take on the political situation back home, and I nodded along as Hadsh went through all his points.

But in the end, did he imagine his future in Eritrea or Israel?

Hadsh was aware of the political debate over the asylum seekers, intensely so, but his mission was just to stay in Israel for the time being, earn a living, buy a condominium or a house, and send money home to his family. "If I had legal residency," Hadsh said, with determination, "I would do a lot of things."

I parted from Hadsh when my train reached the stop closest to Givatayim, and he continued to South Tel Aviv. In his militant national solidarity, as in his gritty fortitude to make his way in a frequently hostile land, Hadsh reminded me of those prior generations of Israelis like Ami and his parents who were single-minded about building their newfound homeland. They, too, had grown up amid warfare and saw their personal survival as linked to their nation's survival, a loyalty that persisted whether they actually lived there or not. I knew Israelis who had lived decades in the United States who were just as loyal to Israel as Hadsh was to Eritrea, just as willing to minimize the homeland's failings while amplifying the threats from external enemies.

21

<u>DAVID</u>

Alam and I had a tentative plan to visit Ramallah on Saturday, when he was off work from the ministry for Shabbat while Palestinian cities were still open, with Friday being the customary day off work for Muslims. That morning, however, Gabi woke me by saying he'd spoken with Alam, and they didn't think it was a good idea to visit Ramallah after all. Though the protests in Jerusalem had ended and Palestinians were praying once more on the Temple Mount, militias in the West Bank were stepping up their demonstrations in public places. On his phone screen, he brought up a news report with a photograph of armed men standing in Ramallah's central square, their faces hidden behind balaclavas and kaffiyehs wrapped around their necks.

Instead, Gabi suggested we attend a protest against Prime Minister Netanyahu that evening in a nearby town, one that his friend David Ben Khalifa had been attending and was helping to organize.

David arrived to pick us up just as it was getting dark, parking his aged but solid Mitsubishi Montero SUV on the sidewalk while we boarded. Nira, her thirteen-year-old son Roe, Gabi, and I all got in, and David steered the Montero out of Givatayim and onto the highway, headed to the nearby suburb of Petah Tikva.

Along the way, Gabi and David explained that the protest was directed at Israel's attorney general, Avichai Mandelblit, who seemed to be dragging his feet in his investigation of Prime Minister Netanyahu for corruption. A former military judge and long-time member of the Likud party whom Netanyahu himself had appointed, Mandelblit was known to be determining whether the prime minister had accepted luxury items, cigars, and champagne as gifts from an Israeli-born Hollywood producer, and also whether he had colluded with American casino magnate Sheldon Adelson to arrange positive media coverage. Netanyahu was also suspected of other wrongdoing, such as receiving a kickback of several hundred thousand dollars for the Israeli navy's purchase of submarines from a German company.

Attorney General Mandelblit lived in Petah Tikva and the protests were being held near his home in a normally sedate section of this town ten kilometers from Tel Aviv. Founded by Haredim in 1878, Petah Tikva included a large industrial sector while also serving as a convenient, family-style suburb of Tel Aviv, and the Mandelblits lived in a cluster of concrete towers. The protests had been started thirty-six weeks earlier by five people who kept returning every Saturday, and David started attending two weeks ago after seeing a television report about the protest and asking his daughter to find it online.

David parked the Montero in a sandy lot between two unfinished towers, and we headed toward the mass of people carrying signs and making a din. "When I started coming, there were fifteen people here," David said, gesturing at the noisy crowd across the street.

David had organized three carloads of people to join him at the protest, and many others had done the same, so that now there were hundreds of people gathered around a two-story outdoor mall, overflowing the public spaces and sidewalks and spilling into the roads and gardens. The bank, toy store, clothing boutique, and grocery were all closed, but the Berlusconi gelato store on the second floor was open, doing a lively business with protesters buying ice cream and cold drinks. It was a decidedly festive affair, with most protesters casually dressed in T-shirts and shorts holding handmade signs with slogans that ranged from direct to witty to biblical: "The People Demand Justice," "Mandelblit Hid Bibi's Crimes That the Police Discovered," and "Corruption Is a Plague, Silence Is Not the Cure!"

A woman with long, curly hair held a pink cardboard cutout designed to resemble a submarine, with the words "Vessel of Corruption"; a few people held signs that read "Brothers in the War Against Corruption"; and a thin, middle-aged man in a plain, white V-neck T-shirt held a placard with just one word, "Enough."

The protesters were not political in the sense of preferring any other party or candidate. Indeed, we found a contingent of about a dozen men wearing white Likud T-shirts, indicating they were members of Netanyahu's own party.

Some of the people around them were incredulous. Were they *really* Likudniks? "Of *course* we're really members," they answered. "What, do you want to see our registration cards?"

I approached one of the Likudniks, a clean-shaven man about my age with a short haircut and fashionable, steel-rimmed glasses, and asked him, "Why do you think is it important to be seen here as a Likudnik?"

He answered earnestly, "It's important for the future of the Israeli people to have a government free of corruption."

We listened to the speakers, including a journalist who had been sued for libel by the prime minister over a story that alleged corruption by his wife, Sara.

Across the street a small counterprotest had formed, fifteen men and boys all wearing kippot, dressed in pants and long-sleeved shirts with fringed prayer shawls underneath, waving Israeli flags and banners with Likud logos and Netanyahu's face printed on them. The counterprotesters called the protesters traitors and idolaters, and frequently broke into chants of "Bibi, King of Israel."

A police car drove around the protest area and parked warily near the counterprotesters, but the groups remained far apart and the officers never left their vehicle. It all wrapped up around 9:30 P.M., the crowd dispersing without incident.

We made our way back to the sandy lot where David had parked and noticed a Toyota pickup truck stuck in a hole in the sand, its rear wheels spinning and whining uselessly. David approached the driver and offered to help pull him out. We stood by on the sidewalk while David attached cables from the Montero, then maneuvered to extricate the pickup from the hole, and finally dragged it to a place in the sand where it could get traction to drive itself onto the sidewalk.

The operation took twenty minutes to complete, and Gabi commented from the sidelines on this "trope of Israeli masculinity."

David, back at the steering wheel, didn't disagree, even as he waved goodbye to the driver of the pickup, grateful but chagrinned.

"Really, he was an idiot," David said, noting that the pickup driver had picked a particularly poor spot to park, but he felt obligated to help.

As we drove back to Givatayim, David recalled an incident from the mid-1980s, just after he'd bought the Montero: He'd driven to the beach in the afternoon just as the tide began to come in, parking at a distance to observe the sunset. But then a brand-new Ford sedan drove past him onto the sand, way too close to the water in David's estimation.

Sure enough, the Ford got stuck in the sand just as the water started to rise, the waves lapping ever closer.

Out of the car came a man, his wife, and a host of children

ranging in age from teens to infants, who all stared at the car silently for a while. Finally, one of the youngest children spoke up, asking, "Dad, how are you going to get the car out of here?"

"Don't worry, sweetie," the child's mother answered, not even looking at her husband, "Daddy got us into this, and he'll get us out of it, too."

It was a volatile situation, and as the odds of successfully rescuing the vehicle were slim, David prepared to make his escape. His girlfriend begged him to stay and help them, however.

Gabi and Nira broke in excitedly. "Which girlfriend was this, David?"

"It doesn't matter which girlfriend." David laughed back, continuing his story.

After delicate negotiations with the family, David hooked up the Montero to the Ford and prepared to pull it out of the sand. He gunned the Montero's engine, pulling the cables taut, but the Ford refused to budge. David kept his foot pressed onto the accelerator as the engine whined until, suddenly, with a dramatic pop, the Ford leapt free of the sand. The family was ecstatic and presented David with a juicy, ripe watermelon in gratitude.

Still thinking about Ramallah, I asked David if he'd spent time in the Palestinian territories. He had worked as a freelance mechanical engineering inspector in hospitals and had often been called to Palestinian towns in the West Bank, he answered. He'd been treated well, and found their medical staffs professional and knowledgeable, though sometimes they were doing their best with old equipment that in Israel would have long since been replaced.

"For the past few years, though," David added, "I haven't been able to go because things just got too tense."

I asked David if the protest tonight had any connection to the occupation, noting that none of the speakers had mentioned it, nor had the topic appeared on any signs.

"Certainly, there is a connection," David said.

Gabi chimed in that Israel's construction companies benefited from the ready access to cheap laborers from the West Bank. Tens of thousands of Palestinians endured long security checks on a daily basis just to come and work low-wage jobs inside Israel.

David agreed, pointing out that the military control of the West Bank as well as the encirclement of Gaza were enormously expensive enterprises that included the IDF but also innumerable private businesses providing services that ranged from construction and utilities to catering, and a whole raft of others.

"The occupation causes corruption the minute you have roads that are only for Jews on Arab lands."

On the morning of my last full day in Israel, I stopped at my mother's and found her in active discussion with Shosh, the home care worker assigned to her by the Israeli government. Shosh arrived every morning at 8:00 A.M. promptly, swept and mopped the floor, helped my mother do the shopping, laundry, and other chores, and usually had enough time for a chat until it was time to go home. A state-sponsored home care worker was a benefit my mother received as an elderly Holocaust survivor, but most survivors wanted someone who would stay with them twenty-four hours, often a young woman from the Philippines or Sri Lanka. Shosh was a middle-aged Jewish native of Iran who lived in Tel Aviv with her husband and had children and grandchildren. My mother, prizing her privacy, appreciated the fact that Shosh had her own life to return to after a few hours of help.

My mother had mentioned to me previously that Shosh had come to Israel only well after the Islamic Revolution, and now suggested I interview her for my book.

I thought that was a great idea, if Shosh agreed.

Shosh considered for a moment, a bemused look on her face. Fit, with jet-black hair, green eyes, and a confident manner, she asked me about the book's title, and the basic concept, before agreeing.

I started by asking her about her arrival in Israel in 1989, a decade after the revolution.

Shosh explained that she was already in her thirties by then, and that she and her husband were part of the large Iranian Jewish community that had stayed on. She came from an observant family with thirteen siblings, and still had a brother and sister in Iran as well as siblings in the United States and Australia. Her children, however, had all been born in Israel.

How did she compare Israel and Iran?

Iran was a much larger country than Israel, ten times larger in population and seventy-five times larger in area, and Persian Jews were sophisticated even by the country's advanced standards. They frequently studied abroad, gaining an expansive worldview, and women actually were freer in Iran than here in Israel. In general, she thought people were more trustworthy there, too.

"You can't trust the people here [in Israel]," she maintained. "Everyone has different motives."

Was she still able to stay in contact with her relatives in Iran?

Of course, she said. Until the revolution, Iran and Israel had always enjoyed good relations, with direct flights from Tehran to Tel Aviv. It was different today, of course. Still, telephone conversations could be held on the Internet through specialized apps, and while it was impossible for Israelis to travel to Iran, it was possible for Iranians to make the journey the other way, though it had to be accomplished by circuitous routes, such as flying to Turkey or Europe before switching planes for Israel. These were mere inconveniences, however. The true crimes of the Islamic Revolution were much worse, Shosh said. She was especially disappointed in Ayatollah Ruhollah Khomeini, who she said had not only interrupted Iran's progress but besmirched its image in the eyes of the rest of the world.

"Khomeini ruined the honor of Iran," she said.

Now Shosh turned the tables and asked me about my book. Why was I calling it *Twelve Tribes*? She was observant and kept a kosher home, and knew that my family was not, so why was I referencing the Tanakh?

I wasn't trying to compare the ancient tribes with the modern people of Israel, I explained. But I thought the Tribes were a good metaphor for the fractious relations among Israel's different sectors. Shosh nodded. Moreover, it was important for me to include religious people in this book, I explained, hence my timing this trip to coincide with the Shtefanisher Rebbe's memorial, for example.

At the mention of the Shtefanisher Rebbe, Shosh's demeanor became very serious.

"*You* went to the memorial?" she asked me.

"I did," I replied. "It was a very powerful experience."

Had she been to the Shtefanisher's memorial celebration as well? I asked.

"Many times," she said. "It really *is* a very moving experience."

I thanked her for the interview and turned to my mother, who was engrossed in a TV news report about violence in Jaffa the previous day. Protests had erupted after police shot and killed a young man and wounded his associate in a confrontation near the port in the morning. By that afternoon, hundreds of Palestinian men clustered in the same spot, blocking streets, setting fires, and throwing stones and other projectiles at officers.

DAVID

Shosh was outraged by the protesters' conduct and urged police to take a tough line, even if that meant using force to shut
down the demonstrations. Her youngest daughter was a police
officer based in Jaffa—studying to be a lawyer—who reported
that the streets were littered with debris from the fighting.

That afternoon, I made a final trip to Jerusalem to have lunch
with a friend and took a taxi back to the bus station afterward.

The driver, a neat, average-size man in a short-sleeved madras
shirt, asked me what I was doing in Jerusalem. I told him about
my book, and the title.

"First, you have to *find* the tribes," the driver opined. "We
lived among the goyim for so long, some became Christian, some
became Muslim, some are maybe Hindus, even Buddhists."

Take his own family, for example: his parents were both from
Morocco, and they liked Arabic music; but the Jews from Europe, they liked classical music. These were the kinds of cultural
differences that were apparent all over the country and were a
challenge to building a sense of solidarity among all citizens.

On the street outside, a large group of Haredim crossed the
street, momentarily delaying our progress. I asked the driver if
he could tell the differences between the different branches of
Haredim.

Of course, he answered. Every branch of Haredim rode in his
cab, and he often overheard their conversations in Yiddish.

"If you really want to understand Haredim," the driver
quipped, "you should drive a cab."

I was enjoying the conversation, but not too much to notice
the cab had passed Jaffa Street, where we should have turned to
get to the bus station.

245

He apologized with a guilty look, but I told him it was fine, and asked him to stop the cab. I could walk easily from here.

I was back in Givatayim by early evening to make a final visit to the Shtefanisher Rebbe's tomb. This time, the desk was manned by a robust younger Haredi man with a curly, light brown beard and piercing blue eyes, from whom I borrowed a kippah. The only other person there was another Haredi man, gaunt and pale, with thick, greasy glasses, who rocked back and forth as he prayed in a murmur barely above a whisper, tears streaming down his cheeks.

The weeping man remained where he was as I took up a corner of a tomb, reading to myself a few lines of a prayer book that had been left there. When I was finished, I returned the kippah to the fellow manning the desk and thanked him.

"*Kool toov,*" he said, using a colloquial expression for "It's all good," though his tone left me wondering if he was mocking me, revealing an affinity for secular culture, or simply using the vernacular.

My flight back to the United States left at 4:00 A.M., and I was bleary while I made my way down the jet's aisle past clots of young adults who were far too excited for this unholy hour. At row 54, I stowed my bag in the overhead compartment and claimed my aisle seat in a three-seat group at the window of the starboard side. My row-mates soon arrived, two slender young women with thick, long hair in glamorous, feathered cuts that swayed as they walked. They took their time placing their bags in the overhead bins, then arranging their various digital devices before finally settling into their seats.

I spoke with my neighbor in the middle seat after breakfast: Avigail, twenty-six, was born in Venezuela but had lived in Miami for the past several years, and was on this trip sponsored by Birthright along with her friend, also from Venezuela, who was sitting next to her.

I asked her about the economic and political situation in Venezuela.

Venezuela was being run by Nicolás Maduro, the successor of the late President Hugo Chavez, Avigail explained. The economy had collapsed, and though Chavez and Maduro were ostensibly socialists, the ultrarich continued to make outlandish profits without interruption, while party members and soldiers all received subsidies and handouts from the government. Maduro and his cohort were, meanwhile, plundering Venezuela's vast oil wealth and other assets as fast as they could before their time ran out. Left behind in the whole equation were the middle class who had no plan B, civil servants whose salaries had been reduced to twenty dollars per month, and those who lived day to day.

"It's a dictatorship," she said, "but not like Cuba."

"You can leave if you want to," her friend in the window seat chimed in, "that is, if you have the means."

The perfidy at the top left a desperate, chaotic situation on the ground, where street crime was ubiquitous. Avigail said she'd been robbed herself six times, on several occasions just for her cell phone.

"So many people have nothing, and have nothing to lose," she explained matter-of-factly, "so they just go on a crime spree."

Still, many Venezuelans felt guilty for leaving while their friends and comrades continued protesting.

I asked what she'd got out of the Birthright experience.

Avigail had attended Jewish day school in Venezuela and was literate in Hebrew, but she didn't know many other Jews in Miami. Her first time in Israel had been ten years ago, when she had participated in a five-day military-style camp, with basic training exercises like crawling under barbed wire and a "mean commander yelling at you."

I asked them about the Birthright itinerary, whether they'd examined any of the political, economic, or social issues that were the focus of news reports about Israel.

Avigail said they had indeed spent an overnight in a Bedouin camp, where they met with a woman who had divorced her husband. She quickly added, however, that the point of her trip was to party, especially in the clubs of North Tel Aviv on the beach, and *that* had not been facilitated by Birthright. She'd had to pay a thousand dollars extra to extend her trip for ten days, a sum that she considered well worth it.

"It's expensive," she said, "but that's when you get to have a good time."

22

ISRAEL IN CHICAGO

In September 2017, just a few weeks after I got home, I was invited to have lunch with the acclaimed Israeli chef, television personality, gay rights advocate, and best-selling author Gil Hovav in Chicago. The Israeli Foreign Ministry was sponsoring Hovav on a tour around North America to coincide with the publication of the English translation of his book *Candies from Heaven,* a collection of autobiographical vignettes about his childhood tracing the birth of his personal appreciation for Israeli cuisine to his grandmother's kitchen.

Within Israel, Gil was an iconoclastic figure with an estimable lineage, a great-grandson of Eliezer Ben-Yehuda, who moved to Jerusalem in 1881 and systematized modern Hebrew to make it the common language of the Jews in the country. In his time, Gil defied convention as an openly gay man with a longtime partner and an adopted child—even though gay marriage was not legal in Israel and adoption required circumvention of multiple bureaucratic obstacles.

An assistant press attaché from the consulate suggested we have lunch at the Little Goat Diner, a fashionable spot that was one of several restaurants owned by Stephanie Izard, the first woman to win the American edition of the *Top Chef* TV contest. I met them at the entrance: Gil, trim at fifty-five, with fashionable, rimless glasses and a shaved head, a brilliant smile and a firm handshake; and the press attaché, Moran Birman, a clean-cut young man in a navy suit and matching tie on a checked shirt.

Little Goat was bright and cheery inside, with plush booths and stools at countertops, and a menu of American classics. French toast, waffles and pancakes, Reuben sandwiches and tuna melts, but also a few of Izard's takes on Asian cuisine, such as the Osaka classic okonomiyaki and Korean-origin bibimbap. Gil ordered a Caesar salad with grilled chicken and a glass of chardonnay.

"I never drink water," he explained, "just wine."

I told him about all the different restaurants where I'd eaten in Israel, Ha Nitzahon in Ashqelon, El Marsa in Akko, and Sami and Susa in Be'er Sheva, and he nodded with a look of resignation. Israel was in a moment of cultural transition, he observed, with the European cuisine of the old days being recast or supplanted.

"The East is taking over in food," Gil said. "Once the European restaurants were dominant. Now there's just a few places to get chicken soup."

He mentioned a Bulgarian restaurant in Jaffa where the owner died, his children weren't interested in taking over the business, and so it was bought by the Arab guy who had worked there, steadily assuming responsibilities for the founder as he himself faded. The new Arab owner made all the old Bulgarian specialties and even spoke Bulgarian.

"Now it's an Arab-Bulgarian place," Gil quipped.

I told him about Ofer, the taxi driver who brought me home from Anna Lou Lou and learned to cook watching his Tunisian mother spice up her mother-in-law's gefilte fish.

Gil nodded. The transition was inevitable, he allowed, a result of Israel's history as well as its demographic realities. Where other Israeli chefs, notably Yotam Ottolenghi, argued that the nation's cuisine was the result of the interaction between Arabs and Jews, Gil said Israel's unique food culture was more the result of Jews from around the world interacting with one another the way Ofer's family had, adapting and experimenting with local ingredients in their own households, playing around with all the spices and fresh vegetables available in Israel. Indeed, this was the story of Gil's own kitchen since, in addition to his descent from the eminent Ben-Yehuda, Gil had Yemenite ancestry as well.

Israel had always been an integral part of the Middle East and North Africa, after all, so the preeminence of European dishes was bound to be fleeting.

"The Israeli kitchen is not naturally an Eastern European kitchen for pickled fish and all that stuff," Gil admitted. In that respect, he embraced the changes to the Israeli national menu, but only to the extent that it incorporated the various food traditions of the Jewish world. He was not a fan of what he saw as an intrusion of East Asian ingredients and flavors. His partner of more than a quarter century, a professor of computer science who was also involved in a tech start-up, traveled to South Korea for business frequently, but Gil never wanted to go, mainly because he detested the food—above all, kimchi, the spicy pickled cabbage ubiquitous there.

Regardless of the use of East Asian flavors, Gil maintained that Israeli cuisine reflected the growing influence of Mizrahim and Russians in politics as well as culture.

Moran, the press attaché, began to squirm uncomfortably in his seat.

I told Gil about the anti-Netanyahu protest I'd attended in Petah Tikva, and asked if he thought it was evidence of a political groundswell.

Gil was thrilled by the prospect of the end of Netanyahu's reign, but warned that politics had already changed Israel irrevocably. It wasn't just the word for "occupation" that couldn't be uttered, it even went into the way people talked about salad. The regular salad of diced vegetables that much of the country ate for breakfast was called an Israeli salad by those on the right wing, and an Arab salad by those on the left.

I cackled a bit. "My brother calls it a chopped salad, but then he's a lawyer."

"Spoken like a true lawyer, yes," Gil replied. "Like calling it 'the territories' instead of 'the occupied territories.'"

Hoping to ask him about the American influence on Israel, I mentioned Jeremy Welfeld of Jem's Fresh Beers, who had succeeded with a decidedly American idea despite the opposition of the country's entrenched beer corporations.

Gil agreed, adding that bars and restaurants had been reluctant initially to serve Jem's as well, because they weren't used to thinking of beer in the same terms as wine or liquor. But really, what Jeremy had to overcome was his American-ness, the stereotype that Israelis had that all Americans were basically "*freiers*"—suckers, that is, which was about the worst sin an Israeli could commit, to be gullible.

Americans were inevitably under suspicion of being *freiers* for even coming to Israel in the first place. What kind of person would willingly leave the prosperity and opportunity of the United States for the deprivation of Israel? Everyone else came to Israel in the midst of tragedy, Gil said. Even if they were motivated by zionism, they came after a pogrom or Holocaust or Farhud or other wave of antisemitic violence, often accompanied and exacerbated by economic collapse.

The reality, however, was that the American Israelis' willingness to put up with the inconveniences of daily life in Israel was an indication of their zeal and determination, Gil said. It was the same reason that so many of them were very right-wing and disproportionately represented among the ranks of the most racist settlers in the Palestinian territories.

Not that the Americans could be blamed for everything, Gil went on. The interminable conflict with the Palestinians had shaken his faith in the country, and he offered a note of pessimism in his assessment of how the national project launched by his ancestor Ben-Yehuda and his comrades would turn out: "When I think about my ancestors and the world they left behind, maybe their dream was appropriate to their time and place, but there never was a country like that and there never *will* be a country like that."

Later that same week, I interviewed Nate Shapiro, a businessman who had played an essential behind-the-scenes role in the movement of tens of thousands of Ethiopian Jews to Israel during the 1980s and 1990s.

I was introduced to Nate by Diane Goldin, the founder of the Goldin Institute, a Chicago-based not-for-profit where I'd recently become the senior adviser for communications and development. Diane started the Goldin Institute in 2002 along with Executive Director Travis Rejman to work with grassroots organizations around the world, and Nate was a member of the institute's advisory board.

Travis and Diane picked me up, and we drove along the arterial highway past the city limits to Highland Park, an upscale, North Shore suburb with a sizable Jewish population. Nate had located his brokerage firm, SF Investments, close to home in Highland Park's small business district, which consisted of just a few boutiques, lunch spots, and cafés.

Diane explained that Nate had been a close friend of her late husband, Morton "Moe" Goldin, owner of a private jewelry salon on Chicago's tony Michigan Avenue, and the two had worked together closely on the evacuation of the Ethiopian Jews. This interview was a rare opportunity, as Nate was usually reluctant to discuss his activities with Ethiopian Jews, but Diane had spoken with him that morning, and he sounded willing, even excited.

We arrived at Nate's office, a spacious, elegantly understated space with a few carefully selected antiques and pieces of artwork. He walked with some difficulty but shook my hand with strength and spoke fluidly for more than two hours, recounting his personal involvement in this extraordinary movement of people.

Nate first read about the Ethiopian Jews in articles in the Jewish press in the midseventies and was outraged because the reports indicated Israeli authorities were blocking them from coming to the country because they were Black. Like other Jewish communities around the world, Ethiopian Jews had functioned as a minority in a nation of Christians and Muslims, subject to discrimination, segregation, and restrictions on their access to education and professions. But the Ethiopians were isolated even from Jewish communities in neighboring countries such as Yemen and the Arabic-speaking countries to the north, and within Israel, their origins were hotly contested among both secular and religious authorities.

The Ethiopian Jews themselves traced their history back to a fateful meeting of Solomon with the Queen of Sheba, recounted in the Tanakh. In 1973, Ovadia Yosef, then beginning his term as Israel's Chief Sephardic Rabbi, issued a ruling that the Ethiopian Jews were indeed part of the Jewish people, descendants of the Tribe of Dan, often described as one of the so-called Lost Tribes because they mostly disappeared after the Assyrian conquest of

Israel in 722 B.C.E. Judaism has no formal hierarchy and Rabbi Yosef's opinion wasn't binding, but it did provide needed support to those who dreamed of bringing the Ethiopian Jews to Israel, and most significantly, it inspired many Ethiopian Jews to begin to organize themselves.

Reading all these reports, Nate could not abide the idea that the Jewish state would practice racism, especially toward fellow Jews, and five months later, he traveled to Israel for the first time to investigate for himself. He stayed at the King David Hotel in Jerusalem, where he was visited by Haim Halachmi, the director of the Israel office of the Hebrew Immigrant Aid Society, a large nonprofit that often worked hand in glove with various government agencies, including the secret foreign intelligence service known as the Mossad. A Jewish native of Tunisia, Halachmi had been involved in the evacuations of Jews from throughout North Africa, and he confided to Nate that Israel was indeed planning to facilitate the removal of the Ethiopian Jews, but that the whole effort had to be kept secret for the time being.

Instead of putting Nate off, however, Halachmi actually accomplished the opposite. He reasoned the Israeli government wouldn't have dispatched a senior official to meet with him if they weren't worried their reluctance to rescue Ethiopian Jews would be exposed. Otherwise, Nate said, "Why would an important guy, Halachmi, spend time talking to a nobody like me for one and one half hours?"

Six months later, he had acquired contacts with Ethiopian Jews, including those who had been through difficult journeys to Israel by way of Sudan, and he was deeply moved when he learned firsthand about their dire situation in Ethiopia. There were many educated, urbanized Ethiopian Jews, especially in the capital, Addis Ababa, but most Ethiopian Jews lived in villages of the

Gondar region, where they were prohibited from owning land and restricted to otherwise taboo professions that handled fire, such as metalworking.

Seeing it as a test of his own ethics and values, Nate felt personally responsible for taking action to help them. "I love Israel, and I love the United States," Nate explained. "The U.S., we believe, stands for the hope of the world. Israel three thousand years ago brought forth the ideals the U.S. was developed on. You can't betray what you believe in."

He added, "You can imagine today if it never happened," referring to the evacuation of Ethiopian Jews. "If the only Jews who didn't get there were Black, it would belie everything Israel was built for."

And so he built a fund-raising network among some of Chicago's wealthiest Jewish families and teamed up with Baruch Tegegne, an Ethiopian Jew who had immigrated to Israel permanently in 1976, served in the IDF, and then worked with the Mossad. In 1980, using fake passports, they succeeded in getting five Ethiopian Jews out of the country all the way to Germany. They called Halachmi in Israel and told him, "Come get them."

Halachmi refused initially, but after German media reports appeared about the Ethiopian Jews, Israel took them in. "We shamed Israel into doing the right thing," Nate said.

Though this was just a tiny number initially, Baruch, Nate, and their partners had proved that it was possible to get Jews out of Ethiopia, and motivated others to leave on their own. Soon there were thousands in refugee camps in Sudan awaiting evacuation.

In 1982, Nate and Baruch were called into a meeting with Israel's then ambassador to the United States, Benjamin Netanyahu, who ordered them to stop trying to help the Ethiopian Jews because their efforts were endangering the Mossad's secret negotiations. Nate remained steadfast, however, and was soon back in Ethiopia, using a rental car to drive people to Sudan himself. Even though Sudan's Muslim leaders were unwilling to publicly support the "zionists," Nate found a general who was willing to accept bribes to release the Ethiopian Jews at the rate of a thousand dollars each, and small groups of Ethiopian Jews flew to Europe and from there to Israel.

Nate simultaneously secured statements of support from 165 members of the U.S. Congress as well as the U.S. State Department. Never publicly critical of Israel, but focusing instead on the discrimination faced by the Ethiopian Jews in their homeland, he became president of the American Association for Ethiopian Jews, an organization founded nearly fifteen years earlier, providing him with an official capacity to continue the work.

The AAEJ proceeded to facilitate the evacuation of eight thousand Ethiopian Jews from Sudan, but the scheme was revealed in the Israeli press, provoking a scandal in Sudan that shut down this path. By then, fifteen thousand more Ethiopian Jews had followed their compatriots into Sudan, at least two thousand dying in the course of the journey. Nate waged an extensive, behind-the-scenes campaign among American and Israeli officials until November 1984, when the Israeli government finally launched Operation Moses, a coordinated effort that over just two months brought out seven thousand Ethiopian Jews aboard specially chartered aircraft, until it, too, was stopped by Sudanese officials due to media revelations. The several thousand Ethiopian Jews who had been left behind were now facing starvation as well as the risk of physical violence from their Sudanese hosts.

"They had no support, no food—nothing," Nate recalled.

Alarmed by the imminent danger these people faced, Nate secured the signatures of all one hundred U.S. senators on a letter to then Vice President George H. W. Bush, who "made arrangements with the CIA to pick them up."

This operation, code-named Joshua, also leaked out to the international media, and riots broke out in the capital, Khartoum, prompting Sudanese military leaders to initiate a coup d'état. The new regime took on an Islamist cast and wouldn't countenance any cooperation with the United States, Israel, or Jewish private citizens.

"That was the end of Sudan," Nate explained. "No more Jews went to Sudan."

More than half of the Jews were still stuck in Ethiopia, where Derg leader Mengistu Haile Mariam resolutely refused to allow their departure. For the next few years, despite persistent efforts to lobby the Ethiopian government, Nate was able to arrange for only a handful of Ethiopian Jews to leave. "There was nothing we could do for the remaining Jews," Nate said. "We took a few out just to keep the issue alive."

By 1989, rebel armies from Eritrea and the hinterlands of Ethiopia were mounting ever more successful attacks against Mengistu's once formidable army, even as the Derg's support from the Soviet Union was ebbing away. Unsure of how the rebels would handle Ethiopia's Jews once they were in power, Nate's CIA contacts urged him to swing into action. With a network from across the United States and Canada, the AAEJ was now collaborating closely with Ethiopian Jewish leaders in Israel and in Ethiopia, and they sent messengers to Gondar, followed by buses and cars, urging all the Jews to come to Addis Ababa. Fifteen thousand soon arrived, in vehicles as well as on horseback and even on foot, and the AAEJ persuaded the Ethiopian government to allow them to stay on property they owned in the city, using tents and food left over from previous waves of refugees. A school was set up teaching Hebrew, Amharic, and math along with employment programs for adults.

While Nate participated in complicated diplomatic negotiations between the Americans, Israelis, and the crumbling Mengistu government, only a few Ethiopian Jews were allowed to leave. Finally, the dictator accepted a ranch in Zimbabwe along with a transfer of $35 million into the Ethiopian government's account, much of it raised by Nate and other wealthy Jewish families in Chicago, and the Israelis began planning a large, coordinated evacuation.

Operation Solomon took place over just thirty-six hours in May 1991, as a fleet of 747s transported nearly the entire gathered mass of Ethiopian Jews to Israel. They had to leave the possessions they brought with them behind, and many were in serious medical distress—several women gave birth on the flights—but the airlift was seen as a humanitarian triumph for Israel.

The AAEJ disbanded in 1993, having fulfilled its mission, but five years later, Nate and other veterans of the organization formed a new organization, Friends of Ethiopian Jewry, to advocate for Ethiopian Israelis with the institutions responsible for their assimilation and to bring over remaining Jews in Ethiopia, relatives of those who had emigrated and some who had converted to Christianity or Islam.

"The 'trouble' with the Ethiopian Jews on its face was that the Jewish Agency and other authorities wanted to treat them like everyone else," Nate explained. In the following decades, the Ethiopian Israelis' situation had improved markedly, he continued, pointing to the election of several Ethiopian members of the Knesset from different parties, while infighting among the community's organizations was diminishing, and Ethiopians increasingly joined other groups with broad agendas on civil rights and environmental issues.

He'd spent decades and expended many millions of dollars on helping the Ethiopian Jews, at least in part because he saw their situation as analogous to the Jews of Europe during the Shoah and the years of Israel's struggle for independence, but in retrospect, it was the personal appeals of Ethiopian Jews that were decisive in getting him involved.

"It was common sense," Nate summed up. "You knew they were being persecuted in Ethiopia because they were Jews. They were people crying out for help. How can you not help? If you're in a position to help someone and you don't do it, what's your life about?"

Remaining behind the scenes was the essential component of the overall strategy's success, he maintained. "We never personalized it. It was entirely about a cause," Nate explained. "If you don't want the credit, you can do a lot of things."

As I prepared to return to Israel, the conversations with Gil and Nate gave me a perspective on the internal machinations among the groups within Israel, as well as the extent of American influence over the country. Gil confirmed that there was an intimate connection between the Polish/Tunisian kitchen of Ofer the taxi driver and the chef's restaurants in Tel Aviv. As mothers and fathers in Jewish kitchens throughout the country refurbished classic dishes with fresh ingredients and flavors, entirely new dishes were concocted and a new cuisine was born. Gil pointed out that Ashkenazi tastes had dominated early on, but the Mizrahim had always been sure to win out in the end, because of their numerical superiority as well as their familiarity with regional ingredients. It was just a matter of time before they asserted themselves, and the nation's restaurants channeled this volatile and dynamic process. The change in Israeli food, moreover, hinted at a parallel social transformation in the broader culture as those who had been previously marginalized struggled for leadership and representation. Gil had succeeded in establishing a public persona celebrating this change, but as a gay man in a nation whose legal system had yet to recognize his full human rights, he was hungry for still more rapid change.

Nate, on the other hand, made it clear that American Jews, despite their reputations as *freiers,* were clever and resourceful enough to outmaneuver their own government along with the Israelis, and could effect change in both nations' policies with their vision of what Israel should be. I had focused on Americans as one of the tribes within Israel, but Nate had demonstrated how much those outside Israel could accomplish precisely because they could pressure their own government's agencies and institutions, and then tacitly use their status as Americans to operate internationally. Nate and his cohort took great personal risks, donated substantial amounts of money, and volunteered their time, but they were operating as American Jews who felt a right and even a duty to help make Israel accord with their image of a righteous nation that would serve as an example to others. I was curious to see just how their expectations had been realized on the ground with the Ethiopian Jews in Israel.

23

PRISONER OF ZION

•

Diane Goldin asked me to organize a ten-day trip to Israel at the end of January 2018 to meet with her Ethiopian Israeli contacts and to visit the West Bank, where the Goldin Institute had engaged in projects with Palestinian partners. She also agreed to let me chronicle the journey for this book, without hesitation or caveat.

Diane and Travis Rejman, the institute's executive director, arrived separately, and we all met at the hotel I booked for us near Rothschild Boulevard in Tel Aviv. On our first full day, we headed for Jerusalem to go to dinner that evening at the home of the parents of Yoni Reuven, an Ethiopian Israeli medical student Diane was sponsoring through a scholarship program.

Yoni had distinguished himself as a star even during his military service as a combat officer in the IDF's elite Sayeret Maktal unit, when he participated in numerous classified, dangerous missions. He followed up his military service by getting admitted to a prestigious medical program where he was the only Ethiopian in his class and one of a very small number across the country. Yoni was earning a Ph.D. in epidemiology and planned to work on diabetes and other illnesses that had become prevalent among Ethiopian Israelis as a result of the abrupt change of lifestyle and diet they experienced upon emigrating from Ethiopia. He further hoped to export the solutions he developed to Africa, where many countries were dealing with similar problems.

I'd corresponded with Yoni in the weeks leading up to our trip, and he had helped me plan the itinerary. When I told him I wanted to include the perspectives of Ethiopian Israelis in my book, he suggested that I might interview his father, who had been a leader of the community in Ethiopia, had been imprisoned for his efforts to help Jews emigrate, and in Israel had become a well-respected teacher and radio personality. Yoni's father agreed, and the plan was that I would interview him after our dinner.

We decided to go early to tour the Old City and left Tel Aviv through the main bus station in Neve Sha'an, one of the South Tel Aviv neighborhoods where many immigrants from Africa and Asia lived alongside Israelis. The bus station itself was a sprawling, seven-story architectural tangle, partially incomplete and partially abandoned, with competing bus companies on different floors and clusters of stores selling second-rate merchandise. Once we navigated the stopped escalators and filthy stairs, we found our line and boarded an old green bus operated by the Egged company.

I sat next to Diane, worried that she'd been put off by the bus station's decrepitude, but she was smiling with delight, her eyes gleaming beneath the tint of her sunglasses. It turned out she liked nothing better than a dilapidated bus station in a foreign city, all the better if it was teeming with noise and commerce, smelling of exotic food and the inevitable waste.

Diane had launched the Goldin Institute just a few years after the death from cancer of her husband, Moe. Neither Moe nor Diane had children or siblings, and the Goldin Institute, growing out of her volunteer activities, became the principal beneficiary of her charitable efforts. In December 1999, she was the volunteer coordinator for the Parliament of World Religions' weeklong gathering in Capetown, South Africa, featuring more than nine hundred lectures, events, and symposia that included major speeches from Nelson Mandela, the Dalai Lama, and other dignitaries.

Underfunded from the beginning, the Capetown conclave received a shot in the arm when Diane stepped in with badly needed dollars at a crucial moment, saving the entire thing from cancellation, though she never claimed credit for this timely intervention. It was at this same event that she first met Travis, who was then the group's director of programming. Travis impressed Diane with his calm and resourcefulness in this chaotic situation, how he ensured that the speeches went on without the speakers themselves becoming aware of how close to disaster it all was, and she made sure to keep in touch with him afterward.

At twenty-two, Travis had already spent several years as a community organizer, including a formative experience working for Michelle Obama while she headed Chicago's Public Allies program. When they met up after Capetown, Travis told Diane about people from grassroots organizations around the world who'd contacted him during his work at the Parliament, groups in some of the toughest places on the planet facing the aftermath of war or natural disaster, combined with entrenched poverty and environmental degradation.

Diane chartered the Goldin Institute to work with these groups and others like them, hiring Travis as executive director. Since then, they'd hosted conferences for thousands of grassroots leaders from around the world in different locations, but mostly, they'd traveled themselves to visit the grassroots organizations: garment workers in Bangladesh, women organizing anti-rape patrols in the earthquake-ravaged refugee camps of Haiti, and former child soldiers in Uganda trying to rebuild their lives in war zones that were still smoldering. The Goldin Institute had a very small staff, usually scattered in different locations, and most of the time, it had been just Diane and Travis on these trips, riding rickety buses on cratered roads to remote places where the cuisine was decidedly unvaried, if generously shared.

"We've eaten lots of goat," Travis interjected, to nods of agreement from Diane. "Lots and lots of goat."

When I'd worried about Diane's comfort in Tel Aviv's crumbling central bus complex, she'd confessed that she found it positively luxurious by comparison with many of the bus terminals they'd seen.

We spent the afternoon in the Old City, the Western Wall complex, and the Jewish Quarter, before emerging at the Jaffa Gate, where there was a small bank of taxis. I approached one of the drivers, a smiling, middle-aged Palestinian man with short, clipped white hair who introduced himself as Rami. He impressed me by gallantly holding the door of his Mercedes taxi open for Diane, who sat in the ample back with Travis while I sat in front.

I told Rami where we were headed, Ben Zakai Street to the southwest, and he confidently took off in that direction. Diane asked him in English how long it would take to get there, and Rami turned back for a moment.

"I'm sorry, madam," he said, "My English is not so good. One moment and I will ask this gentleman to translate."

Rami explained to me in Hebrew that he could manage in English if he had to, but he really preferred Hebrew, if his interlocutor couldn't speak Arabic.

I assured him I didn't mind translating, and helped Diane ask him a few follow-up questions about his life: He lived in East Jerusalem with his wife and five children, thanks be to God. He enjoyed driving a taxi, but business was terrible. It was winter, which usually was slow, but now it was even worse because there were protests and security lockdowns all over the country due to American Vice President Mike Pence's visit.

Thinking ahead to our trips to the West Bank in the coming days, I recalled advice from an academic friend experienced at traveling from Israel into Palestinian territory who suggested that I find a driver from East Jerusalem, as they were permitted to cross IDF checkpoints. I explained to Rami what we hoped to do and asked him if he was interested.

Sure, Rami said, clearly pleased by his improving prospects.

How much would it cost, potentially?

Rami calculated. A full day, beginning with being picked up in Tel Aviv in the morning, driving to the West Bank, and then back in the evening, something like 400 shekels, he said.

It was an entirely reasonable fee, a little more than $100. Could he take us to Hebron the day after tomorrow?

"No problem," Rami said, handing me his card. "Call me tomorrow to make the arrangements."

We reached Ben Zakai Street in Katamon, a Greek Orthodox neighborhood in the Ottoman era that was now solidly Jewish, with middle-class families in rows of midrise apartment buildings built on streets that followed the lilting slopes the way most of Jerusalem did.

Greeting us at the door of his parents' apartment, Yoni embraced Diane warmly and introduced his wife, Niva, and his parents, Mehari and Bracha. The apartment was tidy and packed with books in Amharic, Hebrew, and English, and the dining table was set out for an elaborate dinner. Sure enough, we sat down to a feast all prepared by Bracha, course after course of delicious stewed lentils, spinach, potatoes with carrots, as well as chicken and lamb with eggs, all eaten with the spongy Ethiopian bread known as injera. We had wine as well, but the food put me in a higher state of consciousness all on its own.

After dinner, we sprawled on couches and chairs in the salon while Bracha made three rounds of coffee according to Ethiopian tradition, pouring them from a ceramic *jebena* into small cups. In Ethiopia, coffee is usually served with salt, but she offered sugar as well, and I drank it readily.

It seemed the perfect time to interview Mehari after the coffee, and he began to recount his time in Ethiopia as well as his decades in Israel from his easy chair, while Bracha, Yoni, and Niva interjected occasionally.

Born in 1947 in a village in the Wegera province, Mehari tended to his family's animals and collected firewood as a child. The Jews in his village traded with their Christian neighbors, but Mehari also recalled acts of violence and discrimination perpetrated against the Jews. His grandfather had constructed a cemetery for Jews in the region, and Mehari was familiar with burial traditions as well as the code of purity and rituals of purification. He studied with a *kes,* a spiritual leader who taught Bible and Ge'ez, a classical Ethiopian language still used for liturgy by Jews and Christians. He also learned about other forms of Judaism from teachers dispatched by the Jewish Agency who arrived in his village while he was a child.

Educated at a boarding school and then a government school in a regional center, Mehari began his career as a teacher in the same institution where he himself had been trained, before moving on to schools in other villages in the region. He met Bracha while she, too, was teaching, and began supervising projects for World ORT, a Jewish social services organization which had established educational and agricultural projects in Ethiopia.

The Derg seized control of the country and subsequently murdered Emperor Haile Selassie, and Mehari's status changed dramatically. He was dispatched to teach in far-off locations for several years and increasingly came under pressure because of his activities in the Jewish community and with ORT. He moved to Addis Ababa and tried to stay out of sight but was eventually arrested, imprisoned, and, accused of being an agent of the CIA as well as the zionists, tortured with electric shocks among other abuses. Mehari endured nine months in prison, often hearing people near him being killed, while back home, Bracha continued to raise their two young children, until finally, pressure from foreign and domestic advocates succeeded in getting him released.

Mehari resumed teaching, and Yoni was born while they were in Addis Ababa, but all the while he was working to get the family out of Ethiopia. First he sent Bracha and the children. Then, in 1984, he joined them.

They lived in a small town for the first year and a half before moving to Jerusalem, where Mehari and Bracha began teaching English in public schools. But after a lifetime of dreaming about Israel, he was shocked to find that the actual country was nothing like what he expected, especially when it came to the behavior of the population. Where he expected a nation of pious Jews, he found everyone flagrantly violating the Shabbat, driving and cooking without hesitation or shame. Worst of all were the Israeli students, whom he found lazy and disrespectful.

He left teaching in frustration, and dedicated himself to a new mission, helping other Ethiopian Jews assimilate to their environment through journalism. He wrote articles and books in Amharic, including one volume that explained the aspects of democracy and provided a step-by-step guide on how to participate in it for Ethiopians who had come from a totalitarian regime. But his most popular effort was an hour-long Amharic radio program on a public radio station dedicated to new immigrants, which previously had programs in Russian, Persian, and Arabic, among many other languages. Mehari's program quickly became a community institution, broadcasting essential information and occasionally becoming a forum for passionate debate, and his series on the structure of democracy won several awards.

Designated a former "Prisoner of Zion" by the Israeli government alongside those Jews from the former Soviet Union, North Africa, and the Middle East who had been persecuted for their efforts to promote emigration to Israel, Mehari also continued to advocate for other Jews still in Ethiopia, traveling internationally to tell his own story and urge action. He recalled being on a North American tour in 1991 when he saw a headline in the *New York Times* about the Operation Solomon airlift.

Mehari and Bracha's children adapted readily to Israeli society, finding careers and families, with Ethiopian as well as Ashkenazi and Mizrahi partners. Yoni understood that he was seen as a model of assimilation, as did his wife, Niva, whose father was Moroccan and mother was Ashkenazi, and they took it as both a responsibility and an opportunity to speak out against the prejudice experienced by Ethiopian Israelis and to challenge the stereotypes that predominated in the broader society. Mostly, though, they were busy as parents of a three-year-old boy, with Niva pursuing a Ph.D. in anthropology while Yoni was in the residency phase of his training as a physician.

With his children on the right path, Mehari had expanded his personal mission to rewrite the narrative of the Ethiopian Jews to give them credit for their agency in their own exodus, for the sacrifices they'd made and the international support they'd succeeded in winning. There were still Jews in Ethiopia who hoped to be reunited with their kin and needed his advocacy, but Mehari's ambition now was to build a permanent cultural bridge between the Jewish world and Ethiopia, the oldest nation-state on the Earth in the heart of Africa, with a population of over 114 million people.

24

<u>THE PICTURES ON THE WALL</u>

On our second full day in Israel, I took Diane and Travis to meet my mother at the Babylonian Jewry Heritage Center and adjacent Museum of Babylonian Jewry. The august history of Iraq's Jews is recorded, represented, and made accessible in this unique museum and research center in Or Yehudah, a gritty, industrial city just outside of Tel Aviv and well away from the main tourist districts in Tel Aviv and Jerusalem. My mother had discovered the museum when she lived nearby years earlier, and, knowing that Diane and Travis had been to Israel before and were looking for a new perspective on the country, suggested that I take them there, following which we would all have lunch.

She had already arrived with Shosh when we got to the museum and was waiting in the parking lot in her tiny Daihatsu. I made the introductions and we gazed up at the museum, built to resemble a typical home in old Baghdad, with walls covered by gleaming white plaster and a high, vaulted entrance flanked on either side by *shnashil,* the enclosed, protruding balconies that allowed those in the household to observe those in the street without being seen themselves.

"The Jewish community in Iraq is no more," declared a somber inscription just inside, setting the stage for the main exhibit, a replica of a street in Baghdad's Jewish neighborhood during its height of creativity and prosperity. Facsimile shops reflected the community's predominant professions: silversmith, goldsmith, cloth merchant, embroiderer, shoemaker, and spice trader, as well as a café that might have been the scene for debates, negotiations, and romance. At the end of the "street" was a model of the city's Great Synagogue, scaled down to one-eighth its original size and including a platform for the prayer leader called a *teva* (or *bima*) as well as an ark containing Torah scrolls, echoes of a collection of over one thousand scrolls that were renowned for their gold and silver cases. One display housed musical instruments from a community that for generations had produced some of the most popular songs in the Arab world, while precious photographs— some of the very few that had been saved from destruction— depicted various aspects of daily life.

The connection between the Jewish people and the civilizations at the juncture of the Tigris and Euphrates Rivers goes back to the patriarch Abraham, who came to Canaan from the city of Ur, the Tanakh relates. A Jewish community existed there since at least 586 B.C.E., when the Babylonian King Nebuchadnezzar II conquered Jerusalem, destroyed Solomon's fabled Temple, and carted off thousands of the city's elites back to Babylon. Forty-eight years later, Babylon was defeated by the Persian Emperor Cyrus, who allowed the Jews to return to Jerusalem and rebuild their temple. Yet some remained in the magnificent city-state of Babylon, one of the world's metropolitan centers, fabulously wealthy, technologically sophisticated with ziggurats and other architectural marvels, cosmopolitan and cacophonous, inhabited by an unprecedented assemblage of peoples.

Babylon's Jewish community thrived all the way through the city's seizure by Alexander the Great in the fourth century B.C.E., by which time the Jews had already dispersed throughout the region. When the Romans destroyed Jerusalem in 70 C.E., Babylonia's Jews were numerous and secure, and welcomed many refugees into the midst. In the ensuing centuries, their great scholars compiled oral history, legal argumentation, and historical accounts into the Talmud, the central document of rabbinical wisdom that continues to drive Judaism today. Babylonia's Jewish communities prospered through the era of Islamic conquest and conversion, maintaining academies that were the finest in the Jewish world.

In the nineteenth century, Jews constituted more than one-third of Baghdad's population, nearly one hundred thousand people, while the esteemed rabbi known as the Ben Ish Chai, whose portrait Nathaniel bought for me in Mea She'arim, was the patron of Jewish institutions from Jerusalem to Kolkata, his rulings on religious matters influential across the Jewish world.

This territory was also part of the Middle Eastern lands the British Empire took from the Ottomans and their German allies during the First World War, but where Palestine was governed as a colony, the British sponsored the establishment of Iraq as a semi-independent kingdom. Jews enjoyed full citizenship in the Kingdom of Iraq, serving in the elected parliament, the military, and many ministries. During the Second World War, however, Nazi Germany sent agents to foment resentment against the Jews as a means to undermine the government. A Nazi-inspired putsch failed, but the poison had been absorbed. In June 1941, mobs abetted by police and some military units attacked Baghdad's Jewish community for two days, murdering more than 150, raping and wounding thousands, and looting some 1,500 stores and homes before the British sent in squads of machine-gunners.

The community managed to reconstitute itself afterward, commemorating the riots as the Farhud, or Violent Dispossession, until Israel declared its independence in 1948, after which conditions for the Jews deteriorated markedly. Iraq dispatched soldiers as part of the pan-Arab force that was supposed to squash the new state, and the government passed a series of laws designed to curtail any activity to support the new nation or local zionist movements at home. Police and other authorities who harbored hatred for Jews used the opportunity to seize property, imprison, and harass, even executing one of the most country's most prominent businesspersons on allegations of supporting Israel.

After political turmoil and antisemitic attacks in Yemen, Israel had handled the airlift of 50,000 Jews from that nation in Operation Magic Carpet Yemen in 1949 and 1950. But a mass evacuation of all 130,000 Iraqi Jews was a challenge of a different order, and it took nearly two years to bring them out on flights through Iran and Cyprus. The whole effort was funded by the American Jewish philanthropic organization the Joint Distribution Committee and named Operation Ezra and Nehemiah, for the prophets who led the Jews who returned from Babylon in the fifth century B.C.E. The Iraqi Jews, intellectuals, physicians and scientists, rabbis, traders, and farmers arrived in a newly minted country without the resources to accommodate them, however, and where their intimate connection to Arabic language and culture was a liability rather than an asset.

Beyond the exhibits showing the rich culture of Iraq's Jews, the museum depicted the traumatic departure endured by most of the community through artifacts saved by the exiled families. Iraqi authorities had forced them to surrender their citizenship, prohibited them from taking out more than $140 in cash or any jewelry, and allowed only sixty-six pounds of luggage. Actual suitcases and trunks in the exhibit demonstrated just how little this was. Many families saw their heirlooms seized, stolen, and destroyed at the airport. Another display showed a tent that was the typical housing for the Iraqi Jews on their arrival in Israel, just large enough for two cots, luggage, and cookware. The tent homes had no floor and were fixed into the sand with wooden poles. Indeed, the museum, opened in 1988 as a new generation sought to understand their history, was located in Or Yehudah because this city was the site of several transit camps for Iraqi Jews, and then became home to many of those of Iraqi descent.

I let my mother and Shosh guide Diane and Travis through the exhibits while I went to interview one of the museum's board members, Tsionit Fattal Kuperwasser, whose remarkable journey of self-discovery saw her go from being a retired officer in the IDF to a novelist with a book translated into Arabic that had won a sizable readership in the Arab world. *The Pictures on the Wall* is a drama of a Jewish extended family in Baghdad during the final years before the community's mass departure for Israel, a romantic and tragic tale centering on a young woman who defies tradition as well as her elders to marry the man she loves. Published originally in Hebrew in Israel in 2015, *The Pictures on the Wall* attracted a modest but enthusiastic reception within Israel, but was a real hit two years later, when it became the first book written originally in Hebrew to be sold in Iraq.

"The Zionist Who Occupied Baghdad," read a headline about *The Pictures on the Wall* in the Israeli daily newspaper *Yediot Aharonot,* playing with her first name, the female form of the word for "zionist," as well as her military service by using the word for "occupy," which, while generally used for military conquest, in this case gestured toward her literary success in the land of her parents' birth. Tsionit's former job in the military, the article noted, was to advise on Palestinian affairs, and her husband, Yossi Kuperwasser, was a former brigadier general who had been the head of the IDF's research division.

Before leaving Chicago, I'd contacted Tsionit through her Facebook page to ask if she would agree to an interview. Her

275

page was itself a unique space on social media, full of messages from her fans, some in Hebrew, but mostly in Arabic. In a post a few months after our interview, Tsionit commented on the warm responses from readers when her book was featured at the Iraq National Festival of Books in Erbil, the main city in Iraq's semi-autonomous Kurdish region. Many of her new fans asked if she was planning on visiting in person and appearing alongside the other authors at the festival.

Responding in Arabic, she wrote how much she appreciated reading these warm invitations. "At first, I thought to answer them that the political situation makes it impossible, but in recent years, I've learned that it's possible to overturn the impossible into the possible, so my answer is, 'I *will* come.'"

Her Iraqi fans were thrilled:

"All respect and appreciation," wrote Mohammed Hameed Shukar from Baghdad.

"Please return to your country," added Munasiq Ajil, also from Baghdad.

An Iraqi woman chimed in, "All the best and lasting success."

Tsionit brought me to a conference room in the center's lower level, where a portrait of the Ben Ish Chai gazed down at us while we spoke.

Tsionit's parents were both born in Baghdad, she told me, and were evacuated in 1951 as part of Operations Nehemiah and Ezra. She was born in 1964, and grew up knowing very little about her parents' lives before they came to Israel. Like most Iraqi families, they had no photographs or artifacts from their past. Her parents watched the Arabic movie that was broadcast on Israeli television every evening at six o'clock, but they did not speak

Arabic to her at home. What she understood about Iraq was that it was an enemy country to which she was forbidden to go.

"I didn't know anything about my roots," she explained. "I had a lot of anger, like a lot of the children of Iraqi immigrants. We didn't want to learn about an enemy nation."

Her parents both died in their sixties, within a short time of each other, while she was still in the first years of her military service. She learned to read and write Arabic to help with her work advising on Palestinian affairs, but it was a different vocabulary and dialect from the language her parents had used.

After Tsionit's retirement from the military, she enrolled in a graduate program to get a Ph.D., though not with any plan per se to study Iraq's Jewish history. She found herself missing her parents, however, and organically began to reconstruct their lives in Baghdad, consulting old maps, reviewing photographs, and conducting interviews with surviving Iraqis of their generation. Eventually, she left the Ph.D. program to write full-time, but the novel was just a short-term project, and this experiment with fiction would be finished, she imagined, on the day she turned in the manuscript to a publisher who'd expressed interest in it.

"I thought I would return to my life," she said with a laugh, "but I got caught up in the promotion for *The Pictures on the Wall*. It was a new, second phase of life."

Israel and Egypt have a formal peace agreement, even if relations between the peoples remain cool; still, a few Egyptian publishers remain on the lookout for Israeli books that might appeal to Arab readers. One publisher spotted *The Pictures on the Wall* and thought it might work in the Iraqi market. It was a real gamble, given that no Israeli book had been published in Iraq before. Indeed, in the past, authorities in many Arab countries had boycotted any Israeli product so as to avoid any kind of "normalization" of the Jewish state. But the Egyptian publisher went ahead, translating Tsionit's book into Arabic, and it almost immediately found an enthusiastic reception.

Tsionit understood that the publication of an Israeli author in Iraq was a big deal, but she had written the book for an Israeli audience, and had very low expectations from Arabic readers. Surprised and wary by the positive reception at first, she soon came to understand that her novel had arrived at the perfect moment, just as Iraq was emerging from decades of dictatorship followed by years of violence and turmoil, when many were looking to their past for an example of how their nation could become, once again, a tolerant, peaceful place. *The Pictures on the Wall*, portraying an Iraq before the descent into oppression and then factional warfare, suggested the tantalizing possibility that it just might be able to return to those glory days.

"They want the new generation to learn about Iraqi Jews," Tsionit said, "to help create a new, modern Iraq. They went through a process themselves where war and religious strife destroyed the nation, and they want to restore Iraq to what it was before it was destroyed by sectarianism.

"They are looking at the past to figure out how to move forward."

Tsionit confessed that the warm welcome she received from Iraqi readers was transformative on a personal level as well, allowing her to let go of the grudge she had held on to regarding her parents' exile. "I, too, went through a process of change," she said. "When you normalize your enemy, you make him familiar, not a monster anymore. It opened a big door for me."

Now she communicates daily with Iraqis through social media. Though she personally supports the Two State Solution for Palestinians and Israelis, she avoids talking about politics with her Iraqi fans, and they don't challenge her. "They treat me like an Iraqi. They say I am Iraqi," Tsionit said. "They treat me like a sister, and say, 'Let's put the past aside.'"

She deeply appreciated these sentiments, even if she never felt that Iraq was *her* homeland. Nevertheless, the support of her Iraqi fans had also impacted the way she saw Israel, and especially the way she spoke of her parents to her own children. Her son, twenty-five at the time of our interview, and daughter, twenty-two, had roots in both Iraq and Poland, but knew very little about the lives and accomplishments of the Iraqi side, while the heritage of Polish Jews was celebrated in state holidays and taught in their school curriculum. And the opportunity to correct this narrative with testimony from those who were actually *from* Iraq was fading, with those old enough to remember life in Iraq now almost all over eighty.

"Among the first generation, there are those who are still dealing with what happened, parents who are still nostalgic for Iraq," Tsionit explained. "The second generation, like me, are engaged in a process of repair. We didn't always want to learn about Iraq, but we found our way there through the music and the food, from the sounds and smells of our parents' homes.

"Our kids just absorb it all. They are not like us, the second generation, who grew up with this in our homes."

Tsionit blamed Israeli officials, including founding Prime Minister David Ben-Gurion, for waging a concerted campaign to degrade and obfuscate the cultural, religious, and political contributions of Iraqi Jews. "Ben-Gurion wanted to erase Iraqi history, and focus only on European history," she said. "We are a nation of immigrants. We have to learn to appreciate the wealth of each other's heritage. We can't say the Ashkenazi culture is better than the Mizrahi culture. We are one Jewish people."

Equipped now with real knowledge of her family's past, she was able to point with pride to all her parents had brought with them as well as all they had endured, to her own children and to the broader society: "You leave a home you love, where you were rich, and come to nothing, to the desert, where you don't know the language, live in a tent, lived in mud."

This was a community that included many very sophisticated, highly educated people based mainly in the cultural metropolises of Baghdad, Basra, and Mosul. Iraq's rabbis were known for their liberality and for their advocacy for the education of both boys *and* girls, Tsionit noted. Many Jewish families took advantage of a 1936 law that exempted men getting university degrees from compulsory military service, such that the community was replete with those who spoke French and English or had advanced degrees in science and medicine along with lawyers and bankers. Iraqi Jewish musicians were famed across the region, including superstars like the Al Kuwaiti brothers, and their writers had launched a style known as Arab Realism, while others had been pioneering broadcasters on the new radio technology. Yet, the musicians were deemed too "oriental" by Israeli producers and concert promoters, and just a few writers were able to make the transition to Hebrew, while they were blocked from publishing anywhere in the Arab world.

"They came in suits, and tried to work," she said. "They started with zero in economic terms."

There were cultural clashes on multiple fronts, she noted. The kibbutzim were the locus of political power and prestige in the state's early years, but these were set up to absorb young adults, not entire families such as those who came from Iraq. Most Iraqi Jews were habitually religious, moreover, attending synagogues on holidays, saying prayers daily, and eating only kosher food, practices seen as atavistic among Israel's socialist-leaning elites.

"All the desire of the state was to create the new Israeli," Tsionit explained, "But you can't sever the connection. Therefore, it didn't work. You can't tell someone who ate kosher not to eat kosher. You can't erase their history.

"So now, we are in a process of apology."

In the three years since her novel was published, Tsionit had traveled widely in Europe, Asia, and North America, discovering fellow descendants of Iraqi Jews wherever she went. Meeting these far-flung members of the Iraqi Jewish diaspora convinced her all the more of the significance of the Museum of Babylonian Jewry, and especially of the attached library.

"I meet with Iraqis everywhere," she said. "But the world of Iraqi Jews exists only in books now."

Iraq's Jewish history was systematically erased by the Ba'ath party, which seized power in 1968 under Ahmed Hassan al-Bakr and his deputy, Saddam Hussein. Jews were written out of all official records, such that Iraq's next generation knew songs written by the Al Kuwaiti brothers, but not who'd written them. With the Americans' ouster of Saddam and the Ba'athists, however, Iraqi cultural institutions were now working to restore the nation's Jewish components.

"Now they are fixing that history," Tsionit said.

Most significantly, Tsionit had learned from studying her parents and ancestors that the Jews of Iraq had contributed mightily to Arabic culture while retaining their own integrity.

"We are not a faith," she underscored. "We are a people *and* a religion. You can't change Arabic into our personhood, but it is our base."

After the interview with Tsionit, I rejoined my mother, Diane, Shosh, and Travis, and we went to lunch at the Entebbe Restaurant nearby in Or Yehudah's shopping district, known colloquially as Little Baghdad. The restaurant itself was named for the

1976 commando operation that freed hostages from a hijacked Air France plane. These passengers had been held at the airport in Entebbe, Uganda, by terrorists from the Popular Front for the Liberation of Palestine and an affiliated German organization. Israeli commandos flew secretly into Uganda and overwhelmed the terrorists as well as the Ugandan soldiers helping them, a dramatic rescue that solidified the formidable international reputation of Israel's military, once the incident was publicized. Unfortunately, several hostages were killed in the process, along with one soldier, Lieutenant Colonel Yonatan Netanyahu, the charismatic older brother of now Prime Minister Benjamin Netanyahu.

My mother and I liked the food and the atmosphere at Entebbe, but Gabi absolutely refused to eat there, objecting to what he saw as the substandard hygiene as well as the nationalistic, rowdy patrons.

"They wipe the table with the loaves of pita," he would proclaim (surely an exaggeration) whenever I brought up the prospect of a meal there. The food was, in fact, strictly kosher and quite basic, with hummus, baba ghanoush, and various chopped vegetable salads alongside grilled chicken, beef, and lamb, all washed down by mint-infused lemonade.

We sat down, and my mother ordered while the rest of us reviewed what we'd seen in the museum. Shosh was particularly enthusiastic, smiling broadly as she observed (with me translating her Hebrew into English for Diane and Travis) that the Iraqi Jews lived very similarly to the Iranian Jews, except that the Iranians were, of course, wealthier, more cultured, and more sophisticated generally. She planned to bring her sister from Tehran to the museum the next time she visited.

I was surprised that her sister was able to visit Israel, given the intensely hostile relations with the Islamic revolutionary regime in Iran. Shosh shrugged and explained that while it was impossible for Israelis to visit Iran, her sister simply flew to Turkey first before catching a second flight to Israel, where authorities refrained from stamping her passport.

Diane, intrigued as well, asked Shosh whether her sister ever considered moving to Israel. Shosh answered that even though her sister's two children were themselves in Israel, she was a retired bank manager who was living on a pension and would have no source of income if she left.

Did Shosh's connection to Iran affect her politics? Diane asked. Specifically, did she support Prime Minister Netanyahu's hard line toward Iran?

Shosh said she voted consistently for the Likud, Netanyahu's party, but less because of anything to do with Iran than because of their tough stance toward the Palestinians, who were interested only in endless discussions, not in reaching actual solutions.

"Whenever you give them anything," Shosh said, "you get a knife in the back."

25

ISSA AMRO

Rami, the driver from East Jerusalem, arrived in Tel Aviv promptly at nine the next morning in his Mercedes taxi to take Diane, Travis, and me to the West Bank city of Hebron. Rami was dressed in a brown leather jacket over a green sweater, and he was wearing amber-tinted, aviator-style glasses. Diane and Travis sat in the back, while I sat in the passenger seat up front, translating their words into Hebrew, and Rami's into English.

I'd arranged for us to meet Issa Amro, an independent Palestinian activist who had been featured in several news reports as a grassroots leader specializing in nonviolent protest, earning him the enmity of not only Israeli authorities but Palestinians as well. I contacted him through his Twitter account, and we agreed on a day and time to meet, while Issa provided me with a phone number to get precise directions.

I gave Issa's number to Rami, who called on his cell phone, and they spoke in Arabic for several minutes while the car idled. Finally, Rami hung up, and then put the car in gear.

The fastest way to Hebron, he explained, would be via Kiryat Arba, an Israeli settlement adjoining Hebron, so we drove south and east from Tel Aviv, circumventing Jerusalem before heading sharply east across the border into the West Bank. As with the trip to the Psagot winery, we crossed into Palestinian territory without even seeing a checkpoint or having to stop for a passport inspection, realizing we'd crossed the border simply by the sharp increase in the number and type of cameras as well as armored watchtowers with mirrored windows that bristled with antennae of varying widths and lengths. Within ninety minutes of leaving Tel Aviv, we were passing through the settlement of Kiryat Arba, which looked very much like a typical Israeli suburb, with neat lanes of identical bungalows. On the other side of Kiryat Arba, we crossed into the slice of Hebron controlled by the Israeli military and followed the prominent signs in English and Hebrew that indicated the way to the Tomb of the Patriarchs and Matriarchs, driving downhill until we reached an ample, nearly empty lot constructed for tourist buses, where Rami easily found a parking spot.

Rami shut off the engine, explaining that Issa's office was a short walk away. We got out of the car and looked up at the Tomb of the Patriarchs and Matriarchs at the edge of the lot, an enormous rectangle of stone with a flat roof and several towers jutting out that was said to cover the tomb of Abraham and his wife Sarah as well as other figures mentioned in the Tanakh. We were due at our interview with Issa, though, so decided to visit the tomb afterward. Rami checked in with the owners of several shops selling souvenirs and snacks in the parking lot, and I asked if he wanted to stay here with the taxi, but he preferred to accompany us, adding that he was very curious to meet Issa himself.

We began to walk according to Issa's instructions through a neighborhood of homes and shops, solid two- and three-story buildings made of stone, but where all the storefronts were covered over with metal shutters, the windows covered with steel grates. Most of Hebron was a Palestinian city governed by the Palestinian Authority, but this zone had been tightly controlled by the IDF since 1994, after Baruch Goldstein, an American-born resident of Kiryat Arba, shot and killed twenty-nine Muslim worshippers at a prayer service inside the tomb. In the wake of the massacre, Palestinians protested violently all across the West Bank and Gaza as well as in Hebron, and the army imposed a strict lockdown, ordering the closure of hundreds of stores and welding them shut, all in the name of protecting a few hundred Jewish settlers who had taken up residence among thousands of Palestinians in this area. Palestinian government offices were also closed, and what had been a main bus station was converted into an IDF base. Only those Palestinians who persisted in living in the area were allowed to enter the zone, while Palestinian vehicles were prohibited altogether.

The zone was eerily quiet, the streets devoid of pedestrians or cars, except for a handful of Israeli military jeeps and minivans containing settlers. Settlers were allowed to move freely by foot or car.

We reached a military checkpoint, a beaten shack with shattered windows where two young soldiers inside responded in a casual, friendly way as I greeted them in Hebrew.

They didn't even bother to check my identification, or Travis's or Diane's. Glancing at Rami, however, one of them asked me, "Is he with you?"

I confirmed he was, but they checked his ID card anyway, at once perfunctory and thorough.

Diane looked at the firearm carried by the nearest soldier, a short-barreled rifle, and asked me if it was an upgraded version of the famous Uzi submachine gun.

It was actually a new Israeli-manufactured assault rifle called a Tavor, I said, made to be compatible with various high-tech attachments and other weapons systems. The soldier wagged his finger, however. "This is a Micro-Tavor," he averred, referring to the smaller version of the rifle.

I thanked him for the correction, and he smiled graciously.

We walked along Shuhada Street, once this neighborhood's main thoroughfare, known for its shops and warehouses, and passed another checkpoint, where a group of five soldiers was trying to huddle in the shade of their sandbag fort. This was still the end of the Israeli winter, and there had been a damp chill in the air that morning, but it was now quite warm, and the clearly exhausted soldiers looked sweaty in their Kevlar vests, boots, and helmets. An Ethiopian corporal now conducted a more cursory inspection of our passports, barely even looking at Rami's ID.

"It's hot now, isn't it?" I said.

He shrugged. "It's hotter in the south."

I asked him, "Oh, you're from the Negev area?"

"Be'er Sheva," he said, gesturing to his comrades. "We're mostly from the south, all of us who *serve* here."

They all laughed.

On our left as we continued was a large Muslim cemetery, where we saw a few families laying flowers for memorial services, and Rami told us we should soon see a little lane with a sign pointing to Abraham's Well.

He called Issa to let him know we were close, and a moment later, we indeed reached the lane with the sign and saw Issa walking in our direction, dressed in a black hoodie and matching sweatpants, accompanied by another man in gray jeans and a matching sweater. Only then, just when we were within arm's reach, an Israeli soldier ran toward us from across the street, and interposed himself between us and Issa, his rifle slung in front, his helmet in one hand and his other hand raised, palm forward, gesturing for us to stop.

"You have to turn back," he said in English. "This is a closed military zone."

"It's not a closed zone," Issa countered immediately, then told the soldier in Hebrew, "How is it a closed zone? Show me a map. Show me the legal order."

The man accompanying Issa pulled out a cell phone from his pocket and began filming. Travis pulled out his cell phone as well.

Several other soldiers now emerged from across the street, where a metal gate was emblazoned with paintings of the shields of several military units, indicating this was a base of some kind. These soldiers also had their rifles slung in front and were wearing caps rather than helmets, all of which indicated to me they were acting according to procedure but weren't agitated or particularly on guard.

Issa pointed out that the soldier who stopped us wasn't an officer, alleging that he lacked the authority to tell us to go back.

"Go and tell your commander what you are doing," Issa told the soldier.

I stepped forward and began to speak to the soldier in Hebrew, quietly. I introduced myself, shook his hand. "Look, I'm supposed to take these Americans to meet this guy. I'm American, too, but I speak Hebrew and have family here. This lady here"—I gestured toward Diane—"has done a lot for the State of Israel and the Israeli people. Is it really a closed zone? Could we just go up there and speak with him for a little while?"

The soldier hesitated. He was young and unkempt, with a wispy blond beard of several days' growth.

Issa recommended we simply walk past the soldier. "This isn't your area of responsibility," he told the soldier in Hebrew, arguing that as a Palestinian who lived in this section of Hebron, he was under the jurisdiction of the Israeli police, not the military, according to the agreement that divided the city.

"This is a matter for the police. Go and call the police, or show me something that says this is a closed zone," Issa told the soldier, patting the glass face of his phone.

He switched to English and addressed us, "OK, let's go. It's illegal what he's doing here."

The soldier, still standing between us, faced Issa and said we were forbidden to go forward.

"So, shoot them," Issa said, sarcastically, before turning back to us. "Come on."

Travis was ready to proceed, but now I hesitated. I looked back at Diane, who'd wrapped her head in a silk scarf, and at Rami, who was nervously smoking a cigarette.

I stepped closer to the soldier with the blond beard.

"Look," I told him in Hebrew. "Isn't there any way to figure this out?"

"OK," he answered. "Walk back five hundred meters, go through the checkpoint, and you can meet with Issa there."

It seemed a ridiculous inconvenience, but I was worried about the consequences for defying the soldiers.

"Issa, let's meet where it's OK to meet," I said.

"There is no place that will be OK for them," he answered.

The soldier started to interrupt us, but Issa wasn't having it. "I want to talk to them," Issa objected, in Hebrew.

"If you want to talk to them," the soldier responded, "go meet them over on the other side of the checkpoint."

Just then, two tour buses motored past with Hebrew writing printed on the side, either tourists or supporters of the Jewish settlements in the zone. Issa challenged the soldiers: "Who are they? Why isn't it a 'closed military zone' for them?"

He continued, "You are just a settler in a uniform. You are harming Israel more than BDS."

Issa then turned to us and switched back to English, "This is a good example of their racism and apartheid."

I said, "Let's go meet there where it's OK for you *and* for him."

"I don't like to follow them," Issa said. "I like to challenge and confront them because he is full of lies."

But the soldier was insistent, and several others had by now taken positions all around us, so we shortly walked back around the other side of the Muslim cemetery and found the checkpoint at the end of a short street. This was a fortified facility with high concrete walls on three sides and security booths around a metal turnstile. I expected the guards to scrutinize us, perhaps at the behest of Issa's blond-bearded antagonist, but they were perfectly nonchalant, waving us through after a mere glance at our passports; not even Rami's East Jerusalem ID card seemed to interest them.

The gate was a threshold, and on the other side was Hebron proper, the 90 percent of the city that was governed by the Palestinian Authority, a thriving Arab city of two hundred thousand people known for its health care facilities, industry, and universities, containing one-third of the West Bank's economy. This checkpoint, like any border, had attracted a cluster of related shops and businesses, stalls selling falafel sandwiches, soft drinks, and other snacks, shisha shops, professional offices, and Internet cafés in two- and three-story concrete buildings that held many signs, hand-painted as well as in neon, all in Arabic.

We immediately attracted attention from hangers-on and passersby, mostly men, clean shaven and neatly dressed in sports jackets, sportswear, or tailored shirts, earnest but not unfriendly, responding to my *"Salaam aleikum,"* literally "Peace unto you," with *"Merhaba,"* meaning "Welcome." There were a few women as well, all in hijabs and long coats, moving quickly but confidently, their faces uncovered, chatting freely with their friends or walking alone with a cell phone in hand.

Rami organized a car to take us back to where Issa was located, an aged Subaru sorely in need of a muffler. The mustachioed driver spoke no English, smiling sheepishly when I tried to ask him questions. We drove past office buildings, small factories, workshops, street vendors selling baked goods, T-shirts, and plastic sandals, and many, many car shops, garages with vehicles in widely differing conditions, though mostly hulks, wrecked BMWs, Audis, Toyotas, and Hyundais.

At last, the driver dropped us off in a field that adjoined a mosque at the bottom of a hill, where the man wearing the gray sweater and jeans who'd been with Issa was waiting for us. Concerned the soldiers might once again intervene, he urged us to hurry up the slope along a dirt path through the green grass and olive trees as well as piles of tires with ruined treads and shredded rags and heaps of household trash. While we hiked, the mosque's minaret broadcast the muezzin's beautiful, amplified voice. "Not everyone goes to paradise," Rami translated, "and paradise is a long time. Our lives are just a drop in the ocean."

We arrived at a two-story building at the top of the hill, the headquarters for Issa's organization, Youth Against Settlements. It was a busy place with a clubhouse feel, stacks of plastic chairs near the door, a group of people on couches and makeshift furnishings drinking coffee, others in a kitchen making a pot of stew, and a half-finished anteroom where a few people were smoking cigarettes or taking puffs from a tobacco shisha—Palestinian men and women, mostly unveiled, as well as a few Europeans. The concrete blocks outside the entrance were stamped with the English phrases "This is Palestine" and "Open Shuhada Street."

We all sat down at a folding table outside, talking under the shade of one of the larger trees while the gray-sweatered man brought us strong coffee and Rami smoked cigarette after cigarette. Explaining how his life had been shaped by the conflict with Israel, Issa noted that his grandfather had been killed in 1950 while smuggling animals across the Gaza border, while his father had been injured during the Six-Day War in 1967.

Thirty-seven at the time of our interview, Issa grew up in Hebron, a serious student and a dedicated soccer player. He was thirteen when Baruch Goldstein massacred worshippers at the Tomb of the Patriarchs and Matriarchs, and like many of his generation, he was indelibly affected. Issa recalled that several members of his soccer team were killed or imprisoned during the violent protests that broke out in the aftermath, while his school and stores throughout the city were closed for months.

"We Palestinians were victims of the massacre," Issa stressed, "but we were punished by the Israeli authorities."

By 2003, Issa was a devoted student in his final year at Palestine Technical College in Hebron as the Second Intifada raged on, with widespread protests and Palestinian factions committing terror attacks, including suicide bombings, as the Israeli military regularly engaged civilians in cities and towns and imposed strict protocols. Issa's university was closed, and the engineering program in which he'd been pursuing a degree was shuttered, owing to Israeli fears that the training would be used to make weapons and explosives.

"We were told, 'You are studying dangerous science,'" Issa recounted. "We argued with them. We said, 'It's all online. It's on YouTube.'"

Though he hadn't taken much interest in politics until then, Issa began to study the history of revolutions, focusing on the movements launched by Mohandas Gandhi in India, Nelson Mandela in South Africa, and Martin Luther King Jr. in the United States. Other students were attracted to his approach, and Issa soon found himself leading protest marches, writing letters, and making media appearances. He'd never set out to be a leader, but if it was meant to be, he would rise to the occasion, well aware of the risk he was taking.

"If you come from an educational background, they listen to you, but people follow celebrities, and I was a celebrity," Issa said. "But I was in the front. I was doing the most dangerous jobs first."

After three months, Issa and his comrades decided to take their protest to the next level. Using hammers and other tools, they pried open the sealed doors of their university, cleaned up the buildings, and slept there. They were opposed not only by Israeli authorities, but also by their own professors and university administrators, who approached Issa, urging the student protesters to withdraw. Issa rebuffed them all. "We decided to *occupy* the university," he explained, deliberately using the legal term for Israel's military control of Palestinian territories.

"Students are crazy," Issa added. "Nobody can stop you."

Soon there were three thousand students participating, and they started holding classes, with seniors instructing the younger students. A few professors defied their bosses and taught classes as well. After six months of these protests, Israeli authorities finally relented and allowed the university to reopen.

They'd adopted a similar strategy when it came to the building where we were now sitting, which had belonged to a Palestinian family who were harassed repeatedly by Israeli soldiers and settlers. Issa persuaded the family to rent the building to Youth Against Settlements and allow them to "occupy" it as their headquarters for an ongoing protest against Israeli policies in Hebron. Settlers had already taken over buildings all around this one, sometimes by buying them from their Palestinian owners and other times by more nefarious methods. Meanwhile, soldiers tightly controlled who could come and go to the Youth Against Settlement building, targeting them precisely because they espoused nonviolence. Violence, after all, was an excuse to send in the military, and prolonged military control would allow the settlers to come in and establish themselves.

"That is the classic way to do an occupation," Issa summed up. "Soldiers first, settlers second."

Relying on a robust media strategy to counteract both the overt and the sub-rosa efforts by Israeli authorities and the settlers to remove the Palestinians from this section of Hebron, Issa got his message out through mainstream news outlets whenever possible, while also utilizing social media channels on a daily basis: Facebook, Twitter, Instagram, and WhatsApp.

"The media is a game," Issa said, "and we play the media game well. We teach the community how to be nonviolent. We film *everything*."

Issa understood that the imposition of multiple checkpoints, which caused unpredictable delays, requiring people to pass through metal detectors and other inspections, was a policy designed to humiliate and provoke violence, and he calibrated his response, therefore, to be at once nonviolent and media savvy. During the protests around the increased security restrictions on Al Aqsa Mosque the previous summer, Issa noted that tens of thousands prayed without incident day after day, and ultimately won a reversal of the decision to install the new devices and procedures. Still, they received less mainstream news coverage than the teenagers who confronted the IDF with stones and other makeshift projectiles.

"Fifty thousand people praying, not throwing stones," he said "that wasn't in the media, but ten kids throwing stones; that was all over the news."

The checkpoints were not really about security, he maintained, but about creating an "apartheid state" with two sets of laws for people in the same place. Dispelling the idea that Israel's restrictions on Palestinians were due to "security" was a critical item on Issa's agenda, especially among Americans, who continued to exercise a great deal of influence over Israeli policy.

"Israel is very strong because of American support, but most Americans don't know their tax dollars are used in the wrong way, to strengthen the occupation," Issa said. "Israel is too strong to make peace, so we know that change will come from the U.S."

Then he gestured toward Diane, Travis, and me: "That's why they don't want you here."

In this regard, Issa considered American Jews an especially important constituency who, differing on key political points with Israeli Jews, could play a pivotal role in changing the situation on the ground for Palestinians. Visits like this one, from foreigners ostensibly sympathetic to Israel, could help change the attitudes of the soldiers guarding Hebron, Issa suggested. If American Jews were also saying that the occupation was unjust, Israeli Jews might finally see the light, Issa said hopefully. "[The soldiers] didn't know the occupation was so bad," he said. "They were ready to challenge it."

Issa's success at reaching Americans and other international audiences came at a cost, however. In 2016, shortly after a visit from 120 American Jewish activists, he was indicted in an Israeli military court on eighteen counts, including support of the BDS movement, for an incident that had taken place six years earlier, a confrontation with a settler in which *he* was injured. The following year, he was arrested and charged by Palestinian law enforcement officials for Facebook comments supporting a Palestinian journalist who had criticized President Mahmood Abbas.

Nevertheless, Issa understood that international attention, even if it drew the ire of Palestinian and Israeli authorities, could also be a shield, and that allies around the world were crucial.

"They don't want leadership," Issa said. "They don't want

any movement. More recognition is more protection, so we do more media."

In the short term, Issa was pessimistic about the chances for Palestinian liberation, seeing how the governments in both Israel and the United States were shifting to the right. Having listened to the speeches of Shoah survivors broadcast for that year's Day of Remembrance, Issa heard distinct similarities to the atmosphere in Germany in the 1930s, not least in the racist incitement emanating regularly from Prime Minister Netanyahu and other leaders of the right-wing coalition government he assembled in 2015.

"The general atmosphere in Israel is a racist atmosphere," he said. "They have lost their morals."

Annexation of the West Bank, Issa believed, formal absorption under Israeli law, was imminent. The settlers and their allies in the Netanyahu government would take advantage of a world distracted by the ongoing civil war in Syria and the attendant crisis that had sent millions of refugees into Europe, using fear of the so-called Islamic State as an excuse to seize full control.

"Israel is not *defending* itself. It is too strong," Issa said. "Whether Palestinians want to destroy Israel or not, they can't. The fact is, Israel is strengthening itself by occupying more land, creating more settlements."

President Donald Trump, meanwhile, would approve any such annexation to satiate the apocalyptic impulses of his base among Christian evangelicals. The president may have won many admirers in Israel for his relocation of the American embassy to Jerusalem and his endorsement of Israel's annexation of the Golan Heights, but he was really acting to curry favor with the evangelicals, Issa surmised. This was a constituency who endorsed all Israeli expansion, just as it did the harsh treatment of Palestinians, which aligned with their interpretations of messianic prophesies in the Old and New Testaments. Trump revealed his true intention whenever he used antisemitic code words to appeal to extremist groups, even as Vice President Pence's recent visit to the Holy Land sent all the right signals to evangelicals.

"Come on, Trump loves the Jews?" Issa asked, rhetorically, "He's a white supremacist. Ideologically, [Pence] wants there to be a big war. It will bring the messiah."

In this hostile political climate, Issa was hardly hopeful about the near future. He was open to the idea of a One State Solution, but pointed out that currently settlers were the main advocates for a single entity, which they imagined as a state run according to Jewish religious law. Not that he was particularly hopeful about a Two State Solution either. For one thing, it was not clear if a Palestinian state would be democratic; the Palestinian Authority had not held free elections since 2006.

One thing was for certain: "We won't have free elections under the occupation," Issa said flatly. "Any solution based on equality will be good for me. One state or two states, we should be completely equal."

Inspired by Hebron's history as a place where Jews and Muslims had lived together for centuries, prospering together and often defending each other, Issa had spoken to some of the Palestinian Muslim elders who risked their lives to protect their Jewish neighbors in 1929, when Arab militants massacred Jews throughout Palestine, including in Hebron. Until then, the city had a sizable population of Jews, both those whose ancestors had also lived in the city for centuries and Haredim from several different orders who had come to the city in the nineteenth century, adding their own synagogues and yeshivas to a city that had long attracted Jewish, Christian, and Muslim scholars as well as pilgrims.

Even now, Issa pointed out, his most tenacious organizational partners were Israelis, members of Breaking the Silence: former Israeli soldiers who testified about the treatment of Palestinians they had seen and, in some cases, had themselves engaged in. Breaking the Silence brought tours regularly to Hebron, despite criticism and threats from settlers and their affiliates. He also found allies in the Israeli court systems, attorneys and judges who, opposing the settlements as a transgression of law, sought to implement a global standard of human rights.

"If we implement international law," Issa said, "the occupation will be over tomorrow."

His trials in Israel and Palestine were both still ongoing, requiring frequent court appearances and interactions with his lawyers, all of it complicated by the logistical difficulties of traveling under the occupation. For one case in which he was facing charges for organizing volunteers to help Palestinian olive farmers near Jewish settlements, military authorities refused to provide him with a permit to enter Israel for a court appearance.

"They are making my life harder," Issa confessed. "I don't have a normal life."

The authorities' machinations notwithstanding, a steady stream of Israelis continued to arrive at the Youth Against Settlements headquarters, old friends as well as new generations of former soldiers, many fresh from completing their military service, eager to process and heal from their experiences. The Hollywood actor Richard Gere had visited Issa just the year before, walking all along Shuhada Street and issuing photos and video of support on his social media channels.

In 2017, Issa traveled to the United States to meet with supporters including many Jewish leaders, among them Senator Bernie Sanders from Vermont. Issa advocated a very targeted boycott of those particular enterprises that could be traced to the settlements, rather than the blanket rejection of Israeli products proposed by the BDS movement, but on his American tour, he met many BDS proponents and predicted this more indiscriminate agenda would gain momentum the more Israel cracked down:

"BDS is destroying Israel?" Issa asked, rhetorically. "The *occupation* is destroying Israel. *Netanyahu* is destroying Israel. You give more legitimacy to BDS when you attack BDS—"

Issa suddenly stopped talking, and we heard a dull thud in the distance, followed by a second and a third concussion.

"Those are stun grenades," he said, turning to us seriously. "I can tell from the sound."

But who was firing the stun grenades—IDF or Palestinian police? And who was being fired upon? Regardless of the answers to these questions, it seemed wise for us to get back to Rami's taxi. Another question immediately came up: How should we return to the Tomb of Patriarchs and Matriarchs? Back the roundabout way we'd come, or should we risk trying to walk back along the lane where the soldier had stopped us?

Let's risk it, Diane decided, and so, parting from Issa and his crew, we descended swiftly down the road.

Halfway down, we saw a single soldier in a green beret sitting under a small canopy in a one-man guard station made of sandbags just a few meters away from a hole in the ground with a heavy metal gate open in front. Blond, with plump, rosy cheeks, the soldier smiled at us and waved as we approached. On the wall of a ruined structure just beyond the hole, someone had painted the words "Abraham's Well Preserve," but the site seemed unofficial and even neglected, with food wrappers and other garbage strewn about.

The soldier seemed lonely and welcomed us when we asked if we could examine the well. "Of course," he said, gesturing for us to go ahead.

The hole was narrow, just large enough for one person, and I went down first. A steep staircase made of roughly carved steps descended down, but I didn't bother going all the way to the end, as the "well" had clearly been used as a toilet, judging by the unmistakable stench of human feces and the accompanying flies. Emerging back into the light and fresh air, I urged Travis to forgo the experience, but he stepped inside just the same and went down enough of the stairs to confirm my bleak report. Together, we persuaded Diane to take a pass. I looked quizzically at the soldier with the green beret, who shrugged and shook his head with equal bafflement. Clearly, he didn't know either why this "holy site" he had been assigned to guard was in such terrible shape.

We began to walk down the lane, and the green beret soldier smiled and waved amiably when I looked back. In a few minutes, we emerged onto Shuhada Street, where we had been stopped, confronted, and turned away before, but the soldiers were by now nowhere to be seen, and we strolled casually back to the Tomb of the Patriarchs and Matriarchs past two other checkpoints, neither of whose troops stirred in the slightest.

Rami, thrilled to find his car intact, began to chat with the store owners about our interview with Issa. Diane, Travis, and I decided to do a quick tour of the tomb. Rami, deciding to quit while he was ahead, said he would stay with the car.

26

HUGGING THE TZADIK

The Tanakh describes Abraham purchasing a plot of land in Hebron from Ephron the Hittite, a certain cave where the patriarch
went on to bury his wife Sarah before being interred himself, to
be followed by their son, Isaac, and his wife, Rebecca, and their
son Jacob and his wife, Leah.

In the first century B.C.E., King Herod built a structure in the
style of a Hellenistic temple to house this cave, and this proud
building, the Tomb of Patriarchs and Matriarchs, survived the
Roman destruction to be expanded and transformed into a
church by the Byzantines, partially destroyed by Persians, rebuilt
by Arabs as a mosque, reconsecrated as a church by Crusaders,
and finally turned back into a mosque by the Mamelukes, who
banned Jews and Christians from coming any closer to the structure than the seventh step, a prohibition maintained by the Ottomans and the British.

After Israel conquered Hebron during the Six-Day War, the
tomb was turned over to the Waqf Islamic Trust, the same Jordanian organization that administers the Temple Mount in Jerusalem, and Jews were allowed access for prayers and holidays. After
Baruch Goldstein's 1994 massacre, however, the Waqf segregated
the building so Jews and Muslims had access to different rooms,
ceding several spaces for a regular Jewish presence while keeping
the larger, more ornate chambers, the ones directly above the

caves, as a functional mosque. In addition to regular congregants, the tomb attracts hundreds of thousands of Muslim, Christian, and Jewish tourists every year, people who recognize this as one of the world's most significant religious sites.

I went up the stairs and into the tomb with Diane and Travis, touring the Jewish section, but stepped outside to take a call while they continued to explore. I recognized the number on my cell phone as Rabbi Danny Cohen, who was affiliated with the Chabad-Lubavitch movement, and whom we were scheduled to meet after visiting the tomb.

Rabbi Cohen and I coordinated our meeting, but when I looked into the parking lot for Rami, I saw him in close conversation with a soldier. I rushed over and waved, uttering a friendly greeting in Hebrew.

The soldier was standing next to Rami, holding Rami's ID card tightly in one hand and the grip of his M16 in the other.

"He's my driver," I told the soldier in Hebrew. "Is there any problem?"

"Parking is not allowed here," he said.

"Oh, I apologize. We didn't know," I said, looking at the signs everywhere which indicated this was a parking lot, with a number of other taxis and buses nearby. "We're waiting for an American lady and her aide."

The soldier relaxed noticeably talking to me, returned Rami's ID card, and made no further mention of the parking lot's being off limits.

I asked him where he was from. "Be'er Sheva . . . Well, close to Be'er Sheva," he answered.

I nodded. "Many soldiers here are from the south," I ventured.

The soldier agreed.

Young and slight, with thick, dark curls under his austerely placed beret, this fellow had to have been still in his conscription years. I asked, "What do you want to do for your career?"

"I want to stay in the army," he responded, without hesitation.

"Impressive," I said. "You don't hear that from every young person these days."

The soldier paused for a moment, and glanced at Rami apologetically, "I'm not being racist," he explained, "but this is a sterile zone."

Rami and I both nodded, and the soldier nodded back, sheepishly, before returning to his guard post.

It wasn't long before Diane and Travis emerged from the Tomb of Patriarchs and Matriarchs. We all climbed back into Rami's cab, and drove on to a little park overlooking Hebron to meet with Rabbi Cohen.

With a dark kippah perched on his head, wearing plain glasses and a blue oxford shirt accessorized with a retractable pen tucked into his vest pocket, a casual, studious appearance that was contrasted with a tremendous black beard that was only beginning to gray, Danny Cohen was indistinguishable from other Lubavitcher Hasidim except for the semiautomatic handgun holstered at his hip, right next to the fringes of his prayer shawl hanging out from under his shirt.

Forty-six at the time of our interview, Danny explained that his family was celebrating the bar mitzvah of the fourth of his six children, but that he always took seriously his duty to speak with visitors, especially journalists and writers. He declined to shake Diane's hand, according to the Haredi custom of avoiding physical contact between unmarried, unrelated women and men, but was otherwise open and conversational.

"To share my passion and inspiration," Danny said, with grace and practice, "is my foremost mission."

Born in Brooklyn, Danny had grown up in a home that was observant, though not Hasidic. His father was a product of the freethinking 1960s, a proud graduate of Cornell University who moved the whole family to Israel when Danny was six. First coming to Hebron when he was sixteen, Danny immediately felt a connection.

"It's the history," Danny said. "The resting place of our mothers and fathers. The whole struggle is represented here, the existence of the Jews in this land."

He served as a soldier in the Givati combat infantry brigade, but afterward joined the Lubavitchers. There were thousands of Chabad missions around the world, throughout the United States, Canada, and Europe, but also in places as varied as Mumbai, India, and Kinshasa, Democratic Republic of the Congo, where they were a haven as well as a resource to the small local Jewish communities as well as transient businessmen and tourists. Danny spent a year in downtown Chicago, which his wife quite enjoyed, but then he had a "eureka" moment when he asked, "Why not Hebron?"

The Lubavitchers had a long history in the city, going back to the early nineteenth century, when the movement's second Rebbe dispatched his followers to establish a presence there. Though outnumbered by the city's Sephardim, the Lubavitchers formed the largest group of Ashkenazim in the city and took over a former Sephardic synagogue, which they operated until the 1929 riots, following which the Jews were all evacuated by British authorities.

In 2005, Danny took the position of *shaliach* in Hebron, a title that made him an emissary for the Lubavitch movement, though without support from any central authority. Danny and his family initially took up residence in Kiryat Arba, but they soon reopened the former Lubavitch synagogue in Hebron proper, inside the military-controlled zone and very near Issa's headquarters. Danny and his wife specialized in reaching out to the soldiers who cycled through Hebron, bringing the troops coffee and food at their posts at night, and having them to their home for Shabbat dinner.

Living in Hebron was sometimes dangerous—which is why he carried a firearm—but Danny considered it both a duty and an honor to restore the Jewish presence in the vicinity of the Tomb of Patriarchs and Matriarchs.

"We often have thirty soldiers at the dinner table," Danny said. "It was never easy living in Hebron, but if there weren't Jews living there near the Cave of Abraham, it would have been abandoned."

To Danny, the political conflict with the Palestinians manifested itself most immediately in the restrictions on the growth of the Hebron settlers' community. There was insufficient housing for the seventy-five families who lived in the military-controlled zone, but because of a negotiated freeze on the growth of settlements, they did not receive permits from the government to take over additional properties or to expand the spaces they already had. Setting up new sanitation and electricity services as well as Internet access were all subject to interminable delays and bureaucratic obstacles, so that young adults and families with small children often left in frustration. Danny saw these political constraints as paradigmatic of the whole history of the State of Israel, of Jews capitulating to Arab objections.

"This is a microcosm of the Arab-Israeli conflict that's been going on for seventy-five years," Danny said. "Even collecting garbage is a political issue because it signals ownership."

Meanwhile, the Arab part of Hebron was allowed to grow freely, Danny complained: "I hear the construction all the time."

Danny cited a recent designation from UNESCO, the United Nations cultural agency, of Hebron's Old City as a *Palestinian*

World Heritage Site, which he thought had been calibrated precisely to undermine the settlers' claim to Hebron. UNESCO's declaration had excluded Israel from the designation, which he saw as a preposterous effort to sever the Jewish connection to the tomb of their own forefather. Danny noted that Prime Minister Netanyahu had issued a counterproclamation that acknowledged Hebron's Jewish heritage in unequivocal language but complained that Netanyahu had not really done what was necessary to ease conditions for the Hebron settlers.

As far as the future, Danny was confident that Israel would never agree to a Two State Solution, regardless of what was said by some political leaders. All the conversation by those in the United States and elsewhere was beside the point, he maintained. The experience of the 2005 Israeli withdrawal from Gaza and the area's subsequent takeover by Hamas had shattered the idea that Palestinians could be entrusted with self-government.

"Maybe among American Jews, there is still a discussion, but in Israel, that argument about one state, two states, is all gone," Danny said. "For twenty years, the thinking in the Middle East was 'Give up land, take risks.' But the results are rockets in Ashqelon, people murdered. Peace didn't happen.

"Only in fairy tales is there a happy ending. In the Middle East, there is no such concept as peace. There is a concept of *respect*."

Danny recalled periods of time when the Jews and Arabs got along better, when he and his family were able to shop in the marketplace, but now he had "no relationship at all" with his Palestinian neighbors, a situation he blamed on the peace agreements that granted more autonomy to Palestinians. Instead of alleviating tensions, greater Palestinian self-government had led only to more instability and violence. To him, the obvious solution was to roll things back in the other direction. Israel should become a state run explicitly according to Jewish law and formally annex Hebron and the rest of the West Bank.

"The experiment did not work," Danny said, in reference to Palestinian governance. "[The Israeli government] should make it loud and clear [the West Bank] is ours. That will stop the terror."

I asked Danny for his perspective on the relationship between Israeli and American Jews.

Here, Danny emphasized that he was "not a hard-core settler," in that he maintained his American citizenship, voted in American elections, and was a proud Yankees fan. Israeli and American Jews share many of the same values, he maintained, and the average Israeli feels a kinship with American Jews while also believing that internationally, the United States is Israel's "only friend."

Nevertheless, Danny felt that most American Jews were poorly informed about Israel and supported policies that were patronizing and ill tailored to improving the situation for Israelis on the ground.

"Until two years ago, on one side you felt support," Danny said, "but on the other side, it was a friendship, but 'Do it my way.'"

With the election of Donald Trump to the presidency in 2016, Danny saw a marked improvement in administration policy toward Israel. Trump himself had been "very vocal" in his enthusiasm for Israel's expansion, and his official relocation of the American embassy to Jerusalem had been greatly welcomed by settlers. But Mike Pence's recent speech in Jerusalem, that was "music to their ears," Danny said, particularly when the vice president cited the prophesy that those nations who help the Jewish people will be blessed themselves.

"It meant a lot that support came from representatives of the strongest nation in the world," Danny said.

To him, international acquiescence to Israeli control over the

Palestinians was the only way to avoid the disastrous wars and civil conflicts that afflicted so many other nations in the region.

"Look at Yemen and Syria," Danny said. "It's time to come to our senses and not cut and paste Gaza and Beirut and Hezbollah."

We finished talking with Rabbi Cohen shortly before 3:00 P.M., and since we still had the whole afternoon and evening, Rami suggested we go to Bethlehem, just a forty-minute drive away. We decided to see a new hotel created by the British multimedia artist Banksy as well as the Church of the Nativity, where Rami said he had an excellent contact who could give us a private tour.

Rami drove us on roads that were designed to connect Israeli settlements; uncrowded single lanes in either direction through a landscape of pretty hills covered in rocks and scrub with intermittent groves of trees. Soon we were inside Bethlehem itself, where Rami navigated through the city until we reached the Israeli separation wall, a thirty-foot-tall concrete barrier topped with armored watchtowers that bisected streets and neighborhoods. Israelis restricted access on their side of the wall, while Palestinians maintained a road that ran along the wall but allowed construction right up to the street and encouraged graffiti on their side of the structure. Rami asked several passersby for directions until we found the Walled Off Hotel on a busy corner just across from the separation wall.

Notoriously reclusive, Banksy has been identified in unconfirmed reports as a British artist who first gained significant attention in his homeland for street art he created in the 1990s full of images with ironic, antiwar, and anticapitalist themes. He began exhibiting internationally in the early 2000s and led delegations of other graffiti artists to Bethlehem specifically to decorate the Palestinian side of the separation wall beginning in 2005. He painted a little girl in a frilly dress with her hair in pigtails frisking an Israeli soldier, and another of a young man, his face hidden by a kaffiyeh, preparing to hurl a bouquet of flowers.

Just across from the hotel was Banksy's striking portrait of Muhammad Ali in the triumphant moment of his knockout victory over Sonny Liston in 1965, except with a broken missile in place of Liston at Ali's feet.

Next to Banksy's Ali was a neon angel/smiling Madonna wearing a hijab with an infant in her arms by an Australian artist called Straker, and around these artist-signed paintings were pro-Palestinian slogans in Arabic as well as messages in English criticizing the Israeli government and comparing this wall with other barriers, such as the now demolished wall separating East and West Berlin, or the border wall with Mexico that Donald Trump promised to construct during his 2016 presidential campaign. "No Balls, Build Walls" was printed underneath one of the many critical portraits of Trump.

The Walled Off Hotel—a wordplay on the luxury Waldorf chain—took Banksy's perspective on the Israeli-Palestinian conflict as well as his collaborative approach to art into three dimensions. We were greeted by the statue of a large chimpanzee dressed as an old-school bellhop who welcomed new arrivals. The building itself was fitted with a thin façade that added fake Roman-style columns and printed frilly awnings over real balconies on each floor, touches to enhance the colonial motifs.

Inside, the hotel lobby offered a café as well as a piano bar decked out in Victorian style, with velvet and satin-embroidered furniture, dark patterned wallpaper, lamps with tinted shades, and paintings in ornate frames. On close examination, the paintings frequently had a political theme, such as an image of Jesus rendered in medieval style but with an anachronistic laser point on his forehead, yet the atmosphere was cosmopolitan, festive, and young, a mixture of languages and nationalities. There were many backpackers on long-term trips, just the sort of travelers who, a generation earlier, would have stopped on a kibbutz for a stint as a volunteer. The hotel staff and waiters were all young Palestinian women and men in black bow ties, red vests, and white shirts, serving a menu that had several vegan options and an array of mocktails, nonalcoholic versions of the craft drinks that were popular in the hipster bars of Europe and the United States.

We went through the hotel's museum, a fanciful retelling of Israel's founding that underscored the role of the British Empire, and a second-floor exhibit of local Palestinian artists before checking out the gift shop, where we bought T-shirts, posters, and coffee mugs with Banksy images printed on them.

We got back in the taxi, and Rami drove us a short distance to the Church of the Nativity, where we met his contact, also named Issa, an older Palestinian Christian man and self-taught scholar. Palestinian Christians were now a minority in Bethlehem, a city of about fifty thousand people, but the city's economy depended on tourists coming to see the historic sites, especially the Church of the Nativity, and there was a long line of groups in front of the church complex, thousands of seniors, families, and singles with matching hats following guides with color-coded flags.

Bethlehem Issa escorted us around the throngs to a back entrance of the Church of the Nativity, narrating its history as we went: commissioned originally in the fourth century by the Roman Emperor Constantine, it was destroyed during the sixth-century revolt of the Samaritans, a people who claimed descent from the Israelite tribes of Ephraim, Manasseh, and Levi who had broken with other Jews hundreds of years earlier. The Byzantine Emperor Justinian crushed the Samaritans and rebuilt the church, and when the Persians invaded a few decades later, they spared it. But the Crusaders seized the church from its Armenian caretakers and robbed it of an artifact said to be Jesus's manger, which they shipped back to Rome. Today, the church is jointly administered by the Catholic, Armenian, and Greek Orthodox churches, with accommodations made for Copts and Syriac Christians.

Bethlehem Issa walked us through the adjoining Church of St. Catherine, containing the cave where St. Jerome, a fourth-century monk, locked himself away for thirty-six years to translate the Christian Bible into Latin. From there, we entered the great liturgical hall through Justinian's basilica, where a section of Constantine's mosaic floor had been exposed. There were long lines of tourists leading to the reconstructed grotto where Christian tradition held that Jesus was born, but Bethlehem Issa found an Orthodox priest he knew who escorted us around the queue, outraging those who noticed. A Korean woman wearing a white visor grabbed my arm and told me, "But we have been waiting a long time."

I could only shrug my shoulders and follow Bethlehem Issa and the priest.

We descended a steep staircase into the grotto, which now had a marble floor, walls covered with tapestries and paintings, and a low ceiling from which hung dozens of ornate, metal lanterns. Several stern-eyed nuns in black-and-white habits held back the crowd at the stairs while their colleagues simultaneously urged those in the grotto to perform their prayers and take their selfies quickly. At one end of the grotto was a small incline covered by a canopy, which was itself covered by a thick, embroidered tapestry. This was the little cave where Mary had given birth to Jesus, and everyone took turns stooping down to peek into the space, where many lanterns had been hung to illuminate the miniature paintings on the wall, all around a fourteen-pointed silver star with a Latin inscription: "Here Jesus Christ was born to the Virgin Mary."

The following night, back in Givatayim, I visited the Shtefan-isher's tomb at Nahalat Yitzhak Cemetery. The tomb area was illuminated by an overhead light, and the banner celebrating the Rebbe was still there, as was the table with the charity boxes and a few assorted printed pamphlets with prayers and instructions, but it was unmanned just then.

I could see, however, that someone was lying facedown on the tomb itself, and I decided to make this person aware of my presence rather than approach quietly. I dropped a few coins in the *tzedakah* box, so they clanked when they hit the tin bottom, and looked cautiously at the person on the tomb.

He had been smiling with his eyes closed, but hearing the noise of the *tzedakah* box, he stirred, opened his eyes, and sat up. Youngish, with an unkempt blond beard and thick sidelocks along with a knit kippah perched precariously on the side of his skull, he wore a white shirt and a vest, but his Haredi mien was interrupted by his cargo shorts and hiking boots. He saw me pause, perhaps noticed the query in my expression, and felt the need to explain himself.

"I wanted to hug the Tzadik," he said.

"I totally understand you," I said.

He was embarrassed, though, and leapt off the tomb, dashing off into the darkness of the cemetery at large.

27

BELAYNESH

I was happy to be able to arrange a meeting with Belaynesh Zevadia in Jerusalem on one of our last days in the country. She had
recently completed a tenure as Israel's ambassador to Ethiopia,
the first Ethiopian Israeli to serve at that rank, and was back in
Israel for a while. I first met Belaynesh when she was a junior
diplomat at the consulate in Chicago during the 1990s, and we'd
stayed in touch over the following decades, if only electronically.

We rushed to Jerusalem in the morning and met up with Yoni
Reuven at the Mamila Mall, a newly built, open air arcade of
high-end shops just outside Suleiman's walls around the Old City.
Yoni had a rare day off from the hospital and wanted to see Diane
one more time before she left, and also to meet Belaynesh, who'd
been a student of his father's in Ethiopia.

Just as we met up with Yoni, Belaynesh messaged me to say
she had an urgent meeting, asking to reschedule for a few hours
later.

I apologized to Diane, Travis, and Yoni, quipping that she
surely would have put us off only for a meeting with the prime
minister. A few minutes later, Belaynesh sent a few photos of Netanyahu, close up, speaking in a microphone to her and a small
group of Israeli diplomats.

"You weren't kidding," Diane observed. "She really *is* with
the prime minister."

To kill the time, we wandered lackadaisically among the mall's luxury stores: Zara, H. Stern, Pandora, Swarovski, Padani, Timberland, The North Face, and Adidas, among others.

We sat down on a staircase in the shade, and Yoni asked me where we were supposed to meet Belaynesh.

"Café Rimon," I answered, gesturing at the well-appointed restaurant just across from where we were sitting.

Yoni followed up. "Are you sure it was *this* Café Rimon?"

I wasn't sure, and messaged Belaynesh, who confirmed Yoni's suspicions that she meant the original Café Rimon on Ben Yehudah Street.

Thankfully, it wasn't too far away, just one stop away on the light rail, and with Yoni leading us, we even arrived early, and found a table under Café Rimon's expansive canopy outside on Ben Yehudah, the popular, pedestrian-only street that was the heart of Jerusalem's downtown. Opened in 1952, Café Rimon was a kosher spot that had prospered through the years of Jerusalem's bifurcation, even after Ben Yehudah became a tourist trap. The famous restaurant had been the target of multiple terror attacks, including one in 2001 by a pair of suicide bombers who killed ten people and injured nearly two hundred others, and a poisoning plot the following year.

These attacks were a distant memory now, though, and we enjoyed watching all the people passing by, the backpackers and hordes of tour groups and Jerusalemites of all varieties.

Soon enough, Belaynesh arrived, elegant in a floral printed shirt. I made introductions and called the waitress over to take her order.

"Ice cream," she told the waitress, selecting a combination of flavors.

The conversation with the prime minister had been difficult, she explained, as Netanyahu was often fiercely critical of the foreign service, and she had earned the ice cream with her patience and professionalism.

Belaynesh was born and raised in a village in the Gondar region of Ethiopia without electricity or running water. Her father was the Ethiopian Jewish community's most important *kes,* and her earliest memories are of seeing her father teach Torah and hearing him talk about Israel. One of her older brothers, Joseph, had left for Israel in the 1950s, when he was just ten years old, returned to Ethiopia in 1965, and become a teacher in the high school where Belaynesh studied, the same institution where Yoni's father, Mehari, taught. The Derg regime imprisoned Joseph along with Mehari for their advocacy of emigration to Israel, and he, too, was beaten and tortured.

Another brother and a sister made it to Israel on their own, and two of her older sisters walked out of Ethiopia to Sudan carrying their own young children, enduring a long and perilous journey, until they reached a refugee camp where they languished with other Ethiopian Jews. Then, in 1984, just as Belaynesh finished high school, her brother secured a scholarship for her to study at the Ulpan Etzion in Jerusalem, a language school specifically designed for new arrivals, and arranged for her to fly to Israel via Egypt.

Belaynesh arrived in Israel alone, unable to speak Hebrew at all. She struggled through the first months at the *ulpan,* a boarding school with limited experience assimilating Ethiopians. But her family had primed her to make the sacrifices necessary to bring Ethiopian Jews to Israel, so she persevered though that program for a few months until Operation Moses began, whereupon she went to work for the Jewish Agency facilitating the assimilation of new arrivals, including her two sisters who had been in Sudan. Happily, her parents arrived as well, her venerable, ninety-year-old father by then in a wheelchair, with the whole family settling in Be'er Sheva, so he could be near the tomb of Abraham. He died two years later, and her mother just a few years after that; they were buried in Jerusalem.

Belaynesh's father forbade her from military service, but she set lofty goals for herself, enrolling at Hebrew University in Jerusalem's three-year program to earn a B.A. in international relations and African studies. Her Hebrew was not yet refined enough for academic work when she started, so she took notes in Amharic script, and often had to translate words from Hebrew to English and then from English to Amharic. Though the Ministry of Absorption funded her bachelor's degree only, Belaynesh decided to add an M.A. in Anthropology and worked cleaning houses and babysitting to support herself while also paying her own school fees.

A newspaper ad prompted her to apply to the Foreign Ministry's "cadets course," and in 1992 she became the first Ethiopian Israeli woman to enter that prestigious program. She worked for several years within Israel before her appointment in Chicago in 1996 as the consulate's information officer. This was where we first met. I interviewed her for several publications I worked for at the time, and we maintained a friendship afterward. She was a popular speaker to African American and Jewish audiences, recounting the history of Ethiopia's Jews and their exodus to Israel as well as their current status in the country. Her story resonated equally in North Shore synagogues and South Side churches.

Belaynesh married an Ethiopian-born engineer in a grand wedding in Israel that included many luminaries, including Shimon Peres, then a former prime minister and the future president. Her diplomatic career soared as well: after a term as vice consul in Houston, where she and her husband raised their three young children, she was appointed as ambassador to Ethiopia, Rwanda, and Burundi in 2012. It was both a career achievement and a signal that Israel was stepping up its efforts in Africa, and she was the subject of glowing articles in Israeli and Ethiopian media alike. In 2014, she was selected as one of fourteen "groundbreaking women" and honored to participate as a candle lighter during Independence Day celebrations. Two years later, she joined dignitaries at the Genocide Memorial in Kigali, Rwanda, to commemorate the seventy-first anniversary of the liberation of the Auschwitz concentration camp. A few months after that, she welcomed Prime Minister Netanyahu on an official state visit to Ethiopia and strengthened the connections between Israeli and Ethiopian businesses, especially in the agricultural and medical sectors. Belaynesh also developed strong relationships with other women diplomats, including the ambassadors from Germany and Kenya. In Israel, Ethiopian Israelis frequently faced discrimination when it came to the allocation of public resources, jobs, and even in social settings, but on the world stage, Belaynesh enjoyed a certain celebrity.

"I was everybody's pride," she recalled with a laugh.

Of course, even beyond the professional accomplishment, the return to Ethiopia was meaningful on a personal level for Belaynesh. When she presented her credentials to Ethiopia's president, they spoke in Amharic and he told her she was representative of the many Ethiopians who had gone abroad and become successful.

"You have made history," the president told her, "a native of Ethiopia who returns here as an ambassador."

Addis Ababa had transformed during her absence, adding glittering skyscrapers that now made up the expanding skyline as well as cafés and restaurants, even if electricity and Internet service remained inconsistent. But when she traveled back to the village where she was raised and visited her former school, Belaynesh burst into tears at the sight of the other students.

"It all came back to me at once," she told an Israeli news outlet after her visit. "Every little girl who ran around there barefoot, it was as if she were me."

28

FROM OHIO TO RAMALLAH

On Tuesday, February 6, Rami picked up Diane, Travis, and me in the morning to drive us to Ramallah, the de facto Palestinian capital. We had arranged to meet Sam Bahour, an American-born Palestinian businessman. The journey to Ramallah usually took just over an hour, Rami said, though he had allotted a little extra time in case crossing the Qalandia checkpoint took longer than expected.

We traveled most of the way as if we were driving to Jerusalem before turning north to Ramallah, originally a Christian Palestinian city near Jerusalem. The checkpoint was just outside the city, and as we approached, we could see multiple lanes with bays for cars, like a row of fortified toll booths. These were mostly empty, though, and when we pulled up, the soldiers were calm and professional, checking our passports and asking a few perfunctory questions before waving us through.

Within a few minutes, we were in Ramallah proper, trying to find our way to Sam's office. Before we left Chicago, Travis had consulted with his former boss at the Parliament of World Religions, Dirk Ficca, a Presbyterian minister and international peace activist who had decades of experience working with Palestinians, and whose son was currently in Ramallah. Dirk had generously provided us with a list of potential contacts, and Sam was at the top, described as the "smartest, most connected person in the

West Bank." A Google search revealed that he had been quoted by the *New York Times* and other media outlets, so I felt lucky that he was in town and had accommodated us in his schedule.

Communicating with Sam by cell phone, Rami navigated around the various construction projects for new offices and apartment buildings that had shut down sections of Ramallah. Near the mausoleum for deceased Palestinian leader Yasser Arafat, the streets were blocked off by black-uniformed Palestinian police officers, requiring another significant detour. An international icon in his black-and-white checked kaffiyeh, stubbly beard, and holstered pistol, Arafat had been the principal figure in the Palestinian cause since he was made chairman of the Palestine Liberation Organization in 1969, and he led, organized, and sanctioned countless violent attacks against Israeli civilians and military targets before finally agreeing to the Oslo Peace Accords in 1993. He shared the Nobel Peace Prize the following year with Israeli Prime Minister Yitzhak Rabin and Foreign Minister Shimon Peres, and in 1996, was elected the first president of the Palestinian Authority.

Where his mausoleum is now located, there had been a former British military compound, which Arafat converted into the headquarters for his fledgling Palestinian government after he was elected president. But relations with the Israelis deteriorated in the following years, breaking into all-out revolt in what became known as the Second Intifada, in 2000. The IDF accused Arafat of financing and arming terrorists who'd attacked Israel, including suicide bombers, and surrounded him in his headquarters until he agreed to their terms. Arafat died in 2004 in a French hospital of illness, and the mausoleum and accompanying museum were built on the site of his former headquarters, where he'd held out against Israeli forces for the last time.

Caught in the backed-up traffic around the mausoleum, I

asked Rami how he remembered Arafat's leadership now, more than a decade after his death.

"Arafat is the first and the last," he told me, in English, for emphasis.

With Sam's guidance, we eventually came to a cluster of modern glass, steel, and stone office buildings, and spotted him waiting just outside the front door of his building like a human beacon, unmissable at six foot four with his thick, dark mustache and a ring of neatly trimmed black hair around a bald center. Dressed like a prosperous tech CEO in a blue oxford shirt and dark slacks, he shook our hands vigorously and greeted us in English with a Midwestern accent, a product of his upbringing in Ohio as the child of a Lebanese American mother and a Palestinian-born father. His office was a modest but well-equipped suite, and he introduced us to his small staff, bright young men in business casual shirts and slacks and women with business casual outfits plus hijabs. We sat down in a conference room, and he smiled broadly, confessing that he hadn't been sure we'd make it.

"For foreigners to get here is not given," Sam explained. "Israel puts a lot of restrictions on foreigners coming in."

Sam was speaking from personal experience. After a successful career in software development in Ohio, he'd come to Palestine in the wake of the 1993 peace accords, full of optimism, energy, and ideas to build the economy of what he expected would shortly become a new state.

"When Oslo happened," he said, "I came."

In his first years in Ramallah, he made full use of his American experience and citizenship to work and develop a network of contacts among both Israelis and Palestinians. He built a $100 million telecommunications company employing some two hundred people as well as a $10 million shopping mall that employed hundreds more, even as he earned an M.B.A. at Tel Aviv

University, traveling to Israel two or three times each week in a car with the yellow license plates used by Israeli citizens. He ensconced himself for a couple of years, marrying a Palestinian woman, with whom he had two daughters, and moving into his grandfather's home in Al Bireh, the city where his father's family had lived for generations.

Though he applied to the Israeli government for permanent residency in the West Bank shortly after he arrived, it was more than a decade before he got a response, such that he had to rely instead on renewals of his tourist visa every three months. In 2006, after thirteen years of this routine, Israeli authorities suddenly handwrote in his passport the words "final permit," giving him just one month before he was supposed to leave. Pressing his case with his Israeli contacts—high-level government officials and businesspersons—Sam won renewals for three more years before finally getting approved for permanent residency in 2009. His new status only made things more complicated, however, since his American passport now had a stamp which indicated he had been issued a West Bank ID card, which meant that he was subject to the same restrictions as other Palestinians. No longer could he legally affix the yellow license plates on his car and his entry to Israel now required going through a checkpoint on foot, and was limited to between 5:00 A.M. and 7:00 P.M. Effectively, his access to Israel to do business or meet with friends had been severed.

"My actual interactions with the Israeli population diminished to nothing once I became a Palestinian in the eyes of Israeli authorities," Sam said.

Since then, he'd grown steadily disillusioned and disappointed, convinced that the Israeli government was trying to actively undermine any effort the Palestinians were making to create the infrastructure of a state.

"If you stay here long enough," he said, "you realize that any positive influence is unacceptable to Israel. Coming here is unacceptable. Building is not acceptable. Israel has no interest in allowing a Palestinian state. They demand change, but they hold the tools to *make* the change and won't release them."

Sam saw a concerted Israeli program which he described as a "slow burner ethnic cleansing," not only increasing frustration and anger among Palestinians, but driving some to leave, to the Arab world or, if they were able, to the United States, Canada, or Europe, while others sunk into desperation or resorted to nihilistic violence.

"You lose hope, you lose fear," he explained. "They want you to get up and say, 'This isn't worth it anymore.' But I still wake up every day trying to make jobs in this country."

At Oslo, both sides had agreed to create two states, but in the ensuing years, while Palestinians had lined up international support from governments and populations around the world, Israel had dragged its feet and manufactured excuses to avoid actually implementing the Two State Solution.

"We're beyond the process," Sam said. "We're now at the place where the question is whether Israel has the political will to establish the state.

"All we've been doing the last twenty-five years is to play with the process."

The settlers and their supporters were a major factor in thwarting the Palestinians' aspirations for statehood, but those within Israel and elsewhere who had a financial stake in the occupation were at least as influential. Many products had to be imported through Israel, even water, all of which was taxed and permitted.

"Some people think there's something in the Israeli DNA to kill or oppress Palestinians," Sam said. "I don't buy that. Rather, a lot of people are making a lot of money off this captive population."

Under the extensive rules of the occupation, the Israeli military restricted even consumer goods that were commonly used in businesses. Sam recalled that when he set up his office, the Palestinian contractor who came to set up his IT service could offer only second-rate Wi-Fi routers, though the better devices could be purchased off the shelf in any electronics store in Israel. The effect of these restrictions, when multiplied across the whole West Bank, was to hold back much of the Palestinian consumer economy. Citing research from the independent Palestine Investment Fund, Sam said the cost of the occupation to the overall local economy was $16 billion annually.

To illustrate, Sam noted that after many years of delay, Palestinians were finally approved to set up their own 3G cellular service network—just as the rest of the world, including Israel, was moving up to 5G. But 3G was insufficient to handle the latest popular apps, making it advantageous for any Palestinian so inclined to buy a 5G SIM card and tap into the networks from the settlements. The Palestinian business sector, however, was blocked from profiting from this new technology. Software developers, telecommunications services, and retailers all were effectively prevented from getting started, hiring employees, renting office space, or otherwise reinvesting their money in the society to the tune of tens of millions of dollars each year. The funds went to Israeli companies instead, while creative and entrepreneurial Palestinians were continually frustrated.

"What you don't see is the invisible price of the occupation on our shoulders," Sam said. "Our airwaves are as occupied as our land."

Ironically, the machinery of occupation ensured that Palestinians continued to have contact with Israelis, even as Israelis were increasingly isolated from the realities of daily life among Palestinians.

"The Palestinian community has a much deeper understanding of Israel than Israelis have of Palestinians," Sam explained. "Israel is completely blind to what is going on the other side of the war."

Given these circumstances, I asked Sam whether he still preferred the Two State Solution, or if he was open to one state that included both Israelis and Palestinians.

Sam answered that he continued to dedicate himself to the establishment of two states, and that only a state could realize Palestinians' long-held dreams while acknowledging their ability to manage their own affairs.

"Palestinian agency prior to Oslo defined itself as being for two states," Sam said, "and we need to be able to respect Palestinian agency.

"Today, the only feasible, win-win approach is to recognize Palestinians' own national aspirations."

His vision of two states did not occlude some sort of federation between Palestine and Israel. If a single state was imposed on Palestinians, however, Sam feared Palestinians would turn to violence in their frustration.

"How do those two states exist side by side? They could hate each other, *or* they could be like the U.S. and Canada. If there is one state, the Palestinian struggle becomes an anti-apartheid struggle," Sam said. "I see it heading to a bad place."

Currently, the Palestinians were gaining momentum precisely because they were increasingly eschewing violence and building international support for boycotts.

"BDS, the European Union, and the U.N.—they [the Israelis] don't know how to deal with that," Sam asserted. "Those are foreign to them, but take a knife and charge a checkpoint—they know how to deal with that. Israel is drunk with power."

With the threat of violence looming, Sam saw it as all the more important to create viable economic opportunities for Palestinians, and he was actively seeking out American corporate investors for Palestinian ventures, both to create an economic base and to enlist new allies to end the occupation. Those who invested in a hotel, for example, would soon learn that they weren't allowed to import beds because of military rules that restricted the number of beds as a "security issue." Investors experiencing such arbitrary oversight inevitably became allies, and Sam was determined to link economic empowerment with the Palestinian resistance.

"Trying to create jobs is nonviolent resistance," he said. "A lot of the Israeli side is a haphazard set of actions that got us to this point. But at the end of the day, the military occupation is a conscious effort.

"Keeping people here in poverty leads to violence. It's almost as if our argument today is to save Israel from itself."

The effects of Palestinians' economic isolation were particularly severe for younger generations, whose access to the Internet made them aware of developments around the globe and intensified their hunger to participate in an increasingly globalized society. Meanwhile, the Palestinian economy remained dependent on funds from the United Nations and other international charities, "a donor-propped-up economy," as Sam described it, "a house of cards."

When I asked Sam for his assessment of the Palestinian Authority, he did not hold back, describing them as willing facilitators of the occupation who were failing to build the infrastructure of a future state. Though he praised Palestinian Authority President Mahmood Abbas for recruiting international allies, he noted that within Palestine, all the recognized political parties were connected to the Palestinian Liberation Organization or Hamas with closed memberships and predefined agendas. Sam worried about the inevitable transition from the current generation of leaders to a new generation who have grown up under the restrictions of the occupation but are fully aware of the greater freedoms enjoyed by other people around the world.

"Within their bubble of subauthority, the Palestinian Authority has to be better than a regular government, and they are not there," Sam said. "They have only what Israel allows them to have. Every community in the world has leadership. The question is if your political system is open to include new people. This is a closed system today. Young people can't enter politics, so they go downtown to hold a protest."

Diane asked Sam about the differences between the West Bank and Gaza, the latter of which was governed by the Islamist group Hamas.

Sam explained that the Palestinian Authority and Hamas had been entrenched enemies since 2006, when Hamas won in the Palestinian elections, but the factions of the Palestine Liberation Organization, which had been in control of the authority since Arafat's death, refused to cede power. The ensuing power struggle devolved into a violent conflict, and Hamas's militia seized control in Gaza, while Arafat's former allies in the PLO cemented their rule over the West Bank.

Palestinians remained "one political unit and one economic unit," Sam said, even as Gaza and the West Bank were on different tracks, "like Alaska and Hawaii."

Though there are frequent populist calls for reconciliation, Hamas and the Palestinian Authority remain fiercely opposed, with the Palestinian Authority recently colluding with Israeli forces to arrest Hamas-affiliated students who won university elections. Nevertheless, Hamas retained a strong following among Palestinians, and it was a mistake, Sam argued, to treat them as a small terror organization.

"Hamas is a constituency similar to evangelical Christians in the U.S.," he averred. "It is not a car of bandits that can be hit by a drone. When you close Gaza, it develops in the wrong way."

Travis asked where Hamas, as a movement, was going.

Hamas had achieved their popularity among Palestinians through their attacks against Israel, Sam said, but the group was determined to maintain their governance of Gaza. It was also true that becoming administrators of their mini-state was changing the organization, making them more likely to compromise, even to the point of accepting the Two State Solution. He saw the group distancing themselves from the Muslim Brotherhood in Egypt, for example, from which Hamas had emerged originally, and predicted that they would evolve along pragmatic lines, the same way Arafat and his PLO allies had. As a secular person himself, Sam could not support them and did not think they would win over the majority of those who lived in the more secular West Bank, but he saw them as a legitimate part of the Palestinian whole who could be reasoned with as an "internal political reality."

"They can't be trusted, but they can be *dealt* with," Sam summed up. "Hamas has become very, very political, and they will fully fall in line."

More than the internal rifts among Palestinians, what concerned Sam was the growing power of the right wing in Israel, entrenching the occupation in the West Bank and blockading Gaza even as it was imposing a more religious lifestyle on Israelis. Women were already forced to sit in the back of public buses in many Haredi communities, he pointed out, and so he predicted it would not be long before the rights of those Palestinian citizens of Israel were also eroded.

"Why care about Israel?" Sam asked, rhetorically, before commenting on the status of Palestinian citizens. "Because nobody wants to go from occupation to apartheid. We want Israel to be a democratic state because we won't sell out twenty percent of the citizens of that state."

To this end, Sam was focusing his efforts strategically, based on his sophisticated understanding of Israel's politics, talking with obviously receptive audiences as well as more skeptical types he thought might be persuaded. On social media, he concentrated on Israeli influencers and others who were at least open-minded, if not necessarily well informed, trying to build a coalition that equated to a majority of Israeli society.

"The opposition to the Likud can't articulate an anti-occupation position, though the occupation dominates the budget and the politics."

And so, Sam sought out American Jews as an essential constituency in his efforts, politically influential while at the same time receptive to arguments about civil and economic rights. "That's the audience," Sam said. "They're not observers. They're a vested party in this situation. If they see the reality, the social justice pillars of their tradition will kick in. They will understand there is no status quo here. There is only a deteriorating situation.

"My lobbying is in Jewish America, and in the business community, places where that kind of discussion is not happening. I'm going for the tipping point in Israel, fifty-one percent of the Knesset is all I need, so definitely, we have to stop preaching to the choir."

Historically, Palestinians have drawn much of their support from their fellow Arab states, but Syria and Iraq were currently mired in civil war while Egypt's military rulers were squelching a democratic uprising as well as the Muslim Brotherhood, and even the Saudis and the Gulf states were dealing with the financial fallout of having outspent their oil revenues and accumulated debt. But while the various regimes in control of these countries were held back by these internal and international entanglements, their populations had grown even closer to the Palestinians, with whom they communicated on Facebook and WhatsApp.

"We're in full alignment with the populations of the Arab world," Sam said. "They are too excited about Palestine, if you ask me."

29

ZIMAM

Our second stop in Ramallah was the office of Zimam, which described itself as a "grassroots, progressive movement" of Palestinians who take a nonviolent approach to resisting the occupation and building an independent state alongside Israel.

Zimam happened to be the organization where Reverend Ficca's son Dillon worked, and the young man met us downstairs. Tall and thin with thick, neatly combed dark hair, and wearing a striped business shirt and khakis, Dillon embraced both Travis and Diane warmly before ushering us into the office of Zimam's CEO, Samer Makhlouf, where we sat on plush, deep leather couches as we chatted.

Middle-aged, his hair cut very short, with rectangular glasses and a partial beard, Samer sat behind his desk, relaxed, and leaned back in his chair as we spoke. He had copies of two self-help books in English in front of him, *The Art of Thinking Clearly,* by Rolf Dobelli, and *Do the KIND Thing,* by Daniel Lubetzky, as well as *Civil Disobedience and Other Essays,* by Henry David Thoreau.

Samer explained that Zimam—meaning "Reigns"—was formed in the wake of Israel's 2015 elections, after which Prime Minister Netanyahu established a right-wing government and the prospects for a Palestinian state seemed dim. "We decided to see what we could do internally," he said, in perfectly fluent

English. "We are looking at what is preventing us from reaching our national goals. Traditionally, we blame Israel for everything, but they aren't responsible for the corruption, or the lack of an economy. We oppose all forms of violence and extremism and call for tolerance, acceptance, and democracy in Palestinian society. We want to live so Palestine lives."

Zimam was formed in January 2016 with support from One-Voice Palestine, a NGO funded by private foundations in the United States and the United Kingdom. It was a particularly grim time in which dozens of individual Palestinians had attacked Israeli soldiers and civilians, often with no more than a kitchen knife. Meanwhile, just a few kilometers away in Syria and Iraq, the so-called Islamic State was wreaking havoc, destroying whole cities, and murdering entire populations. It was clear to Samer that Palestinians desperately needed progressive alternatives.

In its first year, Zimam attracted 1,100 active members, including many students, and launched a petition campaign that called for a "rejection of extremism, and an embrace of tolerance, nonviolence, and national unity," logging more than 15,000 signatures from residents of cities and villages across the West Bank as well as from Gaza, from imams and other religious authorities, and from civic leaders and politicians from every party, in four months. Bolstered by the petition's success, Zimam convened a national conference in Ramallah with hundreds of attendees from every sector, a conclave that was graced with a speech, via Skype, from a senior adviser to President Abbas.

Samer was particularly proud of Zimam's Facebook page, which had tens of thousands of visitors, and was one of the rare spaces, virtual or physical, where Palestinians from Gaza and the West Bank were able to communicate freely. There were more than 2.5 million Palestinians on Facebook, he noted, and Zimam had more than 209,000 followers across all its social media channels, second in popularity only to Yasser Arafat's commemorative page. Samer cited a video interview of a teacher in Bethlehem that received more than 700,000 views as an example of the kind of messages that were competing with the knife attackers, many of whom died in the course of their attacks and posted videos exhorting violence or martyrdom before they acted.

"Giving our kids a good education is the resistance," Samer said. "It's not fair for our kids to stab someone, and get killed for nothing. We want people to question everything."

Samer continued to advocate for the Two State Solution, contending that there was still overwhelming support for a Palestinian state, regardless of polls and surveys showing diminished enthusiasm. These were a gauge of the levels of apathy and cynicism over the political stalemate, Samer insisted, but that was why a fresh approach was all the more urgent. In his social media and public speeches, he had been an outspoken supporter of the nonviolent protests the previous summer that had persuaded Israeli authorities to reverse the additional security protocols at the Temple Mount, and he had consistently argued for a unified approach among all Palestinian factions.

"The drop in support for the Two State Solution is not real, not ideological," Samer said. "This is our work, to channel negative energy into something positive, to fix our internal struggle to get unity. The rising extremism in Palestinian society is disturbing. I don't believe what is bad for Israelis is good for Palestinians and vice versa. Extremism is bad for both people."

More than 1,700 young people had been trained in hundreds of Zimam workshops "to be able to build for the future," Samer said, learning strategies absorbed, at least partially, from Barack Obama's successful presidential campaigns. As a result of this training and organizing, Zimam members accounted for half of the members of the student council at Al Najar University, the largest in Palestine, with twenty-two thousand students.

Nevertheless, the ongoing crises in Syria, Iraq, and Lebanon were making it ever more difficult to secure grants as donors' priorities shifted, Samer admitted. Many funders were increasingly wary because there had been so little change on the West Bank. Anticipating that the foreign grants would evaporate, Samer boasted that 78 percent of his budget now came from local sources, including Palestinian tax revenues.

"The Europeans are questioning to what extent they are funding the status quo, a five-star occupation," Samer explained. "At some point, people will not be able to do it. Our internal resources are enough to fund what we need in this . . . do you call it a country? Or an entity?"

Dillon interjected at this point in the conversation to provide his personal endorsement of Zimam's activities. While he was still in Illinois, Dillon had worked with OneVoice, Zimam's principal funder, and saw how it was able to organize students from six area colleges, young Jews as well as Muslims. When he first expressed his interest in going to Ramallah, his father strongly recommended to Dillon that he work for Zimam. It was one of the few organizations with a truly progressive agenda, and it was in touch with young people in Palestine. One-half of the Palestinian population was under twenty-four, Dillon noted, half of whom were unaffiliated politically. Young Palestinians were attracted to Zimam exactly because they were frustrated with the corruption they perceived among older generations of Palestinian leaders, Dillon maintained.

"Living here every day, you can feel the occupation," Dillon said, "but when you go to Zimam events, you can forget the occupation. There's a whole new energy."

Samer agreed that endemic corruption had calcified the polit-ical system as well as the business sector, all of which left young people deeply frustrated. "The current situation is comfortable for everyone in politics," he said. "Why would they change it? Building pressure from the bottom up is the only way to make them change."

Samer's certainty about the efficacy of mass, nonviolent move-ments came from experience and evolution, he explained. Just fifteen years earlier, he had been involved in radical activity and had suffered the consequences. His mother had been born in Jaffa and been displaced from her home, so Samer had been raised with a refugee's sense of loss and injustice. At fifteen, he was imprisoned for six months for radical political activity, during which time he was tortured as well. Not long after this, he was imprisoned a second time for four months. The death of his father in 2006 and the birth of his son both prompted him to rethink his strategy for the future.

"She was a refugee," he said of his mother, "so I was a refu-gee. But when I started thinking of the future, I was freed from the burdens of the past. My father promised, 'Your days will be better than mine,' and when I had my son, I decided to work for the future. People here deserve better. We deserve a proper life."

His newfound support for the Two State Solution and nonvi-olent resistance led him to participate in numerous international events and to give a speech at Hebrew University. He felt he was remaining true to the Palestinian cause by acknowledging the futility of the armed struggle and the political and economic re-alities.

"We are captured by the history of the past," Samer said. "I didn't become a zionist and I will never become a zionist. I am a Palestinian, but I believe we can have a better future."

Samer's fiercest critics in those days were fellow Palestinians who accused him of "normalizing" relations with Israel, though he had no relationship with any Israeli organization. In some towns, his meetings were disrupted by gangs of thugs, but he had also experienced some of his greatest successes among those who had been radicalized as he once had. At one university, Samer said he faced particularly tough questioning from a young man from Nablus who had been incarcerated by the Israeli military for four years; sentenced to eleven years, he had been released early in a negotiated amnesty. In the end, that young man became a particularly successful Zimam advocate.

"The experience of prison is tough, bad, negative, and very destructive," Samer said. "But it is also a learning experience. You find yourself isolated from all your support, in a small room with small windows, crowded with youth leaders. Those who have this experience, when they become advocates, they become very strong advocates. If you show them what happens when they invest their energy in a positive direction, they change quickly. The accusation of normalization is very big, very serious in Palestine, but this is not normalization. We are ending the occupation instead of living with the occupation."

The United Nations and its affiliated international agencies were not allies in liberating the Palestinians from the occupation, Samer argued. Recently, international agencies had paid a lump sum to the Israeli electric utility to bail out the Palestinian government's debt, without paying for the construction of a separate Palestinian electric grid. In effect, the international donors had subsidized impunity and encouraged short-term thinking within the Palestinian government. Samer noted as well that the Palestinian Authority had allocated the largest share of its most recent budget, 35 percent, to security, with just 7 percent going to education and 1 percent to agriculture. The purchase of badly needed sewage-processing equipment had been delayed, but the authority had agreed to buy seven hundred new cars.

"The international donors allow refugees to not pay their electric bills, but there should be rule of law," Samer said. "We want to make sure this money is spent in the right place with the right person. International funding should go into infrastructure."

Even under the present circumstances, however, Samer prophesied, Palestinian entrepreneurs would thrive, since they had successfully grown their sector over the past two decades with relative autonomy.

"The donor economy is a house of cards, but now, the majority of the economy is not connected to NGOs, even though we are not investing in the right places," Samer said. "The private sector is leadership, and we need all components in Palestinian society. The whole situation needs to be rearranged."

With our time running short, Travis turned to Dillon and asked how his work in Ramallah was going.

When Travis last saw Dillon, he was running a recording studio on Chicago's West Side producing the work of young rappers. That section of the city has a notoriously high rate of homicides and other serious crimes, and Dillon saw his role there as helping African Americans broadcast messages that contested the stereotypes of their neighborhoods while directing a spotlight at discrimination and neglect from area institutions.

"Not only are these communities different from how they're presented," Dillon said, "I could use my voice as a white male to speak up for these people."

Nevertheless, when Dillon announced he was headed to Palestine, his co-workers responded with concern. "When I told people I was going to Ramallah, they asked, 'Isn't it a war zone?'"

Palestinians he met upon his arrival, meanwhile, questioned

him about his politics, in particular whether he supported President Trump.

"When I first got here, people said, 'Do you like Trump?' And I said, 'If I liked Trump, I wouldn't be living in Ramallah.'"

At Zimam, he found that he was useful as an American when it came to interpreting the requirements of grants or new information from the American government. He often saw parallels between his work here among Palestinians and what he had been doing on Chicago's West Side.

Travis pressed on, however, smiling mischievously as he asked Dillon about how his *other* project was going.

Dillon blushed slightly and said that he was making progress there, too. He turned to the rest of us again and said that he was courting a young Palestinian woman who lived in Ramallah. They'd met while she was earning a bachelor's degree in Chicago, and when she finished her degree and prepared to go back, he asked if he could go with her. She explained that her father wouldn't even consider him as a potential spouse unless he had a college degree, moved to Ramallah, got a job, and, most important, converted to Islam.

Highly motivated, Dillon had completed all of those steps over the previous two years, earning a B.A. in political science, and even changing his name to Adam when he converted to Islam, before arriving in Ramallah in December 2017 to start working at Zimam. It was a precarious situation as he had to leave the country every few months to renew his visa, and there was a real risk that Israeli authorities would block his reentry if they learned he was actually staying in Ramallah. But every time he entered Israel, Dillon felt awkward and longed to be back among Palestinians.

"I feel at home here. I identify with the Palestinian community," he said. "It's like you're in Switzerland, going into West Jerusalem."

We drove out of Ramallah through its bustling downtown, the streets lined with shops selling clothing, electronics, luggage, furniture, and housewares; restaurants serving falafel, fried chicken, and pizza; and a good number of delectable-looking bakeries offering sweet confections. The traffic and the crowds were thickest around Al Manara (Beacon) Square, a major intersection with a monument in its traffic circle, a stone pillar with four lions at its base. On the walls of a building dominating one corner were a few familiar-looking logos, green circles with white figures in silhouette inside, very similar to the Starbucks sign, but this was actually the Stars and Bucks Café, a popular spot for coffee and other drinks. Starbucks made a brief foray in Israel from 2001 to 2003, but pulled out amid stiff competition from local cafés and a cultural resistance to taking coffee to go in paper cups; Israelis generally preferred to linger with a ceramic cup. But global brands tended to shun the Palestinian territories, so a group of local businesspeople opened the "Stars and Bucks" chain to tap into the international conglomerate's established reputation.

The drivers and pedestrians packing the streets and the roundabout itself reflected a full range of Palestinian society: women in fashionable, patterned hijabs; men in T-shirts and jeans or suits, clean shaven with short haircuts, and often bristly mustaches. There were many women behind the wheels of cars, or walking alone or with their friends or talking on their cells. Of course, there were also street vendors of various types, with handcarts, pushcarts, and a few donkey-pulled conveyances, as well as stalls and tables vying for space with the flow of pedestrians and vehicles.

Rami planned on driving through the Qalandia checkpoint, and as we approached, we saw a retaining wall with a mural of young men in street clothes and makeshift military uniforms, kaffiyeh over their faces, slinging rocks at imaginary Israeli soldiers. Travis asked Rami to stop so he could take some photos, but Rami demurred, explaining that we were driving through the Qalandia Refugee Camp, established by the United Nations in the wake of the 1948 war, but now built up with permanent structures so that it is effectively a section of Ramallah. Israel insists Qalandia falls under their jurisdiction as a part of Jerusalem, but doesn't provide any municipal services in the area. Thus, many of the residents who were already poor, desperate, and politically radical saw their situation made even worse when Israel demolished a section of the neighborhood to make space for the separation wall, the checkpoint, and an accompanying military base. It was no place to tarry.

We drove on and reached the outer layer of the actual separation wall, the tall, concrete slabs of which were covered in art—militant, nationalistic, politically straightforward when compared with the ironic images in Bethlehem created by Banksy and other international artists. An enormous portrait of Yasser Arafat showed the Palestinian leader in his trademark kaffiyeh, a flock of birds and the waves of the ocean over his shoulder. Next to Arafat was an equally large painting of Marwan Barghouti, a popular Palestinian leader who had been imprisoned by Israel since 2002, his hands held forward in handcuffs over the words "Free Barghouti" in rectangular, three-dimensional letters. Secular but militant, Barghouti remained influential even from prison and was sometimes proposed as a potential leader for the new Palestinian state, someone who, if he was ever released, could check the aspirations of the Islamist Hamas.

The volume of cars approaching the Qalandia checkpoint

slowed to a crawl, and Rami grew concerned. Palestinian cars were, for the most part, not allowed in Israel, so almost all the cars had yellow Israeli license plates and were driven by Palestinians who lived in East Jerusalem and worked in the West Bank, not quite citizens but with more mobility than those under military control.

Still, the checkpoints could become a bottleneck, and upon checking WhatsApp, Rami found that the current wait was forty-five minutes and could easily rise to one hour or two. Instead, he suggested we go around Qalandia to another checkpoint near the settlement of Pisgat Ze'ev. It would leave us on the other side of Jerusalem, but we were headed to Tel Aviv anyway.

Of course, we deferred to Rami's expertise, and he took the Mercedes taxi out of the queue for the checkpoint and onto a side road that was totally open. We were continuing along the separation wall under armored watchtowers, but the cars flowed briskly.

As we progressed, I noticed a group of four or five young men in a half-built structure to our right, all wearing black T-shirts and gathering rocks. On our left, I saw an Israeli military jeep stop and several heavily armed soldiers get out, taking up positions around the vehicle.

The truck ahead of us slowed, and as we decelerated, the young men advanced toward the soldiers with rocks in their hands, using the taxi to shield their movements. A moment later, Rami saw an open lane and pressed down on the gas pedal so that we sped out of the scene, watching the young men advance on the soldiers through the Mercedes' rear window.

We reached the Pisgat Ze'ev checkpoint quickly from there. There was no line, thankfully, the gate was up, and we passed through with barely a nod from the soldier inside his booth.

Rami smiled broadly. "We were lucky," he said. "Sometimes, they close the checkpoints for hours, just because."

Diane asked if the checkpoints closed because of actual terrorist threats, or if it was the broader political situation.

Rami shrugged. Sometimes it was for a real security threat, but Israelis had a broad definition of what constituted a danger. "The checkpoints all close when there are Jewish holidays," he said, to cite one example.

The road around Pisgat Ze'ev was quiet, almost eerily so after the clamor and chaos of Qalandia. On a bend, Rami pointed up at a picturesque hilltop and told me, "That's the Psagot settlement. You told me you were there, right?"

A few minutes later, we entered Jerusalem's outermost Jewish neighborhoods, in an area that was contested by Palestinians and their international supporters, but which now featured row after row of neat, solidly built town homes and bungalows housing Israeli Jews. From there, it was just a few minutes more until Rami found the on-ramp to the main highway back to Tel Aviv.

30

RAMI

On our last full day together in Israel, Rami picked up Diane, Travis, and me in Tel Aviv in the morning for a tour of Jericho, the Dead Sea, and East Jerusalem.

It was a little over an hour's drive to Jericho, but a steep descent toward the Dead Sea, where it was distinctly hotter and more humid. Just before the entrance to the city was a large sign with white letters in English, Hebrew, and Arabic against a red background warning that past this point, we would be in "Area A," which was under the control of the Palestinian Authority: "Entrance For Israeli Citizens Is Forbidden, Dangerous To Your Lives And Is Against Israeli Law." There were clashes between Palestinian protesters and the IDF in both Hebron and Nablus that day, and the checkpoint before Jericho looked as if it had been attacked recently, with black soot stains on the road as well as on some of the concrete pillars. But it was unmanned, and we drove straight into town without seeing any soldiers.

Rami was proud that Jericho was the first city to go under Palestinian control in 1994, and he took us first to the Tell es-Sultan, a UNESCO archaeological site on a man-made hilltop that includes ruins from twenty-three layers of the city's long history. Freshwater springs and excellent soil have attracted human habitation in Jericho since the tenth millennium B.C.E., making it

arguably the first town on Earth, and also giving its fruit a distinctive, sweet flavor, especially the dates and pomegranates. At
a nearly empty tourist center, we drank delicious fresh-squeezed
juice and shopped for Dead Sea–related products but declined the
persistent pleading from the owner of a camel to go for a mounted
tour.

From Jericho, it was just a few minutes' drive to the Dead
Sea, the lowest body of water on Earth, where we stopped at one
of the public beaches. Called the Salt Sea in Hebrew, its water is
thick with minerals, and though it was midwinter at the time of
this visit and not exactly balmy, there were many tourists bobbing
on the oily surface, mostly heavyset, Russian-speaking senior citizens. Others were smearing themselves with mud drawn from the
sea, which is said to have therapeutic qualities.

The landscape around the sea was spectacularly barren, nearly
devoid of any plants and resembling another planet, with sharp-
edged, dune-colored rocks twisted into bizarre shapes by the hot,
salty winds. We found a vantage point to take some photos and
tried to take a photo all together by putting our phones in selfie
mode, but we weren't successful at finding an angle that included
us all in the frame with the sea in the background.

Luckily, just at that moment, a minivan pulled up next to
us and parked, and out came a father, mother, and two young
children.

I approached them and asked the man if he might take our
photo, and he obliged, smilingly.

He took a few excellent photos of the four of us, arm in arm,
the pale, turquoise water stretching out behind us, and we chatted
politely afterward. The man was from the United States originally, but the woman was from Switzerland and the couple now
lived there in a small town where they found it advantageous to
raise their children. They'd chosen Israel as a tourist destination

but had done very little research about the country before they left, and had booked a hotel on Ha Yarkon Street in Tel Aviv on the Mediterranean shore. They'd come to the Dead Sea at the suggestion of the hotel's concierge and asked us if there was any-where else they should visit.

"I'm sure you're already planning on going to Jerusalem," I said.

The man frowned. "Oh no," he answered. "The concierge told us it was very dangerous there."

I was incredulous. "Dangerous in Jerusalem? There are mil-lions of visitors every year."

"I live in Jerusalem," Rami added. "It is a wonderful city. You and your family will be very safe."

Diane said she felt very comfortable in Jerusalem as a mature woman and urged them not to miss the opportunity to see the Old City and its historic sites.

The man was unconvinced, however, and his wife was ada-mant that they could not risk exposing their children to a terror attack.

Nevertheless, we parted amiably, bidding them good travels.

From there, we drove a few kilometers inland through the rocky landscape toward one particular plateau, Masada, where King Herod had built a palace, and where Judean rebels later constructed a fortress. According to Josephus, the first-century C.E. Judean military leader who defected to the Romans and subsequently wrote a widely cited history of the Jewish Revolt, Masada was a redoubt for a particularly radical group known as the Sicarii, who resisted a siege by Roman forces for months, and then committed mass suicide as the legions were about to break in. After the Roman expulsion, the mountaintop was used as a Byzantine church for a time, but was otherwise unoccupied until the late 1950s, when Israel's state archaeologists arrived to test Josephus's account. Those archaeologists and their fellows found considerable evidence contradicting Josephus, but by then the legend of Masada was already woven into Israel's national narrative as the moment that ended Jewish sovereignty for nearly two millennia. A few years later, Masada was opened as a tourist site, and it was also used to swear in new members of the IDF's armored corps, who finished their oath with the phrase "Masada shall not fall again."

We considered hiking the seven hundred steps that snaked up to the mountaintop, but chose instead to take the gondola, which brought us soaring over the mountain's jagged cliffs in a packed cable car to a rickety dock. On the mountaintop, we joined the tourists and uniformed soldiers walking through the partially re-constructed chambers in the palace-fortress, imagining the Jew-ish rebels looking down with increasing dread while the Romans assiduously built up a ramp to storm the defenses.

After Masada, we drove on, and made it to East Jerusalem in ninety minutes to have dinner at one of Rami's favorite spots for shawarma, followed by dessert at a nearby pastry shop, a special kanefa that he had promised to Diane. We sat outside in the cool night air next to a few other tables with women in hijabs eating ice cream and cakes. Diane, Travis, and I scarfed down the kanefa—delicious, though a tad oversweet—while Rami smoked Marlboros and told us about the neighborhood, his career, and his hopes for his family.

His true name was Abd al Shayer, though he had gone by Rami since childhood. His grandfather, a native of Syria, bought a home in the vicinity of the Mount of Olives in Jerusalem in 1912. Though this meant Rami's family had been in the area for over a century, they were considered newcomers compared with their neighbors, many of whose ancestors had been in Jerusalem for dozens of generations.

Growing up, Rami had wanted to be an engineer and was an excellent student, but his brother, a chef for the Israeli ambassador to the United Nations in New York City, invited Rami to work alongside him. He learned every aspect of kitchen work and enjoyed New York very much. After a short time, though, his brother had a dispute with the ambassador, and they came back home to Jerusalem.

He secured a job as a chef specializing in Italian food at Jerusalem's Waldorf Astoria Hotel and wore his hair long and slicked back, "also Italian-style," he said with a wry smile.

Rami had many girlfriends in the kitchen of the hotel, including one Syrian woman whose family lived in Riyadh, Saudi Arabia, who spoke Arabic with a particularly sweet accent.

"Sometimes, I still make pasta for my kids and speak to them in that sweet way, which they like very much," Rami said.

His worldly experiences notwithstanding, he found a woman from a conservative Jerusalem family when he decided to get married and approached her properly. He first saw his future wife across the aisle at an uncle's wedding, and they married after a brief courtship.

His wife, a nurse, worked many hours while still finding time to care for their children and maintain their household.

"I greatly appreciate her, really," Rami said, earnestly.

They had five children together, ages nine to twenty at the time. The three oldest were girls, the eldest of whom was studying to become a doctor at medical school in Bethlehem.

"I don't have hope for myself anymore," Rami said. "It's over for me, but I do have hope for my children."

He showed us photos of his family, his wife and three daughters in white hijabs and his two young boys in miniature suits with short haircuts. When I asked if he considered himself religious, he smiled, shook his head, and said no. He took his mother to Saudi Arabia for the hajj, he said, and went to the mosque regularly for one month afterward, but then stopped and hadn't gone back since his mother passed away.

Working as a driver provided an inconsistent income, dependent on not only the season but also the political situation. Still, Rami said he enjoyed the job's cosmopolitan aspects, not least meeting tourists from different parts of the world. He recalled securing a minivan so that he could drive a group of African American Christians to different religious sites in Hebron, Bethlehem, Jerusalem, and at the Sea of Galilee. The whole group was tall and heavyset, Rami recalled, and they prayed passionately before eating meals.

Rami also liked working alongside other drivers from different backgrounds. One of his best friends, for example, was a Circassian, a member of a mostly Muslim people who were expelled by the Russian Empire from their homeland in the Caucasus Mountains during the eighteenth and nineteenth centuries and then absorbed by the Ottomans, who gave them homes throughout their Middle Eastern dominions in what is now Israel, Lebanon, Syria, and Jordan. Rami compared the Circassians to the Druze and Bedouins, in that they practice Islam a little differently, live in different places, do not intermarry with Palestinians or any other group, and have a history of serving in Israel's military and police.

And when they do opt to serve in the IDF or the various law enforcement agencies, Rami said, "they are even meaner than Jewish Israelis."

Palestinian elites were corrupt and dissolute, as far as Rami was concerned, so in terms of politics, he supported moderate Islamists and was an admirer of the Muslim Brotherhood in Egypt, though he could not endorse the militants of Hamas in Gaza, who were engaged in a futile struggle, he felt, one that just left more Palestinians dead. Still, he understood the rage that drove the violence, and didn't have much optimism for the future. Violence from one side or the other was inevitable, he lamented, and the consequences were that people on both sides would grow angry and attack one another, perpetuating the cycle. In his fifty-some years, he had already seen two intifadas and innumerable clashes, army raids, and terror attacks.

"When something bad happens," Rami said, "we forget about all the good years that we lived together in peace."

It was already late when we made it back to Tel Aviv, and we expressed our gratitude to Rami, bidding him a fond farewell. Diane and Travis were scheduled to fly out to Miami the next evening, Thursday, February 8, while I planned to stay through the weekend to spend time with my mother and Gabi.

The next day, Diane wanted to spend her last hours before the flight stretching her legs walking through Tel Aviv, and we soon found ourselves at the Carmel Market. She was in her element examining the market's eclectic offerings—fresh fruit and vegetables, prepared food, candy, clothes, records, costume jewelry, and souvenirs—and bought a few pieces of baklava to eat on the plane.

At the bottom of the market near the bus station, we prepared to hike into Jaffa and paused in front of a strawberry vendor, a bushy-haired man in his early thirties, who urged me to buy a basket.

They were beautiful, plump, and bright red. "Are they sweet?" I asked him.

"The sweetest," he answered, his confidence unwavering.

"Can I try one?"

He was reluctant. "Are you really going to buy some?"

"Well, I can't, really," I confessed, pointing to Diane and Travis. "My friends are leaving today, and I'm flying out in a couple of days myself."

The vendor relaxed and began chatting. He asked me, "Where are you flying?"

"The United States," I told him. "Them to Miami. Me to Chicago."

He nodded. "How long does it take to get there?"

"About eleven hours, twelve or more if you are going to Los Angeles or anywhere on the West Coast."

He nodded again. "Why don't you take some strawberries. It's a long trip."

He reached into his pile and placed a half dozen in my palms.

"Thank you very much," I told him. "Very kind of you."

"Have a good trip," he said, waving.

I distributed the strawberries to Diane and Travis. They were a little underripe, in truth, but I savored what sweetness there was.

31

<u>ERAN</u>

I returned to Israel that August of 2018 for three more weeks, this time with my ten-year-old son. I tried to give him a version of the kind of visits I'd made at his age, which is to say dragging the poor kid about to various relatives, family friends, and "important" sites. He also had plenty of time with his extended family, accompanying his grandmother to her swimming club, playing video games with his cousins, and, when he could stand the heat, playing soccer outside.

We oriented ourselves around Katznelson and Weizmann Streets, main thoroughfares that spanned the Rambam section of Givatayim, where we soon had a favorite French café to eat breakfast, a fresh-squeezed juice stand where I daily got a pomegranate/cantaloupe/orange concoction from a curmudgeonly middle-aged attendant, and several places that served pizza, both triangular slices and squares. We visited one particular corner store frequently enough that the clerk stashed a few liter bottles of still water at the back of the refrigerator to keep them cold for us. Gabi introduced us to the owner of a small sporting goods store that specialized in soccer, where we discussed the latest equipment as well as developments with the top players of all the major European teams. Inside the Givatayim Mall on the corner of Weizmann and Yitzhak Rabin Road, we found a pretzel maker equipped with a little oven that allowed him to bake his twisted dough on order, which always came out hot and delicious.

We adapted to the family's schedule, whose work and school week began on Sunday, or "Day One" in Hebrew, and ended Friday at noon, as everyone prepared for the Shabbat. The cafés and pubs filled up for a few hours as people left work, but by sundown on Friday, everything was shut down in the Jewish parts of Israel, even in secular Givatayim, and most families gathered together for the evening meal. Businesses and services remained closed until the late afternoon Saturday, a shutdown that was more widely and rigorously observed than, say, Christmas or Easter in the United States.

Stopping in at Nahalat Yitzhak Cemetery, we found a half-dozen Haredi men and boys gathered at the Shtefanisher's tomb, led by a youngish rabbi with a thick, black beard. The annual memorial festival had been held several weeks earlier, but the enthusiasm for the Rebbe lingered, and we took our turns putting our hands on the tomb and placing a few coins in the *tzedakah* box.

My son grew close to Nira's now fourteen-year-old son, Roe, who was on his summer break from middle school, and on a free weekday, I conscripted both of them to accompany me to the Western Wall in Jerusalem. We took the bus from the Arlozorov station and arrived in Jerusalem on schedule less than an hour later.

Outside the bus station, I found the old scholar sitting on his stool, and squatted in front of him. "Hello rabbi, how are you today? I brought my nephew and my son from America," I told him.

The old man looked at me pityingly. "America is a fine place," he said, "but you really should come to Israel. This is where everything good happens, where miracles happen. But that said, I wish for you a happy and prosperous new year."

It was still over a month away from the new year on the Jewish calendar, but Rosh Hashana begins the Ten Days of Awe, which ends with Yom Kippur, the Day of Atonement, and is soon followed by the fall holiday of Sukkot, a month of ritual and celebration that the old soothsayer was already anticipating.

He asked me my father's name, and then said a prayer for me before sending us on our way.

I insisted over the boys' protests that we walk along Jaffa Street rather than ride the light rail to the Old City, and by the time we made it to the Mahane Yehudah Market, they were hungry, so we went to lunch at Pasta Basta before moving on.

We reached the Jaffa Gate and passed through the market on the way to the Western Wall complex, placing our own notes in the cracks and visiting the chambers underneath Wilson's Arch. The boys listened patiently to my lecture about the history of the Temple Mount, and why the Western Wall was located just beneath the Dome of the Rock.

We were all tired by the time we emerged from the Old City, and I gladly consented to taking the light rail back to the central bus station. The boys napped in their seats on the ride home and declined my attempt to rouse them when the bus drove by the Elvis Inn.

At the Arlozorov Terminal, they likewise insisted we take a cab home despite the thick traffic. We got into the first cab in the queue, and I spoke with the driver, who introduced himself as Eran—thin, clean shaven, bristle-short haircut, and gold-rimmed aviator sunglasses—about the dangers of the motorized bicycles darting all around us.

Two days later, I dragged the boys to the Tikva (Hope) Market in South Tel Aviv, which Roe recommended as "more authentic" than the Carmel Market. It had been founded by neighborhood residents in the 1930s—Yemenite, Iraqi, Syrian, and Iranian Jews—after clashes with Arabs in nearby Yafo cut off access to those markets. Renovated in 2005, the Tikva Market featured low prices and a no-frills atmosphere that continued to attract working people and senior citizens, Jews as well as Arabs, along with recent Jewish immigrants and those from Africa buying groceries and housewares. The vendors at this *shuq* accepted only cash, however, and I spent all of mine on a half-dozen plump, ripe mangos, bags of snacks, olives of several different varieties, and baklava. Only on our way out, unfortunately, did I notice a Bukharan bakery, a Yemenite restaurant, and a hummus spot, all of which looked delectable.

"Next time," I vowed.

We carried my purchases to the bus stop, but after waiting a half hour in the heat, Roe helpfully reminded me that I could use one of my credit cards to pay for a taxi. Just then, as luck would have it, a cab passed by. We hailed it, got in, and I immediately recognized the driver as Eran, who had picked us up at the bus station two days earlier.

"I'm glad we ran into you," I told him. "We were going to be late to my mother's for dinner."

"I know what you mean," Eran said. "Mothers always treat you like you are a baby. I'm forty-two, and not married yet, so my mother is always in my business."

Boasting of the mangos I bought, I asked him if he ever went to the Tikva Market.

"All the time," he answered. "The Tikva is a *real* market."

We drove along Moshe Dayan Road past new developments of glass and steel that alternated with the old concrete blocks.

"Tel Aviv has become kind of a wondrous city, don't you think?" I asked him.

He frowned a bit underneath the aviator sunglasses. "I was born in this city, and if you ask me," he answered, "I liked the old Tel Aviv better, when air-conditioning was a luxury, toys were expensive, and kids made up their own games."

32

BENNY BROWN

I was back on the bus to Jerusalem a couple of days later with plans to meet the scholar Benjamin "Benny" Brown, one of the world's foremost academic experts on Haredim, with whom my friend Nathaniel Deutsch had recommended I speak. On my own this time, I got on a #480 in the Arlozorov station and found a window seat, but it was a busy time, and the bus filled up quickly. An elegantly overdressed woman in a black wool dress and stockings, her hair fashionably bobbed, took the seat next to me. Pale and a bit damp in the heat, she anxiously retrieved her cell phone from her purse, a black, fake-leather bag that matched her dress.

Alternating between Russian and heavily accented Hebrew, she had a series of intense conversations with what seemed like all of her closest relatives and friends about the meat she was planning to serve that evening at dinner. What kind of meat would be best? What quantity? Which butcher should she get it from? With each call, she grew more frantic and was strangely furious as she listed the merits of each butcher before calculating whether she would have enough time to reach them. When we finally reached Jerusalem's central station, she practically jumped out of her seat.

I passed through the security check unhindered and steered my way through the crowds in the bus station until I got out onto Jaffa Street. The old holy man was seated on his stool as usual, but this time, I had to wait my turn while he gave an extended consultation to a woman in a turban. Behind her, a young man who appeared to be her son waited impatiently, tapping his feet and glaring into his phone, demonstrably standing far enough away that he couldn't actually hear the advice being dispensed. Though dressed in Haredi style, with a white shirt, black suit, and hat, he was clean shaven and looked at his more stolidly traditional mother with embarrassment while she conversed with the holy man. When his exasperation boiled over, he tapped her on the shoulder and insisted it was time to go. My turn.

I knelt down in front of the old man to greet him. He asked me if I was married and was pleased when I answered that I was. He wished me "Peace, love, and prosperity in the new year," and I wished him a happy new year as well.

I found a municipal bus to the National Library easily enough, and rode along through dense urban neighborhoods for just a few kilometers until we reached Givat Ram, an area of large, mostly concrete buildings built in modernist style surrounded by ample green space that included the Knesset, the Supreme Court, the Albert Einstein Institute of Mathematics, and the Israel Museum, among other institutions, as well as one of Hebrew University's several campuses. It was still the university's summer break, so the bus and the streets were uncrowded, and within a few minutes, I arrived at the library, which stood directly opposite the Jerusalem Academy of Dance and Music, and adjacent to several Hebrew University dormitories. Partially concealed amid tall cypress, palms, pines, and even a few imported sequoia trees, the library was an impressive rectangular structure built into a ridge with glass walls on the lower floors.

Benny had suggested we meet in the library's cafeteria on the ground floor, an illustrious meeting place for intellectuals, he mentioned, and I had arrived about forty-five minutes early, with plenty of time to survey the scene. It was still early for lunch, but the seating area inside was already full, each table taken up by people in deep conversation. One-half of the men, at least, were wearing kippot and I heard as much English as Hebrew, though there were many other languages as well. There were many Palestinian men and women here, too, some seated together and others with Jews and foreign students.

Noticing an attractive patio outside, I went to investigate. This, too, was full, with what appeared to be a class in the ancient Semitic language of Ugaritic in one corner, and smaller groups taking up the remaining tables and benches. For all its charm, the patio reeked of cat urine, and I could see a half-dozen cats running around, playing, fighting, and slipping in and out of the cafeteria at will. In one spot against the wall, someone had helpfully set up some water bowls and dishes that had bones and other remnants of food left for the cats.

I decided to get some refreshments and try my luck at a place to sit afterward and ventured inside the cafeteria, which was protected by an unshaven, middle-aged security guard, a pistol holstered at his hip, who checked everyone's bag and even asked for some people's ID cards. He looked at me carefully in the eyes, but waved me through.

I looked through the entire menu of soups, sandwiches, and other lunches before deciding in the end on a *bourekas,* a phyllo dough pastry that was a ubiquitous, savory treat here, and a cappuccino from the self-serve machine. Next to the coffee, I found a dispenser of the granular brown sugar that I preferred in the United States, but which was rare in Israel, and spooned some into my cappuccino. A tiny woman with her hair cut bristle short was refilling the other sugar dispensers, and I commented to her as I replaced the brown sugar container, "This is the best sugar."

She looked away in disgust.

"I have to disagree with you," she said, firmly. "That sugar clumps and sticks."

I laughed nervously, and said, "OK. Point taken."

She looked at me fiercely, however, refusing to break off until I had walked away with my *bourekas* and coffee.

I grabbed a table as soon as one became vacant and sat down, greedily devouring the greasy *bourekas,* which was filled with farmer's cheese, while I eavesdropped on the tables nearby. At one, a Jewish man with a kippah and a thick, unruly beard was holding forth in Arabic to two Arab women in hijabs that matched their long-sleeved, ankle-length coats. At another, a young Israeli graduate student and her American colleague, both in short skirts and short-sleeved shirts, compared their workloads in English and chartered out the careers they wished for.

Professor Brown soon arrived, middle-aged but clean shaven and with a youthful smile under his kippah, and sat down, genially insisting I call him "Benny."

We spent a few minutes getting acquainted, and I summarized for Benny the Haredi sites and events I'd already attended—the Breslover *shul* in Mea She'arim and the Shtefanisher Rebbe's memorial—adding that I still planned on visiting Bnai Brak, the Haredi city next to Tel Aviv, about which Benny had written extensively. I described the public notices I'd seen in Haredi communities reproaching anyone who might use a "forbidden device" to access the Internet, but I surmised the rapid growth of Haredi families also meant a growing demand for jobs, education, and access to the broader world. With all of these internal and external pressures for change, I asked Benny, did the Haredim constitute a force for pluralism in Israel, or divisiveness?

"That depends on your point of view," he answered.

Haredim were in a constant battle to maintain their integrity in the face of massive generational shifts, while their leadership consisted of dynastic rabbinical courts that were often ill equipped—and sometimes ill informed—when it came to guiding their people.

"They are always trying not to lose their basic solidarity," Benny explained. "It continuously feels like they are walking a tightrope. It feels dangerous."

The tension over Haredi leaders' efforts to insulate themselves from the financial and personal motivations to open up to the world was evident in the *pashkevelin*. That so many of these public notices were dedicated to trying to stop Haredim from using cell phones, tablets, and laptops was, contrapositively, an indication of just how common use of these devices was by now. As in any other community, Haredim relied on these devices for work, school, communication with family, entertainment, and, inevitably, accessing news and information.

"Many old-school Haredim still want to stop everyone from using the Internet," he said, "but young people all have their iPads."

Benny's interest in Haredim stemmed from growing up in Bnai Brak. Founded in 1924, Bnai Brak was originally conceived as a religious city and, in its first decades, was politically aligned with religious zionists, rather than the secular-socialist zionists who held the majority in the rest of the country. Haredim who had survived the Shoah later gathered in Bnai Brak as well, especially the Lithuanian branch of the movement, known as Misnagedim, who rebuilt their synagogues as they reconstituted their families, growing in numbers as well as in political confidence. Within Bnai Brak, Haredim increased public pressure for businesses and public institutions to close on Shabbat and for nonkosher establishments, or those deemed to be promoting immodest behavior, to close altogether. Observant, though not actually Haredi,

Benny's family stayed through the transition, adapting to the life-style changes even as many secular families left Bnai Brak for other towns and cities within Israel.

In 1977, when the Likud party won a majority in the Knesset for the first time, Menachem Begin became prime minister and Haredi leaders became a significant component of the government for the first time. Where previously, they had lobbied behind the scenes, they now explicitly demanded increased funding for their schools and exemptions from military service for young Haredi men and women, and put forward an agenda for imposing strict observance of Shabbat on all Israelis, including the shutdown of public transportation and other services, as well as separation of men and women in public.

"It was a stormy time," Benny recalled. "The country was asking, 'Who are these strange people?'"

Benny studied at yeshivot, but also at Hebrew University, where he focused on philosophy and earned a law degree, practicing as an attorney for just one year before returning to academia. He wrote his master's thesis on Da'at Torah, a popular concept among Haredim that the wisdom of great Torah scholars also extends to politics and even to personal matters instead of just religious issues. The paper was published as his first book.

"It was really about the Haredi concept of leadership," Benny said.

In his subsequent works, he has discussed developments in Jewish law, utilizing his knowledge of secular law, while chronicling the lives of some of the most significant rabbis. He won multiple accolades—and generated a fair amount of controversy as well—for his 2011 biography of the Chazon Ish, a seminal figure in rebuilding Haredi institutions in Israel after the Shoah.

Revered among Haredim for his great scholarship and humility, the Chazon Ish's name was Avraham Yeshaya Karelitz, but he was referred to by the title of his magnum opus, which translates as "The Vision of Man." Lithuanian born, he arrived in Israel in 1933, when he was already in his midfifties, held no title at any yeshiva or synagogue, wrote very few publications, and had no children, yet he became Israel's foremost authority on Jewish law and a role model for other Haredi leaders. Generally opposed to the formation of the State of Israel, the Chazon Ish endorsed a protest in April 1948, during the run-up to the Declaration of Establishment, encouraging Haredi Jews to go out in the streets and wave white flags and call for peace with the Arabs.

Nevertheless, he acquiesced to the state's existence after it was established and, in 1952, met with Israel's first prime minister, David Ben-Gurion, in his modest apartment in Bnai Brak, where they debated the status of Haredi Jews. Citing a story about two camels in the desert, one carrying a burden and the other unencumbered, the Chazon Ish argued passionately that yeshiva students and Haredi women should be exempt from military service, comparing Haredim with the camel toting the burden of the spiritual health of Israel. Ben-Gurion retorted that it was secular Israelis who were actually the ones carrying the burden—the military defense of the nation, the integration of new immigrants, and the construction of state infrastructure. Still, he agreed to extend the exemptions to IDF service for yeshiva students.

Benny's book on the Chazon Ish provided a detailed historical biography and a thorough analysis of his teachings as well as a detailed exploration of the much storied meeting with Ben-Gurion, charting his overall influence on Haredim and beyond.

Benny explained that the prevailing attitude about Haredim among elites in government and the academy during Israel's first few decades was that they were an atavism, one that would soon be absorbed by the secular mainstream. Perhaps for this reason, not until the 1970s was there any serious scholarship on Haredim. Not even the Central Bureau of Statistics kept track of the number of Haredim. So when Israel's first prime minister set a precedent by exempting yeshiva students from military service, Ben-Gurion was taking this step because he didn't think the numbers would ever be significant.

"Ben-Gurion imagined the Haredim would disappear," Benny explained.

One of the first scholars to chronicle the most significant personages of Israeli Haredim, Benny was able to get rare access from family members and institutions. The esteemed, elderly Torah scholar Chaim Kanievsky answered his questions on postcards, writing four-word answers in tiny letters, while Rabbi Shmaryahu Yosef Nissim Karelitz, the influential chief judge of the rabbinical court of Bnai Brak and the nephew of the Chazon Ish, invited Benny for a rare face-to-face interview.

Haredim were, in general, deeply suspicious of the academy, and there was a vast difference between the public reception for his books and the private one. Benny's biography of the Chazon Ish was the subject of two articles in the main Lithuanian Haredi newspaper, scathing reviews expressing outrage that he would apply modern historical techniques to a figure of such clear irreproachability. They were furious that Benny dared to analyze poetry written by the Chazon Ish when he was a young man, verse that revealed doubts about his own faith, and the fact that the book mentioned the sage's wife, who, in earlier years, had supported the family by working a menial job. Such critics were also upset that Benny included the Chazon Ish's studies of science and mathematics, and his recommendations that other Jews do the same, since Haredi school curricula had come to de-emphasize the study of math, science, and history in favor of properly religious topics. No question the biography's reminder that the Chazon Ish had studied "secular" subjects extensively was decidedly unwelcome.

"They saw it as diminishing the Chazon Ish," Benny said.

Criticism notwithstanding, Benny's publisher believed the book would find readers among at least the more open-minded Haredim and committed funds to advertise in Haredi publications accordingly. Indeed, the book sold well among Haredim, and Benny continued to receive emails and telephone calls from Haredi readers even six years after publication.

Benny offered to give me a tour of the National Library before I left, and I happily agreed. The entrance hall featured an artistically designed time line that narrated the library's history: its collection dated back to 1892, when the local lodge of the international Jewish philanthropy B'nai B'rith—led by Eliezer Ben-Yehuda, the Hebrew linguist and great-grandfather of Gil Hovav—opened a public library which they named the Midrash Abarbanel, in honor of Isaac Abarbanel, the fifteenth-century Portuguese Sephardic Jewish scholar. The Abarbanel Library soon moved to a new building and rapidly accumulated donations, including at least ten thousand books sent from the Russian imperial city of Bialystok by Dr. Josef Chasanowich, an early disciple of Theodor Herzl, the nineteenth-century Austro-Hungarian founder of European zionism.

Adopted by Hebrew University, the library moved its collection to new facilities built on Mount Scopus in 1925, but when that area was encircled by the Jordanian military during the 1948 war, the books were stashed in several locations, including warehouses in other neighborhoods. The library's holdings by then numbered more than one million volumes. Not mentioned on the time line was that the collection included thousands of books and periodicals that had been taken from vacant Arab homes. From the perspective of the library employees who found them, these books had been rescued from looting and destruction, but to the families who fled their homes during the fighting, the books were stolen from them by the State of Israel.

The building in which we were standing was built specially for the library in 1960. Benny led me up a flight of stairs into a large room on the first floor, a lecture hall the back wall of which was dominated by an enormous, three-panel stained glass window, "Isaiah's Vision of Eternal Peace," by Mordecai Ardon. On the left, the panel depicted a night sky filled with stars, planets, and the Moon over a tangle of roads representing the paths to Jerusalem taken by different nations. Each road has a quotation in a different script, Latin, Greek, or Arabic, from the section of the Book of Isaiah, in which the prophet describes a future of global peace between the nations. The center panel portrays the sky over Jerusalem in a gorgeous range of reds with a bright blue Tree of Sefirot in the middle, a kabbalistic symbol also known as the Tree of Life. At the panel's bottom, the walls of the city were depicted as inscribed with Hebrew script through the passage of Isaiah—the very words that had been found on the ancient parchment scrolls found near the Dead Sea. On the right panel, guns, shells, and tanks are crushed into a heap at the bottom, only to be re-formed as shovels and spades reaching up into the blue sky, bringing life to Isaiah's prophecy of peaceful transformation: "swords into ploughshares and their spears into pruning hooks."

Ardon finished the windows after four years of work, in 1984, when he was eighty-eight years old and Israel was recovering from the brutal war in Lebanon. Born in a Polish shtetl as one of twelve children in an impoverished family, Ardon had fled his home after his bar mitzvah at thirteen, becoming a student of the renowned painter Paul Klee in Berlin before finding his way to Israel in 1933. Like many of the artists who ended up in Israel in those years, Ardon felt a deep familiarity and connection with the place that drew on his religious upbringing but was haunted by the memories of the world he left behind after it was destroyed during the Shoah.

On the same floor as Ardon's windows was the Gershom Scholem Library, named for the brilliant, German-born scholar who applied historical and scientific methods to studying the Kabbalah and other texts of Jewish mysticism. A Hebrew University professor from 1933 to 1965, Scholem built a personal library that now forms the core of the National Library's extensive collection on these topics, and Benny thumbed through a few volumes on the shelves to show me the scholar's own annotations written in the margins in tiny, meticulous script. He went on to show me a climate-controlled room that held handwritten papers from Albert Einstein, who was a patron of the library.

The building's hub, however, was the general reading room, a massive chamber with hundreds of desks on the main floor and on the mezzanine, with expansive reference desks that had designated stations for periodicals in Hebrew and Arabic, Hebrew literature, Islamic texts, and books on many other topics. The reading room was very busy, with most of the desks filled by a seeming cross section of Israel's population all seated in front of a wide array of books, magazines, and newspapers. But it was also an intensely quiet place, where we were quickly shushed for even daring to whisper.

Outside, Benny added that the library also housed maps of Israel and other locations going back to the fifteenth century, an unparalleled collection of Israeli and Yiddish music, and the papers of Jewish artists ranging from the famous (including Franz Kafka) to the obscure, to non-Jewish figures like Isaac Newton, who had been deeply interested in Jewish mystical traditions. All of it would be moved soon, when the National Library received a brand-new building being built nearby, a larger, technologically sophisticated facility adjacent to the Knesset constructed with philanthropic support from the Rothschild family and others. Ground had been broken for the new library in 2016.

As we finished the tour of the library, Benny returned to our conversation about the role of Haredim in Israel. Referring to the left-of-center newspaper favored by secular Israelis, Benny quipped: "If you read the pages of *Haaretz,* you'd think the secular community is a tiny, besieged minority." But for all of secular Israelis' loudly expressed worries about Haredi threats to their lifestyles, surely the library was an indication that they themselves were still very much in charge. For here was a well-endowed, world-class public institution that incorporated Jewish history, literature, and religious texts among its collections, locating Jews and Judaism among the world's most significant religions while elevating Israel to the first rank of nations when it comes to institutions dedicated to scientific research and intellectual achievement.

33

PONEVEZH

Inspired by Benny Brown's description of Bnai Brak, I reserved a full afternoon the following Thursday to visit the Ponevezh Yeshiva, one of the essential institutions of the Haredi world. To get there from Givatayim, I had only to take a twenty-five-minute bus ride from the busy corner of Weizmann and Katznelson, near the French café and the late-night sundry store where I regularly bought cold liter bottles of water.

The bus rolled up Katznelson and wound its way through main boulevards and narrow streets lined with the same three- and four-story concrete buildings, some with space for businesses on the ground floor, but mostly just apartments. The border with Bnai Brak was unmarked, and, unlike Mea She'arim in Jerusalem, there was no gate, no signage warning tourists to dress modestly, and no difference in the architecture of the buildings or the layout of the streets.

Stepping off the bus, I walked in the direction of the yeshiva. It was the last weekday evening before the Shabbat began at sundown Friday, and pedestrians were out and about, including many young families pushing strollers and children racing through the streets on various wheeled toys, everyone dressed in Haredi style. There were fewer businesses generally and no cafés or bars, nor public parks or other spaces, except for small schools and day care facilities. I knew I was close to the yeshiva, but the number of pedestrians thinned out, so when I saw a lone Haredi man on the corner, I asked him if I was headed in the right direction.

Tall and stately, his resplendent black beard fully complimented by a jacket and hat despite the heat, he took a long drag on his vaping device, exhaled a plume of smoke, and responded, "What's going on over there?"

"I want to go learn there," I told him.

He cocked an eyebrow at me, but confirmed that I was just a block away. "Enjoy yourself," he said.

A block farther, I made it to the foot of a hill where I saw few Haredi boys milling about without jackets around a cluster of shops. Above a small sign, defaced with graffiti, that commemorated the Ponevezh Yeshiva and its founder in both Hebrew and English loomed the yeshiva itself, an enormous, three-story concrete structure that sprawled across the entire hilltop. Following the sound of activity, I proceeded up a road to the back of the building and saw a crowd gathered around parked trucks, people being handed large cardboard boxes. On closer inspection, I saw that the boxes were filled with packaged food, staples as well as snacks, and that the people collecting them were mostly adult women in head scarves.

I walked around the building's circumference to the front, where a group of yeshiva students were gathered on a veranda above the main entrance. I found the staircase and ascended with the intent of interviewing the students, but they were engaged in an animated conversation, and my attention was distracted by the spectacular view from this spot on the hilltop, where Tel Aviv's skyscape glittered in the distance.

Sometimes described as being in the "Ivy League" of yeshivas, Ponevezh indeed had the feel of a campus, with affiliated dormitories, prayer rooms, libraries, study rooms, and offices in the blocks around the central building, each inscribed with the name of its benefactor. Also like on a campus, the student areas were littered with the wreckage of abandoned projects, discarded food wrappers, and other detritus.

Originally established in Lithuania in 1908, Ponevezh was reestablished in Bnai Brak in 1944 by Joseph Kahaneman, who had been the head of the yeshiva since the founder died in 1919. Kahaneman had escaped Lithuania just before the Nazi invasion that saw the murder of 95 percent of the country's Jews, including his own family as well as nearly all his yeshiva students. He started the new Ponevezh with just seven students, but he was an indefatigable fund-raiser and recruiter, traveling the world to seek out both students and rabbinical talent, even as he continued to build Ponevezh's reputation and influence.

After Kahaneman's death in 1969, Rabbi Elazar Schach, another native Lithuanian and the yeshiva's longtime dean, made Ponevezh a political base as well by joining other Haredi leaders in the Agudat Israel party in coalition with Menachem Begin's Likud. In 1988, he went on to launch his own political party, Degel Ha Torah. Funded by millions of shekels from the government and attracting thousands of students, including many from the United States and other countries, Ponevezh had thus become a significant institution, not only theologically but in very material, political terms as well. Positions at Ponevezh had therefore become prestigious, and well worth fighting over. Throughout the Haredi world, rabbinical seats were by now essentially dynastic, producing intense contests between rival claimants. For decades, a conflict between supporters of a grandson of Kahaneman and those of his brother-in-law had raged over who was the rightful holder of the job of "Head of the Yeshiva." The battle was strictly over prestige—there were three other senior rabbis who were also "heads" and actually ran the yeshiva—and not even a special rabbinical court ruling in 1999 that both men would have the title was sufficient to resolve the dispute.

One faction of yeshiva students aligned with Kahaneman's grandson called themselves the "haters," while those aligned with his brother-in-law called themselves the "terrorists." Members of the two factions had squared off in the dormitories, and even in the main study hall, not only with harsh words but also with fists as well as volleys of chairs and tables; on several occasions, more serious weapons were used, a tear gas canister and a hand grenade, neither of which, thankfully, were detonated. To keep the peace, each group was assigned their own dorms and classrooms, though space was tight for everyone, and frequent encroachments led to clashes, all of which were well covered in the Israeli media, often with accompanying video provided by the combatants.

There was no fighting on the evening of my visit, however. I wandered the hallways until I found a library, where all the books of commentary and law seemed well thumbed, the edges worn, the paper often grease smeared. But I was alone in the library, so I went back into the hallway, where I followed the flow of students into a study hall, a *beis midrash* large enough for several hundred with high ceilings and, in the front, a large, golden Aron Kodesh—a cabinet for the Torah scrolls—intricately carved and bedecked with a crown on top. The windows were covered with heavy, dirty curtains that didn't move despite the blasting air conditioner, and the room's bare white walls were stained, badly in need of a fresh coat of paint.

The room was filling up, though not full, and I sat down at one of the hundreds of desks, glancing through the prayer book that had been left there. Around me, the students were reading to themselves, praying out loud, davening rhythmically or speaking quietly with their neighbors. From time to time, a student would speak a prayer out loud which was then echoed by many others, so that the whole room erupted into a unified sound.

I'd made a point of wearing black pants and a black baseball cap along with a short-sleeved, collared shirt, so as to be close enough to the general uniform not to stand out too badly, and no one had challenged my presence while I moved about. My camouflage worked better at a distance, however, and the young man who now sat next to me saw right away that I was a stranger, and nodded to me in a manner that was welcoming, if also a bit diffident. Like all the other men there, he wore a black suit and hat as well as a white shirt, and up close, I saw he was wearing the sort of rimless eyeglasses common among Haredi men. In his midtwenties, he had a patchy black beard that was especially wispy between his lip and nose; still, he managed to project a wizened, world-weary demeanor.

I explained in Hebrew that I was writing a book about Israel and wanted to include a chapter about Ponevezh. Would he mind answering a few questions? He dutifully agreed.

I asked him to tell me a little about the history of the yeshiva.

"It was built seventy years ago by a few Haredim," he said, "the remnant of the community left over from the Shoah."

Had the Chazon Ish played a role in founding the synagogue?

"He was not one of the founders, but he was revered by everyone, of course, and whenever the Chazon Ish came, it was a big celebration and excitement."

How did it feel to be part of this community today?

"In the early days, these benches were sparsely filled," he said with a broad smile, waving his hand over the room, where nearly all the desks had by now filled up. "Now we are many thousands."

Did he speak Yiddish?

He didn't. "Thirty to forty years ago, everyone spoke Yiddish," he explained. Now all the classes were in Hebrew, as was their newspaper, and people spoke Hebrew at home as well, except for the very old.

Occasionally, an older man would enter the room and make his way down the aisles between the benches to the front of the room near the Aron Kodesh, prompting the students he passed to stand in respect. My neighbor explained that these men were the leaders of the yeshiva, relatives of the founders.

Behind us, a group of young boys wearing identical T-shirts were being led into the room by a guide who appeared to be one of the students. I noticed a few of the boys taking photos with their cell phones, and asked if I was permitted to take photos, too.

My neighbor looked at me as if my question was ridiculous.

"Tourists come through all day," he said.

The moments when the students prayed in unison came more frequently, and I asked my neighbor if this was a special occasion.

"It's a powerful time," he said, going on to explain that it was the month of Elul on the Jewish calendar, just before Rosh Hashana.

It was daunting how much there was to learn, I mused. Was this something that must be started when one was young, like these students?

My neighbor chuckled, shaking his head. "Rabbi Akiva didn't start learning until the age of forty," he pointed out. "He didn't have children until the age of sixty."

I left a short time later as the prayers became more intense, and my desk was immediately filled by one of the many students waiting at the back of the room. The hallways were filled with even more young men waiting to enter the great hall and participate in the group lesson.

At the bottom of the hill, I stopped in at a bakery and bought a few rugelach before going back to where the bus had dropped me off. I'd planned to take the same bus line in the opposite direction, but as the station was not on the other side of the street, as I'd hoped, or indeed anywhere on the blocks nearby, I just began to walk on Herzl Street until I found a free taxi.

I remained quiet in the taxi's backseat until we turned onto Katznelson, where the cafés, restaurants, and bars were all overflowing with women and men.

"From one world to another," I observed cheerfully.

"Which is better?" quipped the driver, in his T-shirt and jeans, a hipster's hat softening any hair loss on top.

"I'm not sure, to tell you the truth," I answered, explaining that I'd just visited the Ponevezh Yeshiva and found myself actually quite moved by the pride the students there showed at rebuilding a community that had been destroyed during the Shoah.

The driver seemed worried he had offended me, so I quickly explained that I was a writer and had gone to Ponevezh to try to understand the Haredim as a secular person.

"I'm not heading that way religiously," I told him, "but maybe you are more observant?"

He pursed his lips and nodded. He knew some rabbis, and had spent some time recently studying with them.

"I'm strengthening in it," he said.

We'd reached Katznelson just next to the late-night store where I bought water, and I asked the taxi driver to drop me off. The clerk recognized me and greeted me warmly, asking if I wanted my usual six-pack of liter water bottles.

"Not this time, friend," I answered. "I'm going home in a few days."

He nodded and asked, "Where is home?"

"Back to Chicago," I told him. "I was born in the U.S., though most of my family is here in Givatayim."

"What do you do in Chicago?"

"I'm an author—I'm actually writing a book about Israel."

He smiled and tapped his chest. "You should write about *me*," he said. "I've gone through a lot in my life."

Restraining my journalist's skepticism, I sized up this fellow in his early twenties, clean shaven and with a closely cropped haircut as well as a knit kippah on his head. I was really intrigued as to why he was so confident in his story.

I opened my palm toward him, "So, tell me."

He reached into his pocket and produced a small box from which he pulled out a ring with a single, small diamond in the middle. He'd dated a woman for more than two years before giving her earrings and jewelry and finally this ring as a proposal for marriage. Recently, though, he asked for the ring back. He lived at home with his parents and worked at his father's store, and his girlfriend complained frequently that he didn't earn much money.

"She only liked me when I had money," he said.

Two young women in tight crop tops and yoga pants came in just then to buy cigarettes and soda. They tried to chat with the clerk—a good-looking guy—but he kept it brief and businesslike.

We continued our conversation standing at the store's threshold, talking for some time about the best qualities in a spouse, and I pointed to a portrait on the wall of Ovadia Yosef, the former Sephardic chief rabbi.

"I'm not a religious guy," I said, "but the sages like Rav Yosef have a lot of knowledge. A good wife is worth 'a price above rubies,' the Torah says.'"

"My father really likes Rav Yosef," the clerk said. "His name's Eitan, too."

At this point, a man walked brusquely into the store, grabbed something from the cooler, slapped a few shekel coins on the counter, and came over to the clerk. Wearing a sleeveless T-shirt that showed off his biceps as well as a tattoo of a black panther, he seemed impatient to speak with the clerk, and perhaps a bit intoxicated as well, so I bid them both good night.

On my stroll home, I regretted not trying to engage the brusque man, though. I was curious about his tattoo; there had been a very active Israeli version of the Black Panthers in the early 1970s representing Mizrahi Jews, but he was clearly too young to have been part of that movement. I wished I'd asked him what the Panthers meant to him.

34

JAMAL

Earlier that year, the Goldin Institute launched a fellowship called GATHER, a new, online training curriculum for a specially selected group of international grassroots organizers. Twenty individuals were picked from sixteen countries across Africa, Asia, Europe, the Middle East, and North and South America, among them the manager of an orphanage in Kenya, a peace and reconciliation specialist in Colombia, and a rape survivors' advocate in Kentucky. They were each sent an iPad preloaded with software Travis had designed to facilitate their training in principles and techniques he had distilled with the goal of creating a "community of practice" that could share ideas as well as resources.

One of the GATHER fellows was Jamal Al Kirnawi, a Bedouin from the city of Rahat inside Israel who ran an NGO called A New Dawn in the Negev. Jamal had been recommended to Diane and Travis by Yoni Reuven's wife, Niva, who thought he might gain some useful connections and new opportunities through the program. Travis asked me to interview Jamal for the Goldin Institute's newsletter and other communications with its board and supporters, and Jamal was obliging. I scheduled a visit to Rahat the day before before my flight back to Chicago, and Gabi agreed to drive me, one last brotherly adventure before I returned home.

Rahat was even closer to Tel Aviv than Be'er Sheva, a drive of just over an hour, and we left after the rush hour traffic had died down. Historically, the Bedouin were nomads who herded and traded across the deserts of the Middle East and North Africa, but the Ottoman Empire began a policy that translates from Turkish as "sedentarization," using a combination of force and enticement to get them to live in permanent settlements. The Ottomans founded Be'er Sheva in 1900 as part of this effort, connecting it to the rest of their dominion with a railroad in 1915, just before the British conquest. The British Empire continued the Ottoman's tactics, pressuring the Bedouin to give up their travels and become permanent denizens of their towns, building schools to entice them, though meeting with decidedly limited success.

By 1948, there were more than 100,000 Bedouin in the Negev, most of whom fled to Gaza and Jordan during the war. Israel contained the remaining 11,000 in a particular section of the desert under martial law that continued until 1966. When martial law was phased out in the late 1960s, Israel created its own sedentarization policy, providing Bedouin with cash incentives to move into certain designated areas while demolishing villages and towns they deemed illegal.

The second city created under this policy, Rahat, has grown into the largest Bedouin city, its population rising from 28,000 in 1998 to more than 71,000 in 2019, even as the overall population of Negev Bedouin rose to 210,000, fully one-third of the residents in the region. At least 45 percent of the Bedouin live in "unrecognized" villages that do not receive water, electrical, or other services and are at odds with the Israeli government, which has denied most of their claims of land ownership for decades and targeted their homes for demolition.

Rahat itself has earned a reputation for clan-related violence as well as tense relations with police. A shoot-out between officers and armed clan members in 2015 left a twenty-year-old bystander dead and ignited weeks of protests that prompted the

Jewish Telegraphic Agency to ask "Is Rahat the Ferguson of Israel?"

Unemployment in Rahat was as high as 40 percent until 2014, when SodaStream, the manufacturer of home carbonization machines, moved into a new industrial park built on the city's outskirts. A century-old company that was relaunched to great success by a Queens-born entrepreneur, SodaStream originally built its factory in a West Bank settlement and hired Palestinians, but after being targeted by the BDS movement internationally, it moved to a larger facility in Rahat, within Israel, where it employed Bedouin, new immigrants, and some of the same Palestinians who'd worked at the West Bank plant. Still, Rahat's unemployment rate remained at 14 percent, approximately double that of nearby towns, with poverty rates among the highest in Israel.

A few kilometers outside of Tel Aviv, the lush landscape of the coast gave way to arid and rocky desert, and we made it easily to the entrance of town, but when Gabi used Waze to navigate through town to the address Jamal had given me, the app steered us to a dead end. I called Jamal to help us but couldn't explain exactly where we were, since there were no street signs and every block was made up of large homes with courtyards surrounded by high walls. There were no pedestrians to ask either, so I knocked on the door of a random house, but the giggling boys who answered could speak neither Hebrew nor English.

Finally, Jamal was able to guide us through the neighborhood using landmarks including a house that had many visible satellite antennae and a truck parked on a side street. When we turned onto his block, he was standing in the street, and we parked in front of the headquarters of A New Dawn for the Negev, a modest one-story building at the end of a cul-de-sac with its own gate and a courtyard where there were a few shacks and work benches set up.

Of average height, with closely cropped hair, a clean-shaven face, and plastic-framed glasses, Jamal shook our hands vigorously before welcoming us inside, where he introduced us to his staff of a half-dozen employees and volunteers, made us coffee, and told us about his life and work.

When he was born in 1979, Jamal's family lived near Tel Arad in an unrecognized village some kilometers to the east, but they moved to Rahat when he was three. His vision was impaired from childhood such that he had to wear glasses, which prompted his teachers to seat him at the front of the classroom. There, he drew the ridicule of his classmates, who teased him for being "blind."

By the time he was a teenager, Jamal had tired of being singled out and was looking for any way possible to escape. He found his chance when his school welcomed a delegation of students from the Jewish city of Rehovot. Until then, Jamal and his classmates had very limited experience with their Jewish compatriots. Even when his parents went to market in nearby Be'er Sheva, they didn't bring their children.

"We never saw Jewish people before," he explained, "except maybe on TV in black and white."

On the day the students from Rehovot came, his school was cleaned and spruced up, and several of the students' mothers brought lunch. Jamal and his classmates were assembled in a line to greet the Jewish visitors, the teachers matching each student from Rahat with a peer from Rehovot. Jamal, noticing how many of the Rehovot kids were wearing glasses, felt a surge of enthusiasm and goodwill. Without even waiting for the teachers to pair him, he spotted one boy with blond hair and blue eyes, walked up, and introduced himself.

Jamal had learned basic Hebrew from watching television, and was intrigued when the boy, who was likewise sixteen, told him he was president of his school's student council. His school didn't even have a student council, so Jamal inquired about what it was and how it operated, and the Rehovot boy gave him a telephone number for a contact at the Ministry of Education in Jerusalem.

These were the days before social media, and Jamal called the ministry official, identifying himself as the president of the student council in Rahat. The ministry official transferred Jamal to a colleague in Be'er Sheva, who was very friendly and excited to include Jamal in regional activities. "Taking the day off" from school without telling his parents, Jamal went to visit the official in Be'er Sheva, who put him on the national student council and connected him to Jewish teenagers on other student councils in towns and cities throughout the country. He traveled all over, with the ministry reimbursing him for his bus trips.

"I was looking for open windows," Jamal said. "I was hungry for any participation."

His family was wary of Jamal's travels to Jewish areas, especially when he went to Tel Aviv, which they considered a dangerous city, and his teachers tried to discourage his work with student councils. Jamal, however, was as defiant as he was determined.

Despite continuing pressure to abandon his student council work, Jamal created an actual student council when he was in tenth grade. "I didn't care about the teachers or even the principal," he said. "I fought with my family, with everyone.

"My classmates thought I was crazy, but they were just jealous. They were stuck at home with their families, and described me as 'you with your suitcase.'"

The discouragement from the principal and his teachers was Jamal's first encounter with the internal structures of Bedouin society in Rahat, which he would go on to compare with Haredi communities.

"The principal wanted control and didn't want young students as leaders," Jamal said. "It is a very hierarchal world, patriarchal, conservative. They keep everything close to the heart of the power. It behaves like a big tribe, and when you behave as a tribal, you cannot see how things could be."

After becoming one of the handful in his class who passed Israel's high school matriculation exam, he moved to Be'er Sheva by himself, and lived on his own for five years while he attended Ben Gurion University of the Negev, where he earned a bachelor's degree in public health administration. Jamal was particularly excited when President Bill Clinton visited Israel in 1998, which he saw as evidence that Israel was his gateway to the rest of the world. From Be'er Sheva, he went to McGill University in Montreal, Canada, where he garnered a master's in social work.

"The world became bigger," Jamal explained. "I was not just a Bedouin, but part of the whole world. I had become an international."

In his next position, though, Jamal became keenly aware of the obstacles still remaining in his path. He returned to Be'er Sheva and became an academic counselor at his alma mater, Ben Gurion University of the Negev, working with Arab students. In that job, Jamal discovered that while he might have experience and knowledge that he could give back to the community, many would simply refuse his services. Nor were Israel's universities generous to minorities: neither Russians nor Ethiopians, in particular, had an easy time at the university, largely because the university never prioritized resources for these groups. From this experience, Jamal came to understand that universities were not necessarily laboratories of social change.

"There are a lot of enemies for social change. The system is blind, but minorities feel victimized, so even if you offer help, help is not taken. Change has to come from the grass roots. Change will come from Jewish and Bedouin people together."

These often frustrating experiences were what prompted Jamal to launch A New Dawn, an attempt to open up the world to the Bedouin, to allow them to access culture and resources, so that they might participate not only in the labor market at their full potential, but in art and music as well.

"They don't realize they are in a minority," Jamal said of the Bedouin of Rahat. "They live in a great big bubble."

Jamal was thirty-three and not yet married when he founded A New Dawn, thus able to devote himself entirely to the life of a "social activist." For adults, he fostered meetings between Bedouin community representatives and Shoah survivors, and he established a joint forum for residents of Rahat and the surrounding Jewish communities to resolve tensions and work together on regional promotion. Many of A New Dawn's programs were developed for youths, and after building connections with the government of Germany, Jamal launched a new effort bringing German youths to Rahat for cultural exchanges and conversations with young people, as well as in Jewish communities in Israel, to dispel stereotypes and battle prejudice. The German government sponsored volunteers completing national service to come to Rahat for twelve-month stays.

Inevitably, Jamal's success put him on a collision course with Rahat's establishment. In 2014, A New Dawn won a grant directly from Israel's National Insurance Welfare Agency. Then, during a meeting with officials at the agency and the city's mayor, the mayor yelled at Jamal and brought the meeting to a quick and awkward ending. Jamal asked for the leaders of his own tribe to reach out to the mayor, and they were told that he was upset because previous grants from that agency had gone directly to the municipality.

"He wanted to control the project," Jamal explained. "This had become political."

Jamal faced resistance as well from religious authorities, who saw him as an unwelcome competitor. Because he was able to leverage resources from the Israeli government as well as from abroad, many saw him as a "rich NGO."

"Each mosque is another organization," Jamal explained.

To prove himself to Rahat's power brokers, Jamal created a program to work with high school dropouts, a badly needed service in Rahat: 35 percent of the city's high school students dropped out, while less than one-third passed the national matriculation exam. The city had only one community center, where Givatayim had at least five, and there were virtually no public spaces, shopping areas, or even office buildings. The dropouts came to the leased house that served as A New Dawn's headquarters for skills development classes like cooking lessons in the kitchen. Jamal found an anonymous European donor to pay for a classical music teacher, a Russian immigrant, to come to Rahat's schools, but also had to use funds to build a new classroom because all the school buildings were overcrowded.

Jamal's wife had worked as a math teacher in Rahat for years, and she soon joined A New Dawn as its second-in-command. There were no day care facilities in Rahat, so his son, now a second grader, went to one in Be'er Sheva and then a kindergarten in a nearby *moshav*, where he learned Hebrew. He started studying Arabic only in elementary school.

"It's my choice to live here and inspire other people to make the change they deserve," he said. "If you want to be a NGO leading the change, you are not an easy adjustment for the authorities. We are doing good stuff, but instead of welcoming us, we feel suspicion from the municipality. Still, after ten years, New Dawn is going from an entrepreneur to an institution."

Jamal was thinking about the organization's future, which to him meant training new leaders, especially women. "The next step is building our capacity to build leadership," he said.

Jamal wanted to show us Rahat's new market, so we all left A New Dawn's office and got into our respective cars, Gabi following Jamal as he steered through the city's streets. For a couple of kilometers, it was nearly all large family homes surrounded by high walls, with just a few stores and restaurants, Pizza Hut being the single international franchise.

The market itself, made up of dozens of well-equipped stalls under a corrugated tin roof, sold children's clothes, modern dresses for little girls, and the distinctive embroidered gowns of the Bedouin women, as well as toys, school supplies, and housewares. The vendors also included a butcher and a flower shop, among other businesses. From there, we went to a roadside restaurant to eat Bedouin style, using scraps of pita to scoop up portions of grilled meat, stewed vegetables, and rice from a large communal plate. The restaurant's presentation was as basic as its hygiene, but the food was fresh and delicious, and I ate heartily despite the midday heat.

During the meal, I asked Jamal about Bedouin serving in the IDF.

Though Bedouin were exempt from compulsory military service, a few hundred men from the Negev had joined the IDF every year since the state's founding, mainly in a special unit along with Druze and Circassians. While the reputation of the IDF had soured in recent years, Bedouin men in uniform were still safe in Rahat, Jamal said. At A New Dawn, he was working with a high-ranking Bedouin officer to counsel IDF veterans in Rahat on how to access their benefits, which included payment for education and advantages in getting employment. Jamal admitted, however, that fewer Bedouin were willing to serve these days, as tensions rose over inequities with other Israelis, and government leaders made derogatory statements about Arabs and Bedouin.

"They send less to the IDF," Jamal said, "because they have less faith in the government."

That next morning, with just a few hours before my son and I were scheduled to fly home, I stopped in at the corner store on Katznelson to pick up one more bottle of water and a few snacks for the trip, but the friendly clerk was not there. Instead, there was an older man who closely resembled him, save for the thick, black beard anchoring his face.

I asked him, "Excuse me, but is your name Eitan?"

Puzzled, the older clerk answered that he was, indeed, Eitan.

I explained that I'd spoken with his son the clerk a few evenings ago, and that my name was Eitan as well.

We both laughed and chatted for a few minutes, with the older clerk inquiring about Chicago. "But is there any kind of Jewish life there, really?" he asked, skeptically.

"Of course," I answered. "We even have a Haredi neighborhood called Rogers Park."

He pursed his lips and nodded in approval, wishing me luck on my journey, but cut the conversation short because the muscleman with the black panther tattoo had arrived.

As I stepped away, I heard the older clerk admonishing the muscle man for his behavior, staying out all night yet again.

"Look at your brother," the older clerk yelled at the muscleman. "He's here whenever he's supposed to be here."

I turned back and saw the muscleman hang his head in shame, trying to interject weakly, "But, Dad . . ."

EPILOGUE

With a pleasing savor I shall accept you when I take you out of the nations, and I shall gather you from the lands in which you were scattered, and I shall be hallowed through you before the eyes of the nations.

And you will know that I am the Lord when I bring you to the land of Israel, to the land that I lifted My hand to give to your forefathers.

—EZEKIEL 20:41–42

Because two brothers could not get along, we lost our freedom and our liberty to Rome.

—JOSEPHUS, *THE JEWISH WAR*

More than three millennia after the original Twelve Tribes established the first kingdom in the land, Israel remains the focus of international attention for geopolitical as well as religious reasons, and no one is more interested than the Jews of the United States. Even as North America has become home to the largest, most prosperous, and best integrated community in the long history of the Jewish diaspora, Israel remains the vault of Jewish hopes and dreams. Many American Jews see it as their duty to advocate for Israel, while others, for the same reason, feel an obligation to criticize the state: Israel remains at the core of Jewish identity, making it irresistible for American Jews regardless of the vast differences in culture and politics between these two poles of the Jewish world.

In the months since my last trip to Israel recounted in this book, a period of time extended by the COVID-19 pandemic, I followed up with those I interviewed, and found unmistakable evidence of the increasing American influence over Israel as well as similarly clear signs that the country's future will be determined by its ability to synthesize a coherent society from the many different groups who constitute its population, each of whom arrived with their own baggage from the particular nations where their ancestors lived and died for generations.

In September 2017, a little over a month after my meeting with Simona Weinglass, American law enforcement agents arrested one of the kingpins of binary options, a thirty-eight-year-old Israeli woman named Lee Elbaz, when she arrived at JFK Airport in New York City planning to go on vacation in the United States. One month after that, the Knesset finally banned the binary options trade in the country by a unanimous vote, giving companies three months to shut down.

U.S. prosecutors indicted Elbaz along with fifteen of her employees and colleagues at several different companies, five of whom signed plea deals and provided testimony that confirmed everything in Simona's investigation. Elbaz and others had instructed binary options sales staff to use false identities, conceal the location of the companies, use high-pressure tactics to extract as much money as possible from their customers, and obstruct any effort to withdraw accounts. They specifically went after retirees, pension holders, and veterans as clients, according to court filings accompanying guilty pleas by former employees.

"No one here was interested in helping clients," said one of the prosecutors in a press conference during the trial. "It was all a plan to steal money."

Elbaz was convicted of one count of conspiracy to commit wire fraud and three counts of wire fraud after a three-week jury trial in August 2019, and on December 19, 2019, the U.S. district judge presiding over her case sentenced her to twenty-two years in prison and also ordered her to pay $28 million in restitution. By then, U.S. prosecutors had indicted twenty-one Israelis and convicted seven of serious crimes, while Israeli authorities hadn't brought any similar charges, and the binary options companies had disappeared. Many of the individuals who had been involved in these companies had left Israel and either were on the run or had simply moved on to other scams.

Simona took stock in a video for the *Times of Israel,* proud of the modicum of justice she'd been able to win for the victims of the binary options companies. Still, she worried over the lackluster response from Israeli authorities. Elbaz's lengthy sentence had put in stark relief the differences in standards of law enforcement between Israel and the United States, and the extent to which Israel relies on American law enforcement to handle its organized crime.

"One of the reasons it shocked Israelis," Simona said, "is because what Lee Elbaz was doing is something that hundreds of other people, if not thousands of people, are doing. The idea that this could be punished with twenty-two years in prison just emphasized our law enforcement does nothing, and law enforcement in the United States sees things very differently. It was such a breath of fresh air after so many years of frustration of a completely wishy-washy, impotent response from Israeli authorities, someone was finally doing something. Fraudsters finally had to face what they had done. There doesn't seem to be any force in Israel society that will clean this up. We obviously have an industry now that commits Internet fraud and nobody has any idea how big it is.

"When law enforcement is very weak and when prosecutors are not doing their job and prosecuting crime, journalism is the last line of defense. If we hadn't exposed Israel's underground industry of Internet fraud, it would have probably continued the way it's been going."

In the ongoing gentrification in Jaffa, Anna Lou Lou closed its doors in January 2019 with a series of final events and a grand party, issuing a statement to the unique community that had gathered around the little bar. "This was not an easy decision for us to make," it read. "As some of you know, our neighborhood has become a residential area for the ultra-wealthy. We find ourselves spending days and nights dealing with boring neighbors, police, and municipal agencies. What a waste of energy! We are taking a new way forward.

"We have so many great memories from the past eight years. So much dancing, so many beautiful and embarrassing drunk conversations, so much music. And that's just what we remember :) And so, sad though we are to leave our special cave, we are also crazy excited for the new road ahead of us. This is not the end of the Anna Lou Lou story. The future is full of opportunities."

Tsionit Fattal Kupperwasser traveled to London in early July 2019 and connected in person with the Iraqi expatriate community through the nation's cuisine. Ghaith Al Tamimi, formerly a high-ranking Shia cleric in Iraq, hosted her at Al Maskoof Restaurant in the St. George's Fields neighborhood, an establishment that bakes its own bread Iraqi style, flat circles on the walls of a round ceramic oven. As their name suggests, they also grill *maskoof*, a freshwater fish, the traditional way, pinched in a metal grill over a wood fire.

Both of these are Iraqi signature dishes, foods Tsionit ate in her youth but hadn't learned how to make before her parents died. Tsionit posted a film of the bread making and fish grilling on her Facebook page and thanked her hosts for "restoring the aromas of childhood in my parents' home.

"I hope that we will meet soon on Abu Nuwas Street in Baghdad and we'll eat the grilled *maskoof* there."

As usual, the post attracted hundreds of likes and comments, enthusiastic messages in both Hebrew and Arabic. Many of the Israelis commenting were of Iraqi heritage, and were themselves interested to see how the *maskoof* was made, while the Arabic writers warmly invited her to Baghdad and wished her blessings and wellness.

"Blessings and strength to you and your host. I swear to God you are Iraqi," wrote Magid Dawood in Baghdad.

Another commentor from Baghdad wrote, "I wish you would return to the arms of your homeland Iraq and eat the *maskoof* in Abu Nawas."

The political situation within Iraq just then was highly volatile, however, and that fall, large-scale antigovernment protests broke out in Baghdad and other cities, which were met with violent repression from security forces. Tsionit's host, Ghaith Al Tamimi, who had left Iraq after clashing with extremist clerics, became a prominent social media organizer and spokesperson for the protests from London and was subsequently targeted by Iraqi government entities and their allies in the Iranian regime. The Iraqi government, desperate to portray the protests as a foreign instigation rather than a spontaneous, indigenous response to endemic corruption and the pervasive influence of Iran, coordinated closely with Iran's sophisticated propagandists to smear the protest leaders. In October 2019, the *Tehran Times,* an English-language outlet published by the Iranian government, cited the photos of Al Tamimi with Tsionit as "undeniable evidence about Al Tamimi's cooperation with Israel."

Tsionit rejected these accusations in an open letter to the Iraqi people in Arabic posted on Facebook that December, writing that she had been encouraged by the protests "against sectarianism, against corrupt authority, and the penetrating Iranian intervention." She and other Iraqi Jews felt great solidarity with the protesters and were outraged by the deaths of more than 450 people, as well as the injury to thousands. But she had been sorely disappointed by the accusations against her and her host, which drew on the old sectarian hatreds that led to the expulsion of Iraq's Jews, old hatreds she had hoped were finally disappearing.

It was the recent growth of social media networks, she noted, that made it possible for Iraqi Jews to reestablish contacts with Iraqis, and the photo cited by Iranian media, uploaded freely after a casual dinner, was most certainly *not* a meeting of Mossad agents recruiting Iraqi agents.

"It's not a photo taken by a paparazzi photographer or Iraqi or Iranian intelligence agency," she wrote.

Shame on Iraqi politicians and the "court media" who repeat lies again and again. You are the ones who will destroy Iraq.

Neither the Jews nor Israel are the ones who shot guns and tear gas bombs and killed 450 protesters. . . .

The Jews of Iraq have contributed greatly to the development of Iraq, and we from their descendants are hurting your pain and what Iraq has become.

My name is Tsionit Fattal Kuperwasser. Jewish, an Israeli with Iraqi roots and origins for hundreds of years. I am a literary researcher and lecturer. Eleven years ago I was an Israeli army officer. All my activities are public and open to all the broad audience on my Facebook pages in Hebrew and Arabic. And whoever wants more details about me can search my name in Hebrew and English. For what was written in Arabic—check the source of the information.

This post received even more attention than usual, more than six hundred likes, "hearts," and "sad face" emojis, as well as more than eighty shares and over three hundred comments.

Eng Noor Hameed, an engineer in Baghdad, wrote, "Thank you for your noble attitude towards the Iraqi people."

Nabil Al Rubuiy wrote, "My sister, Tsionit, your national attitudes toward the Iraqi people are evidence you are authentically Iraqi."

But if most of the comments were supportive, a handful were laced with antisemitic conspiracy theories, for instance this one from Assad S. of Amara, Iraq, who accused Tsionit of being part of an Israeli scheme to control the entire Middle East, and her supporters of abandoning the Palestinians.

"Jews have an idea they are the best people," Assad wrote. "They are God's chosen people, and their blood is high blood, and the rest of the peoples are supposed to serve them."

Though Tsionit did not react to these commenters, other Iraqis rushed to her defense, calling out Assad for antisemitism and extremism.

Dr. Muzahim Mubarak, another organizer of the antigovernment protests, wrote, "The wonderful lady, Tsionit, is a sweet and spiritual writer, and you answer her with the spirit of empty, ugly animosity inherent against the Jews."

"I'm talking to you about humane and moral principles," wrote Salah Al Hamdani, a poet and playwright who was exiled by Saddam Hussein's regime in 1975. "I told you that you're a fascist like Hitler. . . . If the Arab world does not get rid of the revengeful Islamic ideas, it will remain retarded, just as you are now. Because of people like you, there will be no state for the Palestinians."

Mahdi Mohammed located the effort to blame Israel for the protests in the desperation of the Iraqi and Iranian regimes to remain in control: "We understand their methods and quackery and they will not call us by them. You and other honorable people are our voice abroad and the world. You are from us and we are from you."

In July 2019, Yaakov Berg and the Psagot winery were mentioned in media investigations of the donations of the Falic family, three Florida-based Jewish brothers of Lebanese and Russian heritage who own 180 duty free stores in airports across the United States, including those at JFK, Atlanta-Hartsfield, and Washington, D.C.'s Ronald Reagan and Dulles. The Associated Press found that the Falics had given Israeli causes at least $35 million over the previous decade, funding day care centers, Chabad, and the charity group Friends of IDF, with at least $5.6 million of that sum having been flagged for going to settler groups in the West Bank and East Jerusalem, including the Psgaot Winery. The AP also examined Israeli political documents and revealed that the Falics were the biggest donors, collectively, to Prime Minister Netanyahu's political accounts, providing him with $100,000 over those years. Not coincidentally, the Falics were also major donors to the Republican party and specifically to the Trump campaign.

"We are proud to support organizations that help promote Jewish life all over the Land of Israel," Simon Falic, a Miami-based lawyer, told the Associated Press on behalf of his family.

"The idea that the mere existence of Jewish life in any geographical area is an impediment to peace makes no sense to us."

A subsequent investigation from the British newspaper the *Independent* confirmed the AP report and focused on the Falics' role at the Psagot Winery, determining that the family had become majority shareholders in 2007 when they invested $1 million. The money was used to substantially expand the winery from about 57,000 square meters to 84,000 square meters, and to buy and bottle grapes from other vineyards. Effectively, the Falics' investment made Psagot the hub of the West Bank's settler wineries.

In November of that year, Yaakov received an unfavorable ruling to his suit against the European Union's labeling of his wines from the European Court of Justice. He had pursued the case, an appeal of the European Union's previous decision to affix labels identifying the wines as being from the settlements, against the advice of Israeli diplomats, and, as predicted, the court ruled against him. Fuming over the court's ruling in media interviews, he repeated what he'd told us, equating the labels applied to his wine bottles with the yellow star Jews were forced by the Nazis to wear.

Just a week later, however, Yaakov told the *Times of Israel* he was heartened by a new statement from the Trump administration declaring that Israeli settlements were not illegal, a reversal of decades of American policy that the settlements on Palestinian land were prohibited under international law.

"This is the historical land of the Jewish people—all the Bible stories took place here—how could you say that Jews do not have the right to live here?" Yaakov said. "The U.S. statement is important for the future of this region."

To thank the administration, Yaakov named a "special label" after U.S. Secretary of State Mike Pompeo, who issued the statement, and placed stickers that read "#MadeInLegality" on the bottles, which contained a blend of shiraz, cabernet sauvignon, and merlot.

In November 2020, Secretary Pompeo visited Israel to announce yet further policy changes, though President Trump had lost the national election two weeks earlier and a new administration would be coming in soon. Pompeo declared during a press conference in Jerusalem with Prime Minister Netanyahu that the BDS movement henceforth would be treated as antisemitic. Pompeo topped off this trip with a provocative visit to Psagot, becoming the first American secretary of state to set foot in a West Bank settlement. Previous American leaders had resisted visiting the settlements because official policy regarded them as impediments to peace that did not deserve the legitimacy of official recognition, but Pompeo arrived by helicopter while a small group of protesters from the activist group Peace Now stood outside the winery's gate with signs like "USA Stop Undermining Peace" and "Occupied Territory Can't Be Normalized."

"He won't succeed," said Peace Now's spokesperson, Brian Reeves. "Just as the Trump plan failed, this will fail, too. In a couple months, this whole policy will change, but we're here to send him a farewell. We're telling the U.S., 'Stop undermining peace' and we're telling them that settlements cannot be normalized."

Pompeo's tour of Psagot was billed as a private visit, so media were barred, and no Israeli government ministers attended, though the secretary's office did release an official photograph that showed him speaking with Yaakov and U.S. Ambassador David Friedman, all wearing masks due to the COVID-19 outbreak in the country. Afterward, Pompeo issued an official statement that products manufactured in the West Bank and imported to the United States could from then on be labeled "Made in

Israel," regardless of the legal position of the EU and many other nations that the settlements were not properly Israeli territory. The controversial visit to Psagot was covered extensively by international media, and in its report, the *New York Times* interviewed Munif Treish, a seventy-year-old Palestinian American whose family claimed to own a portion of the land Yaakov used for grapes.

"By law, Pompeo is supposed to protect the property and interests of American citizens all over the world," Treish told the *Times*. "But he is coming here to give legitimacy to the Israeli settlers who are trespassing, grabbing, and cultivating our land illegally."

Yoni Reuven became a star of Israeli TV in the summer of 2020 with the debut of the new season of *The Interns*, a docudrama that followed young doctors as they complete a crucial phase of their medical training. The series recorded Yoni as he made the rounds in the emergency room at Beilinson Hospital, part of the Rabin Medical Center in Petah Tikva, and dealt with the external and the internal conflicts he faced as an Ethiopian Israeli physician.

Some patients flatly refused to be treated by an Ethiopian doctor, and a few asked hopefully if he was "Cochini," meaning an Indian Jew from the city of Cochin, a community with a reputation for having many physicians. Yoni handled these situations with professionalism, remaining self-possessed despite the discrimination.

"There are people whose confusion I dispel and answer their questions of who I am, but really very briefly," Yoni told a magazine published by the producers of *The Interns*. "And there are people who I leave confused, 'Go home. You're fine. I treated you. I did my work to the best of my ability. Now the rest is on you.'"

Yoni was frank about having to carry an extra responsibility, often trying to compensate for the deficiencies in research or policies from health authorities and government agencies in addressing the needs of Ethiopians. Participating in *The Interns* was part of his personal mission to challenge the stereotypes about Ethiopian Jews and to accord appropriate respect to the role of Ethiopian Jews in their own emigration, including the work of his father. Where the general public knew about Natan Sharansky and other Russian "refuseniks" and were quite familiar with the heroism of the Israeli military's airlift of the Ethiopian Jews, they did not necessarily appreciate that Ethiopian Jews had been working inside Ethiopia for decades to bring their compatriots to Israel, and that the airlift was really the culmination of those efforts. Yoni's appearance on *The Interns* was a chance to tell the story of his father and others, but also to demonstrate that Ethiopian Jews were working at the most sophisticated levels of Israeli society. In Hebrew, the word for immigrating to Israel translates as "ascension," and Yoni played with the double meaning in his interview:

It bothered me that there is a whole generation of heroes here who do not get the recognition they should get. The story of the Ethiopians has yet to be told. We talk about the air force's role in our ascension, the Mossad's role in our ascension, but the narrative I tell is that no one lifted me, I raised myself.

That is always the question—did they ascend on their own or were they raised up? What isn't understood in the whole story is the very meaningful activism of Ethiopian Jews, within Ethiopia, to facilitate the ascension of the Jews to Israel. My father is defined as a Prisoner of Zion for the emigration from Ethiopia, but when I tell my friends, they say, "There are Ethiopian Prisoners of Zion?" They don't fully understand.

The effects of the COVID-19 pandemic in the spring of 2020 were felt disproportionately among Israel's Haredim and its Palestinian citizens, a result, according to public health experts, of the extremely crowded conditions among both populations that allowed the virus to spread easily among family groups while preventing the isolation of infected people. Through Passover, Haredi institutions stayed closed, but as the months went on, Haredi leaders and whole communities strongly resisted efforts to keep yeshivas closed and restrict large gatherings—holding large weddings, for instance, but also funerals and prayers. In Bnai Brak, Mea She'arim, and other Haredi neighborhoods, large groups of men confronted police in the streets, often leading to violence and arrests.

Haredim regularly accounted for more than 40 percent of COVID cases, more than double their share of the general population, and videos of Haredim defying social distancing conventions spread widely on social media, while pundits in Israeli media criticized the community's leading rabbis for instructing their followers to defy social-distancing regulations and keep yeshivas open, warning that they would overwhelm the health system. It was yet another example of Haredim rejecting state authority and failing to do their part as citizens, these pundits declared. Haredi politicians, meanwhile, countered that their communities were being held to a separate standard, and that secular gatherings—for instance the anti-Netanyahu protests that had proliferated in recent months—were not being stopped.

At Ponevezh, amid the virus's continuing spread and the

mounting controversy, Rabbi Gershon Edelstein, the senior head
of the yeshiva, issued a video address from his home in Bnai Brak
at the beginning of May, calling for his students to study together
remotely using their phones and for general adherence to health
ministry regulations. While the battles between the factions of
students who called themselves "terrorists" and "haters" raged
over which rabbi would hold the title of head of the yeshiva,
ninety-seven-year-old Edelstein was the institution's true authority as well as the chairman of the Council of Torah Sages and
spiritual leader of the Degel Ha Torah faction of the United Torah
Judaism party in the Knesset. He also controlled the party's influential daily newspaper, *Yated Ne'eman.*

Speaking in Hebrew before a professional microphone with
plain white curtains in the background, Edelstein said the students who studied together on their phones would receive great
merit for their effort. But his comments were also geared to a
broader audience, and he attributed the greater rate of infection
among Haredim to divine punishment for their sins. The behavior of secular Jews was judged less harshly, Edelstein said, because they lacked a proper religious education which would have
allowed them to avoid sin.

"There is an issue here that we have to speak about, here in
Israel, the Haredim who died, relative to the public, it's a much
larger percentage, abroad too. What does that mean?" Rabbi
Edelstein said. "Praise God, some yeshivas have already started
learning, but the main thing is to be very careful and maintain all
Ministry of Health precautions."

So Ponevezh was closed, and learning continued in alternate
facilities that summer in pods, with students assigned to small
groups behind plastic barriers and wearing masks. The "terrorists" took up the officially closed main study hall, while the "haters" had to go temporarily to a yeshiva in Jerusalem. Students

were supposed to be confined together to minimize the chance of infection.

The schools were completely closed again in September, and late that month, with the imminent approach of Rosh Hashana and Yom Kippur, normally a period of prayer and celebration, Rabbi Edelstein described that year's Yom Kippur as "a trial delivered by God," reiterating his call to follow Health Ministry rules. Instructing Haredim to pray "either in courtyards or in their homes," he went on with specific details about how to adapt group prayer requirements—Jews usually require a minimum quorum of ten men to form a prayer group—with masking and ventilation. Again, he emphasized that those who made the extra effort would receive additional spiritual merit.

"Pray in a quorum that takes place in the open air while maintaining the required distance and wearing a mask. Care must be taken to hold the prayer group in a shady and ventilated place to prevent, God forbid, the danger of dehydration during fasting."

Even as other Haredim defied the government and reopened their schools, Rabbi Edelstein kept his schools closed through the fall, leaving 150,000 boys and girls at home. But as infection rates dropped in late November, he told his administrators to reopen "while taking all precautions."

Along with Haredim, Palestinian citizens of Israel accounted for a disproportionate share of COVID cases, and during the first outbreak, Jamal Al Kirnawi set up a virus hotline at A New Dawn for the Negev's office in Rahat to dispense advice and information to a community where social distancing went against custom and tradition.

Jamal understood that almost all Bedouin families lived in close, multigenerational households, similarly to Haredim, where it was impossible to quarantine the elderly or others especially vulnerable to the virus. Language was a barrier to information about health care access, and many low-income Bedouin families didn't have basic Internet access, so they couldn't get their children online for school, and were blocked from communication with doctors, employers, and authorities. Bedouin in the many unrecognized villages of the Negev often lacked running water, sewage treatment facilities, or electric utility service, let alone pharmacies, clinics, and easy access to emergency care.

A New Dawn trained volunteers and established the hotline in the spring of 2020, when the virus began to spread widely throughout the country. Its call center also did proactive outreach to offer advice and resources to families it knew were in complicated scenarios.

"This is a population that is accustomed to contact, a population that is collective and tribal, in which their whole life revolves around a big family," Jamal told the newspaper *Makor Rishon*. "The concept of social distancing, of preventing contact, doesn't exist in their lexicon. This is going to require a major change of social norms. We have many Bedouin families who report to us a feeling of helplessness. These are families who live with many children in the house with their grandmothers and grandfathers, a situation with great danger."

On April 1, A New Dawn joined other NGOs in filing a petition to the Supreme Court from the Legal Center for Arab Minority Rights in Israel, calling for more testing centers for Bedouin villages and increased access to emergency care, including ambulance services.

"It became very clear to me that if we won't be proactive about containing Corona in the Bedouin community," said Jamal, "the consequences could be tragic."

In the second wave of COVID-19 in the fall, Palestinian citizens at first made up more than 30 percent of the new cases, but as local officials imposed curfews and ordered cancellations of weddings and other mass events, the numbers dropped precipitously, and Palestinian citizens were just 10 percent of new cases by the end of November.

In Hebron, Issa Amro was continuing to film and publicize his confrontations with Israeli soldiers, but by the fall of 2020, his social media channel was focused on the American national elections. In a video statement issued through his Twitter account on November 2, Issa addressed "Americans who care about the Palestinian issue" and urged them to vote against the incumbent.

"Mr. Donald Trump made our lives very hard in the last four years," Issa said. "He gave backup and political power to Israeli occupation and to Israeli settlers. He supported them and encouraged them to attack us violently, steal our land, demolish our houses, worked hard to make our cause disappear."

Were he to win a second term, Trump would "make us live in apartheid and discrimination and segregation," Issa warned, citing the administration's official relocation of the American embassy to Jerusalem, reduced funding for Palestinian office in Washington, D.C., and, worst of all, the demand that Palestinians accept a "fake peace deal" that included the annexation of Hebron, Jerusalem, and other essential places.

After the election, Issa tweeted out his congratulations to Americans who "got rid of the Idiot Trump," then got right back to work confronting soldiers and settlers. That afternoon, he posted video to his social media accounts of settlers destroying Palestinian olive trees in nearby Tal Rumeida.

In January 2021, an Israeli military court convicted Issa on three counts—protesting without a permit, disrupting Israeli soldiers' activities, and assault—but acquitted him on twelve other charges. The incidents occurred between 2010 and 2016, and Issa's Israeli lawyer said there were still additional hearings to determine sentencing and appeals.

"It doesn't make sense to punish someone for nonviolent resistance," Issa told the Reuters news agency. "The Israeli military system exists only to oppress Palestinians and restrict freedom of speech."

My mother continued to go to the Saturday morning brunches, even after the fall of 2019, when Esti, Mordi's wife, died after a short illness. She missed Esti greatly, but the conversations remained as political and engaged as ever, critical of the prime minister and his cronies in the Knesset, especially of their hypocritical treatment of Holocaust survivors, paying verbal tribute while declining to actually provide resources that could help the many who were living in impoverished circumstances.

Shmulik Berger, Gretti's husband, died at ninety-two in December 2019 after many months of deteriorating health. My mother was able to travel to Ashqelon to console Gretti only a few times before the pandemic lockdowns began; after that, she tried to console her high school friend with frequent phone calls. Shmulik was buried in a small ceremony, but with all the honors appropriate to a veteran of Israel's first war.

My mother spoke often with Chava Lustig, at the Hungarian museum in Safed, who did her best to keep busy despite the lack of visitors. Chava always asked about my progress on the book. My mother also spoke occasionally with Amnon at Ma'agan, who remained in robust health, with his life on the kibbutz barely interrupted by the pandemic.

When she turned ninety on May 16, 2020, during the lock-down, my far-flung, multigenerational family celebrated my mother by Zoom, with people logging in from California, New York, and Chicago as well as from multiple locations across Israel. We toasted and sang and told stories for several hours, a happy enough occasion that we almost forgot the reason that we could not be physically together.

The multiple lockdown periods and general restrictions changed my mother's lifestyle drastically, forcing her to give up swimming, her shopping routine, and her social events, even the occasional concerts and movies she attended in Tel Aviv. She did her best to keep in touch with family and friends through social media but was sometimes lonely and frequently worried, more for her family than herself. She refused to give up Shosh, however, who continued to come and clean the apartment, help with chores, and argue over the day's news along with essential family matters. Shosh also kept tabs on my writing and was one of those especially pleased to learn that I was finally finished after all these years.

Israel began its vaccination drive relatively early, and my mother received her first dose in early January 2021. Along with the rest of the country, she slowly returned to her normal activities, though she waited until the spring warm-up before swimming again. Most of all, she was excited to see her first great-grandchild, Dor, Gabi's daughter Maya's son.

In May, a new conflict broke out with Hamas, the Islamist group in control of Gaza, after a few days of street battles between Palestinian protesters and police in Jerusalem. Announcing that they were striking to defend the Haram al Sharif, Hamas, whose militia was still led by Mohammed Deif, began firing barrages of rockets at targets all over Israel, attempting to use a large number of projectiles to overwhelm the Iron Dome.

One of the first nights of the conflict, a helpful neighbor, who realized my mother had slept through the phone alerts and the blaring air-raid siren, knocked on her door to wake her up and escorted her down to her building's shelter. She sat there listening to the sounds of explosions in the distance with a few other families, mostly crying children, some because they were too little to understand what was going on and others because they understood precisely what was going on. The Iron Dome successfully intercepted most of the Hamas missiles, but one home was destroyed nearby, leaving its occupant, who had been in the shower, naked in the street but for a towel, though otherwise uninjured.

She was scared, of course, but more angry than scared. She thought of her family and friends, especially Gretti in Ashqelon, who was under near constant fire, but she couldn't stop thinking that on the other side of the firing line in Gaza, there was a ninety-one-year-old Palestinian great-grandmother hiding because bombs were being dropped on her neighborhood. Both sides were firing missiles at old ladies and children. And nothing would change. Hamas would not make Israel disappear, and Israel would not make the Palestinians disappear.

During previous military conflicts, Israelis had rallied around the prime minister, but this time the latest battle ended up being the final blow. Attorney General Avichai Mandelblit, defying the suspicions of those who saw him as Netanyahu's toady, had indicted the prime minister on charges of criminal corruption related to his acceptance of bribes and manipulation of media institutions more than a year earlier, and the trial was well underway. Even after the indictment, Netanyahu had held on after another indeterminate election in March 2020 by cutting a deal with an erstwhile challenger, but that government fell apart and another election was held, the fourth in two years.

At first, the results of this new election seemed just as murky as the previous ballots. But Netanyahu's rivals were concerned by the renewed warfare with Hamas and by fighting in the streets of Israel, where vengeful mobs of Palestinian citizens attacked Jews in mixed towns and destroyed synagogues, while Jewish mobs attacked Palestinian motorists in several places as well. Some suspected Netanyahu had fanned the flames, or even orchestrated the violence somehow, in a desperate bid to stay in power.

Finally, at the beginning of June, Naftali Bennett, a former protégé of Netanyahu's who headed a small, right-wing party, announced that he would join a wide-ranging coalition of other parties and unseat Israel's longest serving prime minster. Bennett warned that Netanyahu would "take the entire country to his own private Masada," referring to the Jews who fought the Roman Empire until their collective suicide. He was acting "to stop the madness and take responsibility."

The new government was composed of representatives of almost all of Israel's tribes: secular leftists; Russian immigrants; defectors from Likud; and Ra'am, a party of Palestinian citizens who identified themselves as Islamists. It had been assembled by Yair Lapid, a former television broadcaster who headed the centrist Yesh Atid ("There Is a Future") party, and it excluded the Likud, ever loyal to Netanyahu, and all of the Haredi parties as well as other parties representing Palestinian citizens. Reflecting the complexity of the whole deal, Bennett had been given the prime minister's seat for the first two years, with Lapid scheduled to take over after that.

Like Netanyahu, Bennett had lived much of his life in the

United States and espoused many of the same policies, but it was unclear if he would be able to hold on to the prime minister's job for long. Netanyahu was an outsized figure who had dominated Israeli politics for a generation after all, and many were already predicting he would beat the charges against him and return to power shortly. Nevertheless, his departure had been coming for a long time, and those who wished for change at the top would not waver either, with certain consequences for the country's all-important relations with the United States. Any successor would be unlikely to have Netanyahu's confidence handling the U.S. Congress, business interests, Jewish communities, and evangelicals, among all the others who feel they have a stake in Israel.

Since Israel's victory in the 1967 Six-Day War, America's defense industries have ensured Israel has one of the world's most formidable militaries, American universities have educated Israel's elites, and American philanthropists have facilitated the migration of millions of Jews from the former Soviet Union and Ethiopia, among other locations. The American role has grown only more complex and intricate in recent years, as American donors have paid to expand Israel's settlements in Palestinian territories and American federal prosecutors have targeted Israel's organized criminals as part of their jurisdiction.

An ever increasing number of Palestinians have their own American education and work experience as well, and they are using their connections with the Palestinian American community to advocate for an independent Palestinian state. Nevertheless, the American government's policy toward Israel/Palestine now and in the future will be calculated as a balance of domestic interests as well as a component of an overall strategy toward the Middle East, one that prioritizes control over the supply of oil and other fossil fuels from the Gulf.

With the trips that I made for this book, I saw firsthand the

American superstructure imposed on Israel/Palestine's economy and politics, but also, beneath that, the reality of Israeli Jews' reconnecting to their family's erstwhile homelands in the Middle East, Europe, Central Asia, North Africa, and East Africa. I have documented Israeli tribes of all types challenging one another, borrowing from one another, and forging unlikely alliances in a dynamic, sometimes violent process with highly unpredictable results. While it is common for commentators to focus on the points of tension between secular and observant Israelis, or between Mizrahim and Ashkenazim, I have also endeavored to point out how porous these borders really are, and how the interactions between tribes can yield results as often sweet as bitter, whether through the unique cuisine emerging from the country or by the Haredi rabbis attempting to guide their communities through the shifting realities of modern life.

The conflict between Israelis and Palestinians on the West Bank has likewise been much chronicled and all too frequently mythologized, but up close on the Israeli side, it is an inchoate set of often arbitrary policies carried out by teenage conscripts, with predictably tragic results that serve only to deepen hostilities and inject rage into the relations between neighboring peoples. To call it an "occupation" was increasingly controversial within Israel, but I saw the extensive military infrastructure required for the settlements and reckoned the effect of the army's presence on the population on the West Bank.

For all of that, the Palestinians I spoke with in Ramallah, Jericho, Bethlehem, Hebron, and East Jerusalem were by no means sanguine about the prospects for Palestinian self-governance. Instead, they protested the perfidy of the political class while building up their own business sector and forming grassroots advocacy groups. After more than seventeen years without an election, the Palestinian Authority headquartered in Ramallah agreed to allow balloting in the spring of 2021 and then canceled those elections a short while later. Still, few were disappointed, as there was little hope the result would unify Gaza and the West Bank or reform the deeply corrupt government in Ramallah.

Meanwhile, Palestinian citizens of Israel were asserting their rights, rejecting second-class citizenship through political organizing, community development, and personal success. They were voting in unprecedented numbers, and the entry of the Ra'am party into the government gave hope to all of those who shared a vision for an Israeli future that provided truly equal rights to all of its citizens. Those Palestinian citizens who opted not to vote found their own ways to protest and prosper, through public service, as Jamal and Alam had, or through private enterprise, as Abu Kaf and Razallah had.

Israel/Palestine is known as a war zone, and I surely glimpsed the political violence, but it never eluded me that every time I came back to Chicago, I was returning to a city of 3 million people that suffered more than 500 homicides annually, a number that was *down,* in fact, from the 1990s, when I was a newspaper reporter and there were more than 900 killings every year. Yet, contrary to Chicago's reputation as a hub of violence, I knew that it was in fact in the middle of American cities when it came to homicide rates, lower than Baltimore or New Orleans or nearby St. Louis and Detroit, but higher than Miami, Boston, New York, or Los Angeles. Overall, there were 14,123 homicide victims throughout the United States in 2018 alone, an overall rate of 5.35 per 100,000 people. In Israel, by contrast, 103 people were the victims of homicide in 2018, a rate of 1.14 per 100,000, typical for the years in which there was no war.

Murder and crime rates are just one measure of a society, of course, but these statistics argue that it would be presumptuous for the United States to prescribe methods of fostering harmonious relations among all the residents of Israel/Palestine. Indeed, we live in an age when the institutions of every nation are being challenged by multiple existential forces: technology and the increasingly free movement of people, goods, money, and information, as well as organized crime, transnational banditry, political rebellion, religious extremism, and, as has just been so painfully revealed, disease. In Israel, just as in the United States, individual identity has become an epic contest between tribal loyalties, respect for diversity, and national solidarity fought in legislative bodies and governments, the courts, and in the streets.

Judaism is a resilient system, a faith and an identity that has survived so long because it adapts, defends its integrity, and replicates under circumstances that are adverse as well as diverse. Jews—and the Jewish attachment to Israel—will remain as they have for millennia. Whether this State of Israel ultimately succeeds, however, will depend on the internal resources to resist every variety of international manipulation and innovate its own solutions to its particular problems.

Neither a cautionary tale nor an international role model, Israel is a microcosm, a tiny domain that contains the truth of how the world really works. The state's survival will be determined, then, by the extent to which it is able to accommodate all its tribes, creating a system that respects each tribe's integrity, but ensures that all are able to contribute to the collective. Surely, this will be the basis for a pragmatic solidarity that acknowledges twenty-first-century realities: allowing individuals to take pride in their heritage while living in peace with their neighbors, collaborating to maximize their collective resources while expanding their mutual opportunities.

ACKNOWLEDGMENTS

This book was finished in the midst of fire and plague, and there is simply no way I could have done it without the love and support of my wife and son. Indeed, my entire family helped me at every stage of this project. My mother, Chana Michaeli, introduced me to her close friends, took me around Israel, and housed and fed me. My older brother, Gabi Michaeli, and his partner, Nira Ashkenazi, utilized all of their resources, including a network all over Israel, and took me to places whose purpose I didn't always perceive until I'd done extensive research, and then found that they were perfect for what I was trying to understand. My younger brother, Dani, was with me even when he couldn't be there physically, and I couldn't have finished this without him either, or without the good wishes of Diane and Carmela Michaeli. Sadako and Ken Naka and everyone in Okinawa watched over Kobo and Kimiyo on my first trip for this book, and their kindness and generosity kept me going throughout.

Love and gratitude for meals, advice, introductions, and making sure I didn't get too lost to Judith Michaeli, Maya Michaeli, Orian Michaeli, and Shmulik Szeintuch. My cousin Rony Zohar is the pilot extraordinaire mentioned in the preface; he and his wife, Idit, have always been generous and incisive hosts with a bird's-eye view. Rony's brother Amnon Sonnenfeld knows Israel better than anyone else and has always shared it all without hesitation, while his wife, Anat, and daughters, Gal and Noam, helped me understand things from totally different perspectives. Special thanks to Julie and Dan Horton for their counsel and compassion as well as to T and Tracey Felkay.

With heartfelt affection and gratitude to Nira's children, Shira Shabbat and Roe Shabbat; parents, Rina and Leon Ashkenazi; grandmother, Ester Boyd; and sister and brother-in-law, Tali and Eran Bezalel.

Nathaniel Deutsch was invaluable to every stage and facet of this book, but I have been the beneficiary of his wisdom, insight, and, most of all, his devoted friendship for more than three decades now. This book, therefore, is only a partial tribute to a great scholar, intellect, and mensch.

My agent, Rob McQuilkin, who has believed in my talent as a writer long before he had evidence to do so, believed in this book before anyone else, guided its gestation at every phase, and even edited its pages. No writer can have a better champion.

To those who appeared in the book, or contributed directly or behind the scenes, thank you for your openness and understanding, patience and trust (in completely random order): Amnon Ben Shoushan, Miriam Hajnal, Belaynesh Zevadia, Vered Dayan, Chava Lustig, Yosef Lustig, Ron Lustig, the staff of Memorial Museum of the Hungarian Speaking Jewry, Yoni and Niva Reuven, Mehari and Bracha Reuven, Tsionit Fattal Kupperwasser, Lainie Blum Cogan, Sam Cogan and Mimi Cogan, Jeremy Welfeld, Shosh Skufa Natan, Alam and family, Yaakov Berg and the staff at Psagot Winery, Nate Shapiro, Simona and Ilan Weinglass, Eli Noy and the vendors at the Shuq Bezalel, Adiva Geffen, Yitzhak Bar-Yosef and the staff at the Genazim, Razallah and Ali Al Heib, Hadsh Berhane, David Ben Khalifa, Taysir Abu Kaf, Ester and Mordechai Gidron, Mari Tavor, Jaakov Kessler, Chava Katz,

Lezer Becker, Dillon Ficca and Dirk Ficca, Gil Hovav, Sam Bahour, Issa Amro, Ahmadiel Ben-Yehuda, Avidaliah Rafa Afrah, Prince Immanuel Ben Yehudah and the entire Village of Peace, Rabbi Danny Cohen, Samer Makhlouf, Abd al Shayer and family, Diane Goldin, Travis Rejman, Jamal Al Kirnawi, and Professor Benny Brown.

In the years that it took me to write these pages, some of you listened to me as I worked through ideas, read drafts, and gave me ideas or critiques as I proceeded. I have endeavored to do justice to your confidence. Thank you all sincerely from the bottom of my heart: Eric Hudson, Kristen Harol, Tem Horwitz, Sandra Barreto, Yuval Taylor, Ruth Welkovics, Rabbi Bruce Elder, Peter Levavi, Jonathan Rothstein, Rachel Haverlock, Jonathan Eig, Mary Piemonte, Joslyn DiPasalegne, R. Eugene Scott, Beverly Reed-Scott, Andre Moriel McClerkin, Donnica Zimrah Gordon, Sayed Kashua, Brent Staples, Rick Perlstein, Robert K. Elder, Shimri Zameret, Admir Kusran, Elizabeth Taylor, Alex Kotlowitz, Jonathan Alter, Ben Austen, Dave Lundy, Brian Gladstein, Chemi and Nili Shalev, Herbert Quelle, Shulem Deen, Stelios Valavanis, Sunil Garg, Yuri Lane, Rhoda Stamell, Demario Jones, Crystal Carjaval, Manny Carvajal, Benjamin Marcial, Ashley "Oz" Ozburn, Burrell Poe, Jimmie Briggs, Delasha Long, Tom Cross, Holly Ramos, Bernie Del Giorno, Henri Peretz, Mary Hidalgo, Kyle Mccullough, Greg Mermel, Liza Wickersty, Mayer Horn, Jeff Levy, Evan Osnos, Mary Wisnewski, Shlomo Papierblatt, David Maraniss, Dale Russakoff, and Matt Weiner.

The team at Custom House/HarperCollins somehow demonstrated total commitment and unflagging professionalism through all of the unexpected challenges of publishing during a pandemic. With offices closed, all the regular tools and resources that help publishers do their jobs were unavailable, and yet Peter Hubbard and Molly Gendell took the manuscript I submitted, edited it, and then shepherded it through the process of becoming a book without a hint of the extra burdens they carried. Likewise, Jamie Lescht, Ryan Shepherd, Dale Rohrbaugh, Mumtaz Mustafa, and Lucy Albanese created the actual print, made sure it would reach readers, and made sure it received the public's attention. It wouldn't have happened without Geoff Shandler's initial investment.

For my father, Avraham Michaeli; aunt and uncle, Zusanna and Abraham Sonnenfeld; and for Henri Zvi Deutsch, David Welkovics, Gil Friedman, Ester Gidron, Shmulik Berger, Alon Niv, Beauty Turner, and Seth Cogan. May their memories always be a blessing.

INDEX